Dave Gibbons
WRITER

Steve Rude
PENCILLER
ORIGINAL COVER PAINTINGS

Karl Kesel
INKER

Steve Oliff
COLORIST

Bill Oakley
LETTERER

SUPERMAN CREATED BY
Jerry Siegel & Joe Shuster

BATMAN CREATED BY
Bob Kane

SUPERMAN · BATMAN
WORLD'S FINEST

Mike Carlin
Editor – Original Series

Anton Kawasaki
Editor

Robbin Brosterman
Design Director – Books

Bob Harras
VP – Editor-in-Chief

Diane Nelson
President

Dan DiDio and Jim Lee
Co-Publishers

Geoff Johns
Chief Creative Officer

John Rood
Executive VP – Sales, Marketing
and Business Development

Amy Genkins
Senior VP – Business
and Legal Affairs

Nairi Gardiner
Senior VP – Finance

Jeff Boison
VP – Publishing Operations

Mark Chiarello
VP – Art Direction and Design

John Cunningham
VP – Marketing

Terri Cunningham
VP – Talent Relations
and Services

Alison Gill
Senior VP – Manufacturing
and Operations

Hank Kanalz
Senior VP – Digital

Jay KoganVP – Business
and Legal Affairs, Publishing

Jack Mahan
VP – Business Affairs, Talent

Nick Napolitano
VP – Manufacturing
Administration

Sue Pohja
VP – Book Sales

Courtney Simmons
Senior VP – Publicity

Bob Wayne
Senior VP – Sales

WORLD'S FINEST

DC Comics, 1700 Broadway, New York, NY 10019
A Warner Bros. Entertainment Company
Printed by RR Donnelley, Salem, VA, USA. 7/6/12. First Printing.
ISBN: 978-1-4012-3477-5

SUSTAINABLE
FORESTRY
INITIATIVE

Certified Chain of Custody
At Least 25% Certified Forest Content
www.sfiprogram.org
SFI-01042
APPLIES TO TEXT STOCK ONLY

INTRODUCTION

BY DAVE GIBBONS

Transitional objects.

That's what psychiatrists call them. Things saved from childhood to ease the transition into adulthood. Reminders of an earlier, more innocent world.

Transitional objects. Comic books, for example.

I'm standing in Woolworth's, looking up at my grandfather. He's smoking a cigarette and, although it's summer, wears a hat and a dark suit. He holds out sixpence for me to buy a SUPERMAN comic, the first I've ever seen. On the cover, Superman pours gems into a treasure chest while Lois Lane looks on in surprise.

I'm sitting in the ABC Café with my mother. She sips tea from a green china cup, enjoying the pause. Across the table, I suck orangeade through a straw and read a BATMAN comic. On the cover, the Mad Hatter is trying to add Batman's cowl to his collection of hats.

I'm at the back door of a friend's house. The smell of frying comes from inside. It's after school and we still have our itchy gray trousers on. We're showing each other our latest comics. At the top of my pile is a SUPER ADVENTURE COMIC. On the cover Batman holds onto a giant arrow, which Superman is firing from a bow. At the top of the first page runs the legend "Your two favorite heroes, SUPERMAN and BATMAN, in one story TOGETHER!"

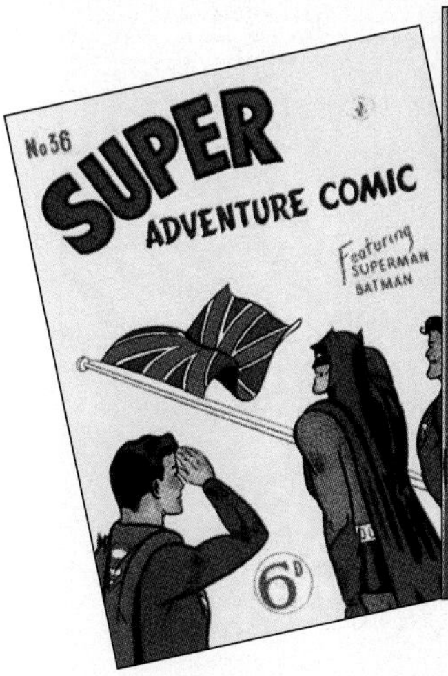
No 36
SUPER
ADVENTURE COMIC
Featuring SUPERMAN BATMAN
6D

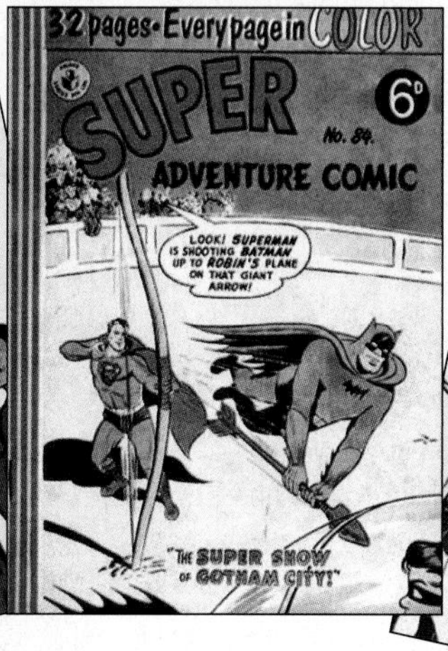
32 pages-Everypage in COLOR
SUPER
No. 84.
6D
ADVENTURE COMIC
LOOK! SUPERMAN IS SHOOTING BATMAN UP TO ROBIN'S PLANE ON THAT GIANT ARROW!
"THE SUPER SHOW OF GOTHAM CITY!"

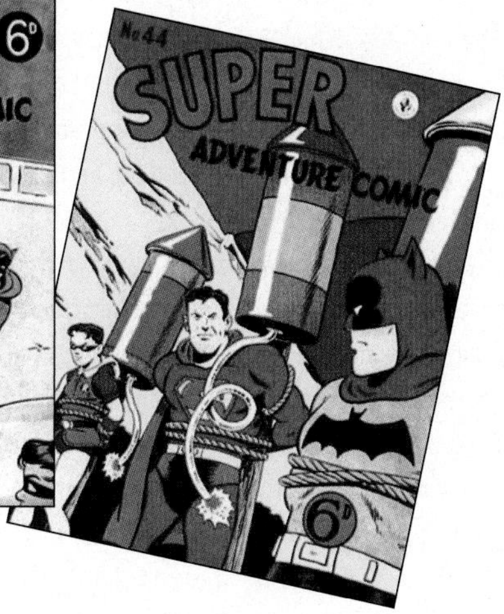
No 44
SUPER
ADVENTURE COMIC
6D

That's right, SUPER ADVENTURE COMIC, not WORLD'S FINEST.

You see, I grew up in England where, until the end of the fifties, American comics were not available. Instead we got Australian reprints, published monthly, with Annuals and Summer Specials to take up the overflow. There were four titles featuring the Superman and Batman "families": SUPERMAN, SUPERBOY, BATMAN, and my personal favorite, SUPER ADVENTURE COMIC, which featured stories from WORLD'S FINEST.

As I discovered later, WORLD'S FINEST was only published bimonthly in the States, so half of these monthly SUPER ADVENTURE reprints carried separate tales of Superman and Batman. However, even these issues generally featured Superman and Batman together on the covers, presumably drawn by an unknown Australian artist.

It's hard to appreciate today, when a comic book is unusual if it *doesn't* feature guest stars, just how thrilling those Superman-Batman team-up stories were. It was as if, in this one magical place, the vast yet separate Superman and Batman universes could meet; only here Superman and Batman could enjoy each other's friendship and share each other's secrets.

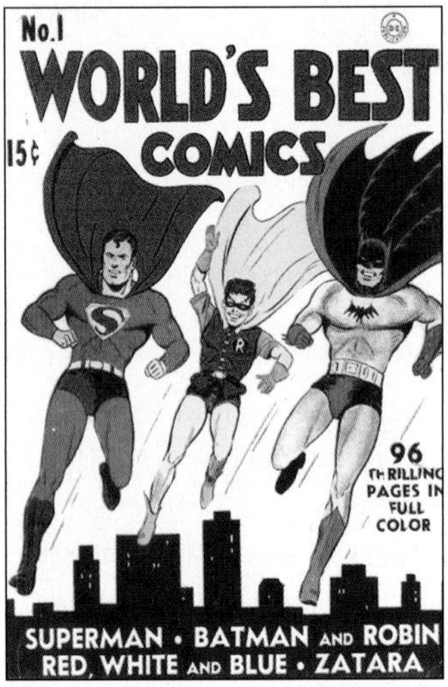
No.1
WORLD'S BEST
COMICS
15¢
96 THRILLING PAGES IN FULL COLOR
SUPERMAN • BATMAN AND ROBIN
RED, WHITE AND BLUE • ZATARA

And if that wasn't enough, the team-up tales were drawn by the "good" Batman artist, as Dick Sprang was universally known in those days before creator credits. On the strength of these stories alone, he became my favorite Superman artist, too.

I liked his work so much I once copied an entire twelve-page story onto a huge sheet of paper, picture for picture, line for line, and word for word. Except, that is, for changing Superman into Atoman, Batman into Birdman, and Robin into Raven. Just so no one would suspect, you understand. Believe it or not, the villain of that issue was called Duplicate Man.

Thirty-five years on, I'm sitting at a keyboard, writing an introduction to a Superman-Batman story of my own and leafing through those very same comic books. They're tattered and worn now, but I'll never throw them out.

Transitional objects, saved from childhood. Reminders of an earlier, more innocent world.

Thirty-five years on, Superman has been reinvented, Batman made grimmer, Robins have come and gone, and the four-color universe has become so crowded that periodic house-clearing is necessary.

Not that I'm complaining. Thirty-five years on, I gladly accept that change is the stuff of life itself. In adulthood, I believe that it is the nature of the universe to be in constant cyclical flux between extremes.

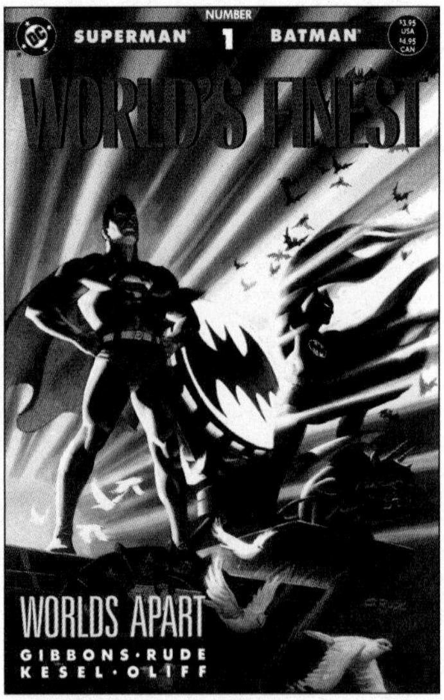
SUPERMAN
NUMBER 1
BATMAN
WORLD'S FINEST
WORLDS APART
GIBBONS • RUDE
KESEL • OLIFF

Furthermore, in the microcosm of super-hero comics, it seems to me that Superman and Batman have grown to become the resident manifestations of this elementary polarity, the yang and yin of its existence. Superman embodies all that is powerful, clear and bright; Batman, all that is subtle, obscure and dark. Their primal, complementary qualities have given rise to the entire field and, arguably, they define its parameters.

Offered the chance to express some of these feelings in a story, at a point where I was attempting another transition, from just drawing comics to writing them as well, my response was inevitable.

And if I felt daunted at having my debut script appear under the title WORLD'S FINEST, I was at least secure in the knowledge that my collaborators' skills merited the description.

So, my grateful thanks go to Steve R., Karl, Steve O., Bill and Mike. And to Daniel, the world's finest son, for his contribution.

These days, new names have been coined for this new medium of ours: "graphic novels," "pictorial fiction," and so on. All well and good. However, I like to think of this volume as being, unashamedly, a *comic book*. Or more accurately, three comic books collected under one cover.

Transitional objects? Perhaps. Reminders of an earlier, more innocent world?

I hope so.

Dave Gibbons

This introduction first appeared in the WORLD'S FINEST trade paperback, 1992.

WORLD'S FINEST

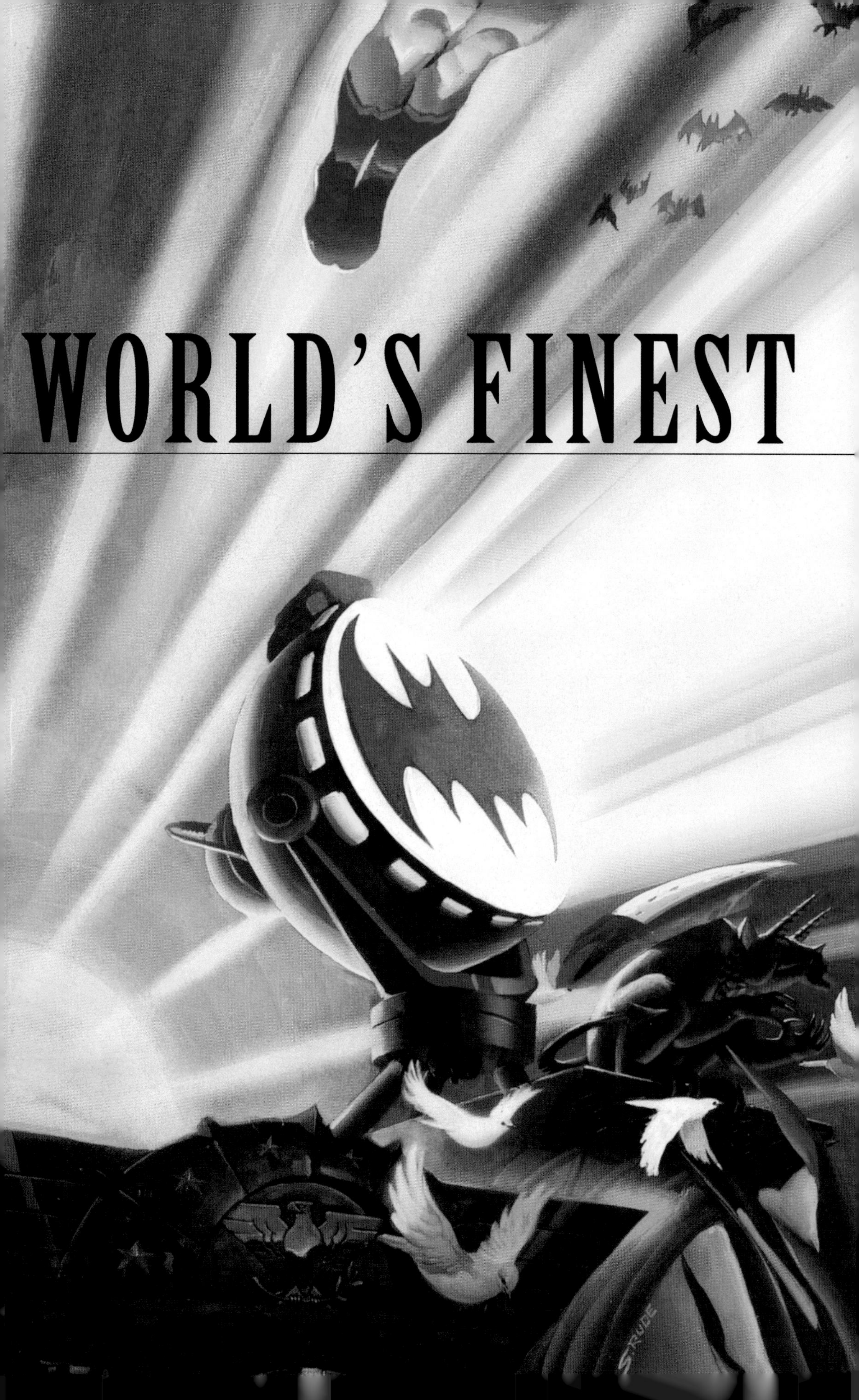
S.RUDE

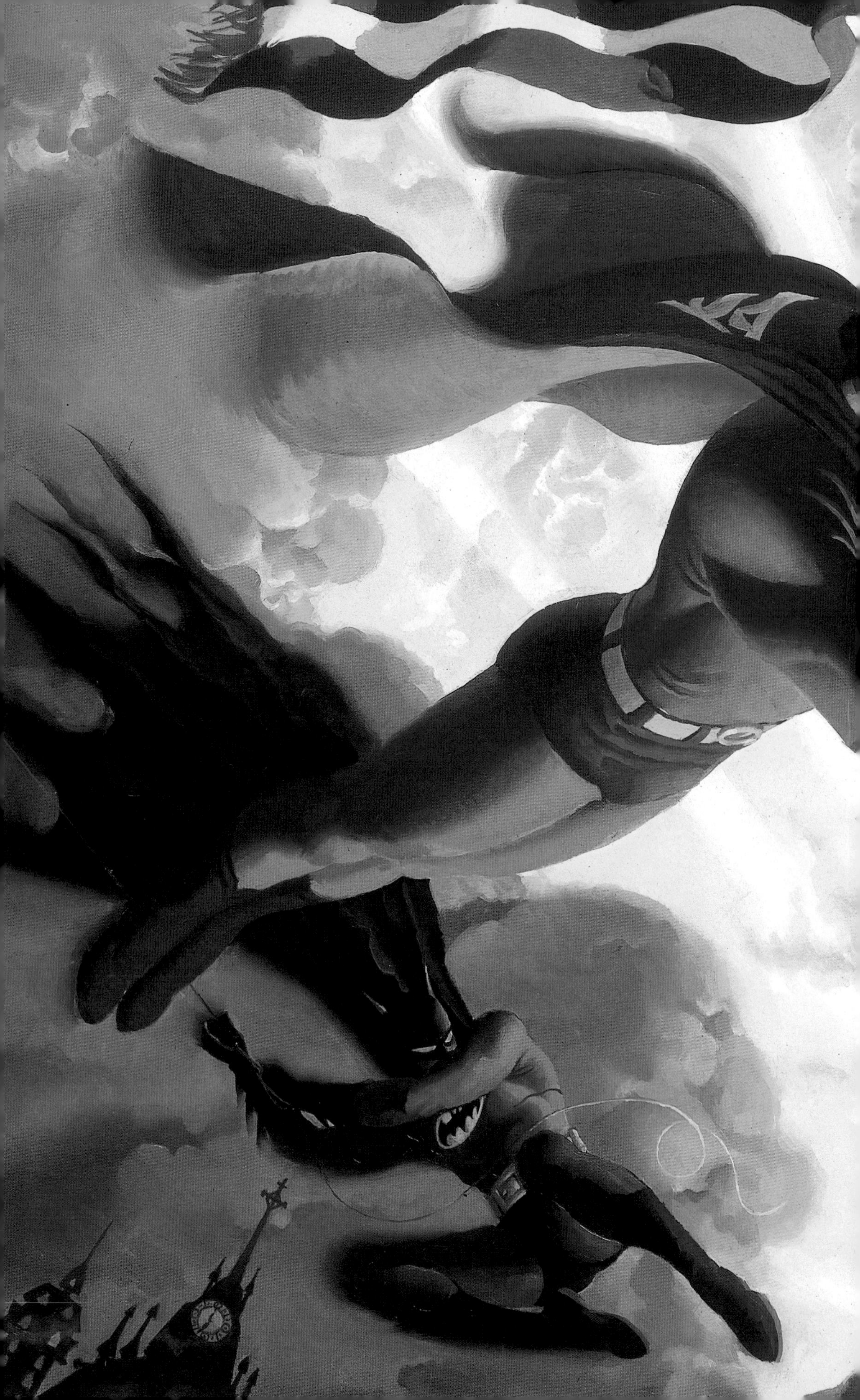

BOOK ONE

WORLDS APART

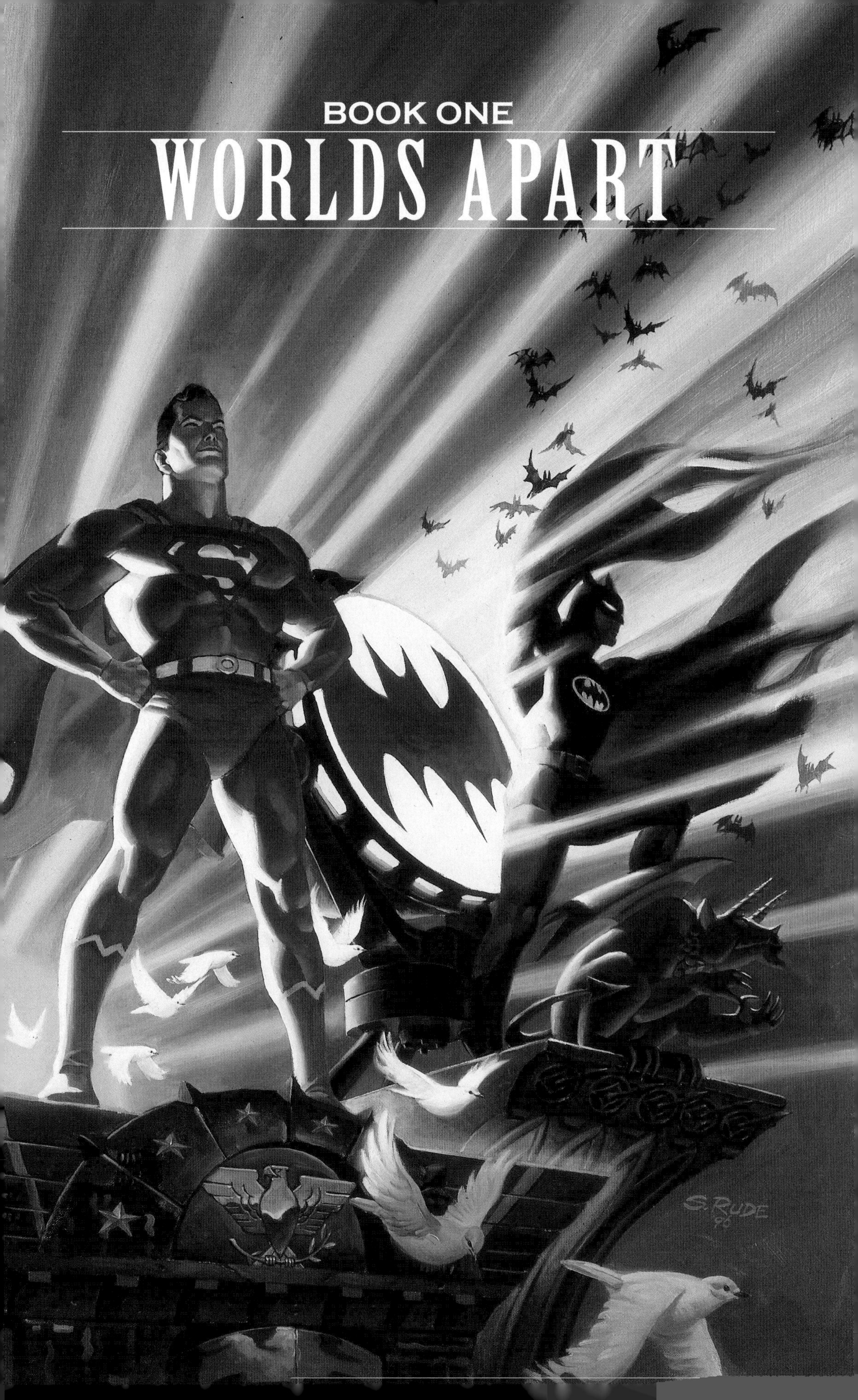
S. RUDE
90

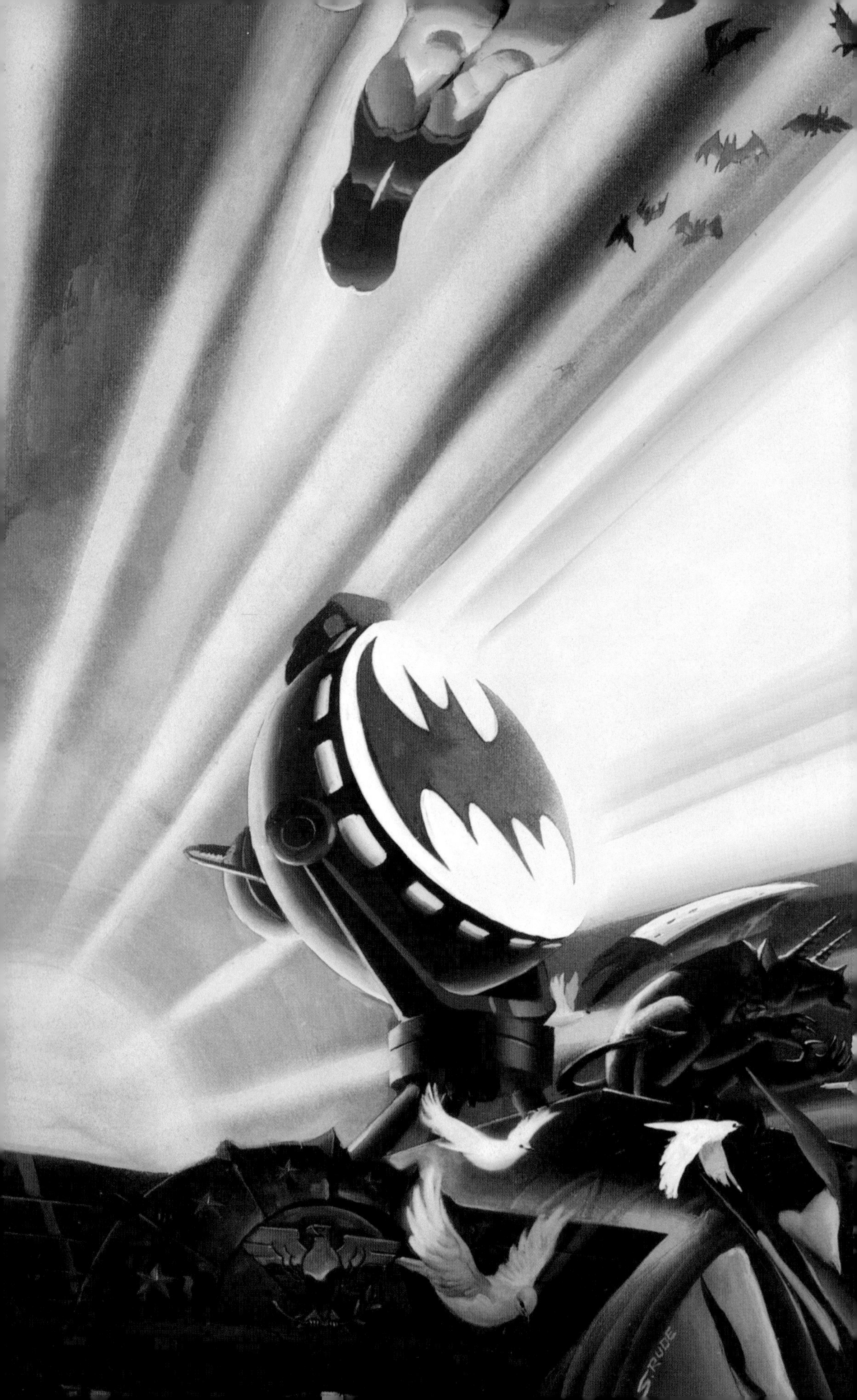
S.RUDE

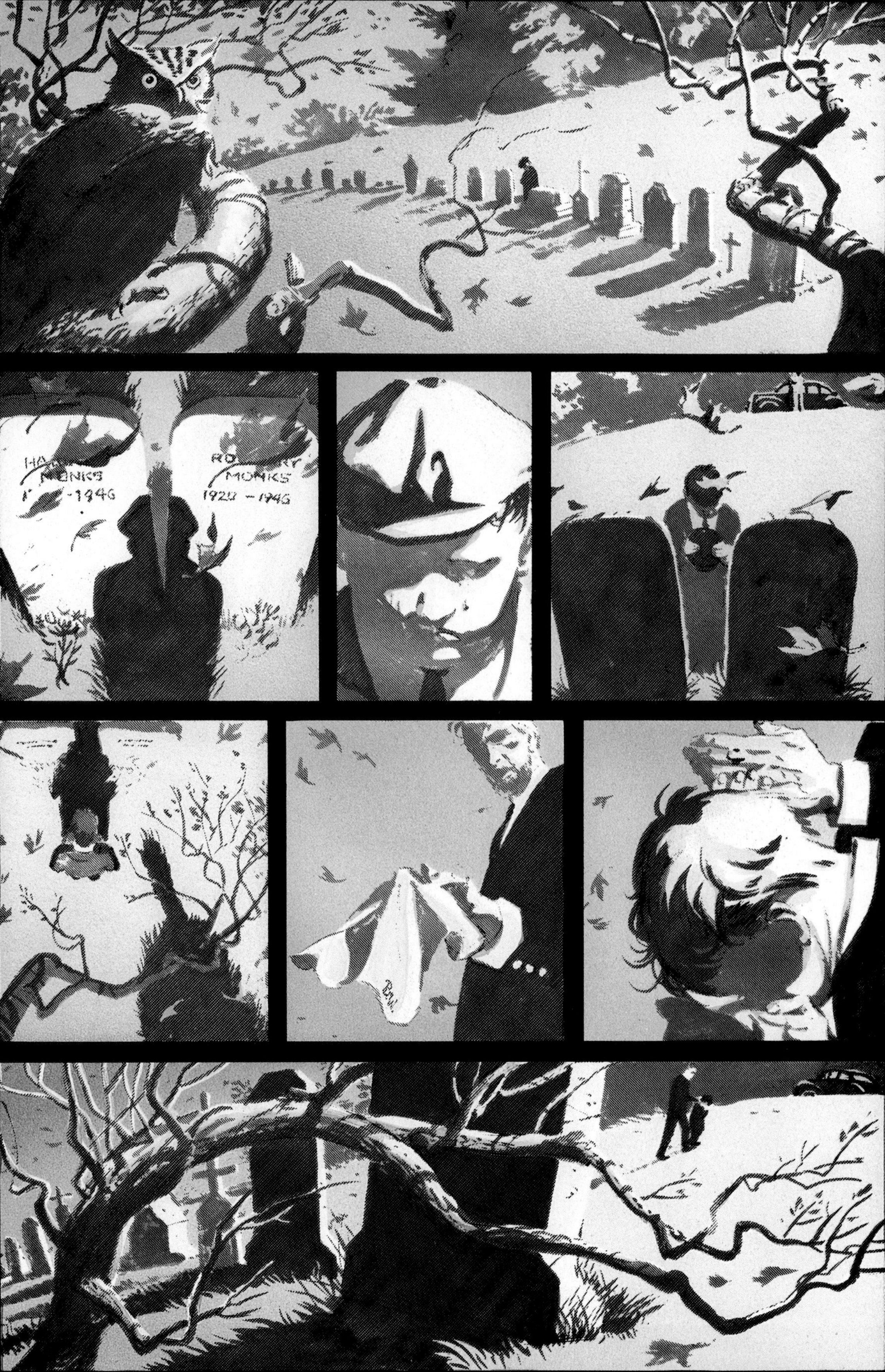
MONKS
MONKS
1920 - 1946

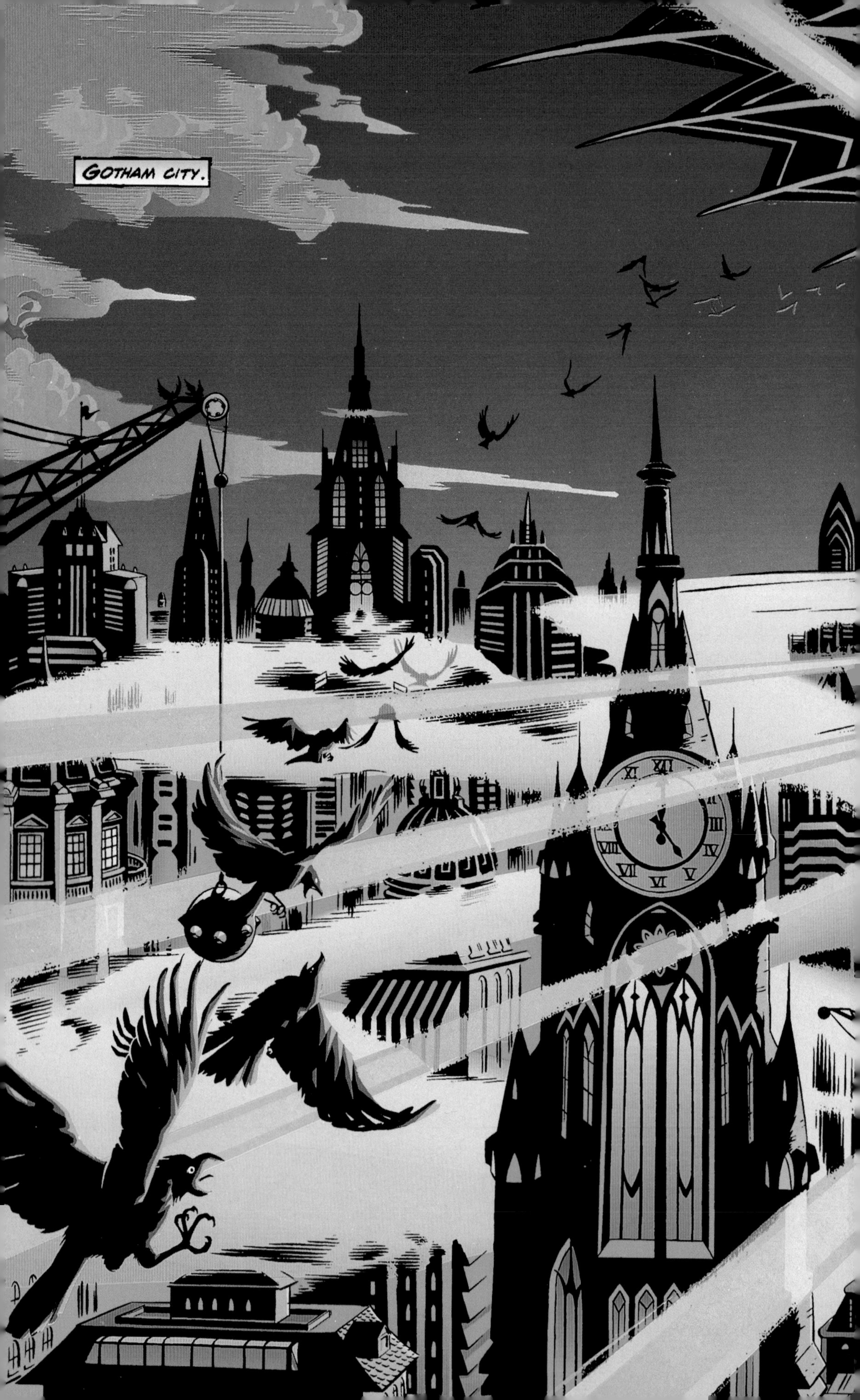
GOTHAM CITY.

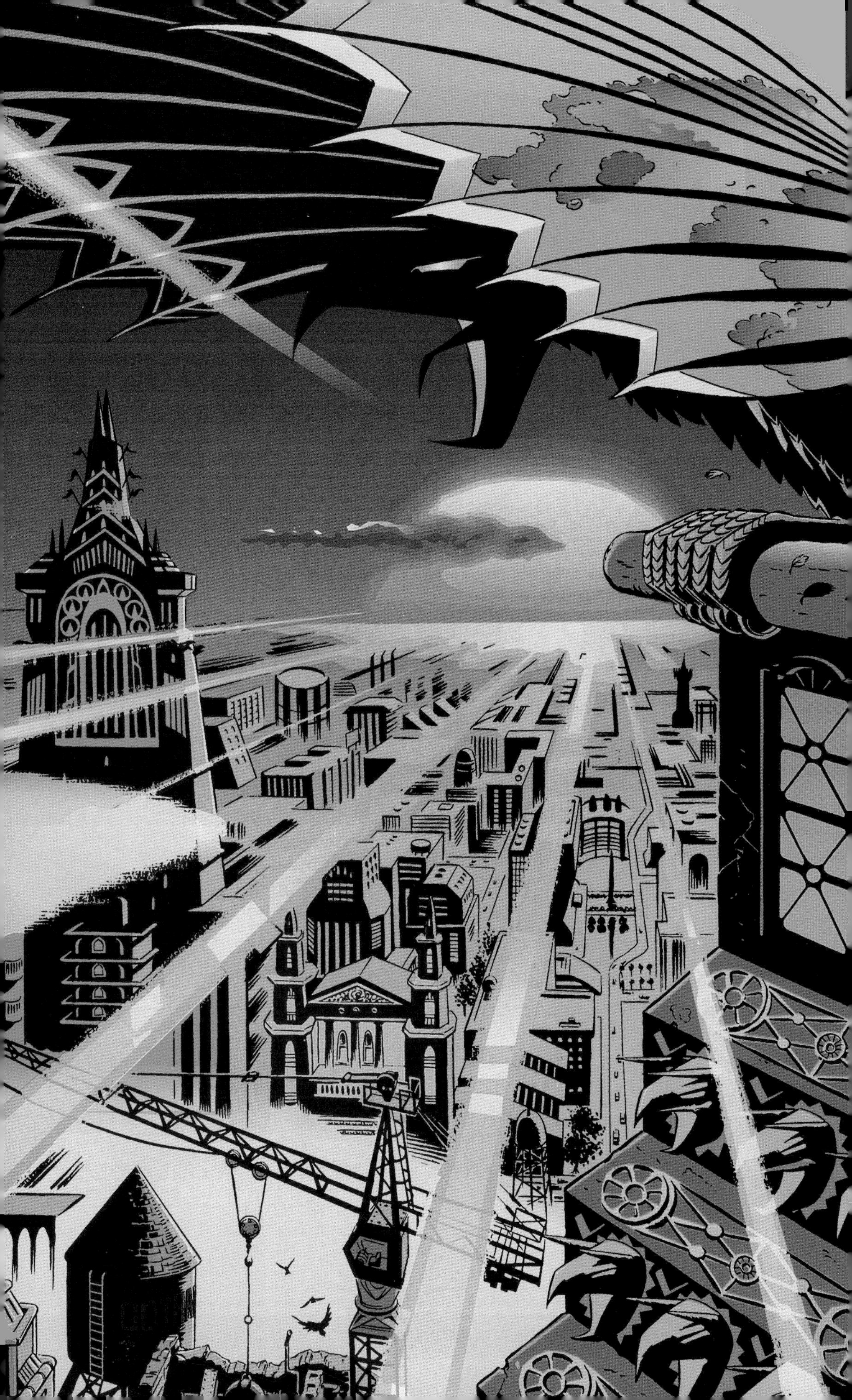

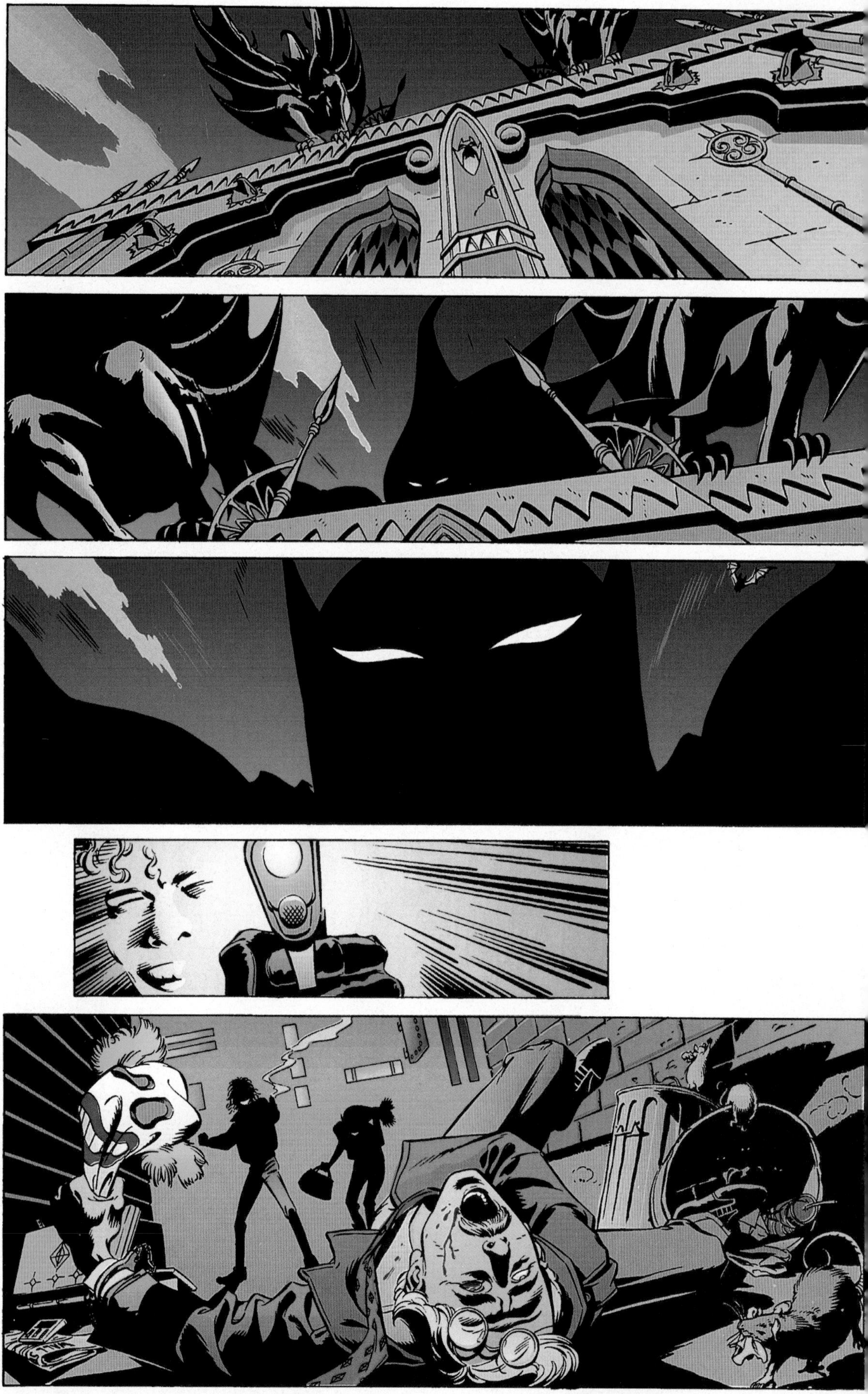

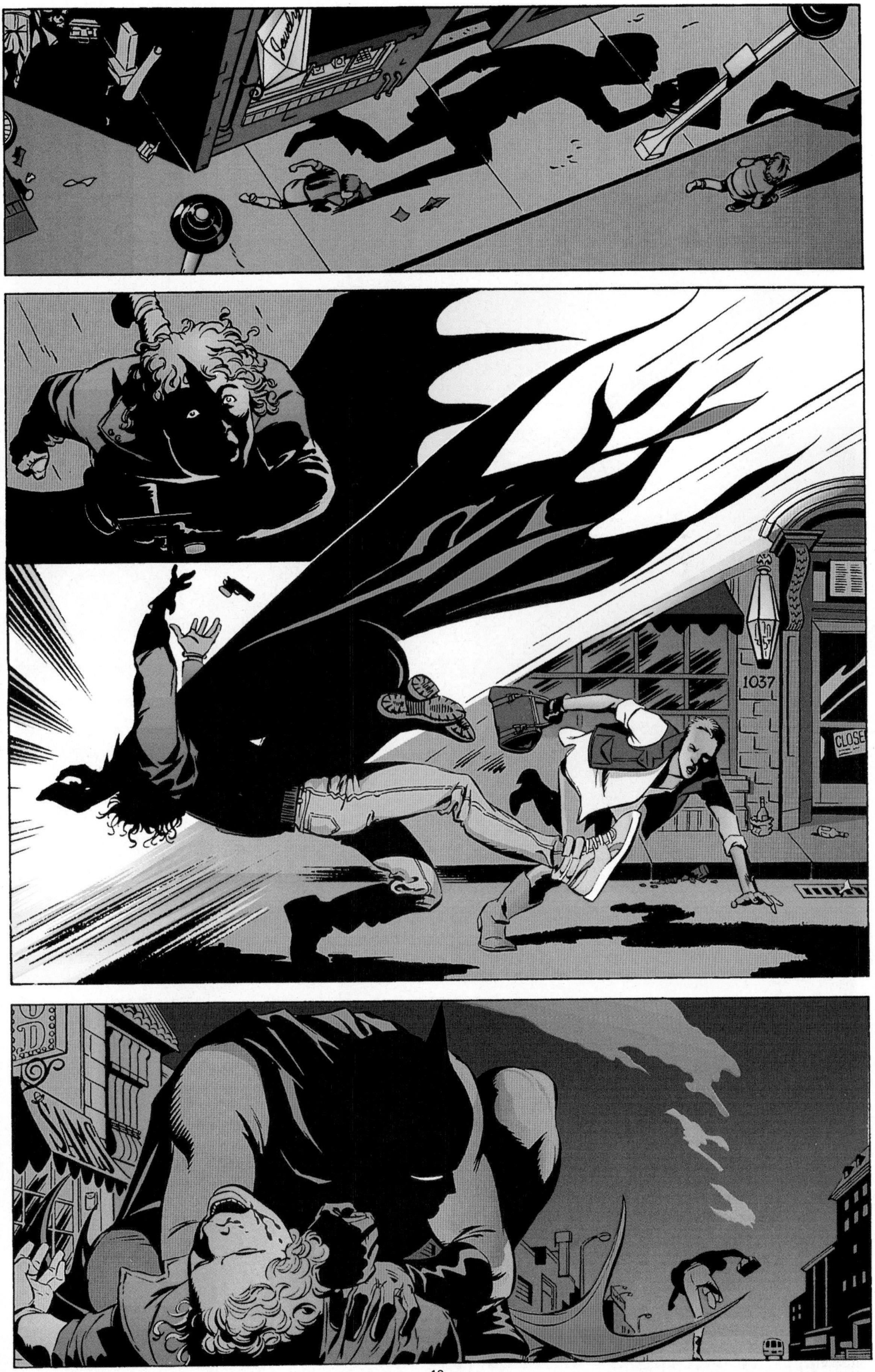
1037

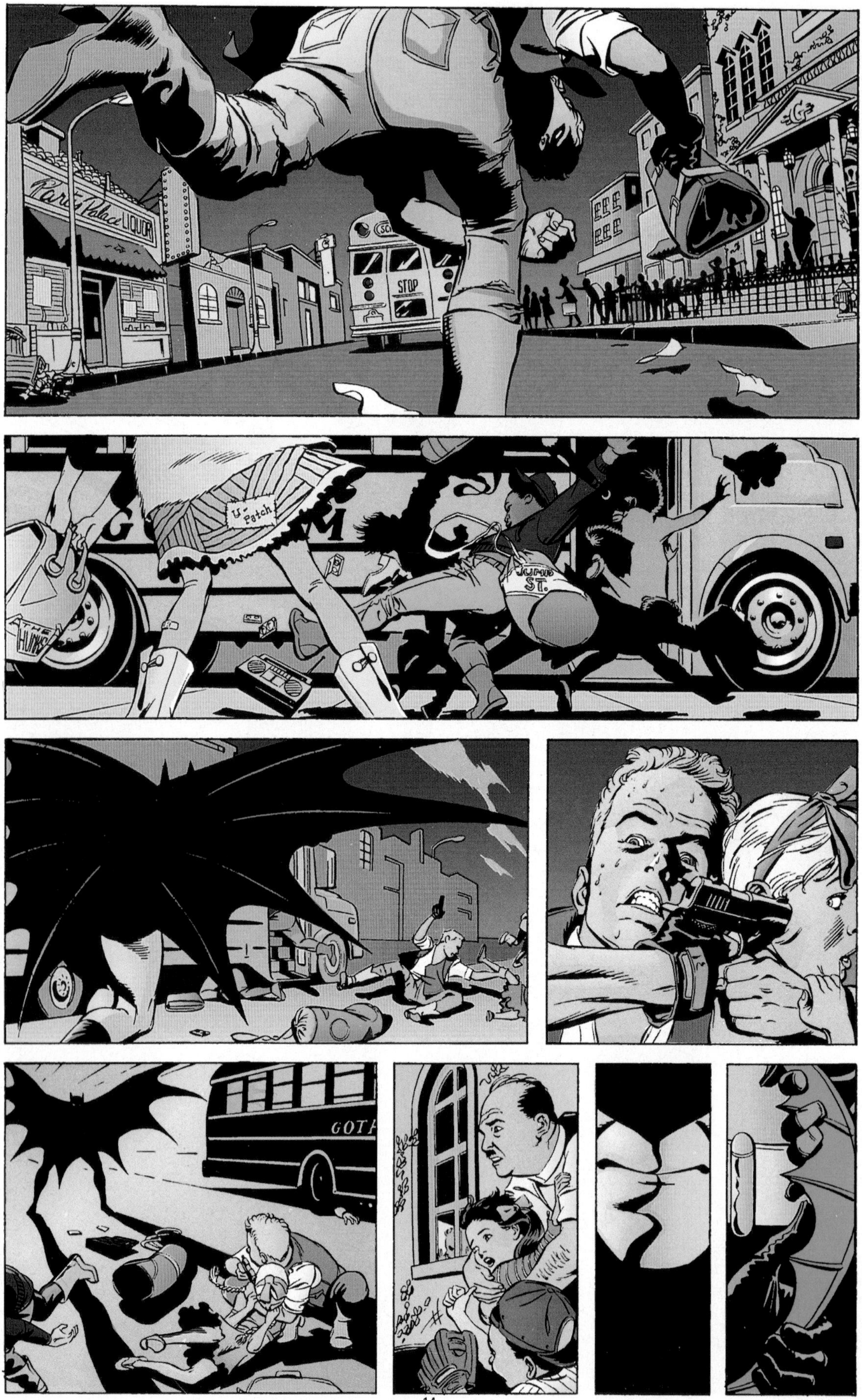
LIQUOR
STOP
U-Patch

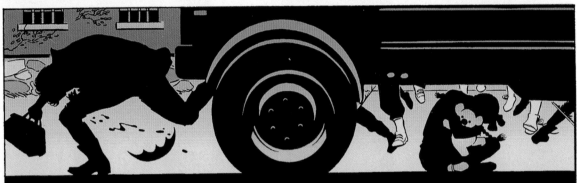

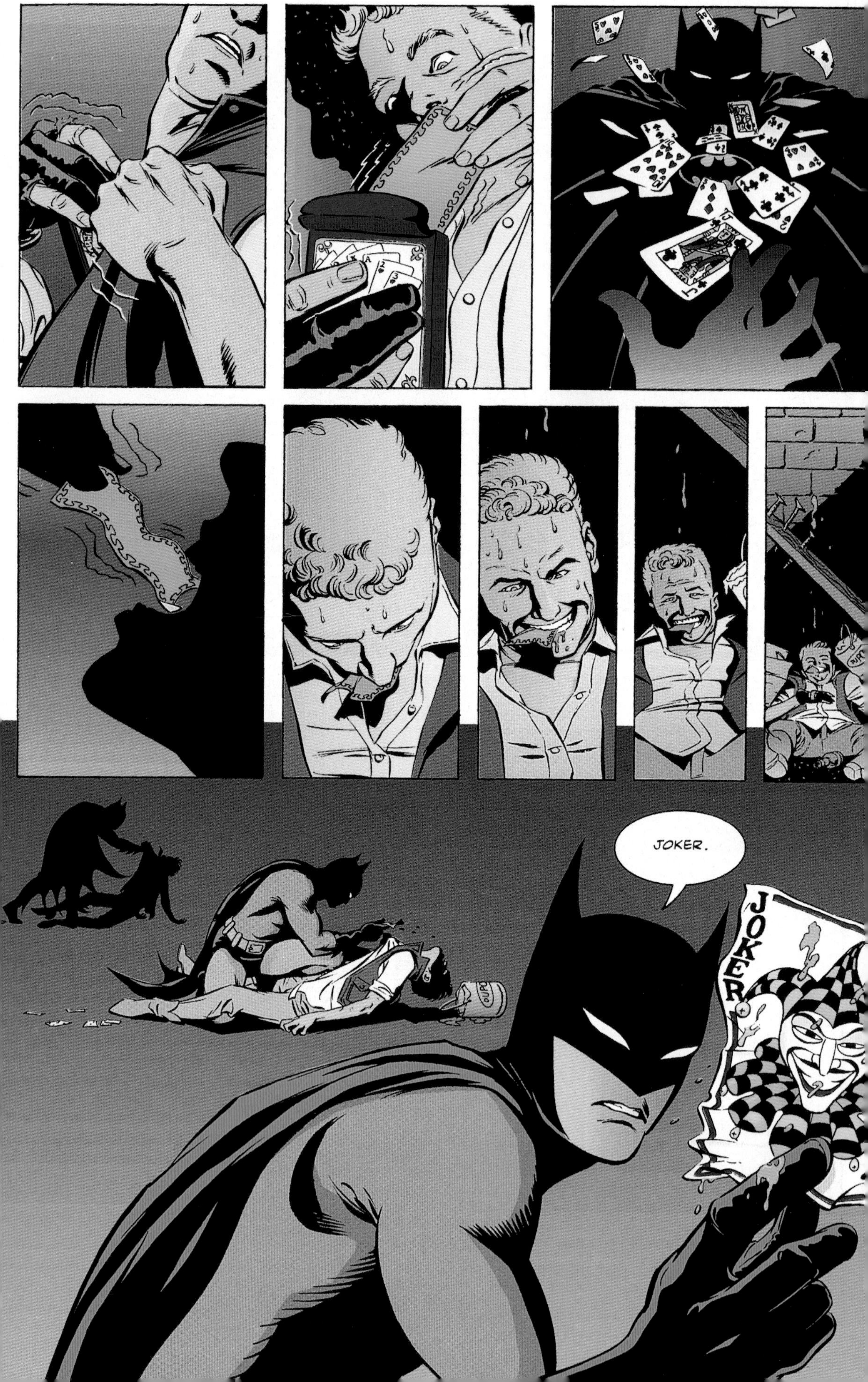
JOKER.
JOKER

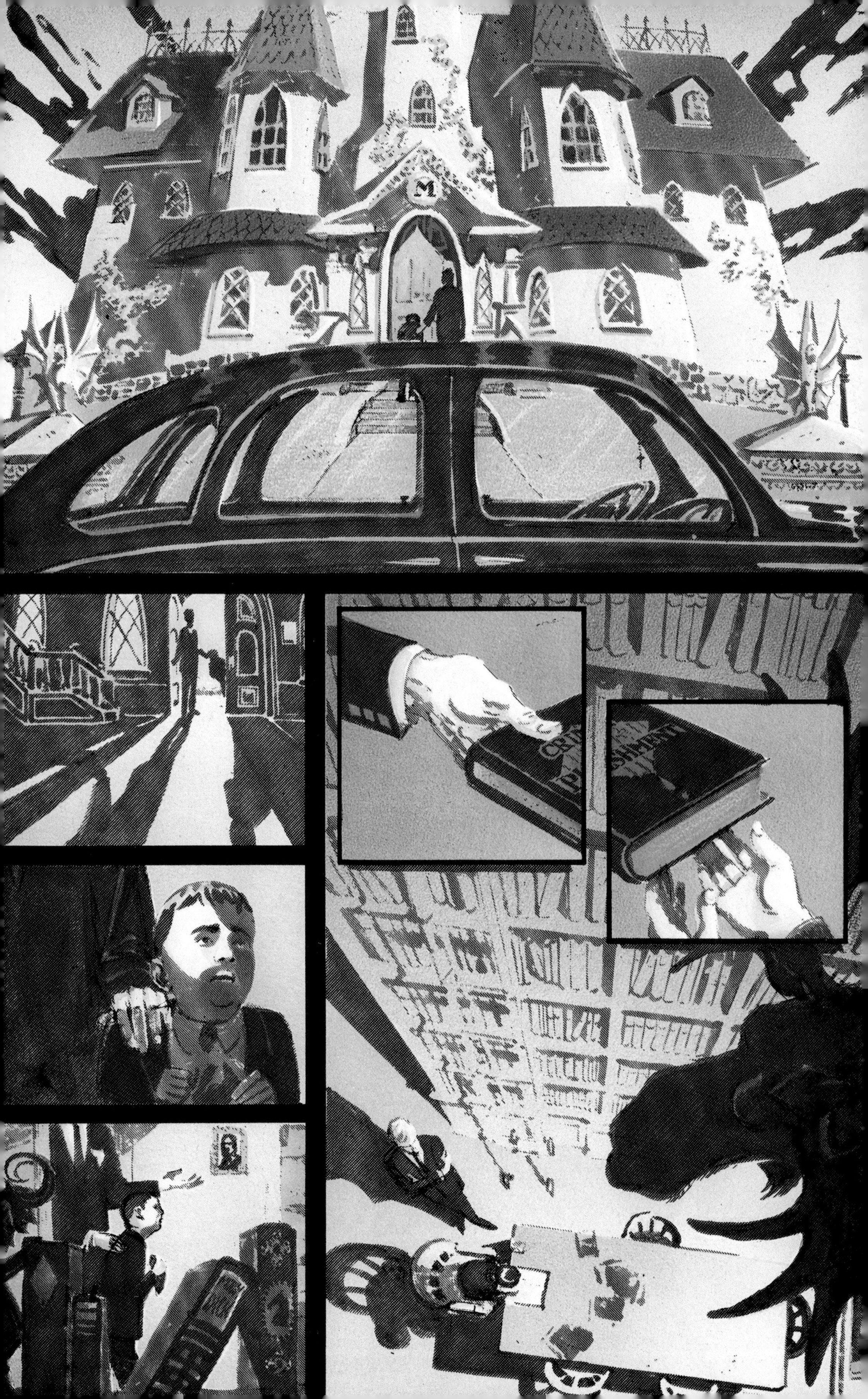

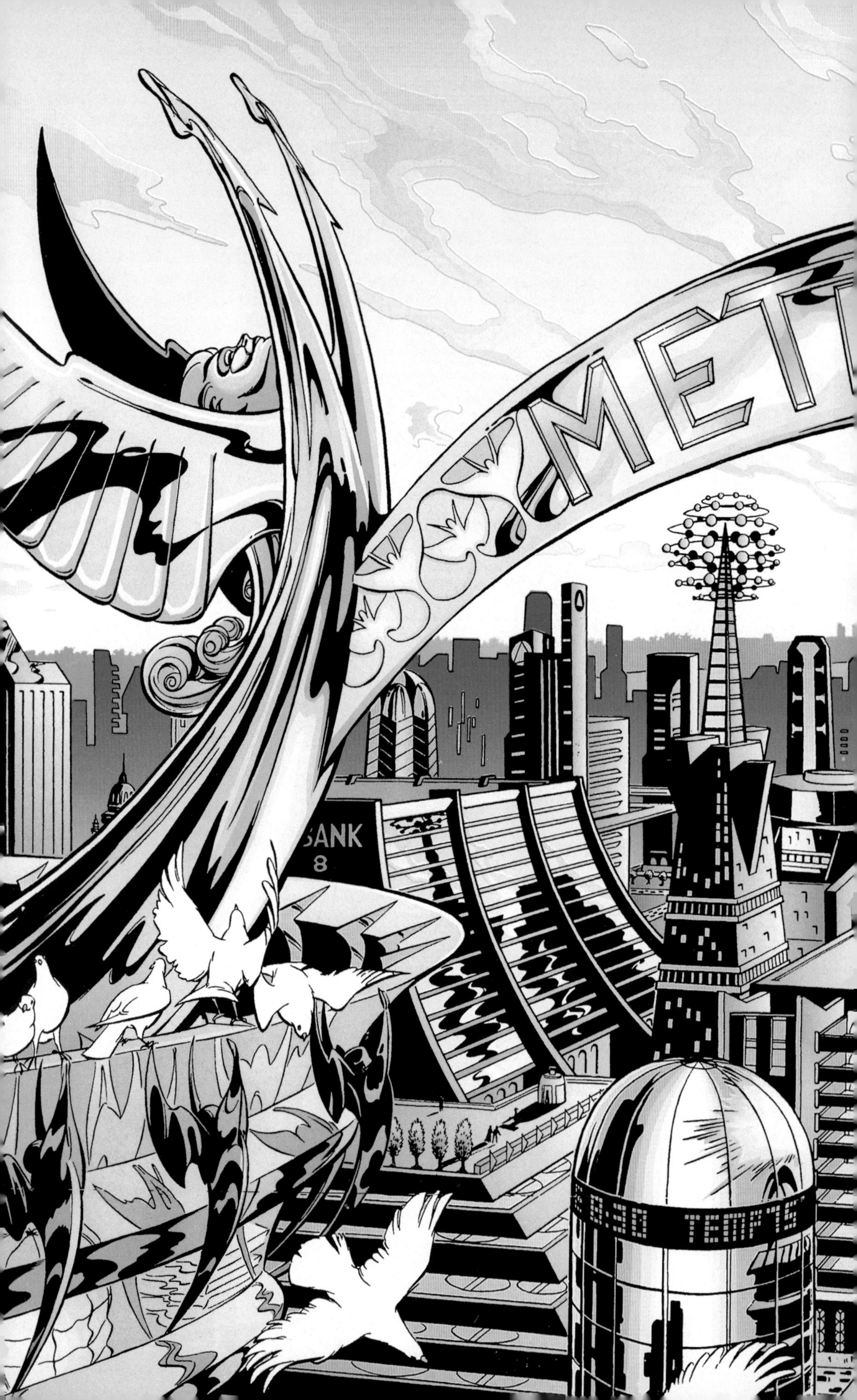
MET
TEMP 75

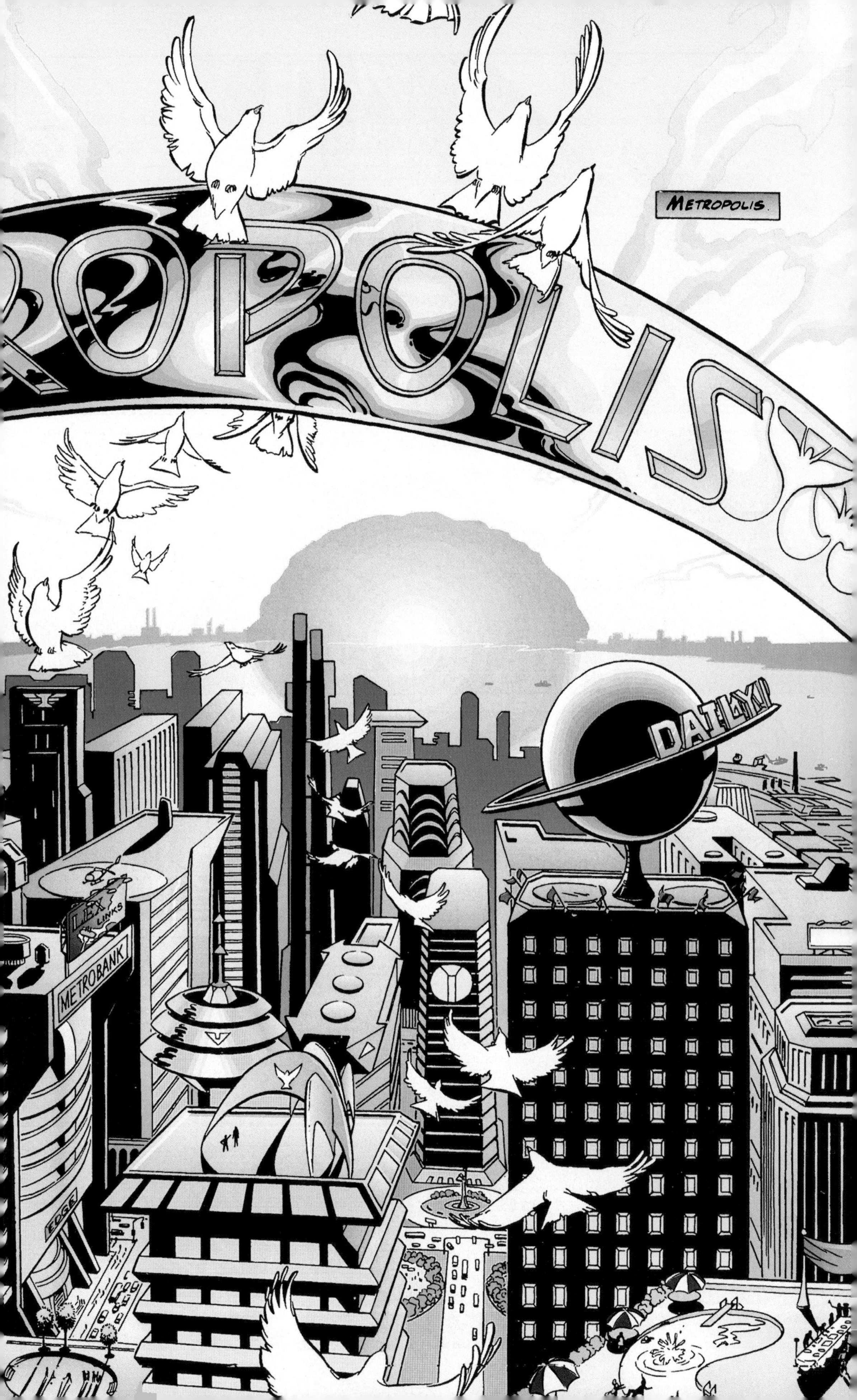
METROPOLIS.
ROPOLIS
DAILY
LEX LINKS
METROBANK
EDGE

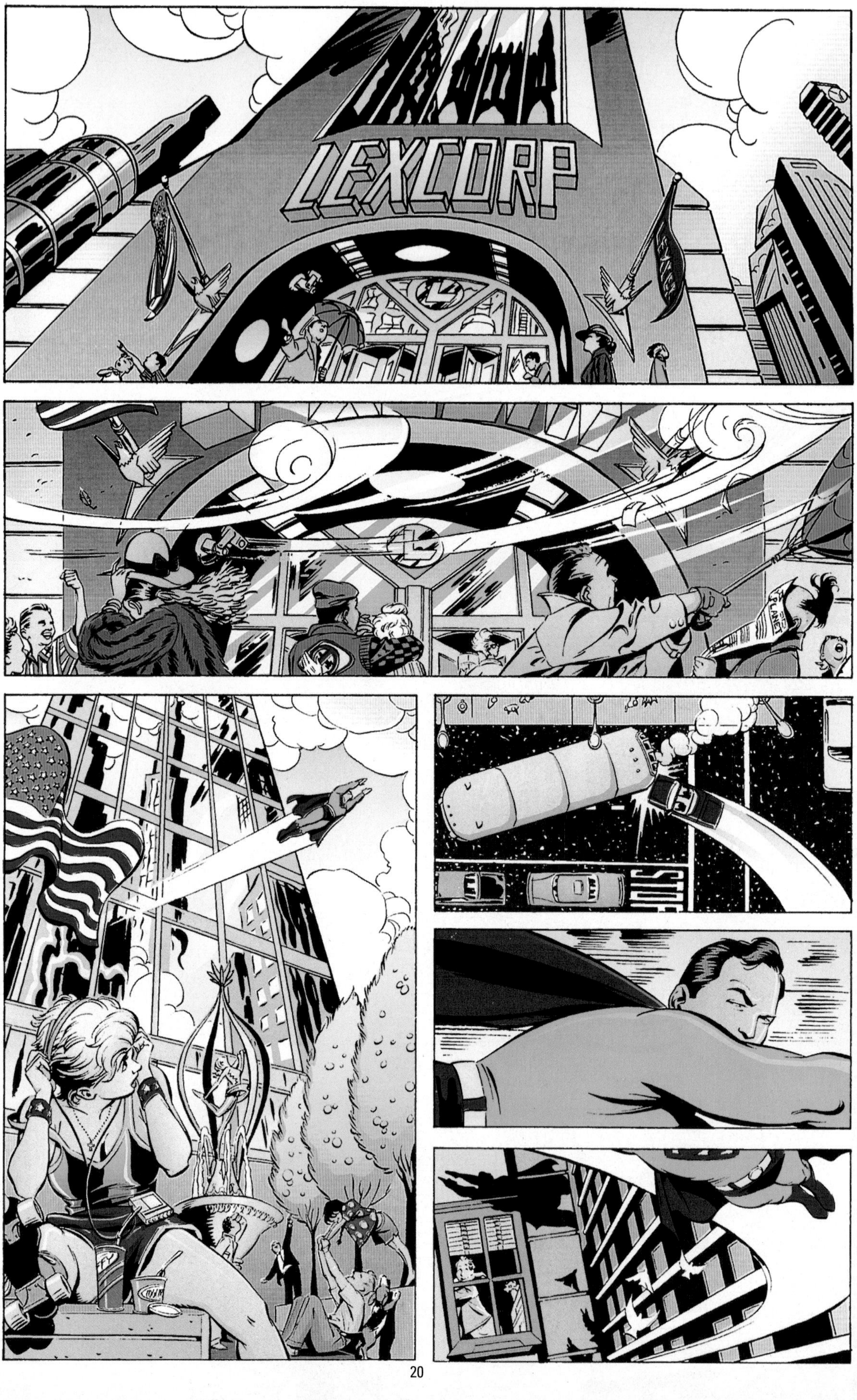
LEXCORP

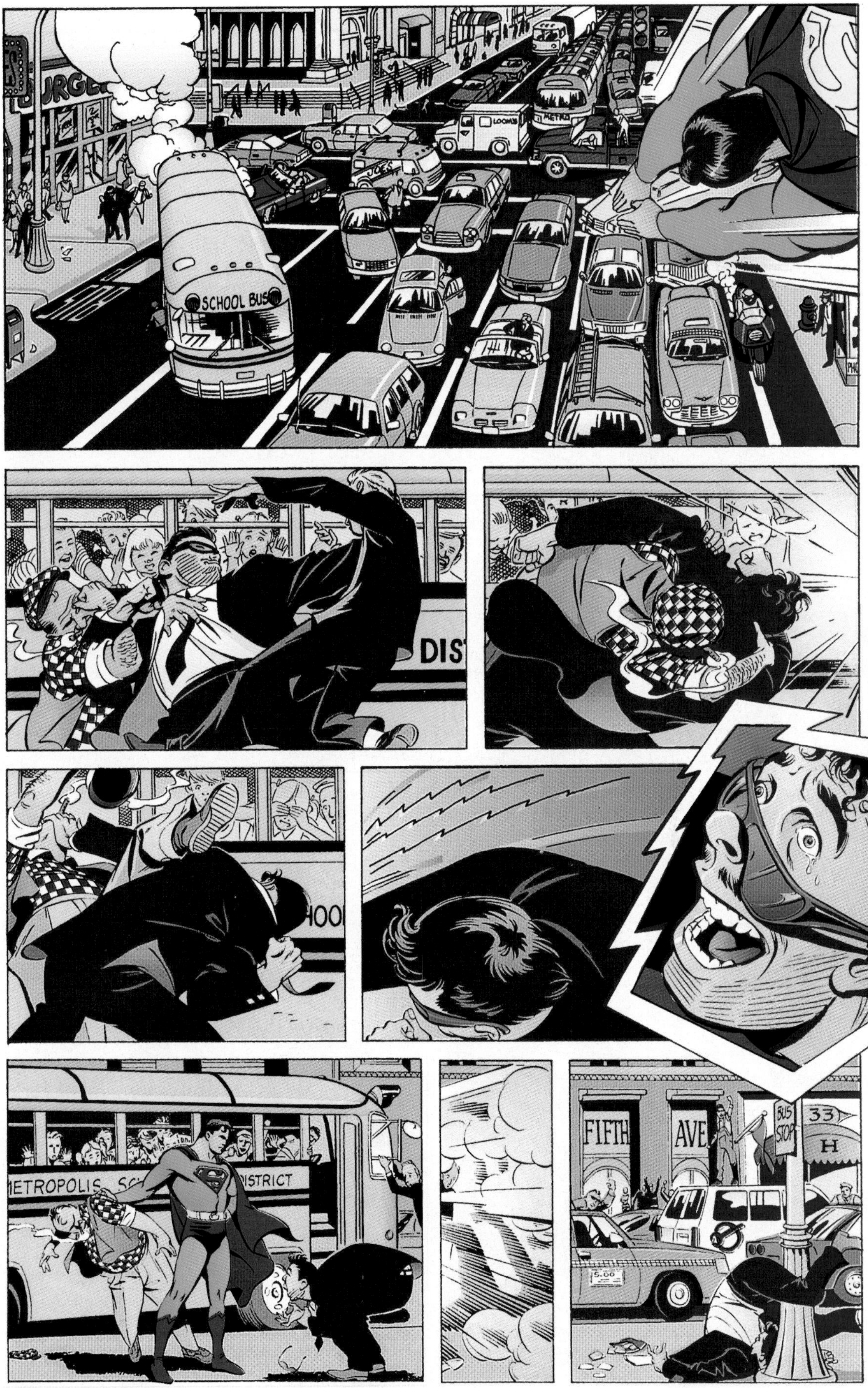

SCHOOL BUS
FIFTH
AVE
BUS STOP
33

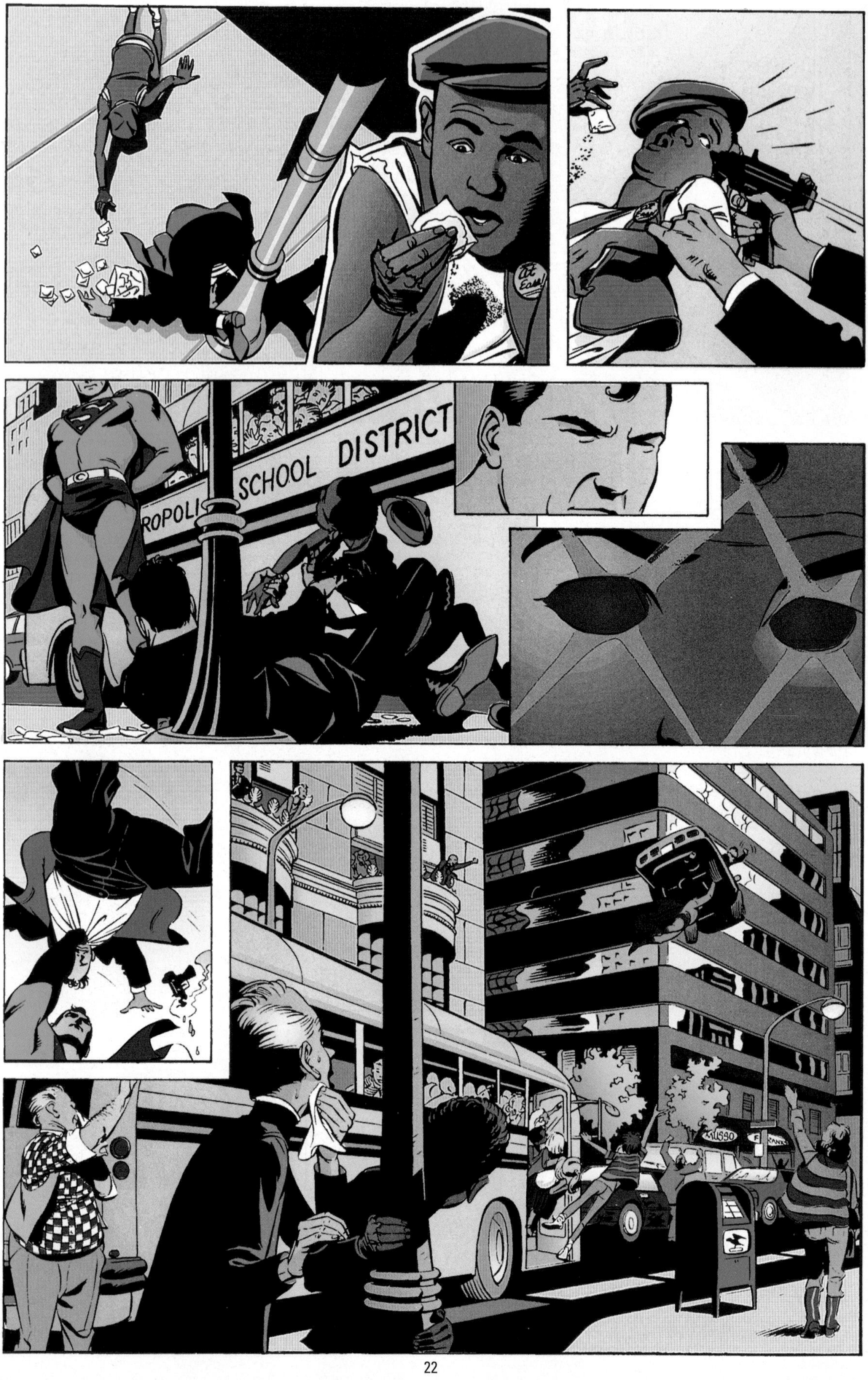
ROPOLI SCHOOL DISTRICT

SGT. PHILCO
DESK SERGEANT

BAIL BOND

JOANA DA COSTA
MARSHALL, A
BURR · LEX
PICKERN · CORP.
ATTORNEYS · LEGAL

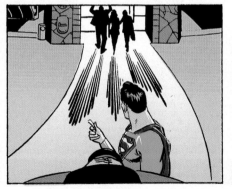

LUTHOR.

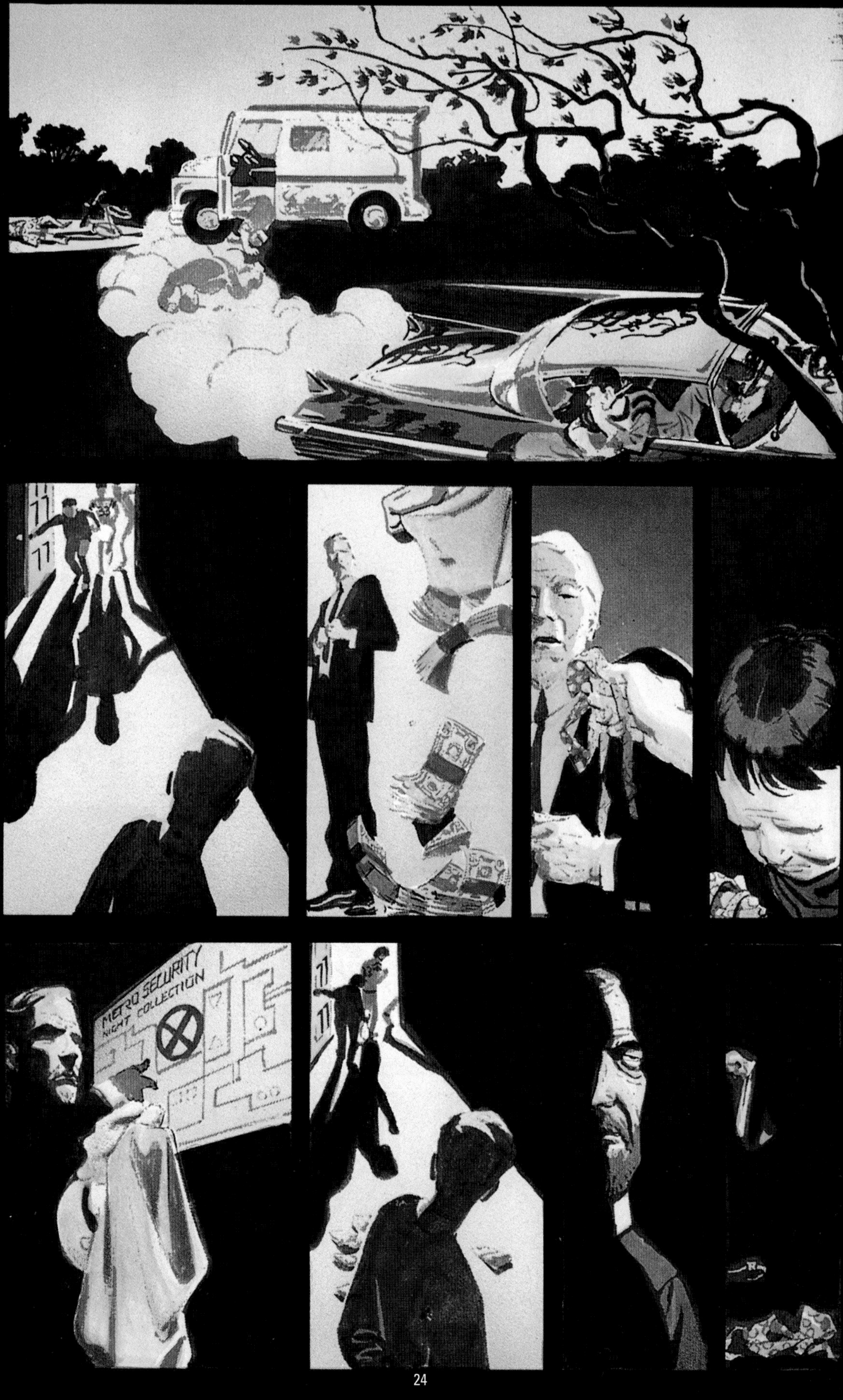
METRO SECURITY
NIGHT COLLECTION

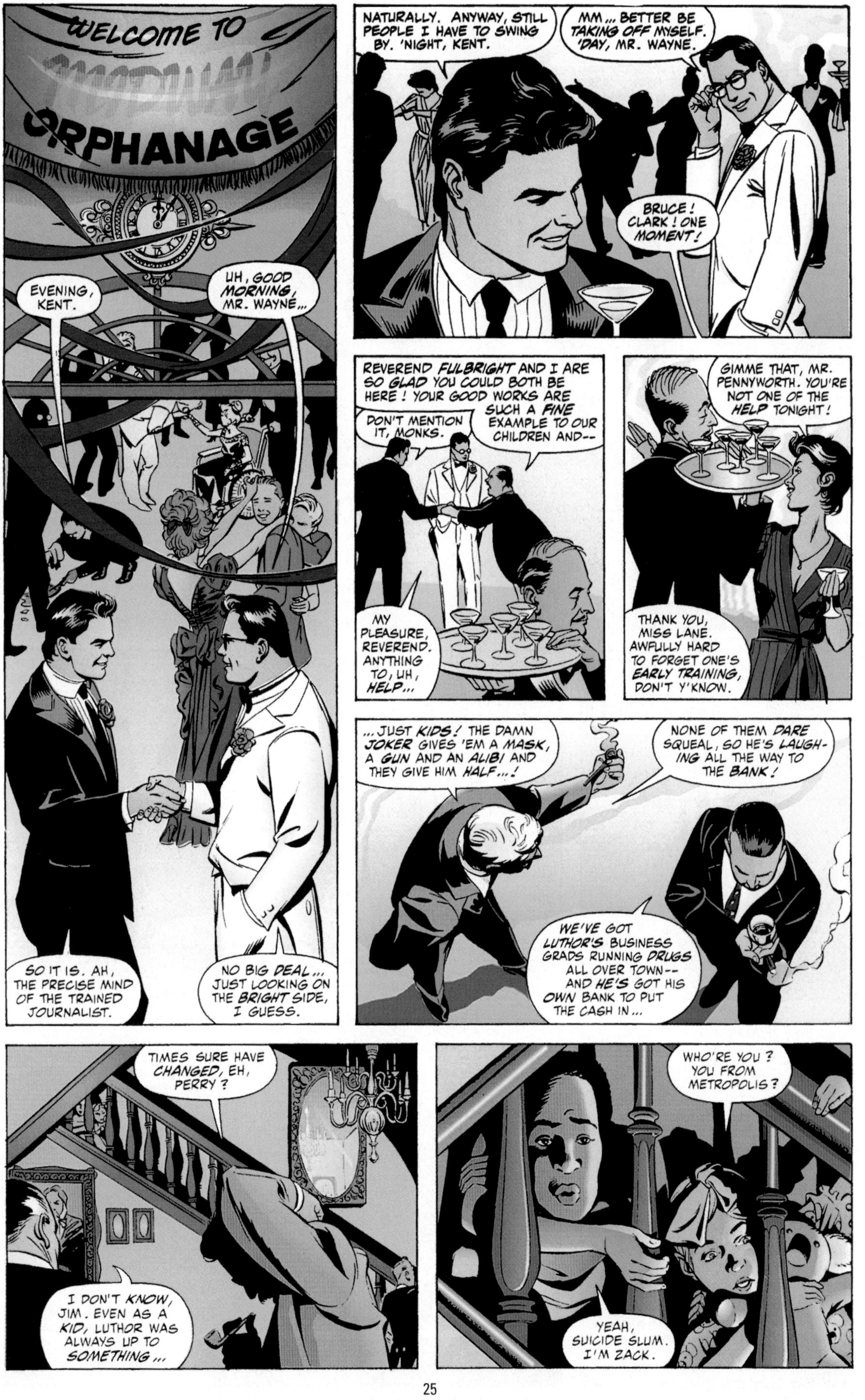
WELCOME TO
ORPHANAGE
EVENING, KENT.
UH, GOOD MORNING, MR. WAYNE...
SO IT IS. AH, THE PRECISE MIND OF THE TRAINED JOURNALIST.
NO BIG DEAL... JUST LOOKING ON THE BRIGHT SIDE, I GUESS.
NATURALLY. ANYWAY, STILL PEOPLE I HAVE TO SWING BY. 'NIGHT, KENT.
MM... BETTER BE TAKING OFF MYSELF. 'DAY, MR. WAYNE.
BRUCE! CLARK! ONE MOMENT!
REVEREND FULBRIGHT AND I ARE SO GLAD YOU COULD BOTH BE HERE! YOUR GOOD WORKS ARE SUCH A FINE EXAMPLE TO OUR CHILDREN AND--
DON'T MENTION IT, MONKS.
MY PLEASURE, REVEREND. ANYTHING TO, UH, HELP...
GIMME THAT, MR. PENNYWORTH. YOU'RE NOT ONE OF THE HELP TONIGHT!
THANK YOU, MISS LANE. AWFULLY HARD TO FORGET ONE'S EARLY TRAINING, DON'T Y'KNOW.
...JUST KIDS! THE DAMN JOKER GIVES 'EM A MASK, A GUN AND AN ALIBI AND THEY GIVE HIM HALF...!
NONE OF THEM DARE SQUEAL, SO HE'S LAUGHING ALL THE WAY TO THE BANK!
WE'VE GOT LUTHOR'S BUSINESS GRADS RUNNING DRUGS ALL OVER TOWN-- AND HE'S GOT HIS OWN BANK TO PUT THE CASH IN...
TIMES SURE HAVE CHANGED, EH, PERRY?
I DON'T KNOW, JIM. EVEN AS A KID, LUTHOR WAS ALWAYS UP TO SOMETHING...
WHO'RE YOU? YOU FROM METROPOLIS?
YEAH, SUICIDE SLUM. I'M ZACK.

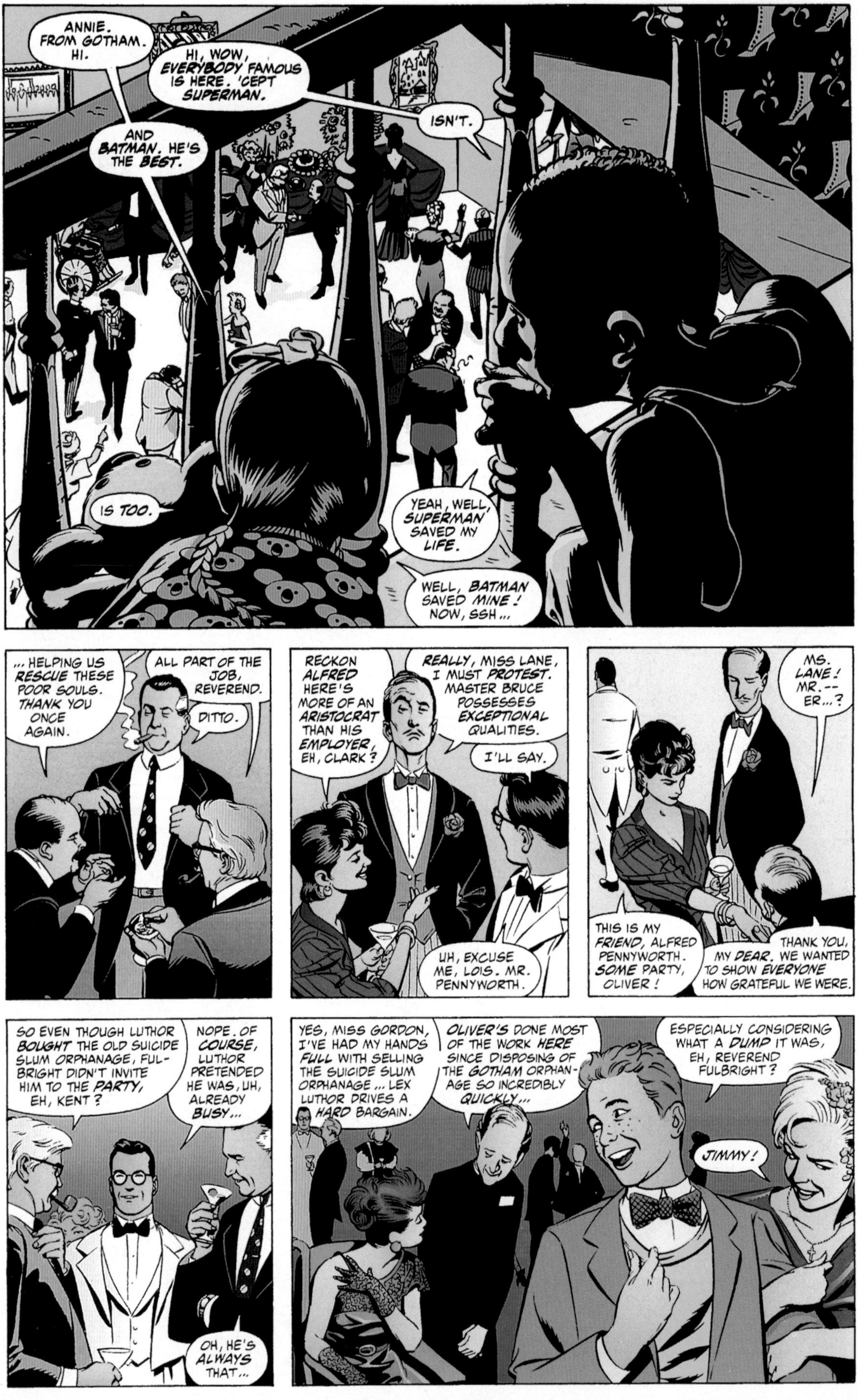
ANNIE. FROM GOTHAM. HI.
HI, WOW, EVERYBODY FAMOUS IS HERE. 'CEPT SUPERMAN.
AND BATMAN. HE'S THE BEST.
ISN'T.
IS TOO.
YEAH, WELL, SUPERMAN SAVED MY LIFE.
WELL, BATMAN SAVED MINE! NOW, SSH...
...HELPING US RESCUE THESE POOR SOULS. THANK YOU ONCE AGAIN.
ALL PART OF THE JOB, REVEREND.
DITTO.
RECKON ALFRED HERE'S MORE OF AN ARISTOCRAT THAN HIS EMPLOYER, EH, CLARK?
REALLY, MISS LANE, I MUST PROTEST. MASTER BRUCE POSSESSES EXCEPTIONAL QUALITIES.
I'LL SAY.
UH, EXCUSE ME, LOIS. MR. PENNYWORTH.
MS. LANE! MR.-- ER...?
THIS IS MY FRIEND, ALFRED PENNYWORTH. SOME PARTY, OLIVER!
THANK YOU, MY DEAR. WE WANTED TO SHOW EVERYONE HOW GRATEFUL WE WERE.
SO EVEN THOUGH LUTHOR BOUGHT THE OLD SUICIDE SLUM ORPHANAGE, FULBRIGHT DIDN'T INVITE HIM TO THE PARTY, EH, KENT?
NOPE. OF COURSE, LUTHOR PRETENDED HE WAS, UH, ALREADY BUSY...
OH, HE'S ALWAYS THAT...
YES, MISS GORDON, I'VE HAD MY HANDS FULL WITH SELLING THE SUICIDE SLUM ORPHANAGE... LEX LUTHOR DRIVES A HARD BARGAIN.
OLIVER'S DONE MOST OF THE WORK HERE SINCE DISPOSING OF THE GOTHAM ORPHANAGE SO INCREDIBLY QUICKLY...
ESPECIALLY CONSIDERING WHAT A DUMP IT WAS, EH, REVEREND FULBRIGHT?
JIMMY!

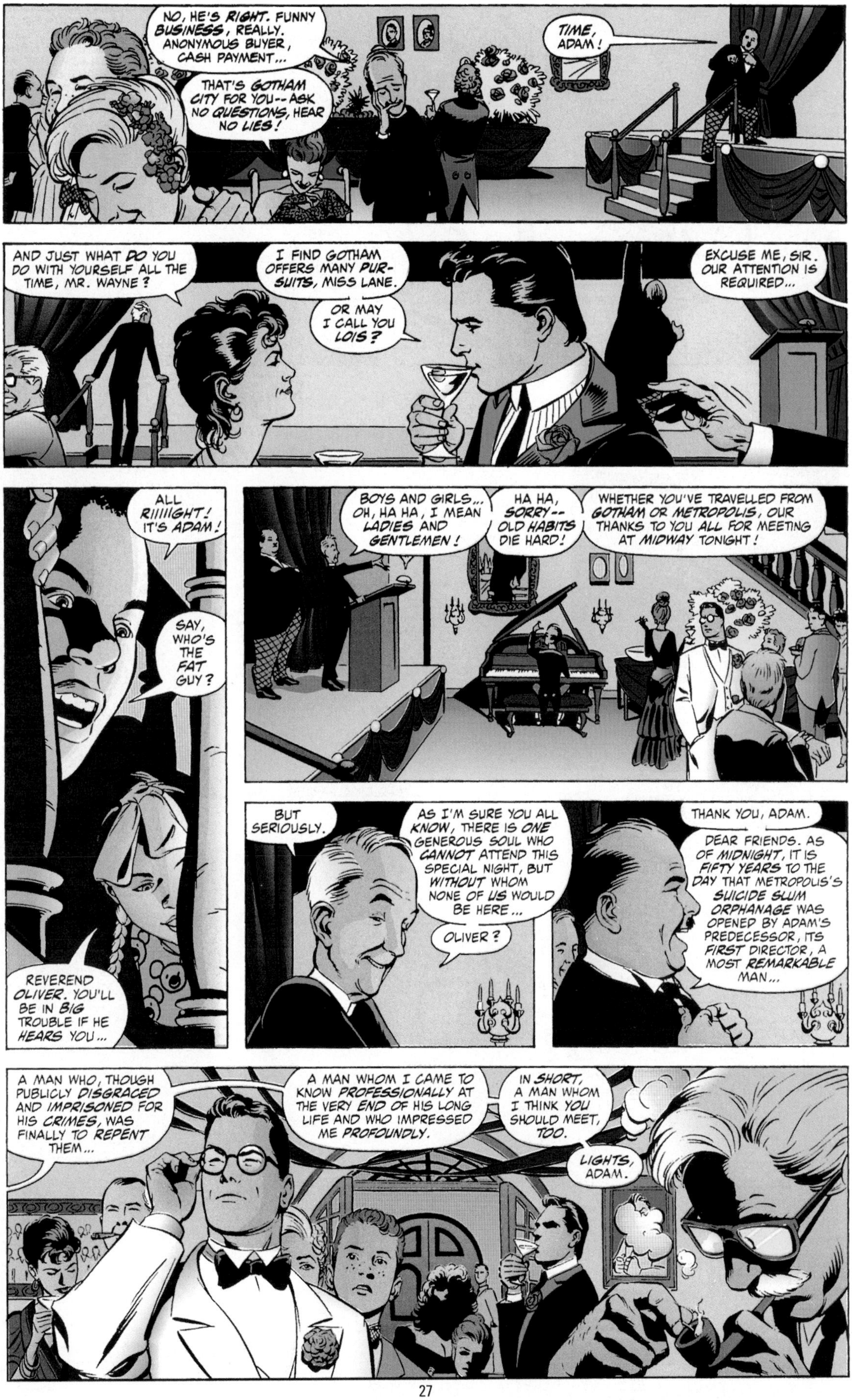
NO, HE'S RIGHT. FUNNY BUSINESS, REALLY. ANONYMOUS BUYER, CASH PAYMENT...
THAT'S GOTHAM CITY FOR YOU--ASK NO QUESTIONS, HEAR NO LIES!
TIME, ADAM!
AND JUST WHAT DO YOU DO WITH YOURSELF ALL THE TIME, MR. WAYNE?
I FIND GOTHAM OFFERS MANY PURSUITS, MISS LANE.
OR MAY I CALL YOU LOIS?
EXCUSE ME, SIR. OUR ATTENTION IS REQUIRED...
ALL RIIIIIGHT! IT'S ADAM!
SAY, WHO'S THE FAT GUY?
REVEREND OLIVER. YOU'LL BE IN BIG TROUBLE IF HE HEARS YOU...
BOYS AND GIRLS... OH, HA HA, I MEAN LADIES AND GENTLEMEN!
HA HA, SORRY-- OLD HABITS DIE HARD!
WHETHER YOU'VE TRAVELLED FROM GOTHAM OR METROPOLIS, OUR THANKS TO YOU ALL FOR MEETING AT MIDWAY TONIGHT!
BUT SERIOUSLY.
AS I'M SURE YOU ALL KNOW, THERE IS ONE GENEROUS SOUL WHO CANNOT ATTEND THIS SPECIAL NIGHT, BUT WITHOUT WHOM NONE OF US WOULD BE HERE...
OLIVER?
THANK YOU, ADAM.
DEAR FRIENDS. AS OF MIDNIGHT, IT IS FIFTY YEARS TO THE DAY THAT METROPOLIS'S SUICIDE SLUM ORPHANAGE WAS OPENED BY ADAM'S PREDECESSOR, ITS FIRST DIRECTOR, A MOST REMARKABLE MAN...
A MAN WHO, THOUGH PUBLICLY DISGRACED AND IMPRISONED FOR HIS CRIMES, WAS FINALLY TO REPENT THEM...
A MAN WHOM I CAME TO KNOW PROFESSIONALLY AT THE VERY END OF HIS LONG LIFE AND WHO IMPRESSED ME PROFOUNDLY.
IN SHORT, A MAN WHOM I THINK YOU SHOULD MEET, TOO.
LIGHTS, ADAM.

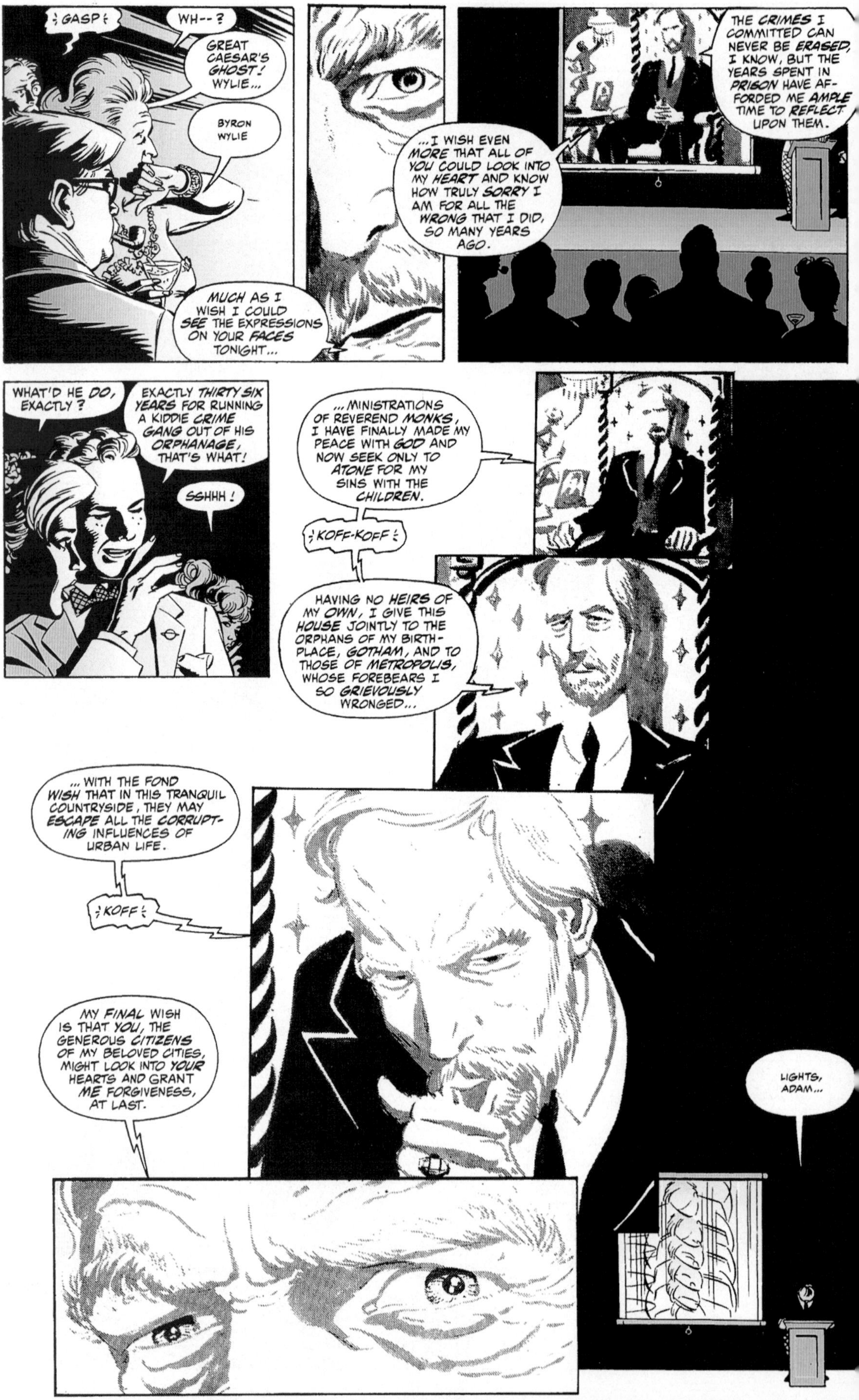

GASP
WH--?
GREAT CAESAR'S GHOST! WYLIE...
BYRON WYLIE
MUCH AS I WISH I COULD SEE THE EXPRESSIONS ON YOUR FACES TONIGHT...
...I WISH EVEN MORE THAT ALL OF YOU COULD LOOK INTO MY HEART AND KNOW HOW TRULY SORRY I AM FOR ALL THE WRONG THAT I DID, SO MANY YEARS AGO.
THE CRIMES I COMMITTED CAN NEVER BE ERASED, I KNOW, BUT THE YEARS SPENT IN PRISON HAVE AFFORDED ME AMPLE TIME TO REFLECT UPON THEM.
WHAT'D HE DO, EXACTLY?
EXACTLY THIRTY SIX YEARS FOR RUNNING A KIDDIE CRIME GANG OUT OF HIS ORPHANAGE, THAT'S WHAT!
SSHHH!
...MINISTRATIONS OF REVEREND MONKS, I HAVE FINALLY MADE MY PEACE WITH GOD AND NOW SEEK ONLY TO ATONE FOR MY SINS WITH THE CHILDREN.
KOFF-KOFF
HAVING NO HEIRS OF MY OWN, I GIVE THIS HOUSE JOINTLY TO THE ORPHANS OF MY BIRTHPLACE, GOTHAM, AND TO THOSE OF METROPOLIS, WHOSE FOREBEARS I SO GRIEVOUSLY WRONGED...
...WITH THE FOND WISH THAT IN THIS TRANQUIL COUNTRYSIDE, THEY MAY ESCAPE ALL THE CORRUPTING INFLUENCES OF URBAN LIFE.
KOFF
MY FINAL WISH IS THAT YOU, THE GENEROUS CITIZENS OF MY BELOVED CITIES, MIGHT LOOK INTO YOUR HEARTS AND GRANT ME FORGIVENESS, AT LAST.
LIGHTS, ADAM...

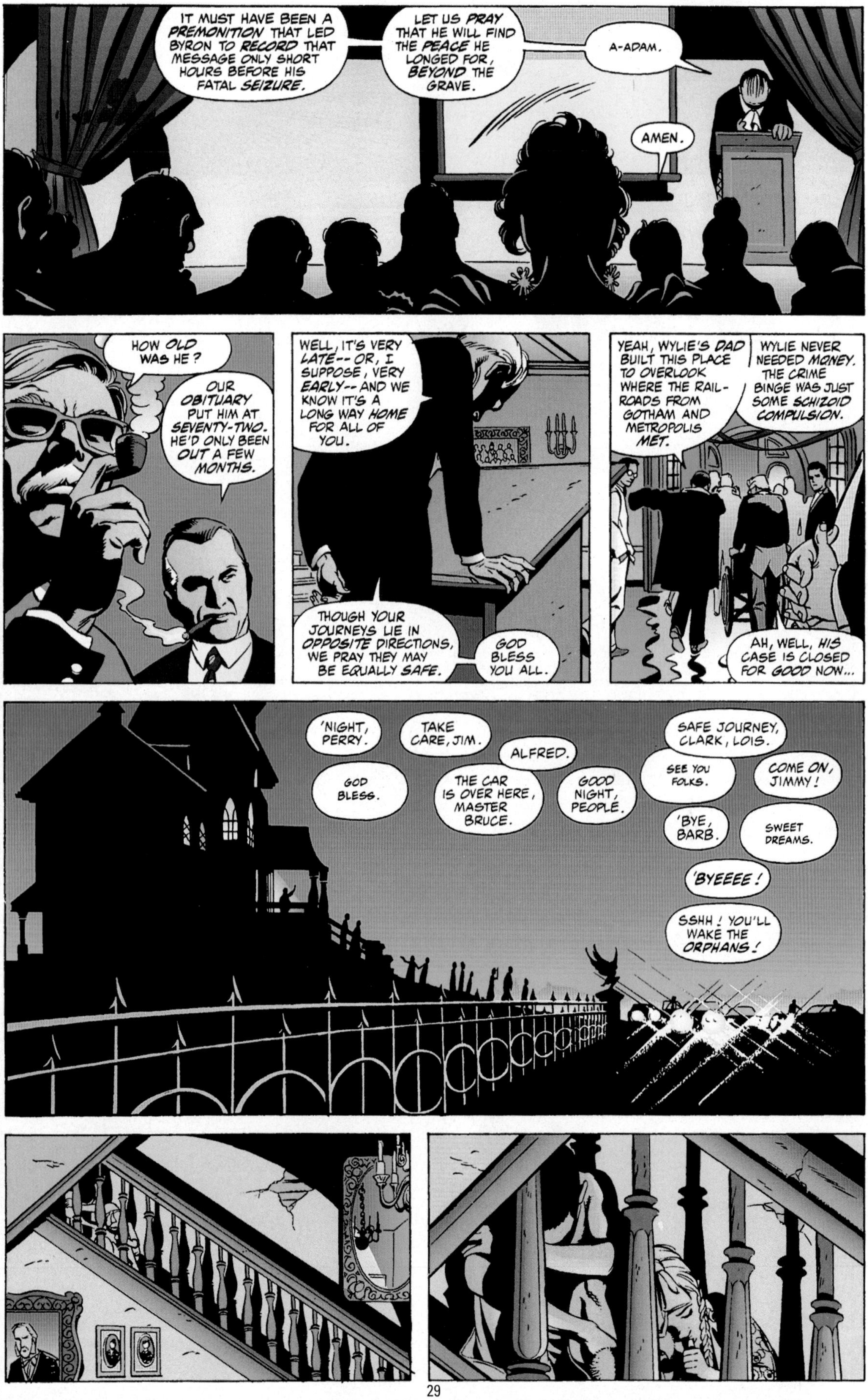
IT MUST HAVE BEEN A PREMONITION THAT LED BYRON TO RECORD THAT MESSAGE ONLY SHORT HOURS BEFORE HIS FATAL SEIZURE.
LET US PRAY THAT HE WILL FIND THE PEACE HE LONGED FOR, BEYOND THE GRAVE.
A-ADAM.
AMEN.
HOW OLD WAS HE?
OUR OBITUARY PUT HIM AT SEVENTY-TWO. HE'D ONLY BEEN OUT A FEW MONTHS.
WELL, IT'S VERY LATE-- OR, I SUPPOSE, VERY EARLY-- AND WE KNOW IT'S A LONG WAY HOME FOR ALL OF YOU.
THOUGH YOUR JOURNEYS LIE IN OPPOSITE DIRECTIONS, WE PRAY THEY MAY BE EQUALLY SAFE.
GOD BLESS YOU ALL.
YEAH, WYLIE'S DAD BUILT THIS PLACE TO OVERLOOK WHERE THE RAILROADS FROM GOTHAM AND METROPOLIS MET.
WYLIE NEVER NEEDED MONEY. THE CRIME BINGE WAS JUST SOME SCHIZOID COMPULSION.
AH, WELL, HIS CASE IS CLOSED FOR GOOD NOW...
'NIGHT, PERRY.
GOD BLESS.
TAKE CARE, JIM.
ALFRED.
THE CAR IS OVER HERE, MASTER BRUCE.
GOOD NIGHT, PEOPLE.
SAFE JOURNEY, CLARK, LOIS.
SEE YOU FOLKS.
COME ON, JIMMY!
'BYE, BARB.
SWEET DREAMS.
'BYEEEE!
SSHH! YOU'LL WAKE THE ORPHANS!

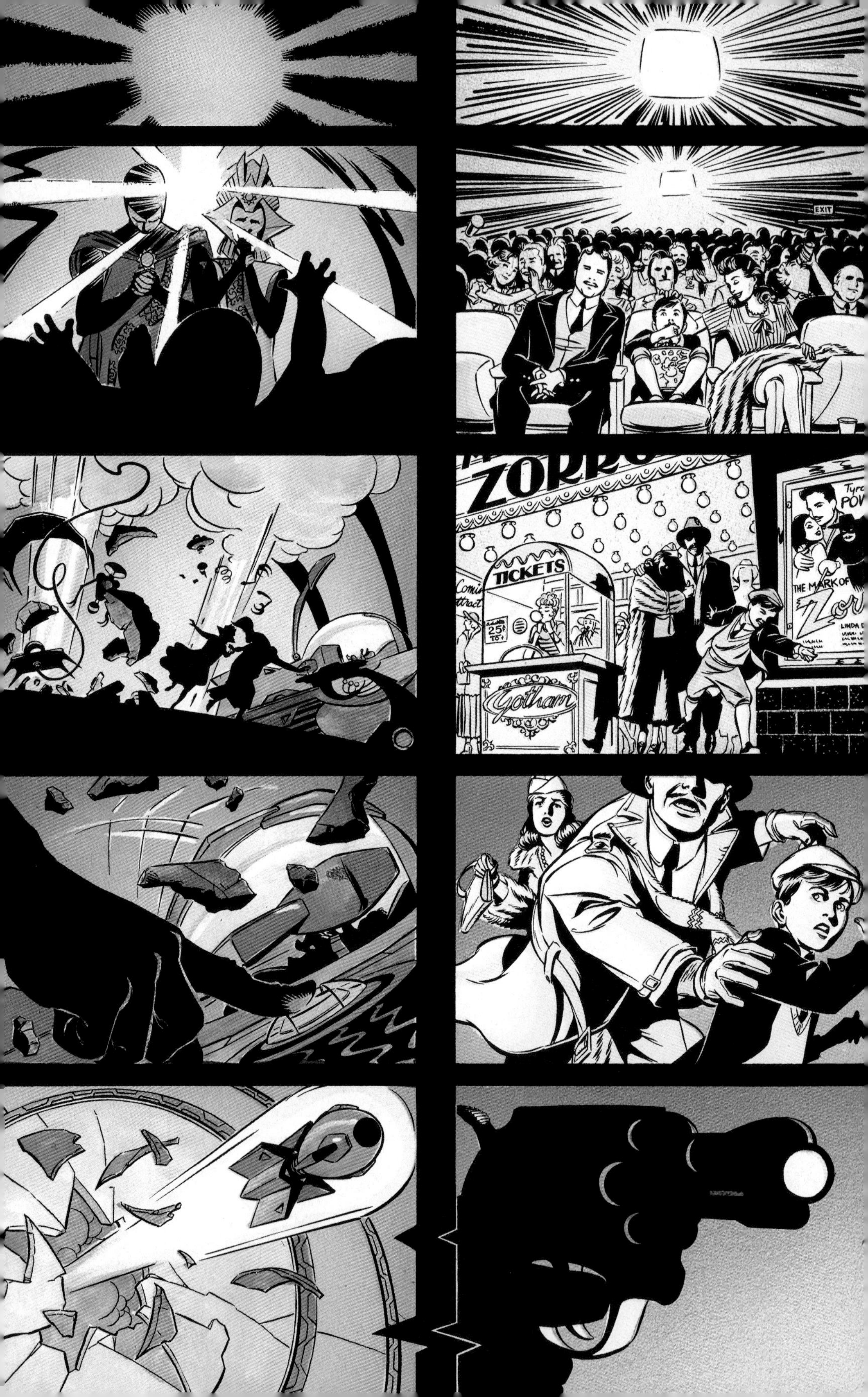
EXIT
TICKETS
Gotham
THE MARK OF

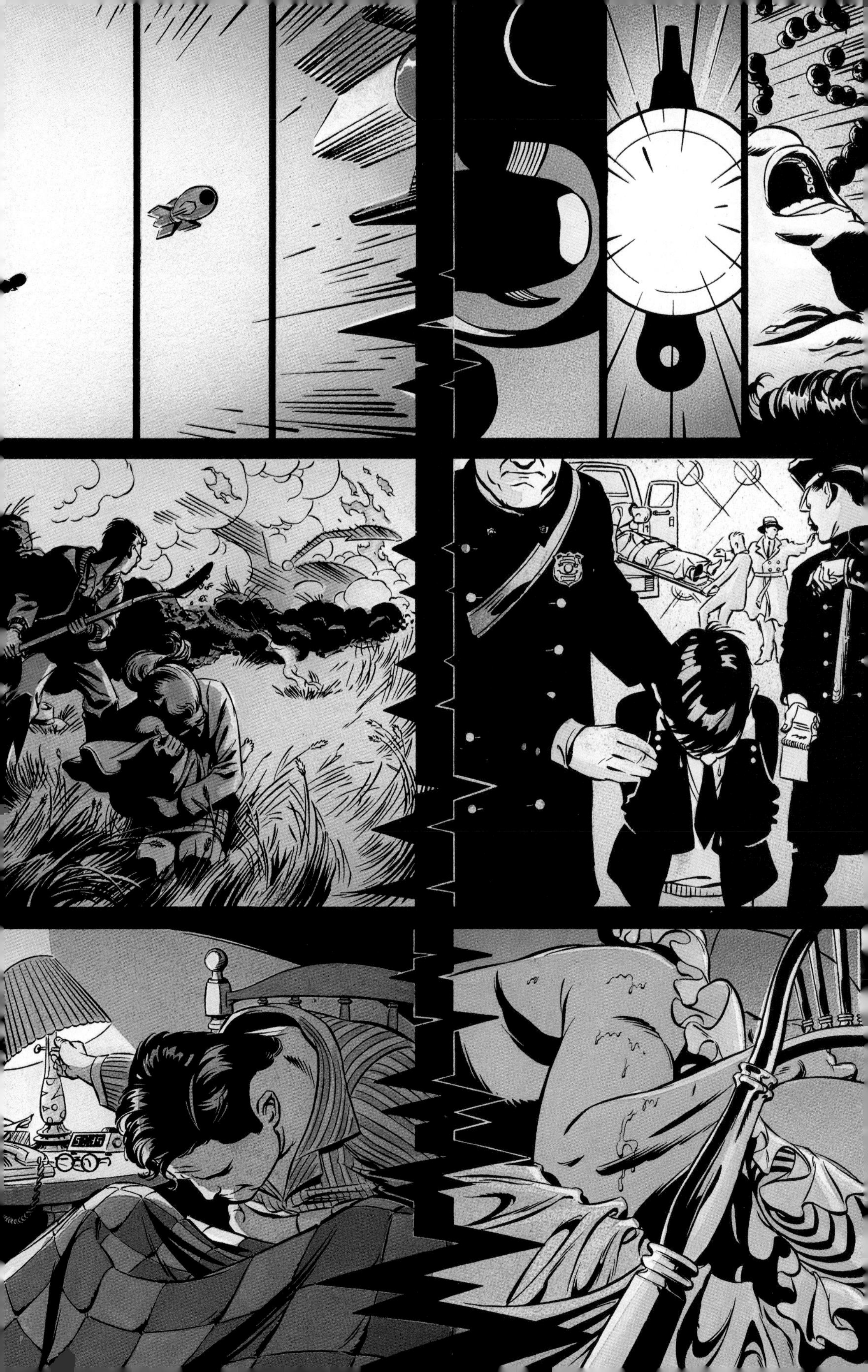

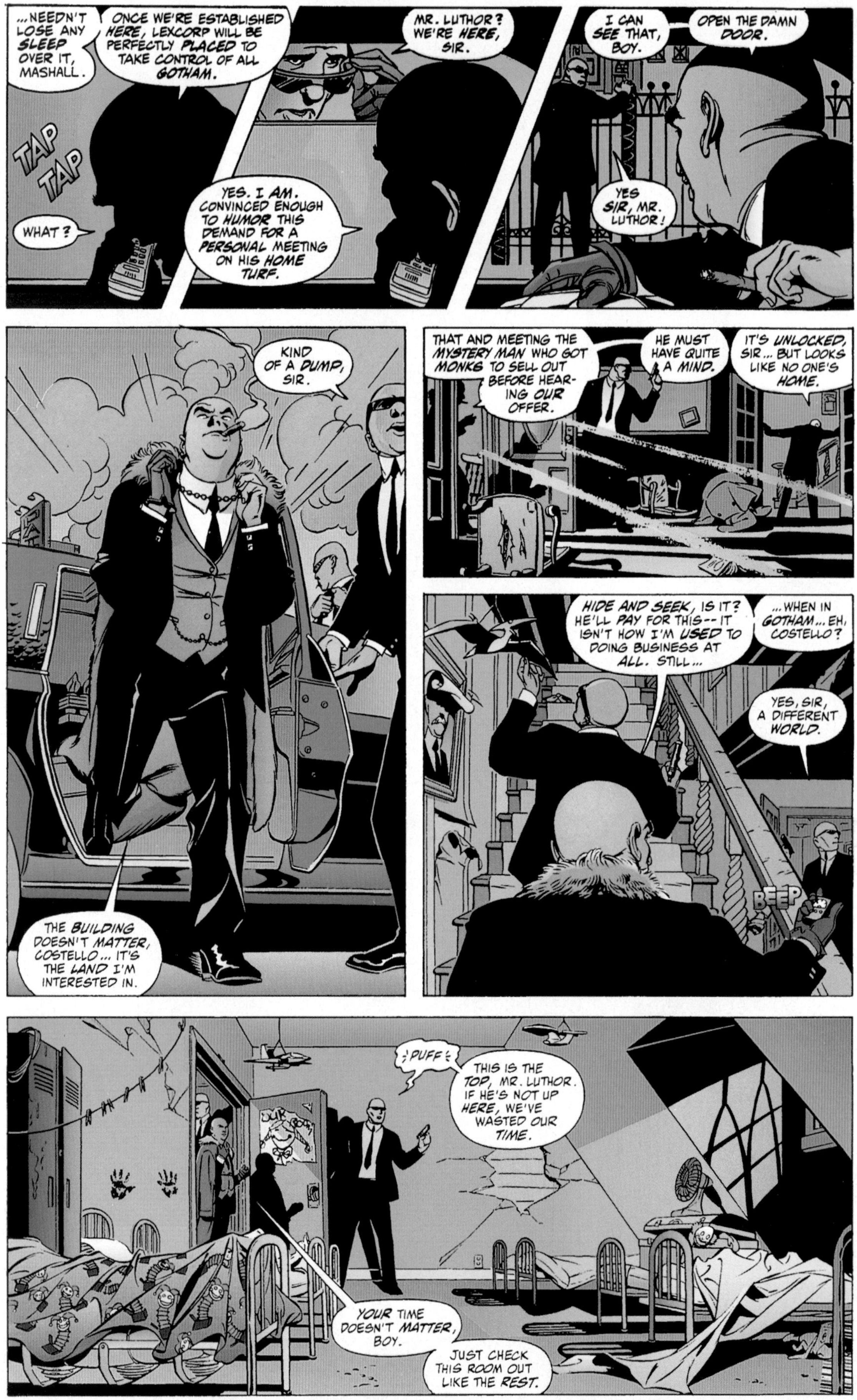

...NEEDN'T LOSE ANY SLEEP OVER IT, MASHALL.
ONCE WE'RE ESTABLISHED HERE, LEXCORP WILL BE PERFECTLY PLACED TO TAKE CONTROL OF ALL GOTHAM.
TAP TAP
WHAT?
MR. LUTHOR? WE'RE HERE, SIR.
YES. I AM. CONVINCED ENOUGH TO HUMOR THIS DEMAND FOR A PERSONAL MEETING ON HIS HOME TURF.
I CAN SEE THAT, BOY.
OPEN THE DAMN DOOR.
YES SIR, MR. LUTHOR!
KIND OF A DUMP, SIR.
THE BUILDING DOESN'T MATTER, COSTELLO... IT'S THE LAND I'M INTERESTED IN.
THAT AND MEETING THE MYSTERY MAN WHO GOT MONKS TO SELL OUT BEFORE HEARING OUR OFFER.
HE MUST HAVE QUITE A MIND.
IT'S UNLOCKED, SIR... BUT LOOKS LIKE NO ONE'S HOME.
HIDE AND SEEK, IS IT? HE'LL PAY FOR THIS-- IT ISN'T HOW I'M USED TO DOING BUSINESS AT ALL. STILL...
...WHEN IN GOTHAM... EH, COSTELLO?
YES, SIR, A DIFFERENT WORLD.
BEEP
PUFF
THIS IS THE TOP, MR. LUTHOR. IF HE'S NOT UP HERE, WE'VE WASTED OUR TIME.
YOUR TIME DOESN'T MATTER, BOY.
JUST CHECK THIS ROOM OUT LIKE THE REST.

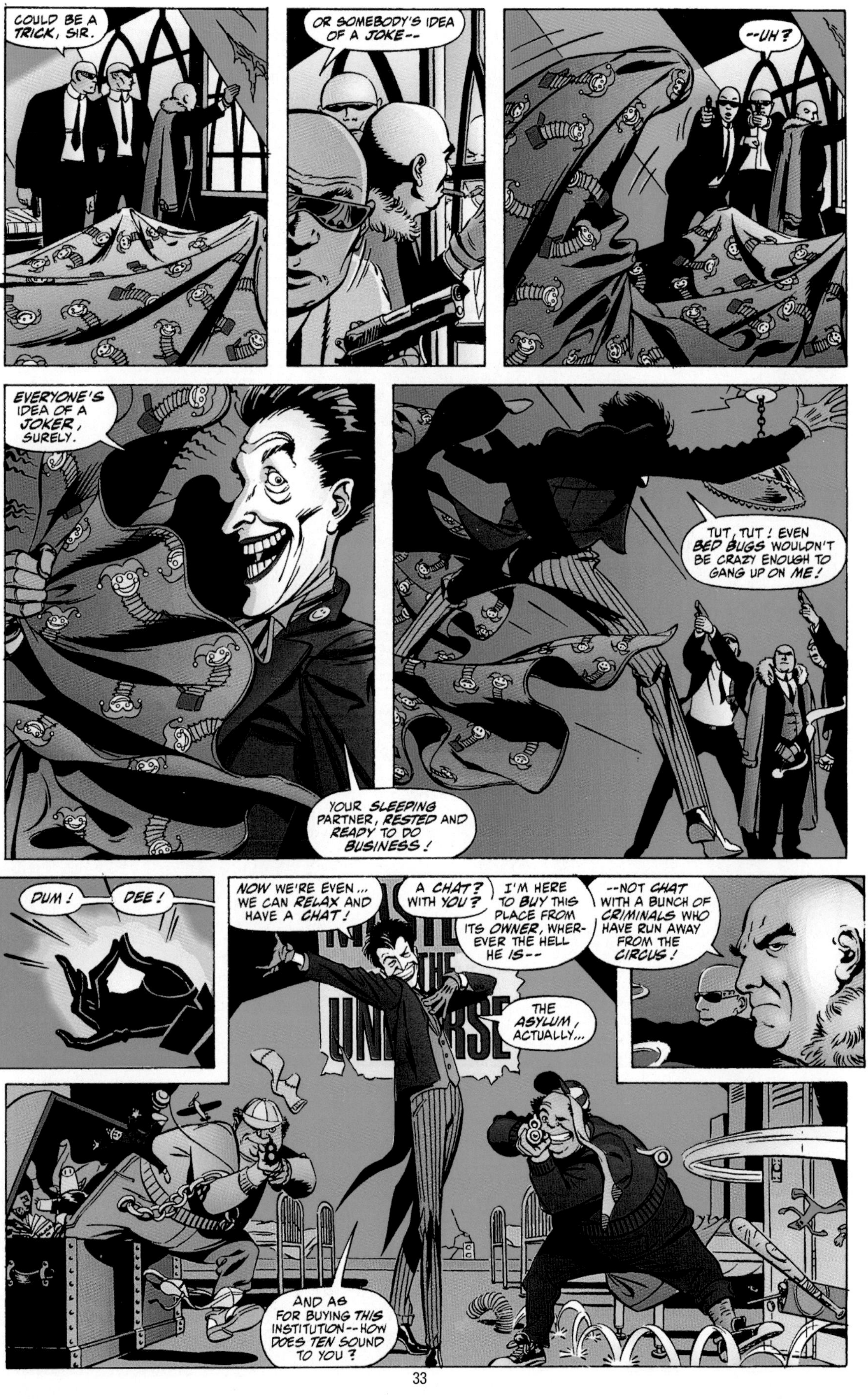
COULD BE A TRICK, SIR.
OR SOMEBODY'S IDEA OF A JOKE--
--UH?
EVERYONE'S IDEA OF A JOKER, SURELY.
YOUR SLEEPING PARTNER, RESTED AND READY TO DO BUSINESS!
TUT, TUT! EVEN BED BUGS WOULDN'T BE CRAZY ENOUGH TO GANG UP ON ME!
DUM!
DEE!
NOW WE'RE EVEN... WE CAN RELAX AND HAVE A CHAT!
A CHAT? WITH YOU?
I'M HERE TO BUY THIS PLACE FROM ITS OWNER, WHEREVER THE HELL HE IS--
--NOT CHAT WITH A BUNCH OF CRIMINALS WHO HAVE RUN AWAY FROM THE CIRCUS!
THE ASYLUM, ACTUALLY...
AND AS FOR BUYING THIS INSTITUTION--HOW DOES TEN SOUND TO YOU?

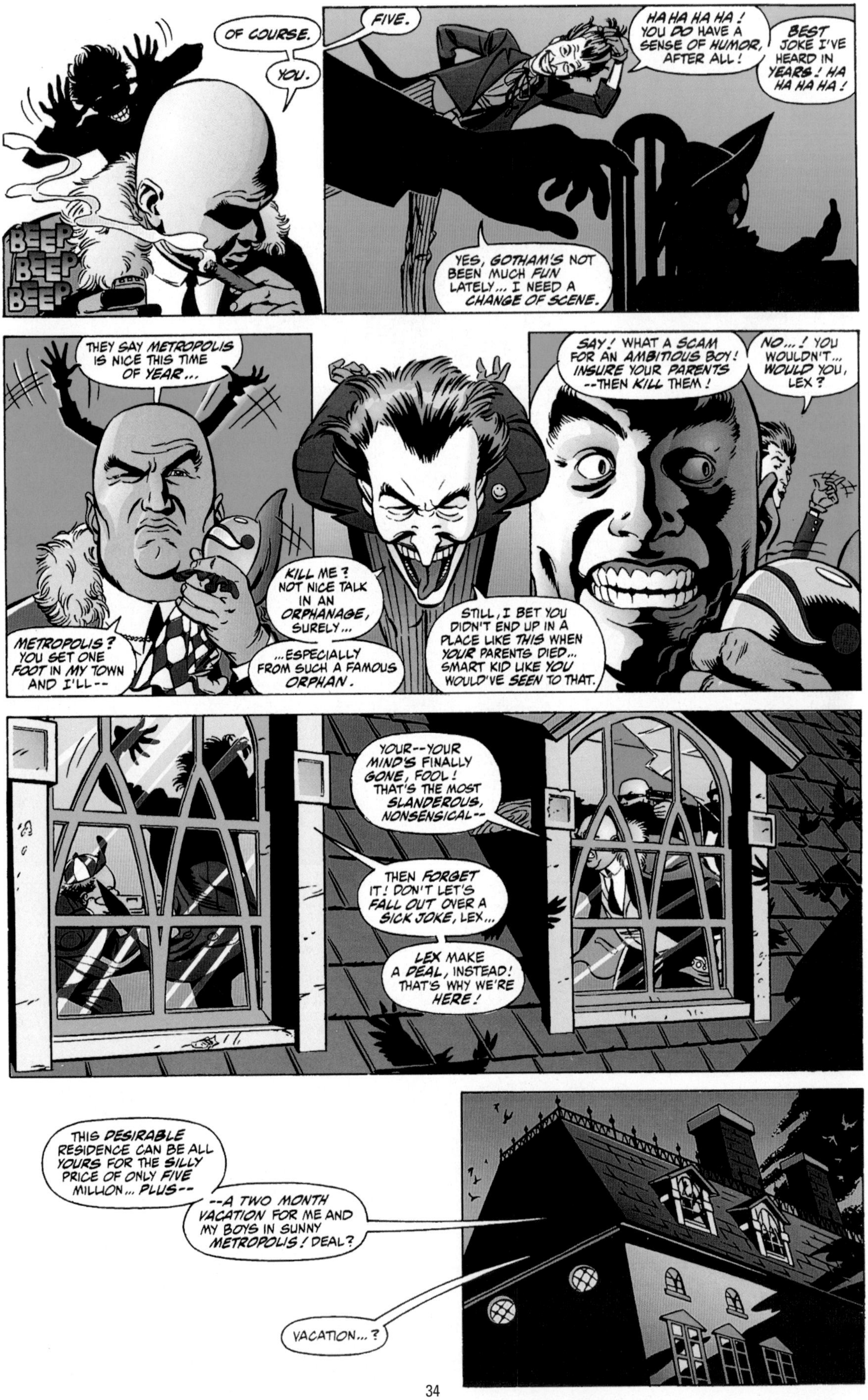
BEEP BEEP BEEP
OF COURSE.
YOU.
FIVE.
HA HA HA HA! YOU DO HAVE A SENSE OF HUMOR, AFTER ALL!
BEST JOKE I'VE HEARD IN YEARS! HA HA HA HA!
YES, GOTHAM'S NOT BEEN MUCH FUN LATELY... I NEED A CHANGE OF SCENE.
THEY SAY METROPOLIS IS NICE THIS TIME OF YEAR...
METROPOLIS? YOU SET ONE FOOT IN MY TOWN AND I'LL--
KILL ME? NOT NICE TALK IN AN ORPHANAGE, SURELY...
...ESPECIALLY FROM SUCH A FAMOUS ORPHAN.
STILL, I BET YOU DIDN'T END UP IN A PLACE LIKE THIS WHEN YOUR PARENTS DIED... SMART KID LIKE YOU WOULD'VE SEEN TO THAT.
SAY! WHAT A SCAM FOR AN AMBITIOUS BOY! INSURE YOUR PARENTS --THEN KILL THEM!
NO...! YOU WOULDN'T... WOULD YOU, LEX?
YOUR--YOUR MIND'S FINALLY GONE, FOOL! THAT'S THE MOST SLANDEROUS, NONSENSICAL--
THEN FORGET IT! DON'T LET'S FALL OUT OVER A SICK JOKE, LEX...
LEX MAKE A DEAL, INSTEAD! THAT'S WHY WE'RE HERE!
THIS DESIRABLE RESIDENCE CAN BE ALL YOURS FOR THE SILLY PRICE OF ONLY FIVE MILLION... PLUS--
--A TWO MONTH VACATION FOR ME AND MY BOYS IN SUNNY METROPOLIS! DEAL?
VACATION...?

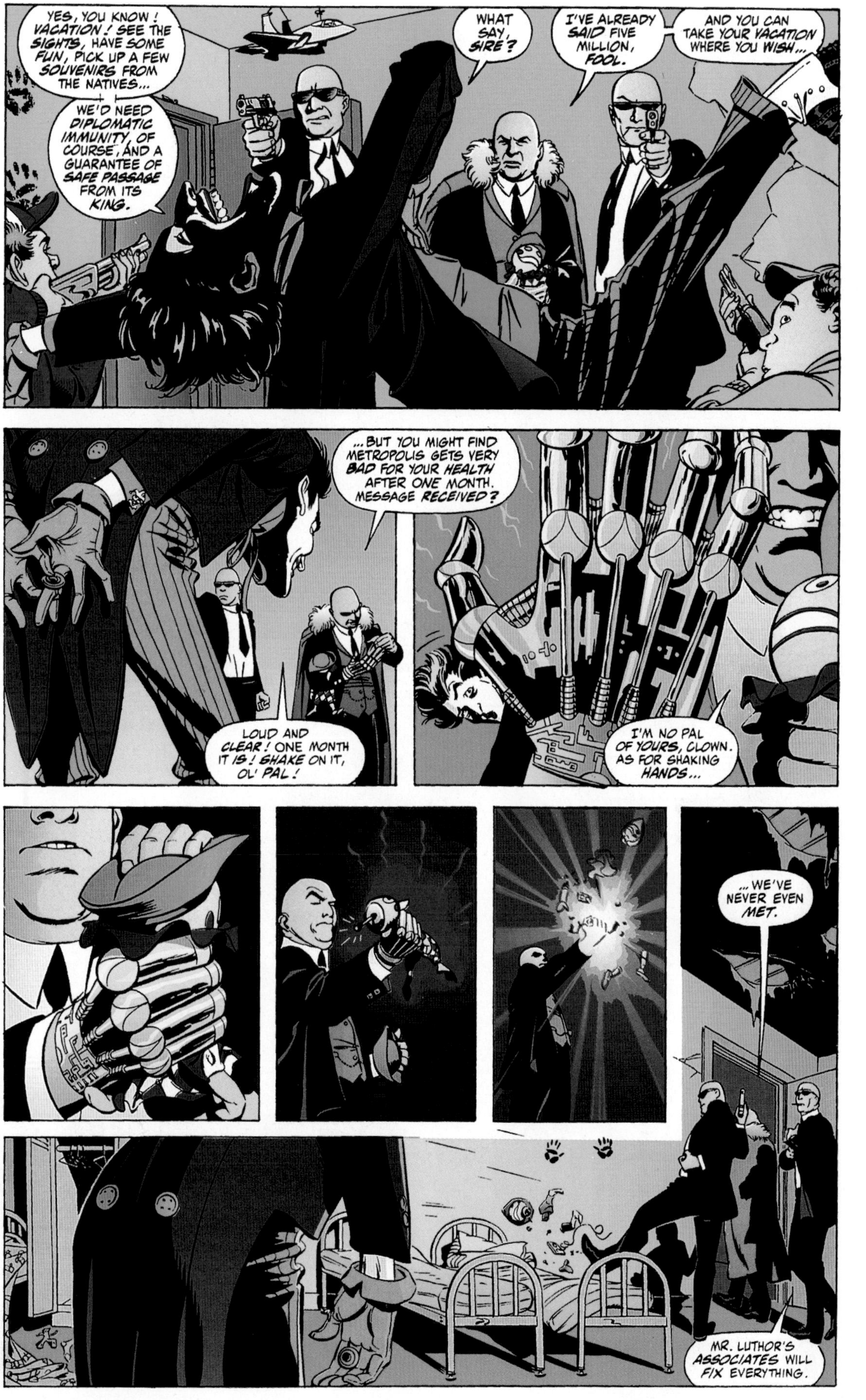
YES, YOU KNOW! VACATION! SEE THE SIGHTS, HAVE SOME FUN, PICK UP A FEW SOUVENIRS FROM THE NATIVES...
WE'D NEED DIPLOMATIC IMMUNITY, OF COURSE, AND A GUARANTEE OF SAFE PASSAGE FROM ITS KING.
WHAT SAY, SIRE?
I'VE ALREADY SAID FIVE MILLION, FOOL.
AND YOU CAN TAKE YOUR VACATION WHERE YOU WISH...
...BUT YOU MIGHT FIND METROPOLIS GETS VERY BAD FOR YOUR HEALTH AFTER ONE MONTH. MESSAGE RECEIVED?
LOUD AND CLEAR! ONE MONTH IT IS! SHAKE ON IT, OL' PAL!
I'M NO PAL OF YOURS, CLOWN. AS FOR SHAKING HANDS...
...WE'VE NEVER EVEN MET.
MR. LUTHOR'S ASSOCIATES WILL FIX EVERYTHING.

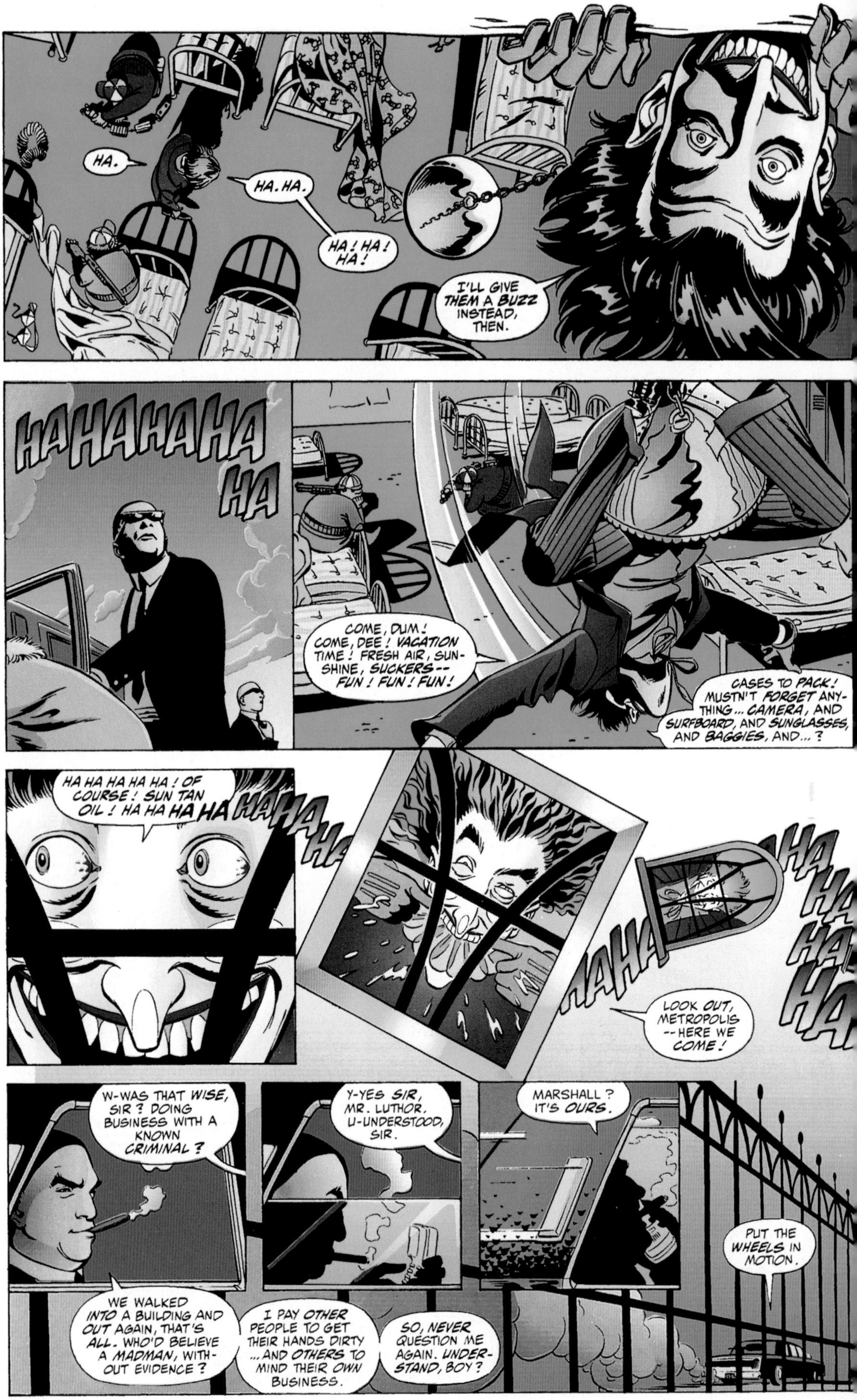
HA.
HA. HA.
HA! HA! HA!
I'LL GIVE THEM A BUZZ INSTEAD, THEN.
HAHAHAHAHA HA
COME, DUM! COME, DEE! VACATION TIME! FRESH AIR, SUNSHINE, SUCKERS-- FUN! FUN! FUN!
CASES TO PACK! MUSTN'T FORGET ANYTHING... CAMERA, AND SURFBOARD, AND SUNGLASSES, AND BAGGIES, AND...?
HA HA HA HA HA! OF COURSE! SUN TAN OIL! HA HA HA HA
LOOK OUT, METROPOLIS --HERE WE COME!
W-WAS THAT WISE, SIR? DOING BUSINESS WITH A KNOWN CRIMINAL?
WE WALKED INTO A BUILDING AND OUT AGAIN, THAT'S ALL. WHO'D BELIEVE A MADMAN, WITHOUT EVIDENCE?
I PAY OTHER PEOPLE TO GET THEIR HANDS DIRTY ...AND OTHERS TO MIND THEIR OWN BUSINESS.
SO, NEVER QUESTION ME AGAIN. UNDERSTAND, BOY?
Y-YES SIR, MR. LUTHOR. U-UNDERSTOOD, SIR.
MARSHALL? IT'S OURS.
PUT THE WHEELS IN MOTION.

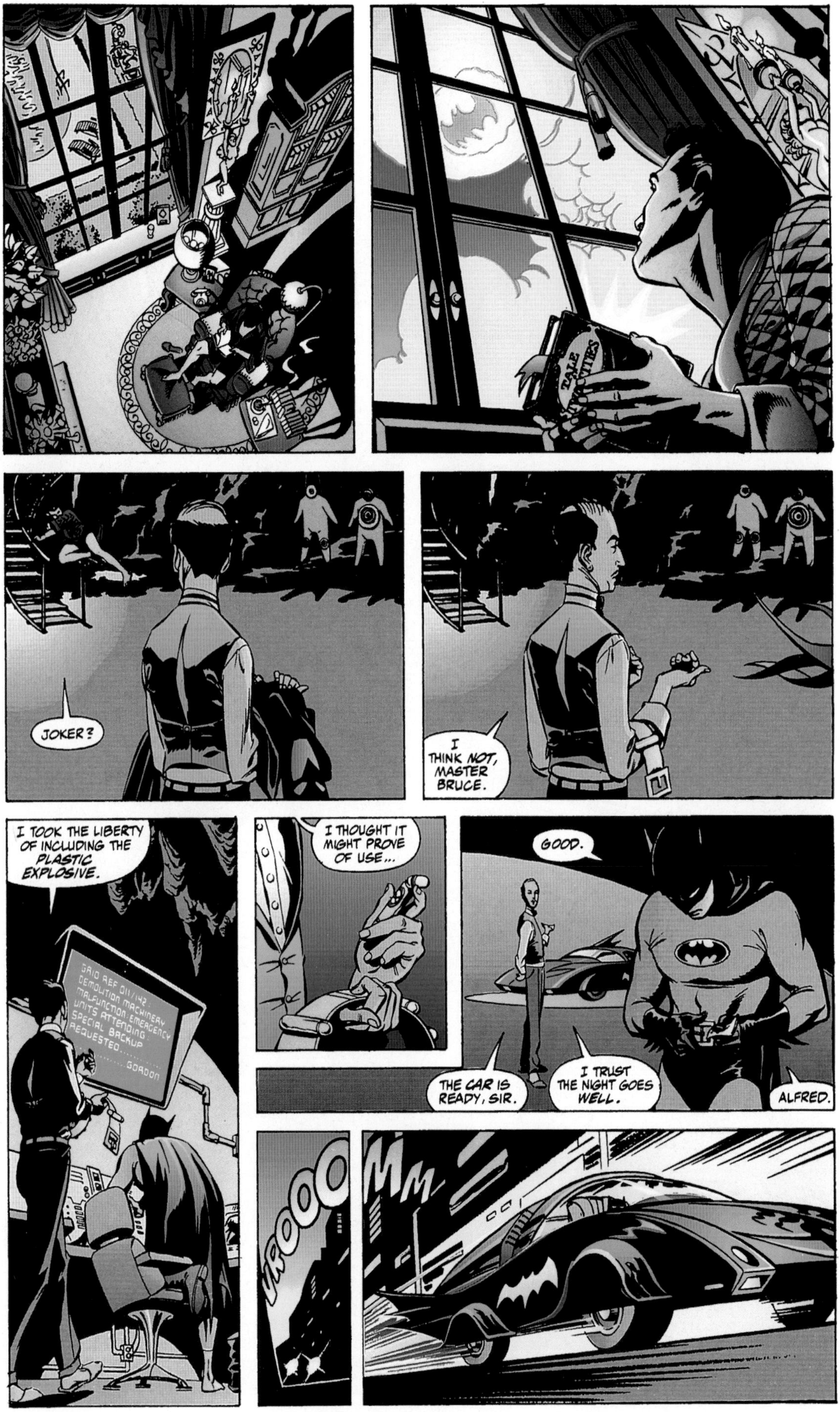
JOKER?
I THINK NOT, MASTER BRUCE.
I TOOK THE LIBERTY OF INCLUDING THE PLASTIC EXPLOSIVE.
GRID REF 011/142: DEMOLITION MACHINERY MALFUNCTION: EMERGENCY UNITS ATTENDING: SPECIAL BACKUP REQUESTED.................GORDON
I THOUGHT IT MIGHT PROVE OF USE...
GOOD.
THE CAR IS READY, SIR.
I TRUST THE NIGHT GOES WELL.
ALFRED.
VROOOMMM

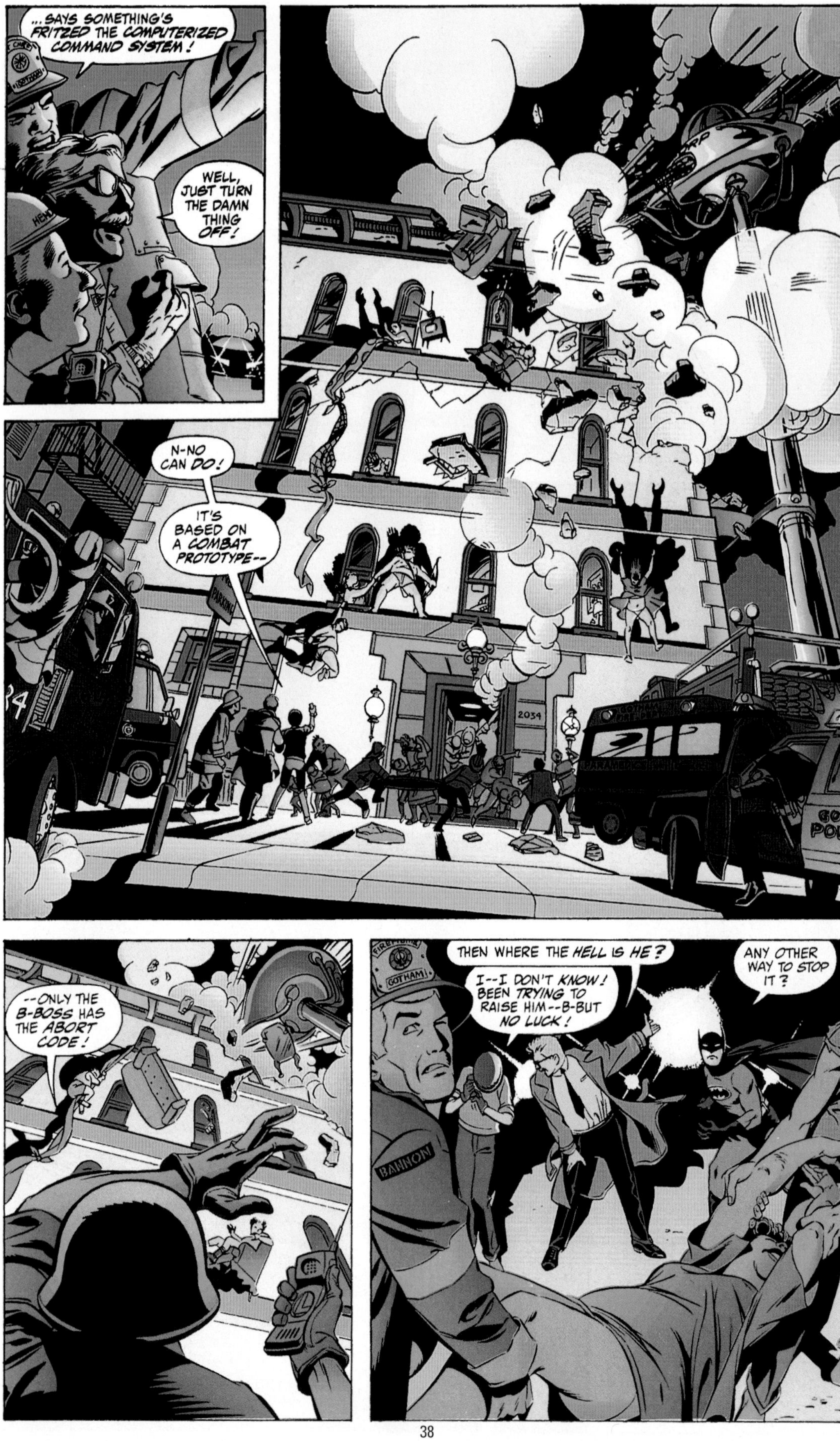
...SAYS SOMETHING'S FRITZED THE COMPUTERIZED COMMAND SYSTEM!
WELL, JUST TURN THE DAMN THING OFF!
N-NO CAN DO!
IT'S BASED ON A COMBAT PROTOTYPE--
--ONLY THE B-BOSS HAS THE ABORT CODE!
THEN WHERE THE HELL IS HE?
I--I DON'T KNOW! BEEN TRYING TO RAISE HIM--B-BUT NO LUCK!
ANY OTHER WAY TO STOP IT?

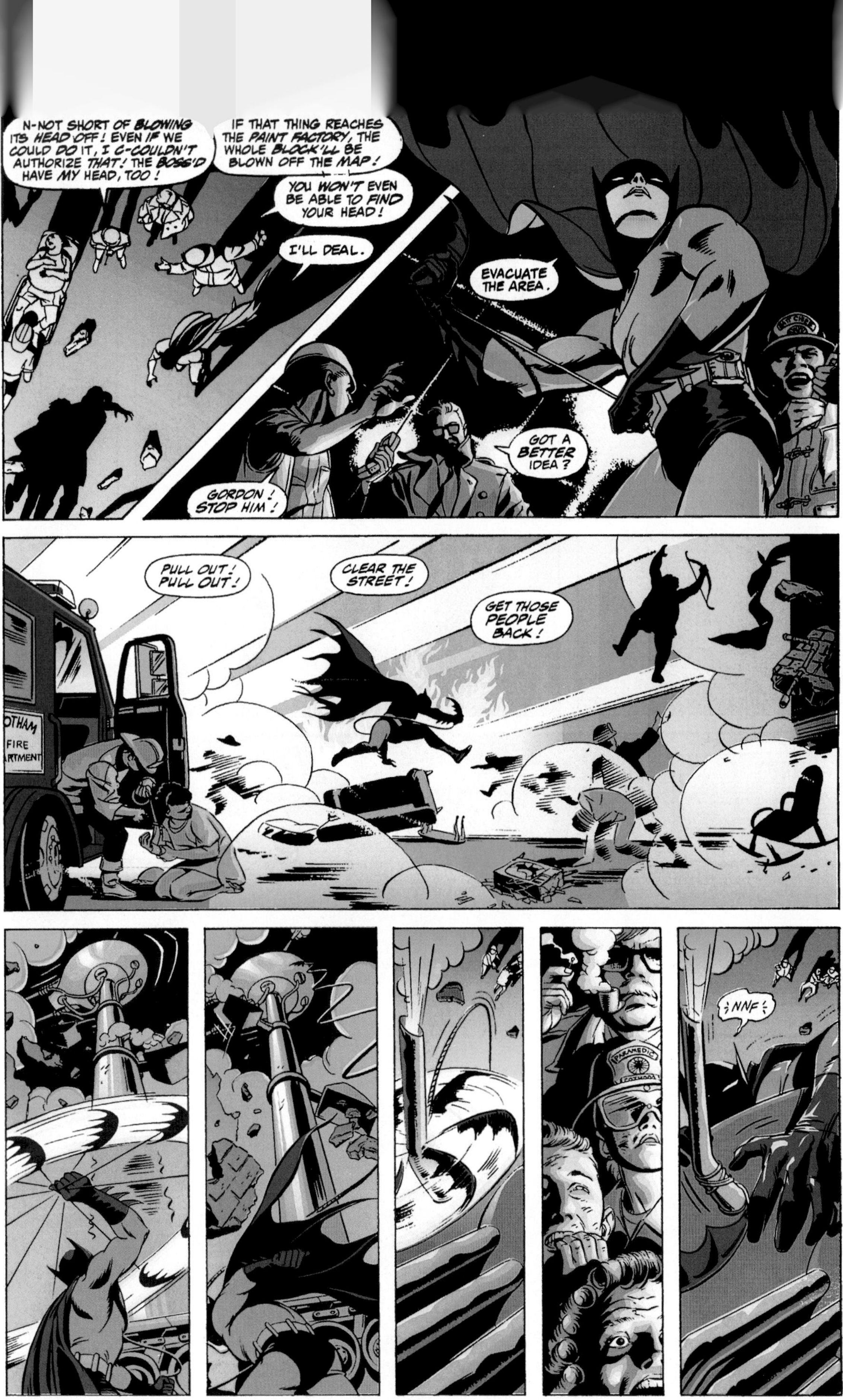
N-NOT SHORT OF BLOWING ITS HEAD OFF! EVEN IF WE COULD DO IT, I C-COULDN'T AUTHORIZE THAT! THE BOSS'D HAVE MY HEAD, TOO!
IF THAT THING REACHES THE PAINT FACTORY, THE WHOLE BLOCK'LL BE BLOWN OFF THE MAP!
YOU WON'T EVEN BE ABLE TO FIND YOUR HEAD!
I'LL DEAL.
EVACUATE THE AREA.
GORDON! STOP HIM!
GOT A BETTER IDEA?
PULL OUT! PULL OUT!
CLEAR THE STREET!
GET THOSE PEOPLE BACK!
GOTHAM FIRE DEPARTMENT
PARAMEDIC
NNF!

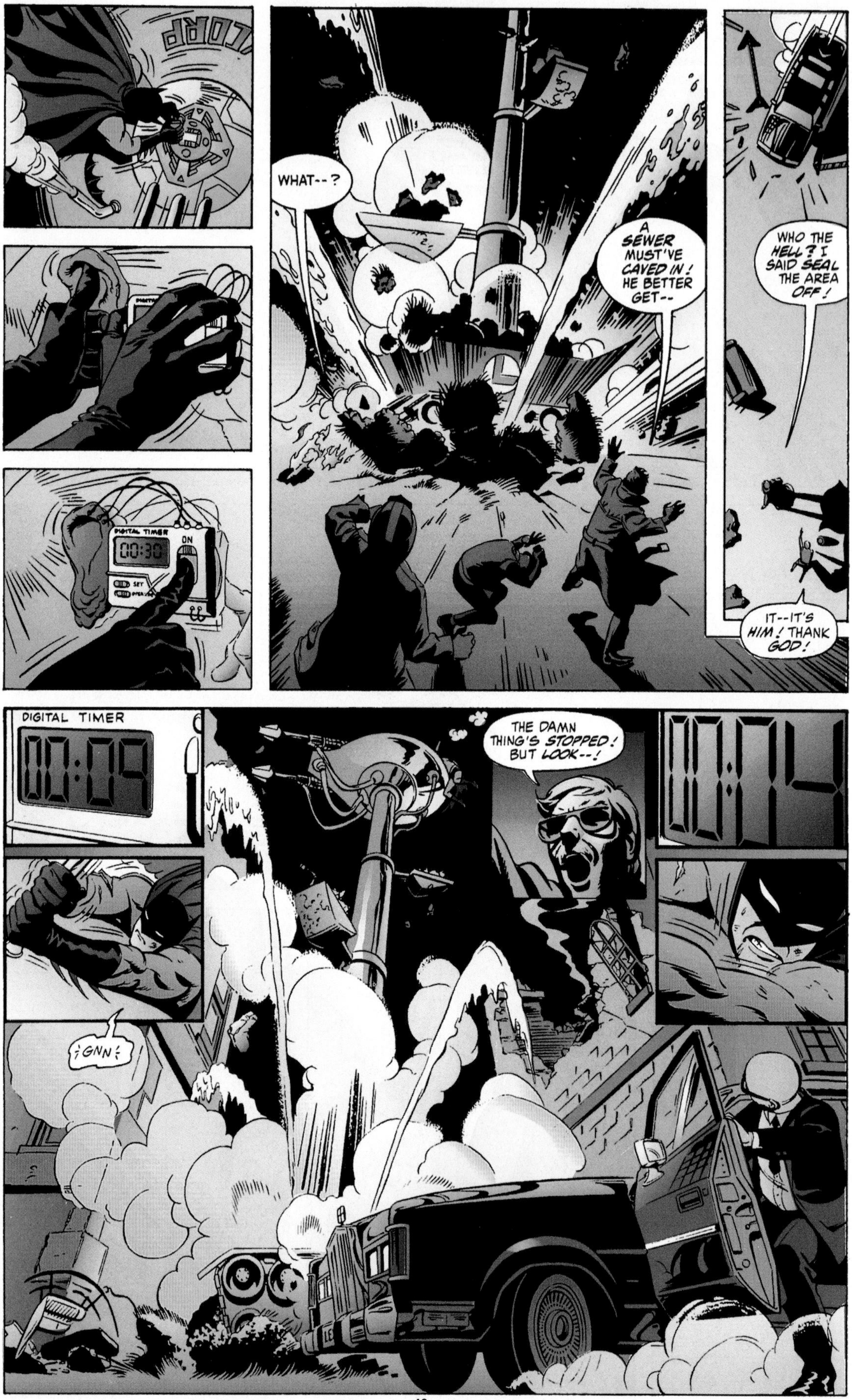
DIGITAL TIMER
00:30
ON
WHAT--?
A SEWER MUST'VE CAVED IN! HE BETTER GET--
WHO THE HELL? I SAID SEAL THE AREA OFF!
IT--IT'S HIM! THANK GOD!
DIGITAL TIMER
THE DAMN THING'S STOPPED! BUT LOOK--!
GNN

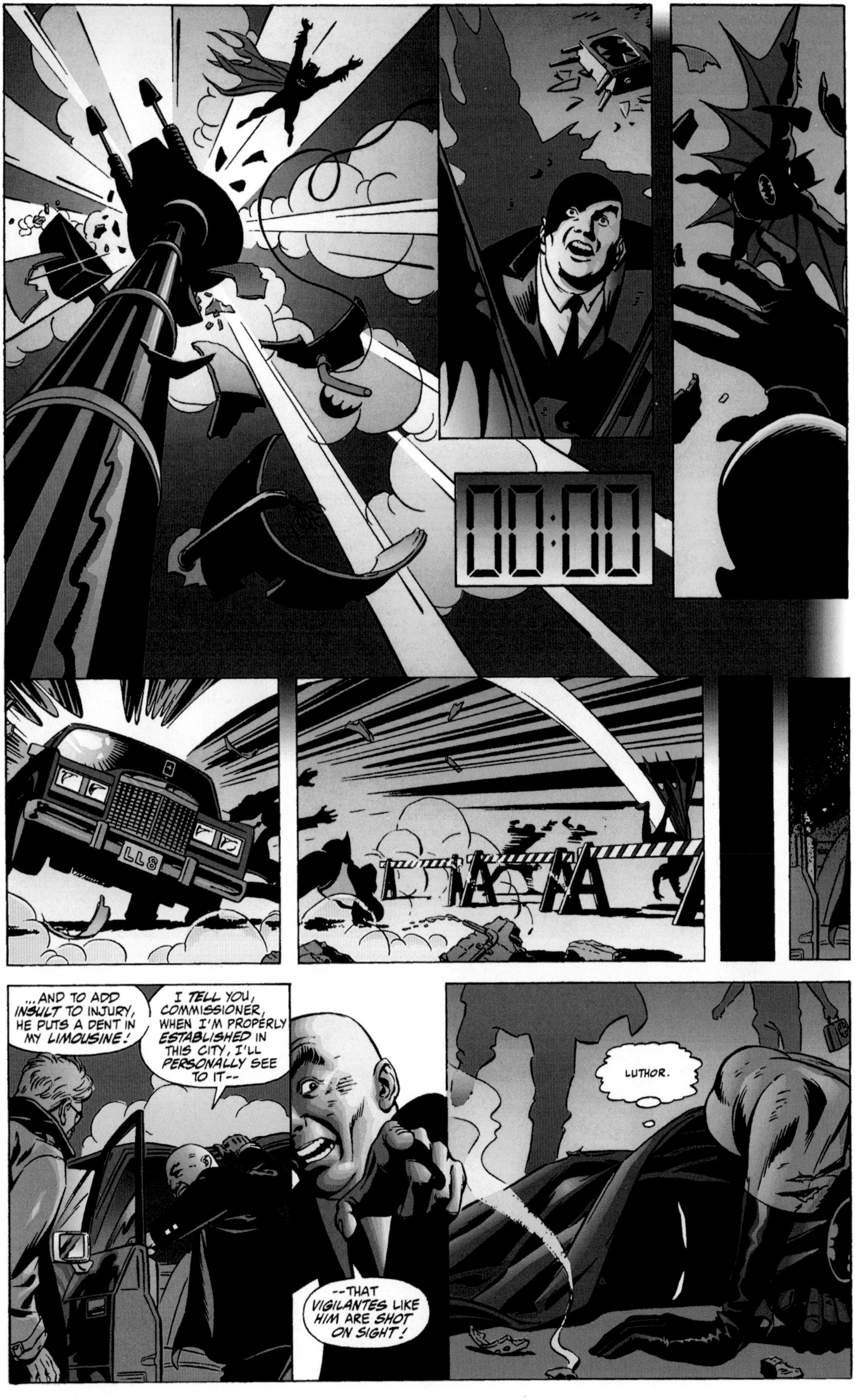
00:00
LL8
...AND TO ADD INSULT TO INJURY, HE PUTS A DENT IN MY LIMOUSINE!
I TELL YOU, COMMISSIONER, WHEN I'M PROPERLY ESTABLISHED IN THIS CITY, I'LL PERSONALLY SEE TO IT--
--THAT VIGILANTES LIKE HIM ARE SHOT ON SIGHT!
LUTHOR.

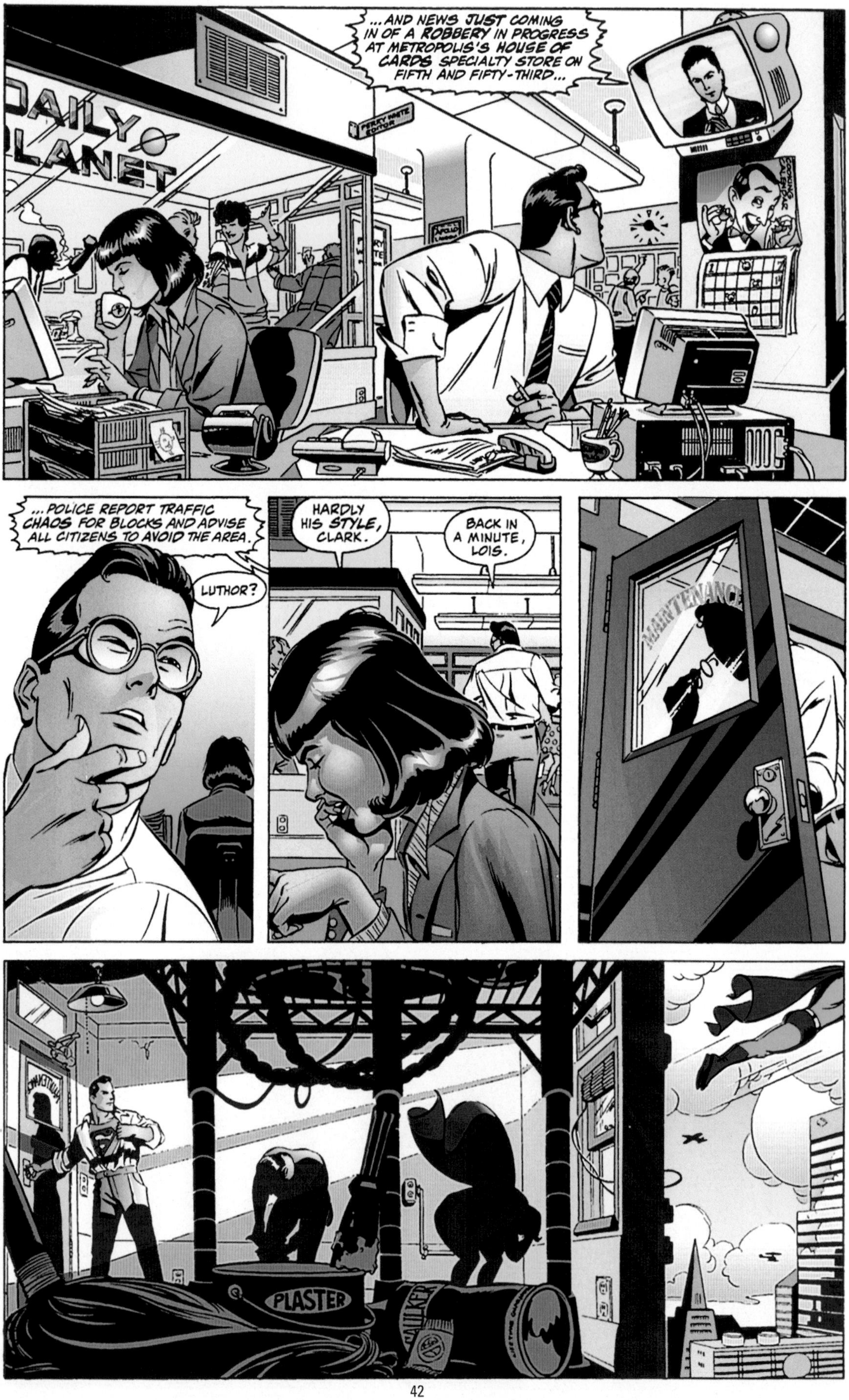
...AND NEWS JUST COMING IN OF A ROBBERY IN PROGRESS AT METROPOLIS'S HOUSE OF CARDS SPECIALTY STORE ON FIFTH AND FIFTY-THIRD...
PERRY WHITE EDITOR
...POLICE REPORT TRAFFIC CHAOS FOR BLOCKS AND ADVISE ALL CITIZENS TO AVOID THE AREA.
LUTHOR?
HARDLY HIS STYLE, CLARK.
BACK IN A MINUTE, LOIS.
MAINTENANCE
PLASTER

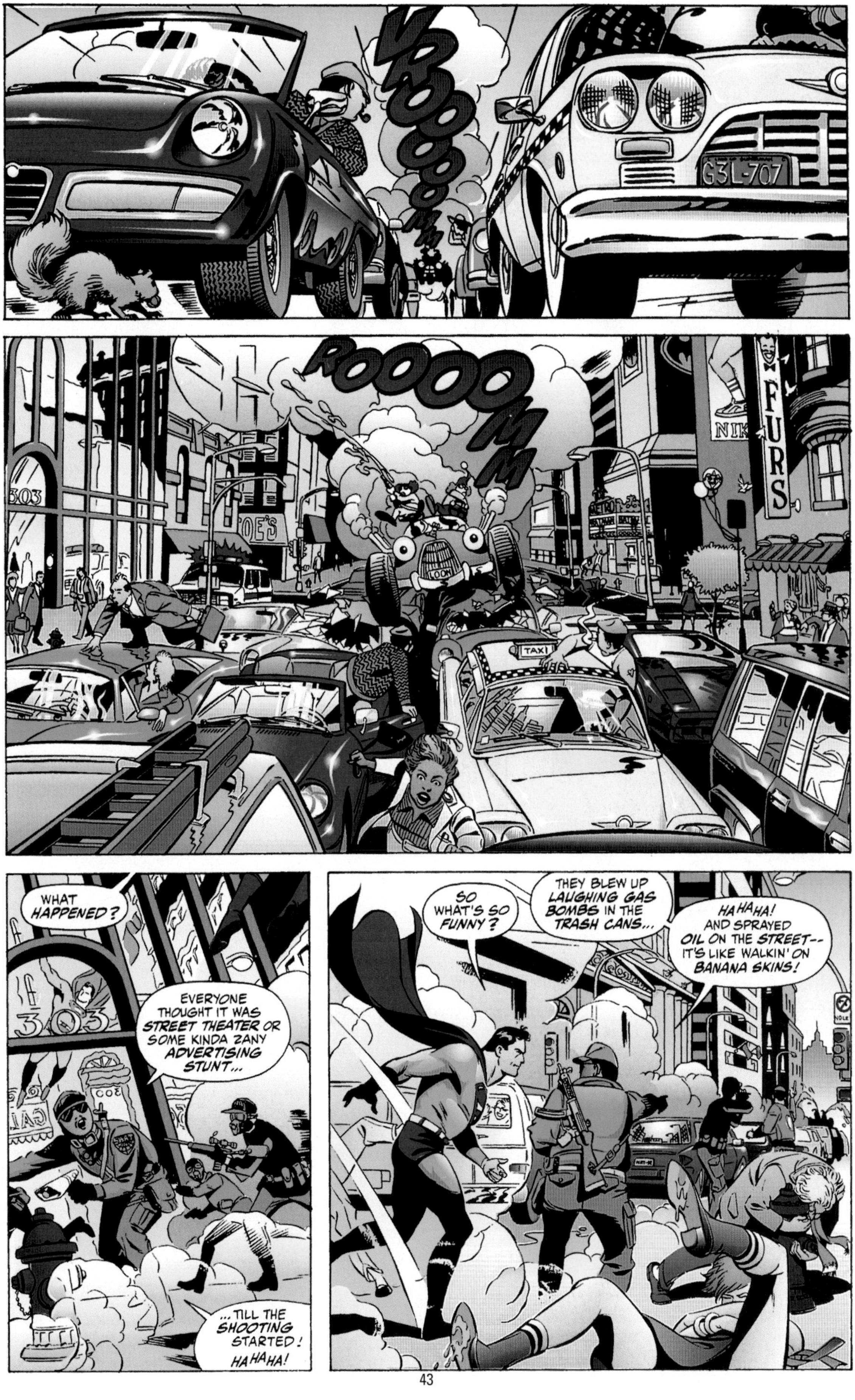
VROOOOOMM
G3L-707
ROOOOMM
303
FURS
LOON
TAXI
WHAT HAPPENED?
EVERYONE THOUGHT IT WAS STREET THEATER OR SOME KINDA ZANY ADVERTISING STUNT...
...TILL THE SHOOTING STARTED! HA HA HA!
SO WHAT'S SO FUNNY?
THEY BLEW UP LAUGHING GAS BOMBS IN THE TRASH CANS...
HA HA HA! AND SPRAYED OIL ON THE STREET-- IT'S LIKE WALKIN' ON BANANA SKINS!

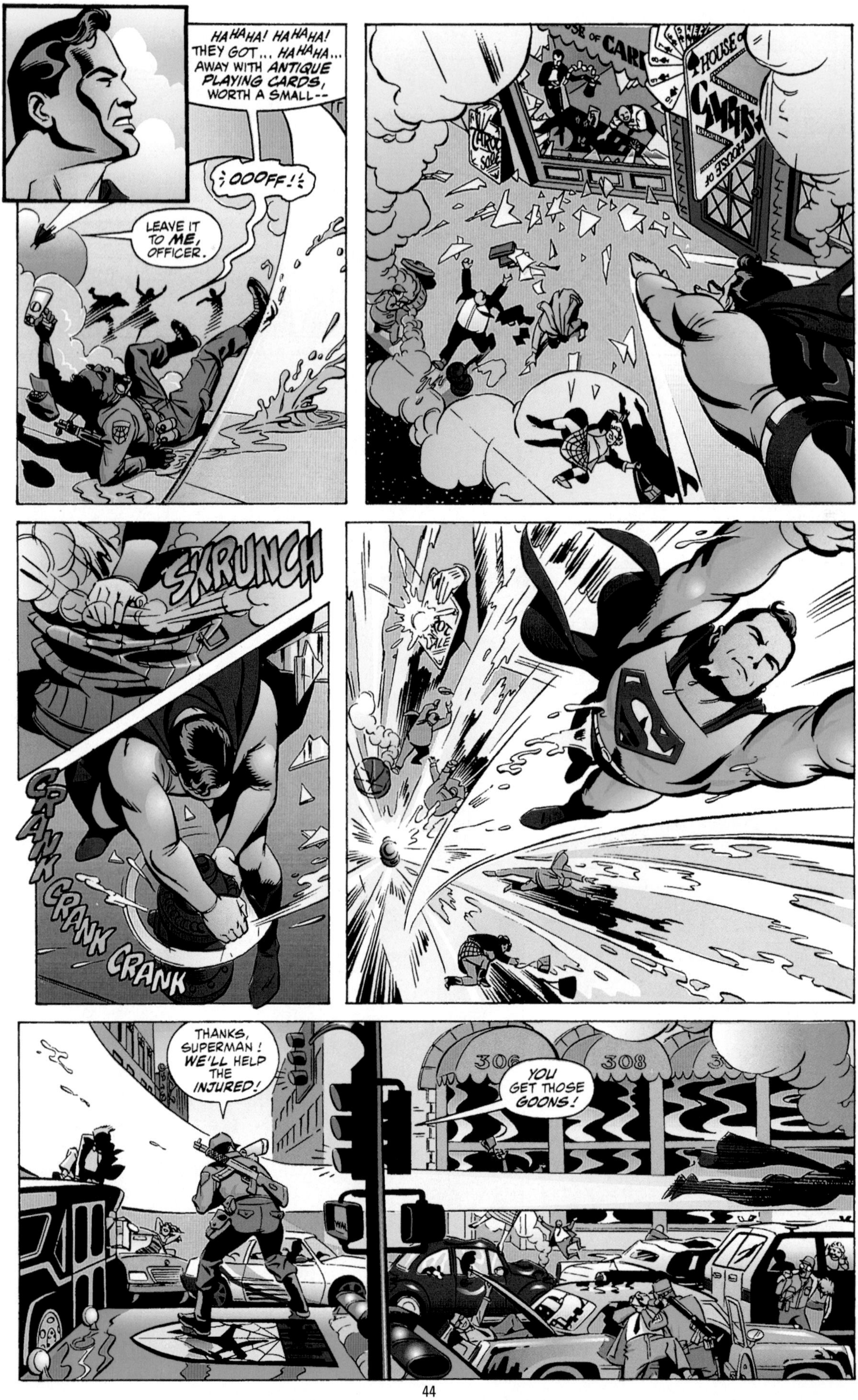
HAHAHA! HAHAHA! THEY GOT... HAHAHA... AWAY WITH ANTIQUE PLAYING CARDS, WORTH A SMALL--
OOOFF!
LEAVE IT TO ME, OFFICER.
HOUSE OF CARDS
HOUSE OF CARDS
SKRUNCH
CRANK CRANK CRANK
THANKS, SUPERMAN! WE'LL HELP THE INJURED!
YOU GET THOSE GOONS!
306
308
WALK

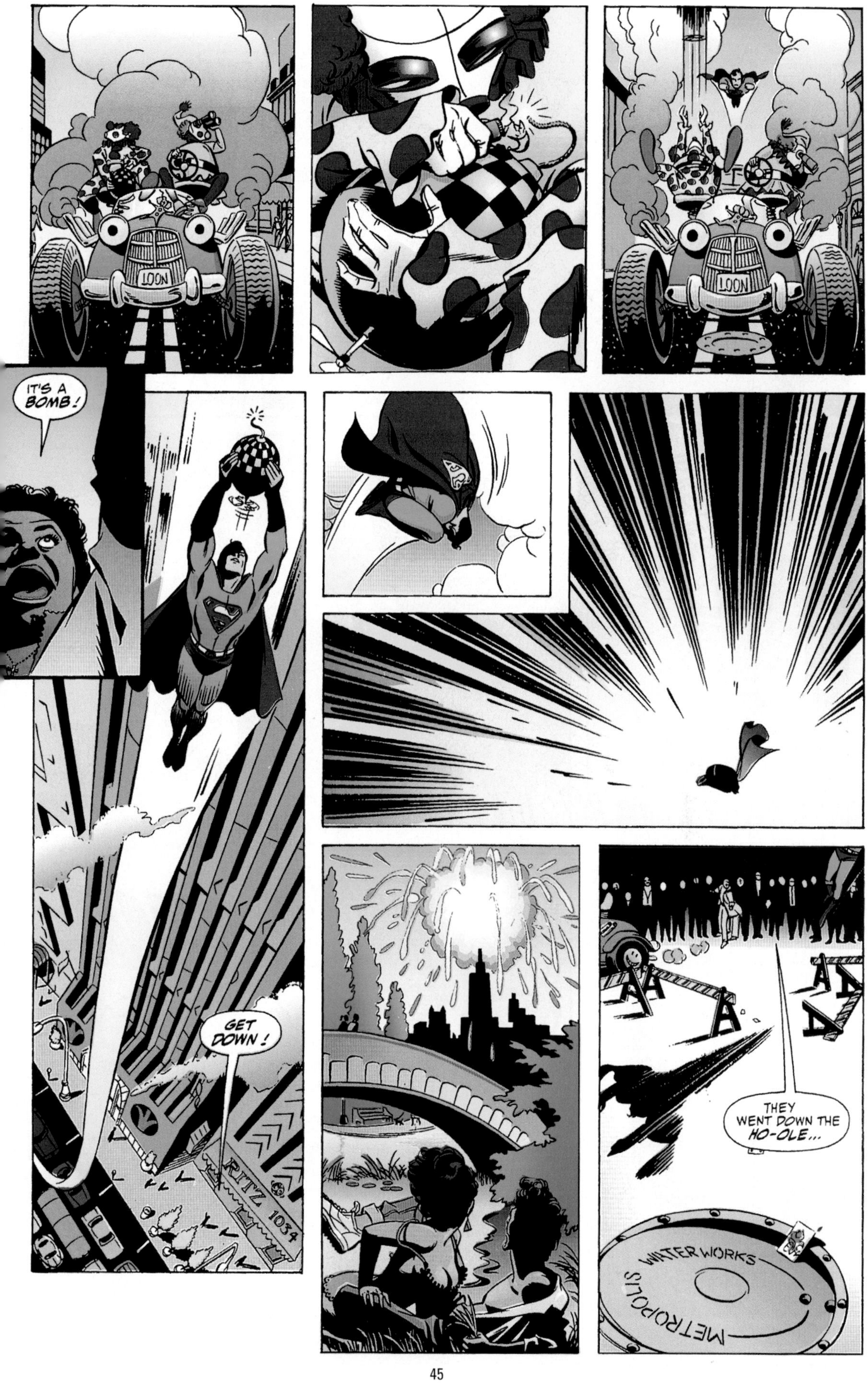
LOON
LOON
IT'S A BOMB!
GET DOWN!
RITZ 1034
THEY WENT DOWN THE HO-OLE...
METROPOLIS WATERWORKS

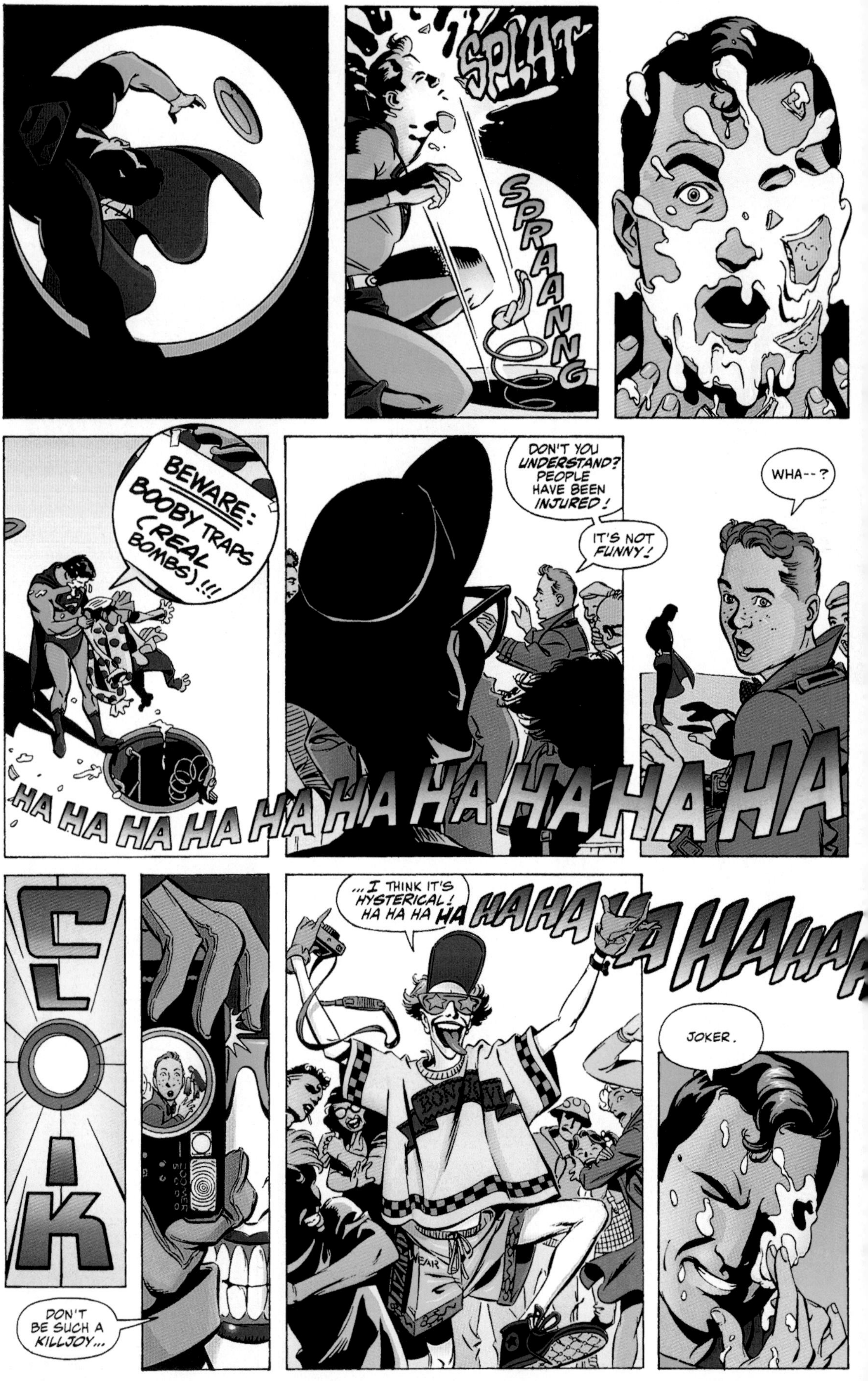
SPLAT
SPRAANNG
BEWARE: BOOBY TRAPS (REAL BOMBS)!!!
DON'T YOU UNDERSTAND? PEOPLE HAVE BEEN INJURED!
IT'S NOT FUNNY!
WHA--?
HA HA HA HA HA HA HA HA HA HA HA
CLOIK
DON'T BE SUCH A KILLJOY...
...I THINK IT'S HYSTERICAL! HA HA HA HA HAHAHA HAHAHA
JOKER.

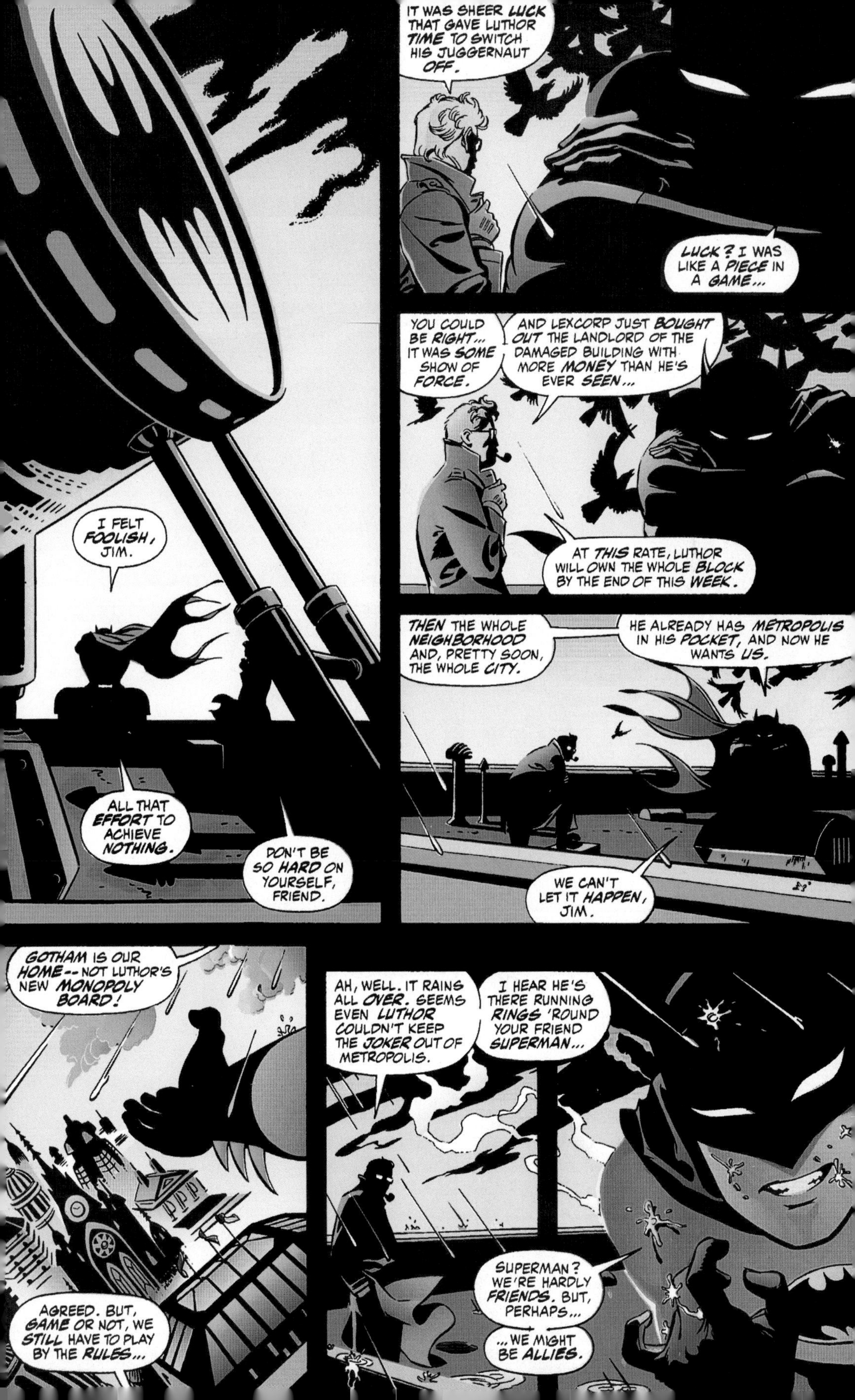
IT WAS SHEER LUCK THAT GAVE LUTHOR TIME TO SWITCH HIS JUGGERNAUT OFF.
LUCK? I WAS LIKE A PIECE IN A GAME...
I FELT FOOLISH, JIM.
ALL THAT EFFORT TO ACHIEVE NOTHING.
DON'T BE SO HARD ON YOURSELF, FRIEND.
YOU COULD BE RIGHT... IT WAS SOME SHOW OF FORCE.
AND LEXCORP JUST BOUGHT OUT THE LANDLORD OF THE DAMAGED BUILDING WITH MORE MONEY THAN HE'S EVER SEEN...
AT THIS RATE, LUTHOR WILL OWN THE WHOLE BLOCK BY THE END OF THIS WEEK.
THEN THE WHOLE NEIGHBORHOOD AND, PRETTY SOON, THE WHOLE CITY.
HE ALREADY HAS METROPOLIS IN HIS POCKET, AND NOW HE WANTS US.
WE CAN'T LET IT HAPPEN, JIM.
GOTHAM IS OUR HOME--NOT LUTHOR'S NEW MONOPOLY BOARD!
AGREED. BUT, GAME OR NOT, WE STILL HAVE TO PLAY BY THE RULES...
AH, WELL. IT RAINS ALL OVER. SEEMS EVEN LUTHOR COULDN'T KEEP THE JOKER OUT OF METROPOLIS.
I HEAR HE'S THERE RUNNING RINGS 'ROUND YOUR FRIEND SUPERMAN...
SUPERMAN? WE'RE HARDLY FRIENDS. BUT, PERHAPS...
...WE MIGHT BE ALLIES.

NO. JUST FOR A *MOMENT*, METROPOLIS WAS AS LAWLESS AS *GOTHAM*.

VERY *KIND*, PERRY, BUT IT WASN'T *ONLY* THE GAS...

AND HAVING TO LET THAT *MANIAC* GO, BECAUSE OF A *LOOPHOLE* IN HIS LAST *COMMITTAL PAPERS*, WAS THE FINAL STRAW.

YEAH. I GUESS BEING IN *PUBLIC VIEW* GIVES HIM THE *PERFECT ALIBI* FOR THIS ROBBERY.

I FELT *POWERLESS*, PERRY.

STANDING THERE WITH *PIE* IN MY FACE AND EVERY-BODY *LAUGHING* AT ME.

THE *JOKER* WOULD LAUGH AT HIS *PARENTS' FUNERAL*, SUPERMAN-- AS FOR THE *REST*, WELL, THERE WAS ALL THAT *LAUGHING GAS*.

SO UNTIL HE *BREAKS* THE LAW, NOBODY CAN DO A DAMN *THING* ABOUT HIM.

NOT *LEGALLY.* BUT IT'S *ODD* THAT *LUTHOR* SEEMS TO BE TURN-ING A *BLIND EYE*, TOO...

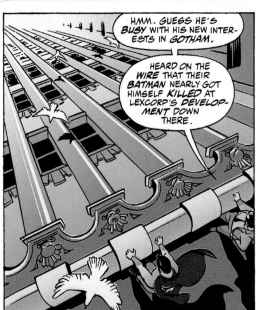

HMM. GUESS HE'S *BUSY* WITH HIS NEW INTER-ESTS IN *GOTHAM*.

HEARD ON THE *WIRE* THAT THEIR *BATMAN* NEARLY GOT HIMSELF *KILLED* AT LEXCORP'S *DEVELOP-MENT* DOWN THERE.

HOPE HE'S *OKAY*. I DON'T APPROVE OF HIS *TACTICS*, BUT, AGAINST *LUTHOR* AND THE *JOKER*...

... WE'RE ON THE SAME SIDE.

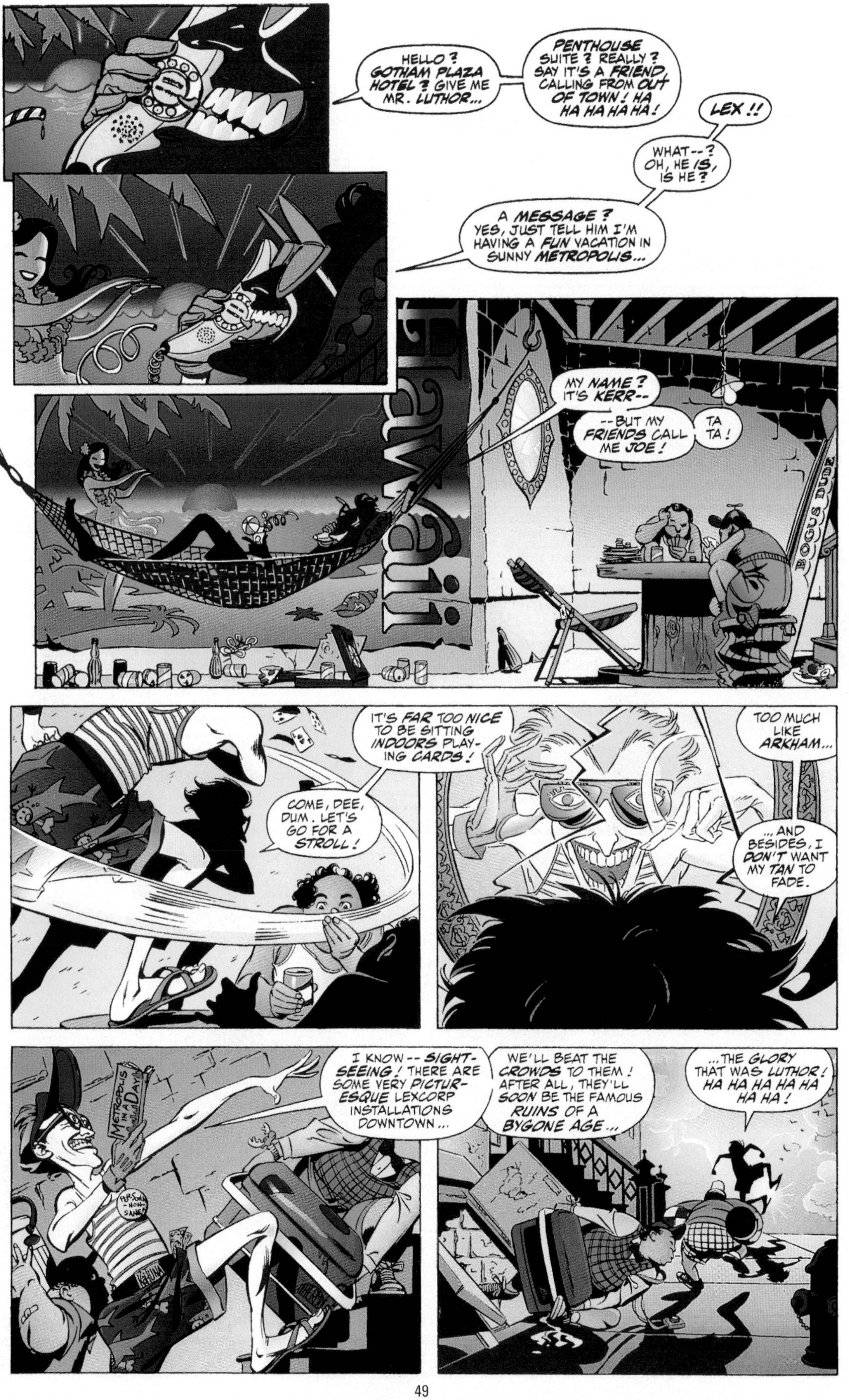
HELLO? GOTHAM PLAZA HOTEL? GIVE ME MR. LUTHOR...
PENTHOUSE SUITE? REALLY? SAY IT'S A FRIEND CALLING FROM OUT OF TOWN! HA HA HA HA HA!
LEX!!
WHAT--? OH, HE IS, IS HE?
A MESSAGE? YES, JUST TELL HIM I'M HAVING A FUN VACATION IN SUNNY METROPOLIS...
MY NAME? IT'S KERR--
--BUT MY FRIENDS CALL ME JOE!
TA TA!
BOGUS DUDE
IT'S FAR TOO NICE TO BE SITTING INDOORS PLAYING CARDS!
COME, DEE, DUM. LET'S GO FOR A STROLL!
TOO MUCH LIKE ARKHAM...
...AND BESIDES, I DON'T WANT MY TAN TO FADE.
I KNOW -- SIGHT-SEEING! THERE ARE SOME VERY PICTURESQUE LEXCORP INSTALLATIONS DOWNTOWN...
WE'LL BEAT THE CROWDS TO THEM! AFTER ALL, THEY'LL SOON BE THE FAMOUS RUINS OF A BYGONE AGE...
...THE GLORY THAT WAS LUTHOR! HA HA HA HA HA HA HA!

HA HA. JOE KERR. VERY AMUSING.

FOR HIS *INDISCRETION* ALONE, THAT *FOOL* DESERVES *EVERYTHING* HE'S GOT COMING.

STILL, *LET* HIM TAKE A FEW *NIBBLES* AT OUR *APPLE*...

...WHILE *WE'RE* TURNING HIS *JUNGLE* INTO OUR *ORCHARD*.

EVERYTHING *TIDY* DOWN AT THE *ORPHANAGE*, MARSHALL?

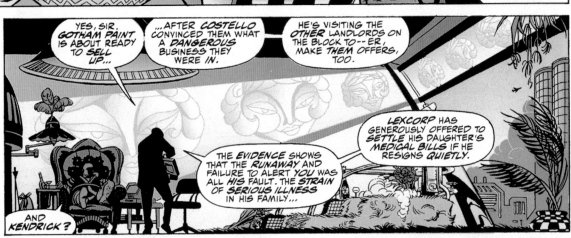

YES, SIR. *GOTHAM PAINT* IS ABOUT READY TO *SELL UP*...

...AFTER *COSTELLO* CONVINCED THEM WHAT A *DANGEROUS* BUSINESS THEY WERE *IN*.

HE'S VISITING THE *OTHER* LANDLORDS ON THE BLOCK TO-- ER, MAKE *THEM* OFFERS, TOO.

LEXCORP HAS *GENEROUSLY* OFFERED TO *SETTLE* HIS DAUGHTER'S *MEDICAL BILLS* IF HE RESIGNS *QUIETLY*.

THE *EVIDENCE* SHOWS THAT THE *RUNAWAY* AND FAILURE TO ALERT *YOU* WAS ALL *HIS* FAULT. THE *STRAIN* OF *SERIOUS ILLNESS* IN HIS FAMILY...

AND *KENDRICK*?

MEDIA COMMENT?

EVEN BETTER THAN WE *PAID* FOR, SIR. OUR PERFECTLY TIMED *SEWER COLLAPSE* WAS *"A LUCKY ACCIDENT..."*

YOUR *DRAMATIC* ARRIVAL WITH THE *REMOTE DISARM DEVICE* WAS *"AN ACT OF SELFLESS HEROISM"... WHILST CONSCIENTIOUSLY CHECKING THE PROGRESS OF WORK..."*

AND-- YOU'LL *LOVE* THIS-- *BATMAN'S* UNSCHEDULED *INTERFERENCE* WAS *"RECKLESS AND UNNECESSARY..."!*

I'D SAY THE NIGHT WENT *WELL*.

THANK YOU, MARSHALL. ON YOUR WAY *OUT*, HAVE THE SWITCHBOARD *HOLD* MY CALLS...

...I'LL BE *BUSY* HERE FOR QUITE SOME *TIME*.

LEXCORP

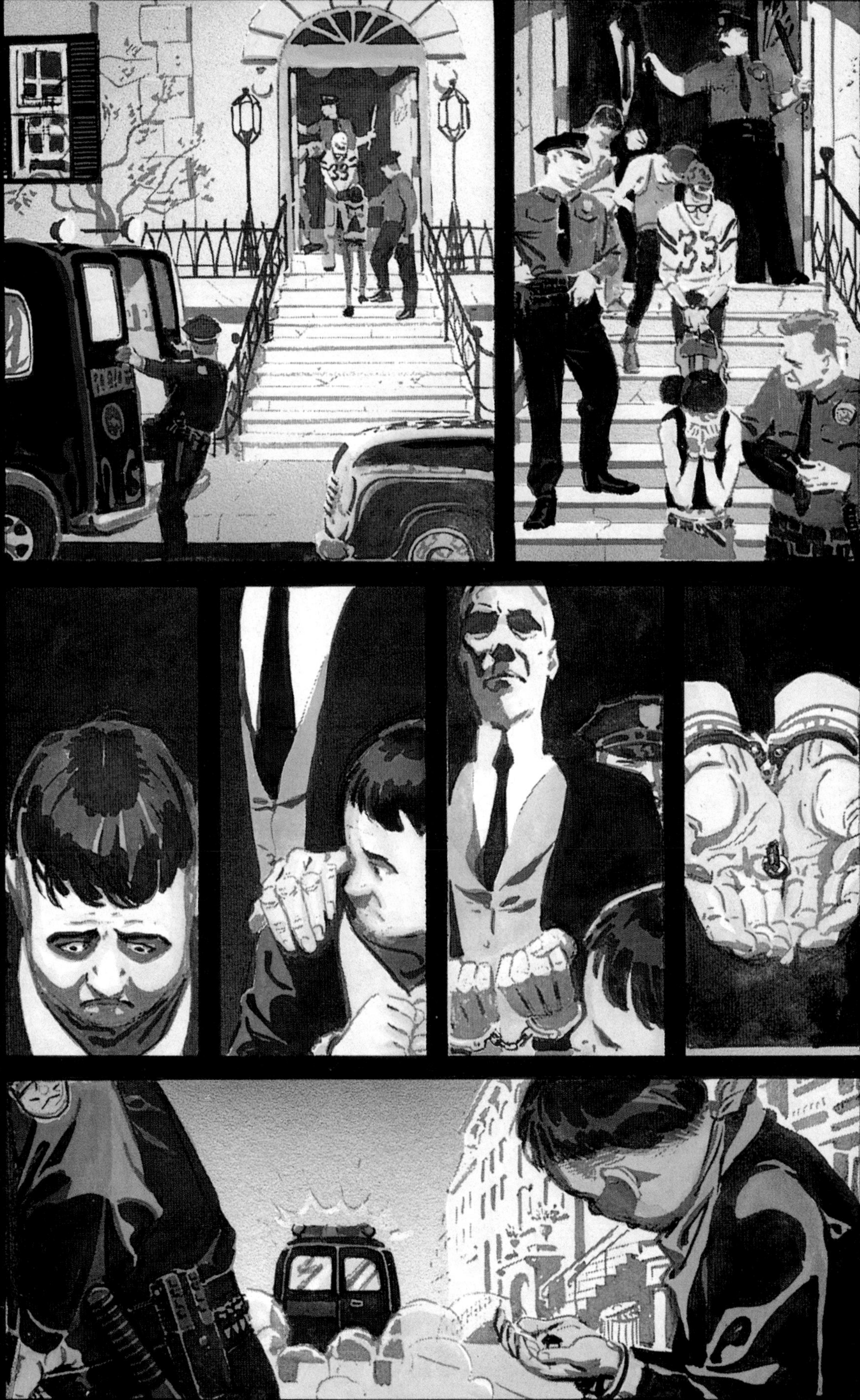

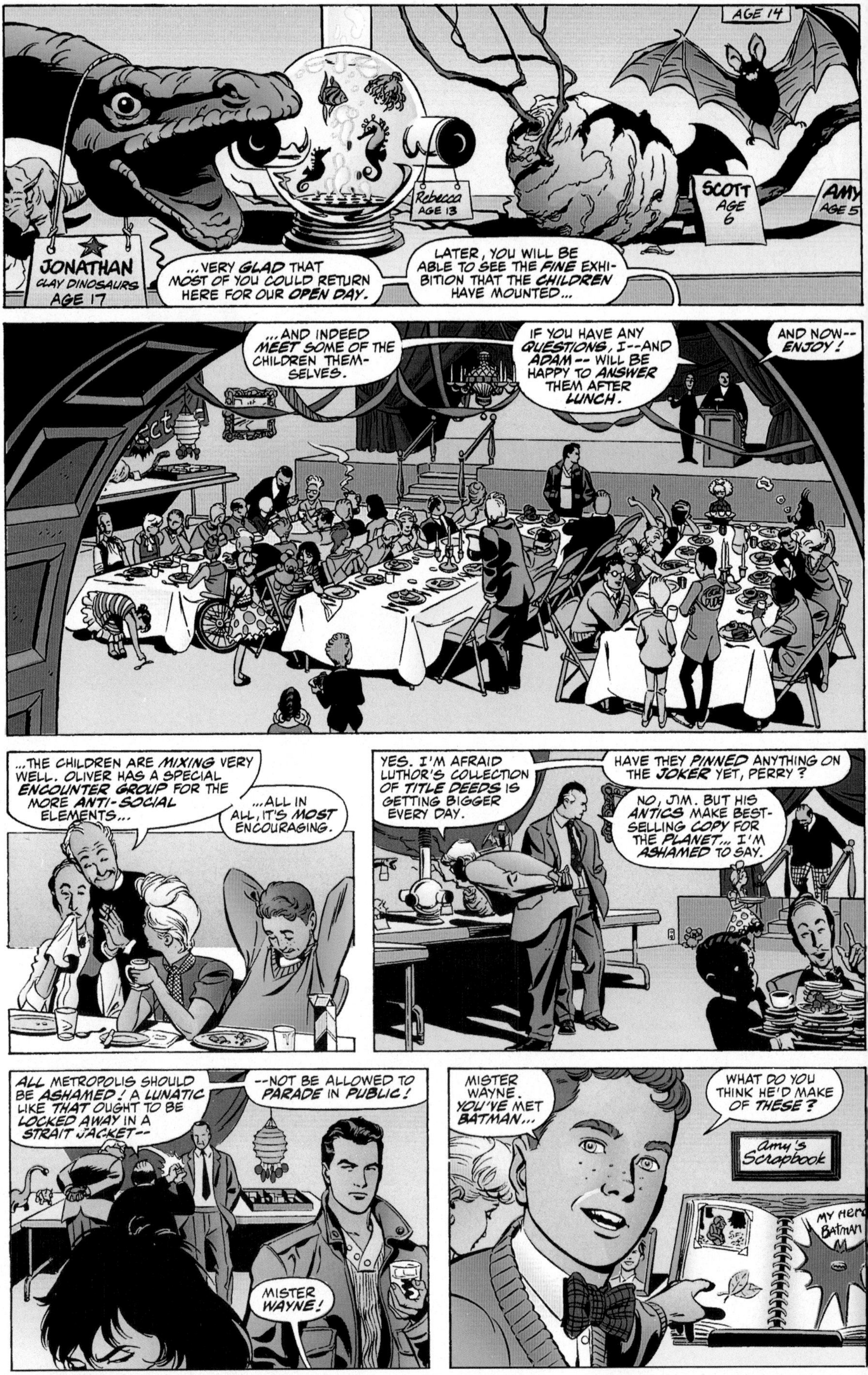
AGE 14
Rebecca AGE 13
SCOTT AGE 6
AMY AGE 5
JONATHAN CLAY DINOSAURS AGE 17
...VERY GLAD THAT MOST OF YOU COULD RETURN HERE FOR OUR OPEN DAY.
LATER, YOU WILL BE ABLE TO SEE THE FINE EXHIBITION THAT THE CHILDREN HAVE MOUNTED...
...AND INDEED MEET SOME OF THE CHILDREN THEMSELVES.
IF YOU HAVE ANY QUESTIONS, I--AND ADAM-- WILL BE HAPPY TO ANSWER THEM AFTER LUNCH.
AND NOW-- ENJOY!
...THE CHILDREN ARE MIXING VERY WELL. OLIVER HAS A SPECIAL ENCOUNTER GROUP FOR THE MORE ANTI-SOCIAL ELEMENTS...
...ALL IN ALL, IT'S MOST ENCOURAGING.
YES. I'M AFRAID LUTHOR'S COLLECTION OF TITLE DEEDS IS GETTING BIGGER EVERY DAY.
HAVE THEY PINNED ANYTHING ON THE JOKER YET, PERRY?
NO, JIM. BUT HIS ANTICS MAKE BEST-SELLING COPY FOR THE PLANET... I'M ASHAMED TO SAY.
ALL METROPOLIS SHOULD BE ASHAMED! A LUNATIC LIKE THAT OUGHT TO BE LOCKED AWAY IN A STRAIT JACKET--
--NOT BE ALLOWED TO PARADE IN PUBLIC!
MISTER WAYNE!
MISTER WAYNE. YOU'VE MET BATMAN...
WHAT DO YOU THINK HE'D MAKE OF THESE?
Amy's Scrapbook
MY Hero Batman

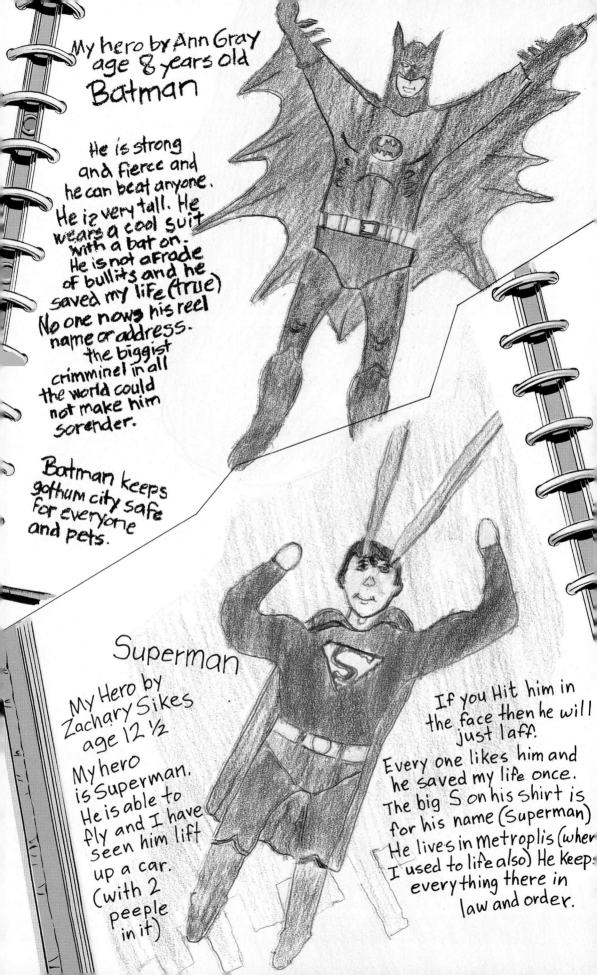

My hero by Ann Gray
age 8 years old
Batman

He is strong and fierce and he can beat anyone. He iz very tall. He wears a cool suit with a bat on. He is not afrade of bullits and he saved my life (true) No one nows his reel name or address. the biggist crimminel in all the world could not make him sorender.

Batman keeps gothum city safe for everyone and pets.

Superman

My Hero by Zachary Sikes age 12 ½

My hero is Superman. He is able to fly and I have seen him lift up a car. (with 2 peeple in it)

If you Hit him in the face then he will just laff. Every one likes him and he saved my life once. The big S on his shirt is for his name (Superman) He lives in metroplis (wher I used to life also) He keeps everything there in law and order.

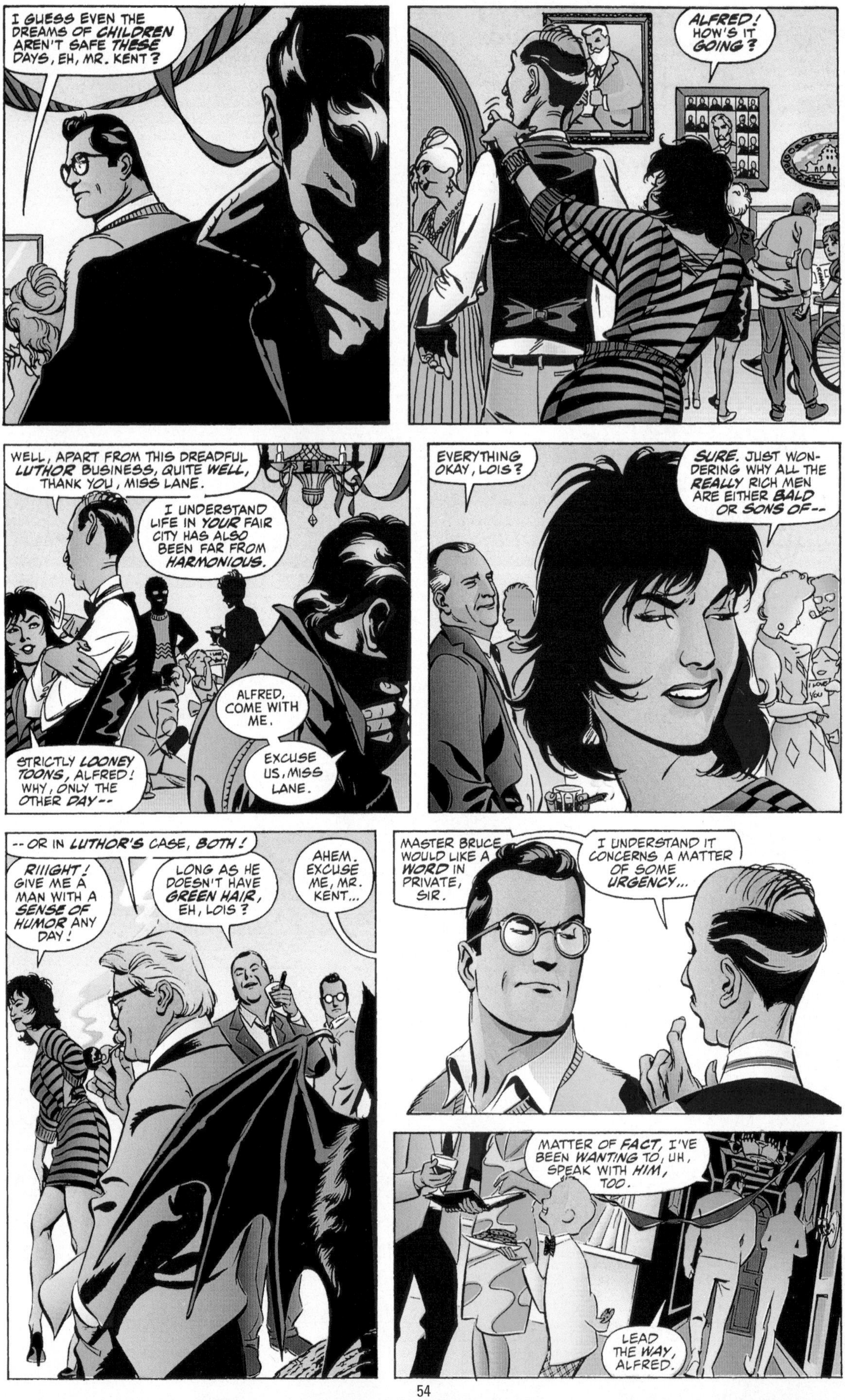
I GUESS EVEN THE DREAMS OF CHILDREN AREN'T SAFE THESE DAYS, EH, MR. KENT?
ALFRED! HOW'S IT GOING?
WELL, APART FROM THIS DREADFUL LUTHOR BUSINESS, QUITE WELL, THANK YOU, MISS LANE.
I UNDERSTAND LIFE IN YOUR FAIR CITY HAS ALSO BEEN FAR FROM HARMONIOUS.
STRICTLY LOONEY TOONS, ALFRED! WHY, ONLY THE OTHER DAY--
ALFRED, COME WITH ME.
EXCUSE US, MISS LANE.
EVERYTHING OKAY, LOIS?
SURE. JUST WONDERING WHY ALL THE REALLY RICH MEN ARE EITHER BALD OR SONS OF--
I LOVE YOU
--OR IN LUTHOR'S CASE, BOTH!
RIIIGHT! GIVE ME A MAN WITH A SENSE OF HUMOR ANY DAY!
LONG AS HE DOESN'T HAVE GREEN HAIR, EH, LOIS?
AHEM. EXCUSE ME, MR. KENT...
MASTER BRUCE WOULD LIKE A WORD IN PRIVATE, SIR.
I UNDERSTAND IT CONCERNS A MATTER OF SOME URGENCY...
MATTER OF FACT, I'VE BEEN WANTING TO, UH, SPEAK WITH HIM, TOO.
LEAD THE WAY, ALFRED.

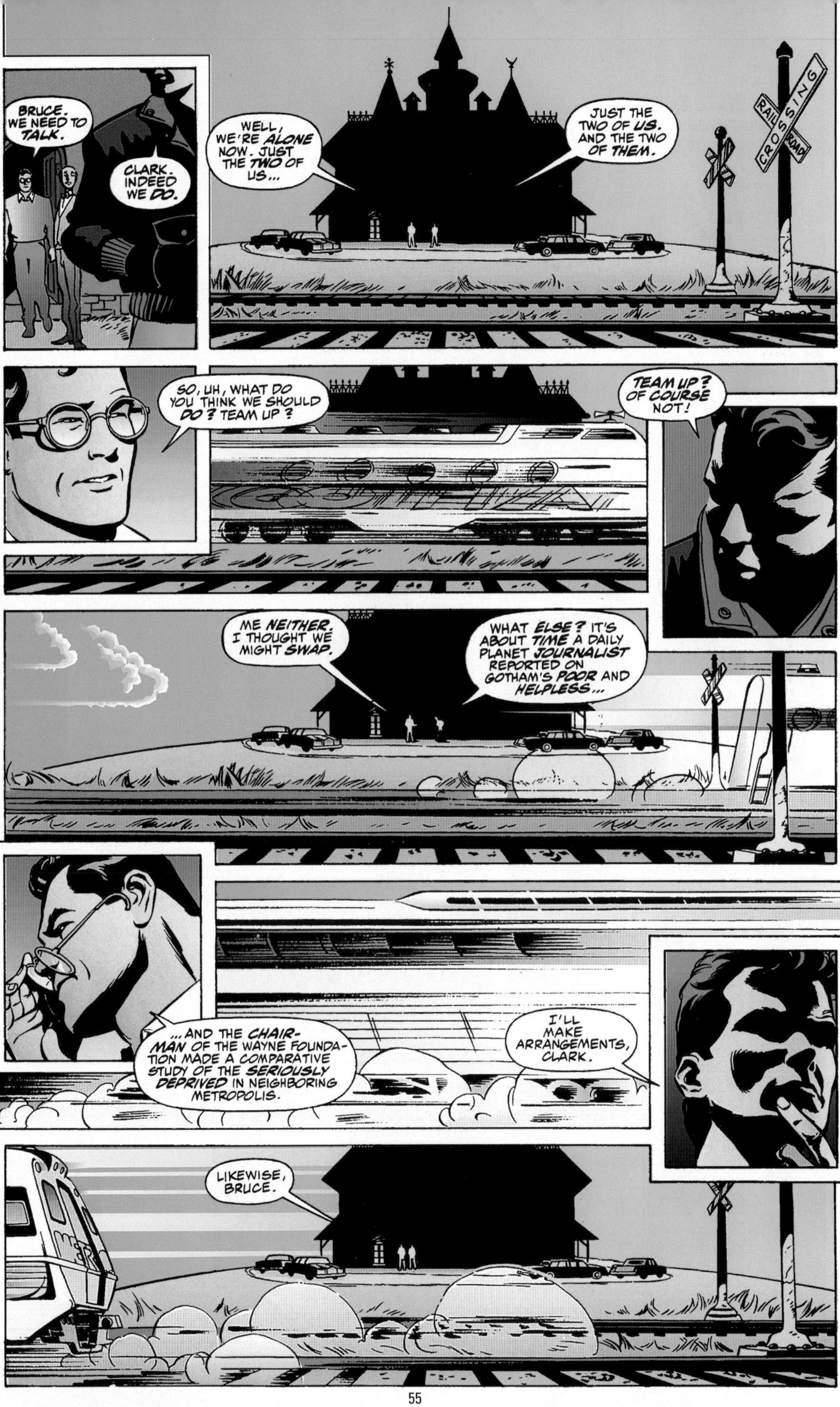
BRUCE. WE NEED TO TALK.
CLARK. INDEED WE DO.
WELL, WE'RE ALONE NOW. JUST THE TWO OF US...
JUST THE TWO OF US. AND THE TWO OF THEM.
RAIL ROAD CROSSING
SO, UH, WHAT DO YOU THINK WE SHOULD DO? TEAM UP?
TEAM UP? OF COURSE NOT!
ME NEITHER. I THOUGHT WE MIGHT SWAP.
WHAT ELSE? IT'S ABOUT TIME A DAILY PLANET JOURNALIST REPORTED ON GOTHAM'S POOR AND HELPLESS...
...AND THE CHAIRMAN OF THE WAYNE FOUNDATION MADE A COMPARATIVE STUDY OF THE SERIOUSLY DEPRIVED IN NEIGHBORING METROPOLIS.
I'LL MAKE ARRANGEMENTS, CLARK.
LIKEWISE, BRUCE.

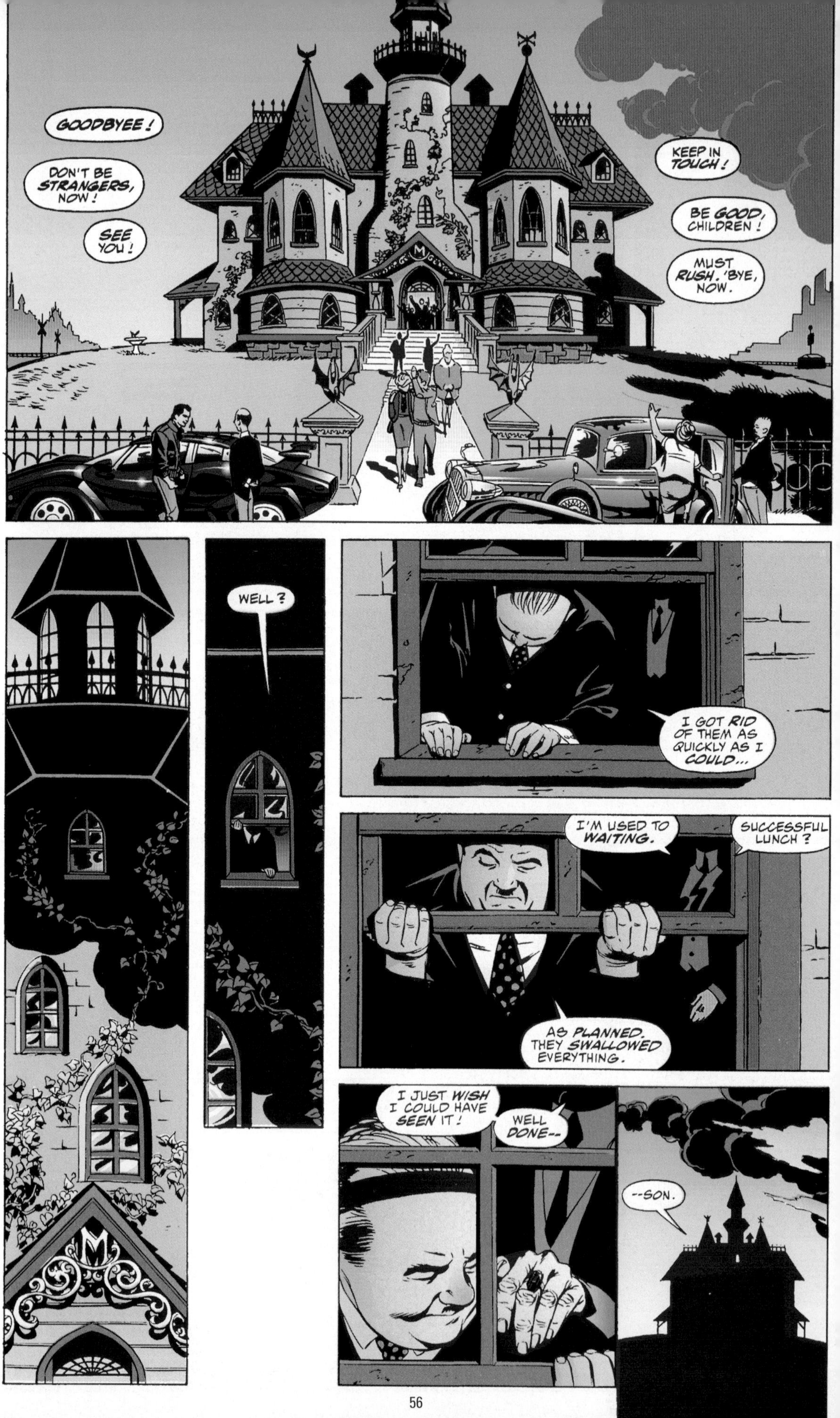
GOODBYEE!
DON'T BE STRANGERS, NOW!
SEE YOU!
KEEP IN TOUCH!
BE GOOD, CHILDREN!
MUST RUSH. 'BYE, NOW.
WELL?
I GOT RID OF THEM AS QUICKLY AS I COULD...
I'M USED TO WAITING.
SUCCESSFUL LUNCH?
AS PLANNED. THEY SWALLOWED EVERYTHING.
I JUST WISH I COULD HAVE SEEN IT!
WELL DONE--
--SON.

BOOK TWO

WORLDS COLLIDE

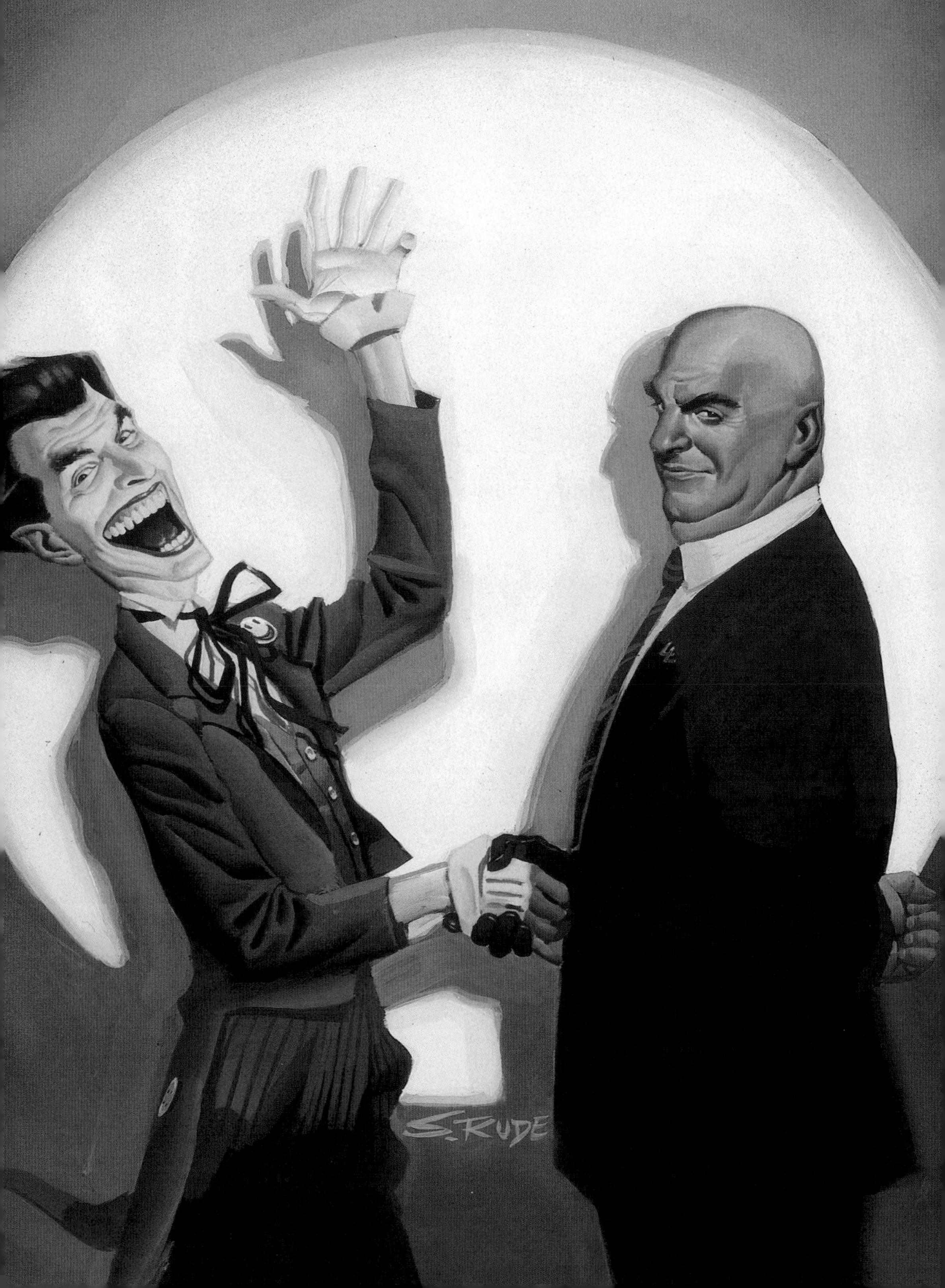
S. RUDE

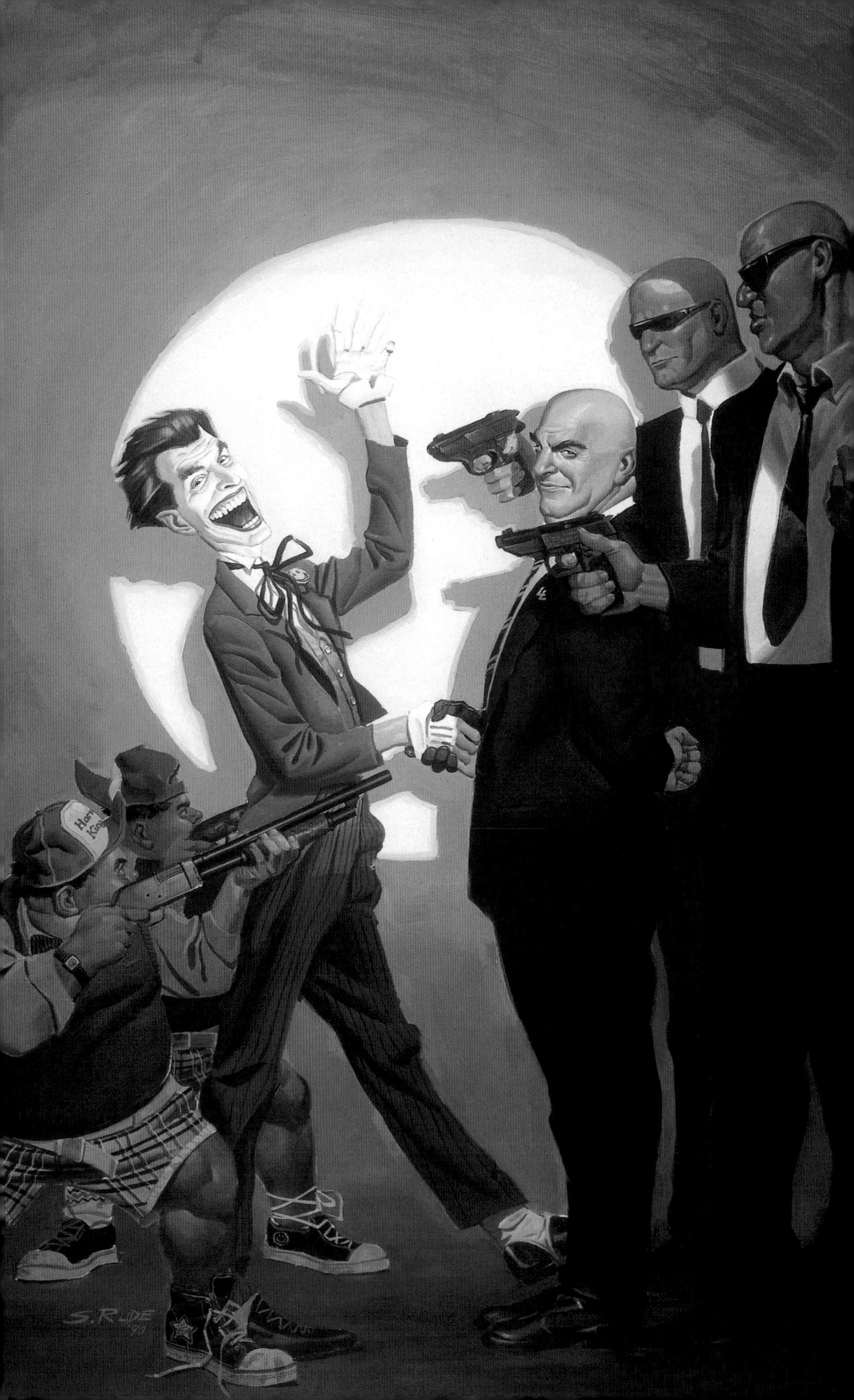
S.RUDE

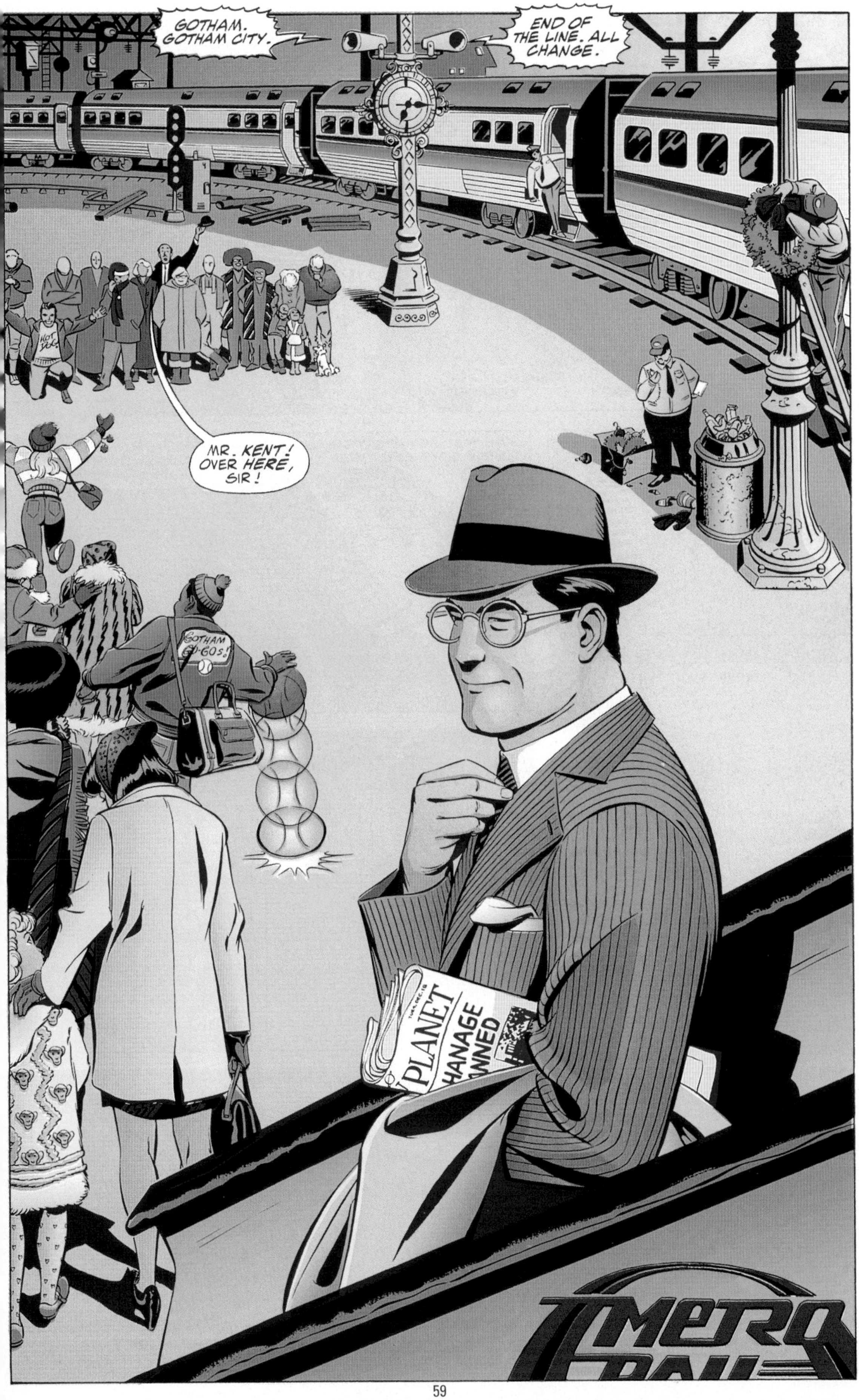
GOTHAM. GOTHAM CITY.
END OF THE LINE. ALL CHANGE.
MR. KENT! OVER HERE, SIR!
HOT DOG
GOTHAM GO-GOS!
PLANET
HANAGE
ANNED
METRO
RAIL

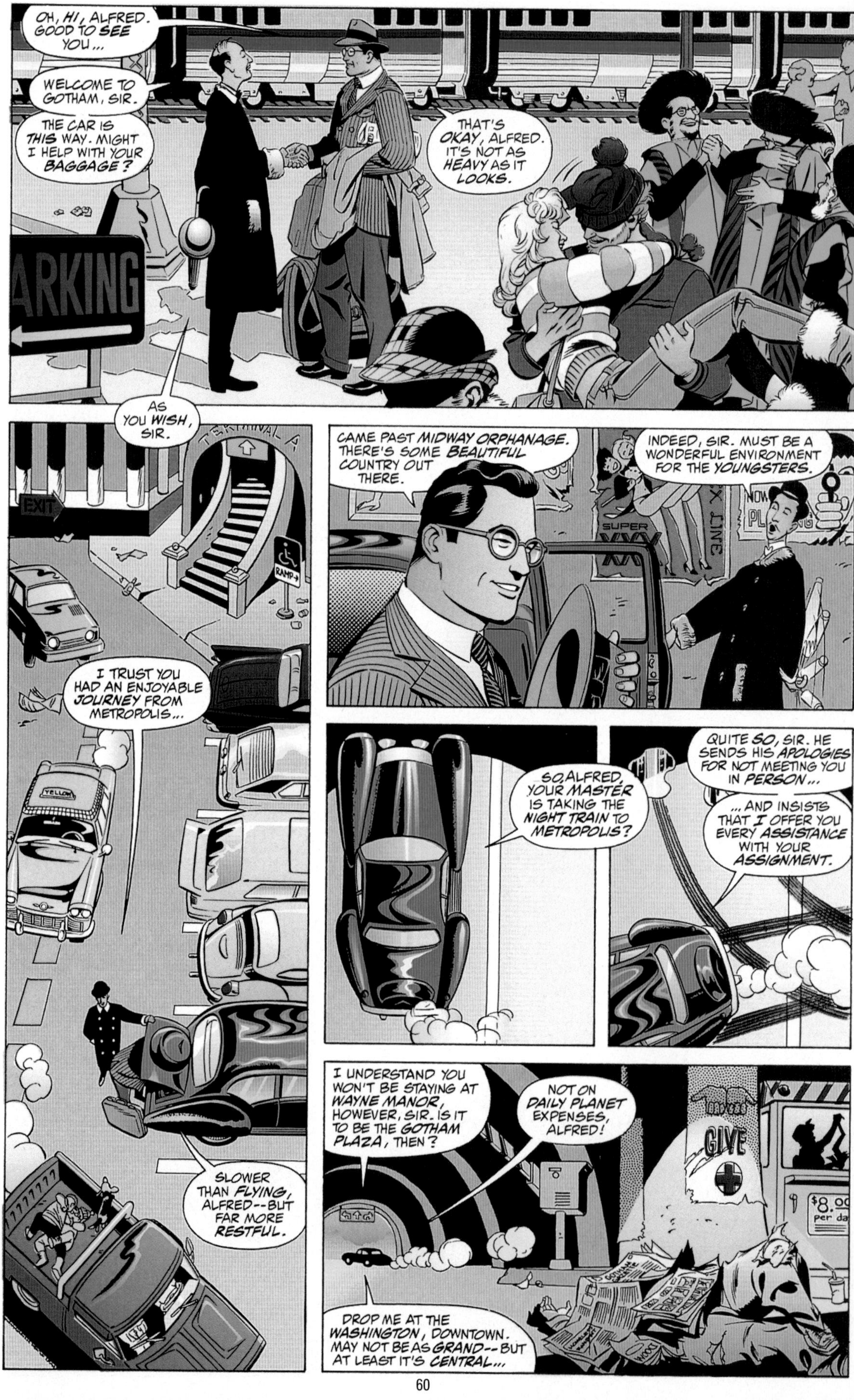
OH, HI, ALFRED. GOOD TO SEE YOU...
WELCOME TO GOTHAM, SIR.
THE CAR IS THIS WAY. MIGHT I HELP WITH YOUR BAGGAGE?
THAT'S OKAY, ALFRED. IT'S NOT AS HEAVY AS IT LOOKS.
AS YOU WISH, SIR.
PARKING
TERMINAL A
EXIT
RAMP
I TRUST YOU HAD AN ENJOYABLE JOURNEY FROM METROPOLIS...
YELLOW
SLOWER THAN FLYING, ALFRED--BUT FAR MORE RESTFUL.
CAME PAST MIDWAY ORPHANAGE. THERE'S SOME BEAUTIFUL COUNTRY OUT THERE.
INDEED, SIR. MUST BE A WONDERFUL ENVIRONMENT FOR THE YOUNGSTERS.
SUPER XXX
SO, ALFRED, YOUR MASTER IS TAKING THE NIGHT TRAIN TO METROPOLIS?
QUITE SO, SIR. HE SENDS HIS APOLOGIES FOR NOT MEETING YOU IN PERSON...
...AND INSISTS THAT I OFFER YOU EVERY ASSISTANCE WITH YOUR ASSIGNMENT.
I UNDERSTAND YOU WON'T BE STAYING AT WAYNE MANOR, HOWEVER, SIR. IS IT TO BE THE GOTHAM PLAZA, THEN?
NOT ON DAILY PLANET EXPENSES, ALFRED!
GIVE
$8.00 per day
DROP ME AT THE WASHINGTON, DOWNTOWN. MAY NOT BE AS GRAND--BUT AT LEAST IT'S CENTRAL...

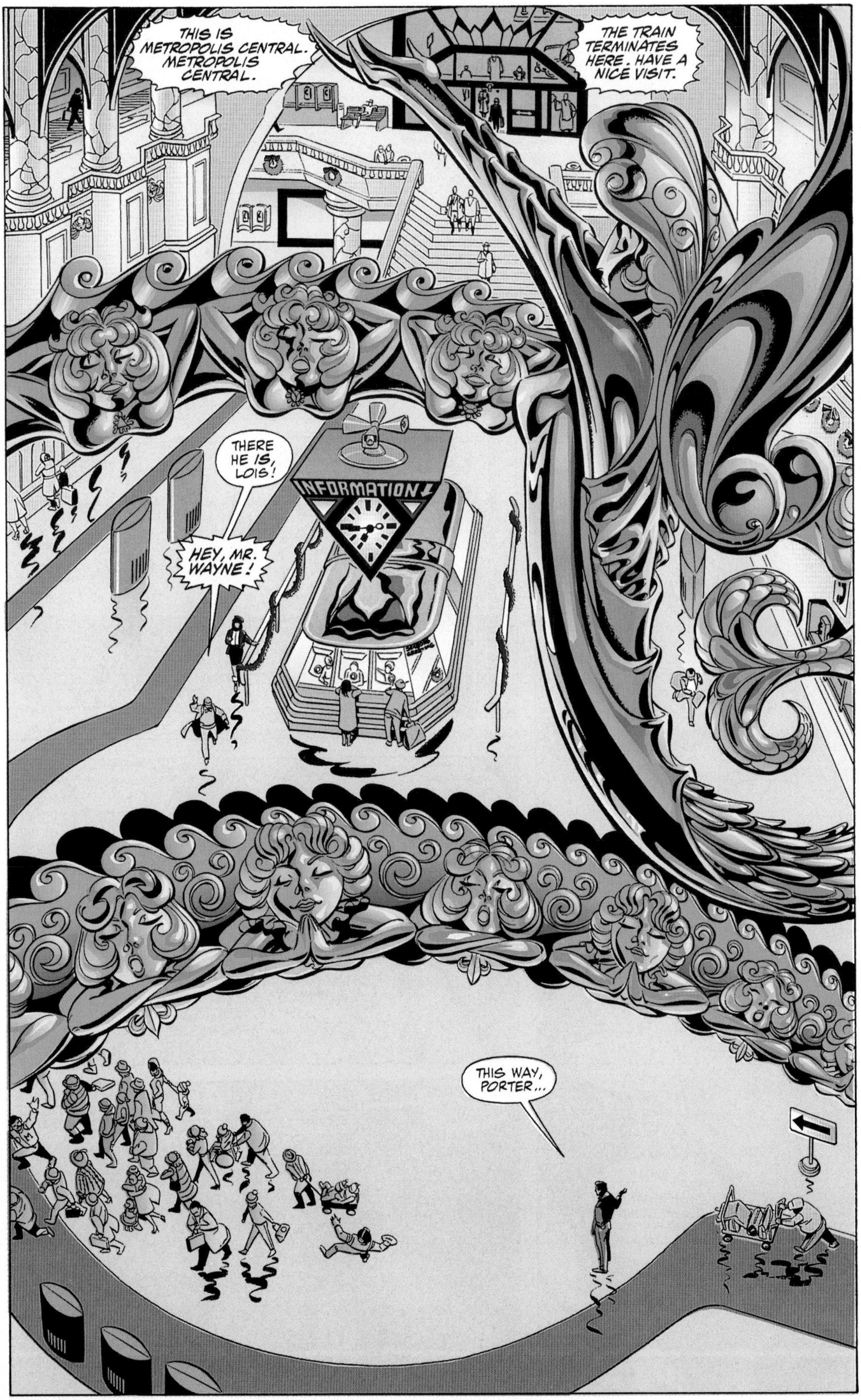
THIS IS METROPOLIS CENTRAL. METROPOLIS CENTRAL.
THE TRAIN TERMINATES HERE. HAVE A NICE VISIT.
INFORMATION
THERE HE IS, LOIS!
HEY, MR. WAYNE!
THIS WAY, PORTER...

HI! PERRY ASSIGNED LOIS TO COVER YOUR STAY, BUT I THOUGHT I'D SAY WELCOME, TOO!

HOW WAS THE TRIP?

BEARABLE, THANK YOU, OLSEN.

LOIS.

÷PHHHT!÷

MS. LANE, THANK YOU.

metropolis

DIRECTORY

V.I.P.

LIMO SERVICE

LEX'S

SPICKLES ECONOMY

LUXURIOUS METROPOLIS PLAZA

SURELY YOU COULD AFFORD BETTER THAN THE TRAIN, MR. WAYNE...?

A PLANE MAYBE, MS. LANE?

EQUALLY POETIC-- AND I HAVE BEEN CONSIDERING BUYING ANOTHER ONE, I ADMIT...

WOW! STILL, I LIKE RIDING ON TRAINS! GIVES YOU TIME TO THINK--

OOPS!

YES, WE ALL NEED THAT, OLSEN.

MY CAR'S RIGHT OUTSIDE, MR. WAYNE.

SO IS MINE, OLSEN.

VIP

I'LL BE IN TOUCH, LOIS.

METROPOLIS PLAZA HOTEL, DRIVER.

C'MON, JIMMY, BACK TO THE PLANET-- I'VE GOT TO START ON THE DEATHLESS PROSE...

SUPERMAN SAYS KEEP METROPOLIS CLEAN

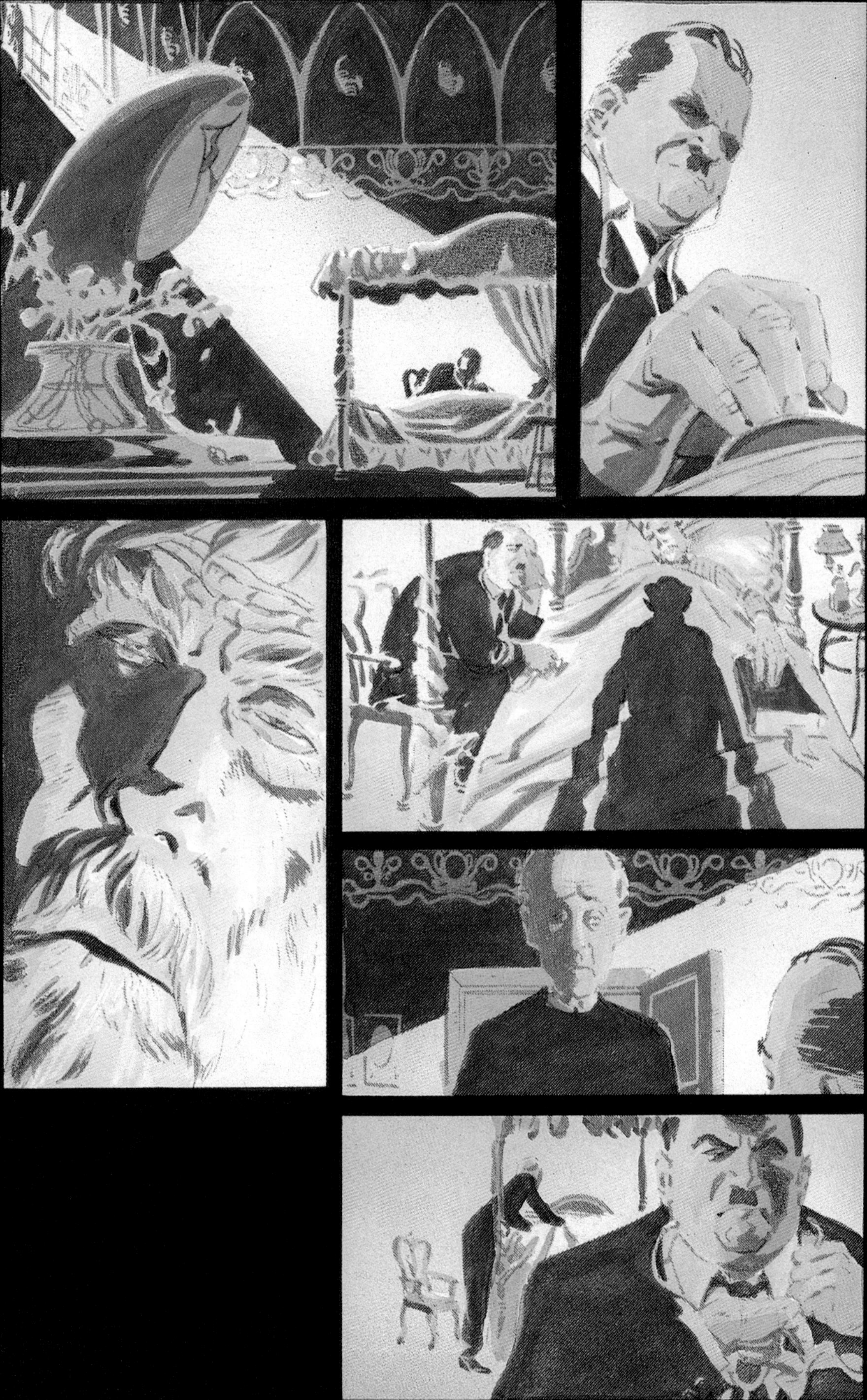

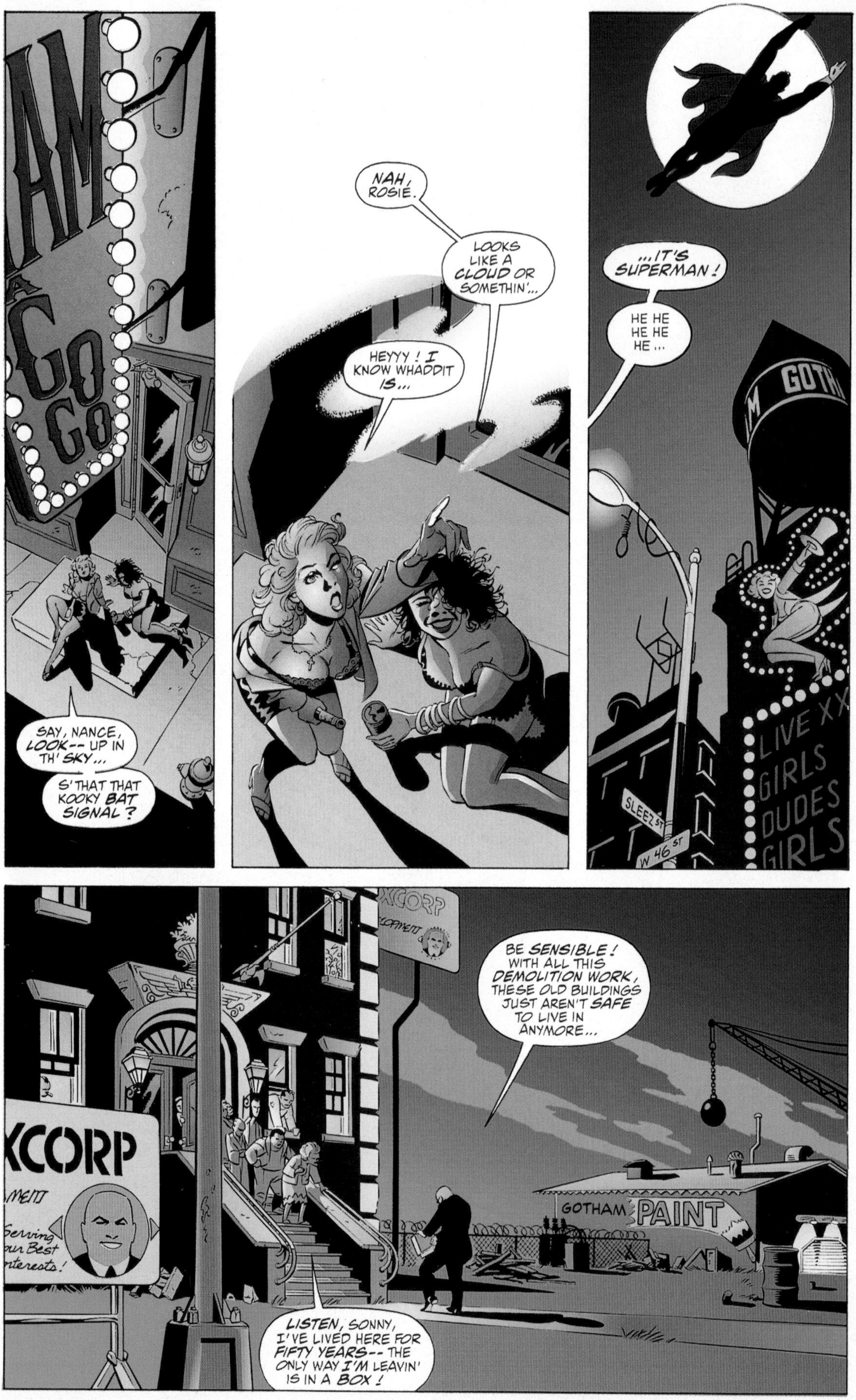
SAY, NANCE, LOOK-- UP IN TH' SKY...
S'THAT THAT KOOKY BAT SIGNAL?
NAH, ROSIE.
LOOKS LIKE A CLOUD OR SOMETHIN'...
HEYYY! I KNOW WHADDIT IS...
...IT'S SUPERMAN!
HE HE HE HE HE...
GIRLS
DUDES
GIRLS
SLEEZ ST
W 46 ST
BE SENSIBLE! WITH ALL THIS DEMOLITION WORK, THESE OLD BUILDINGS JUST AREN'T SAFE TO LIVE IN ANYMORE...
LISTEN, SONNY, I'VE LIVED HERE FOR FIFTY YEARS-- THE ONLY WAY I'M LEAVIN' IS IN A BOX!
XCORP
GOTHAM PAINT

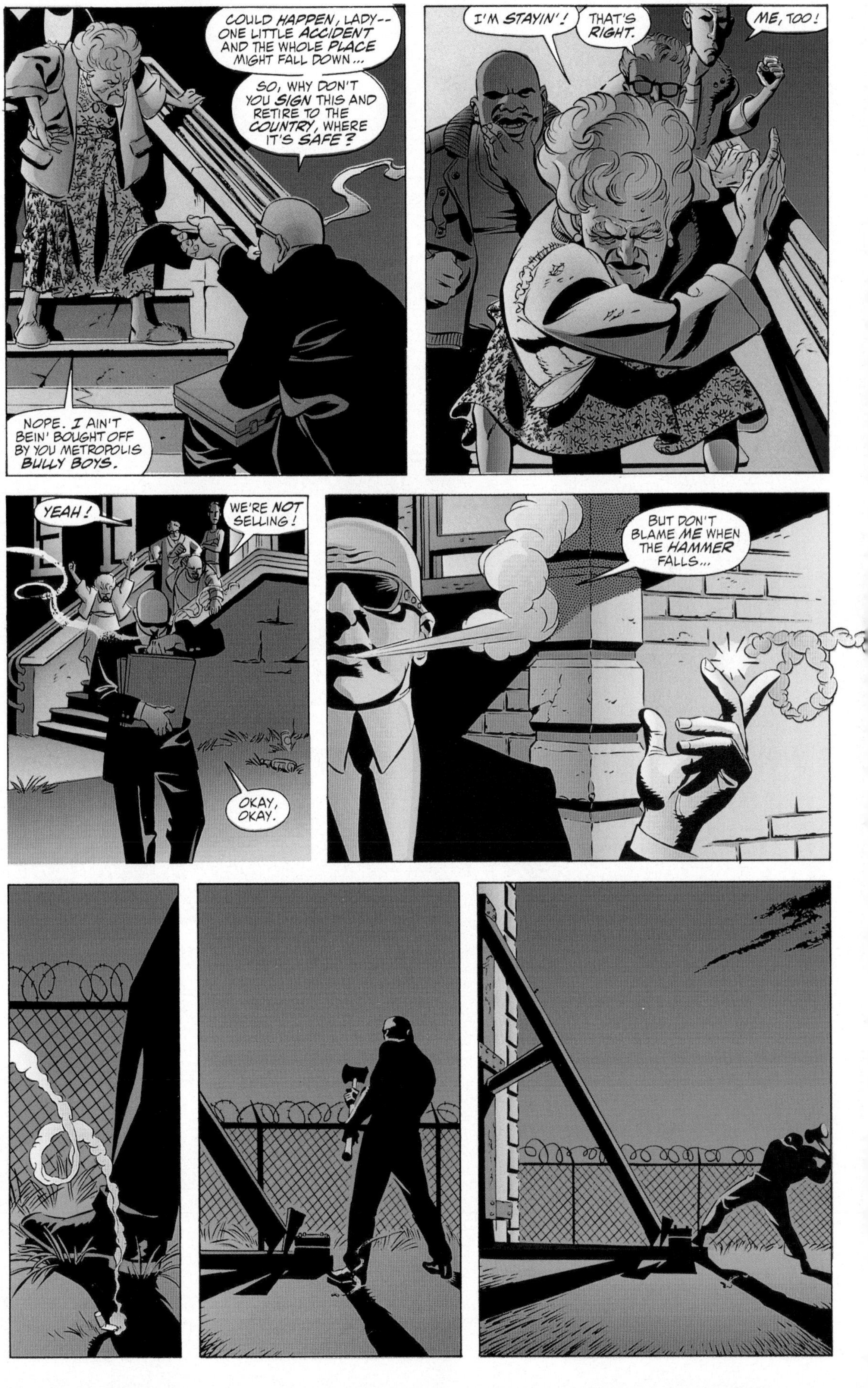
COULD HAPPEN, LADY-- ONE LITTLE ACCIDENT AND THE WHOLE PLACE MIGHT FALL DOWN...
SO, WHY DON'T YOU SIGN THIS AND RETIRE TO THE COUNTRY, WHERE IT'S SAFE?
NOPE. I AIN'T BEIN' BOUGHT OFF BY YOU METROPOLIS BULLY BOYS.
I'M STAYIN'!
THAT'S RIGHT.
ME, TOO!
YEAH!
WE'RE NOT SELLING!
OKAY, OKAY.
BUT DON'T BLAME ME WHEN THE HAMMER FALLS...

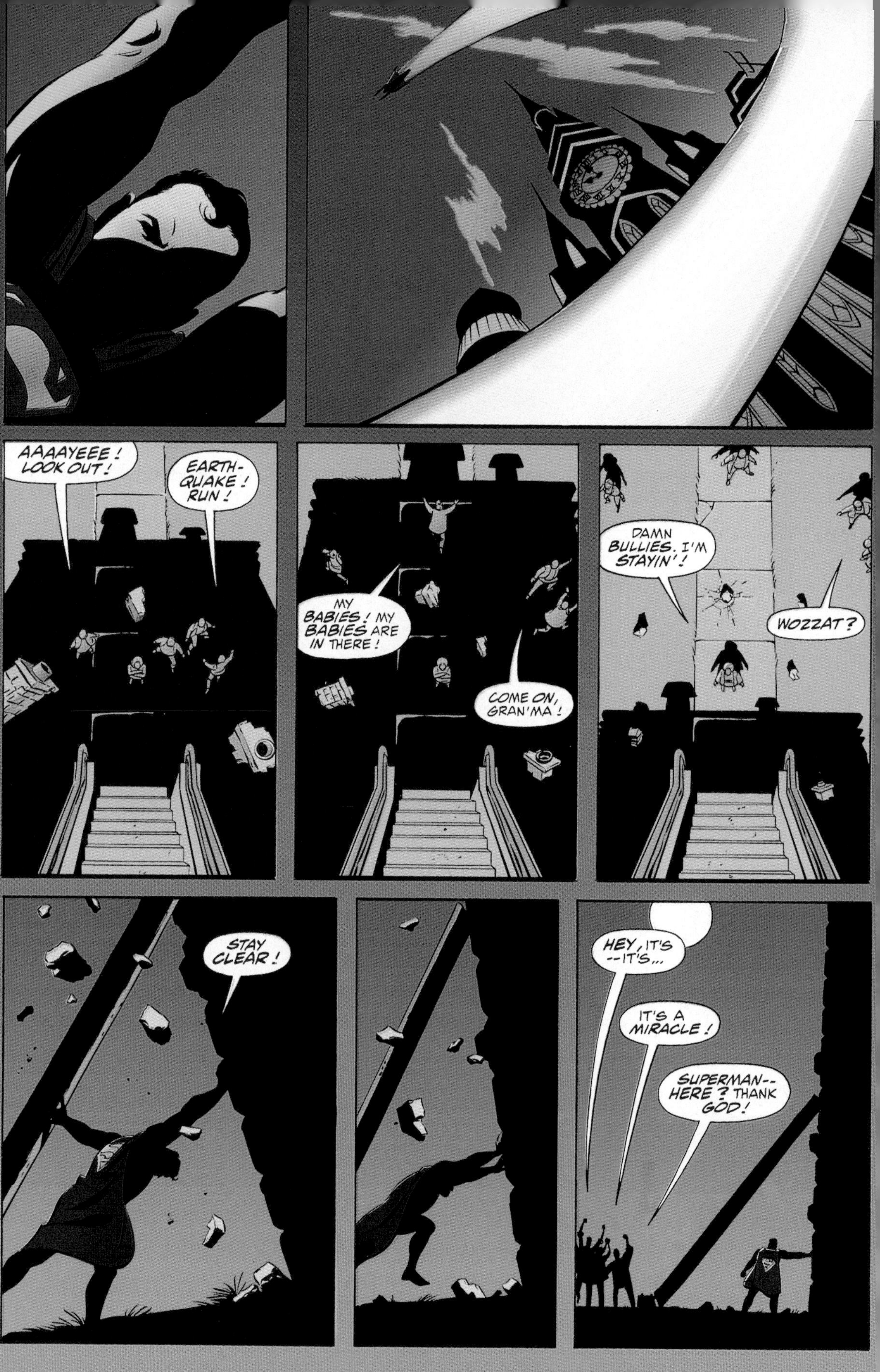
AAAAYEEE! LOOK OUT!
EARTH-QUAKE! RUN!
MY BABIES! MY BABIES ARE IN THERE!
COME ON, GRAN'MA!
DAMN BULLIES. I'M STAYIN'!
WOZZAT?
STAY CLEAR!
HEY, IT'S --IT'S...
IT'S A MIRACLE!
SUPERMAN--HERE? THANK GOD!

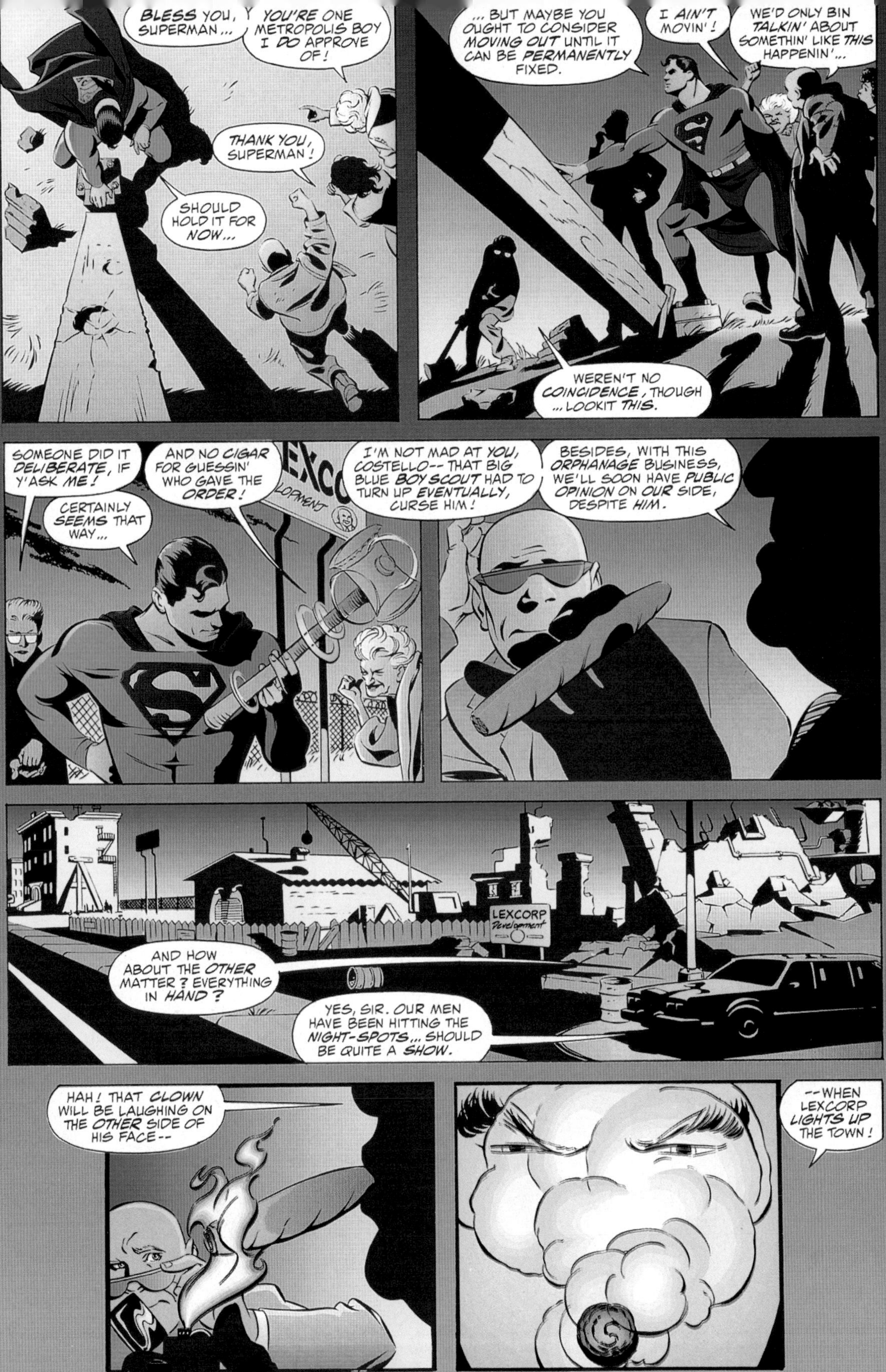
BLESS YOU, SUPERMAN...
YOU'RE ONE METROPOLIS BOY I DO APPROVE OF!
THANK YOU, SUPERMAN!
SHOULD HOLD IT FOR NOW...
...BUT MAYBE YOU OUGHT TO CONSIDER MOVING OUT UNTIL IT CAN BE PERMANENTLY FIXED.
I AIN'T MOVIN'!
WE'D ONLY BIN TALKIN' ABOUT SOMETHIN' LIKE THIS HAPPENIN'...
WEREN'T NO COINCIDENCE, THOUGH ...LOOKIT THIS.
SOMEONE DID IT DELIBERATE, IF Y'ASK ME!
CERTAINLY SEEMS THAT WAY...
AND NO CIGAR FOR GUESSIN' WHO GAVE THE ORDER!
I'M NOT MAD AT YOU, COSTELLO-- THAT BIG BLUE BOY SCOUT HAD TO TURN UP EVENTUALLY, CURSE HIM!
BESIDES, WITH THIS ORPHANAGE BUSINESS, WE'LL SOON HAVE PUBLIC OPINION ON OUR SIDE, DESPITE HIM.
LEXCORP Development
AND HOW ABOUT THE OTHER MATTER? EVERYTHING IN HAND?
YES, SIR. OUR MEN HAVE BEEN HITTING THE NIGHT-SPOTS... SHOULD BE QUITE A SHOW.
HAH! THAT CLOWN WILL BE LAUGHING ON THE OTHER SIDE OF HIS FACE--
--WHEN LEXCORP LIGHTS UP THE TOWN!

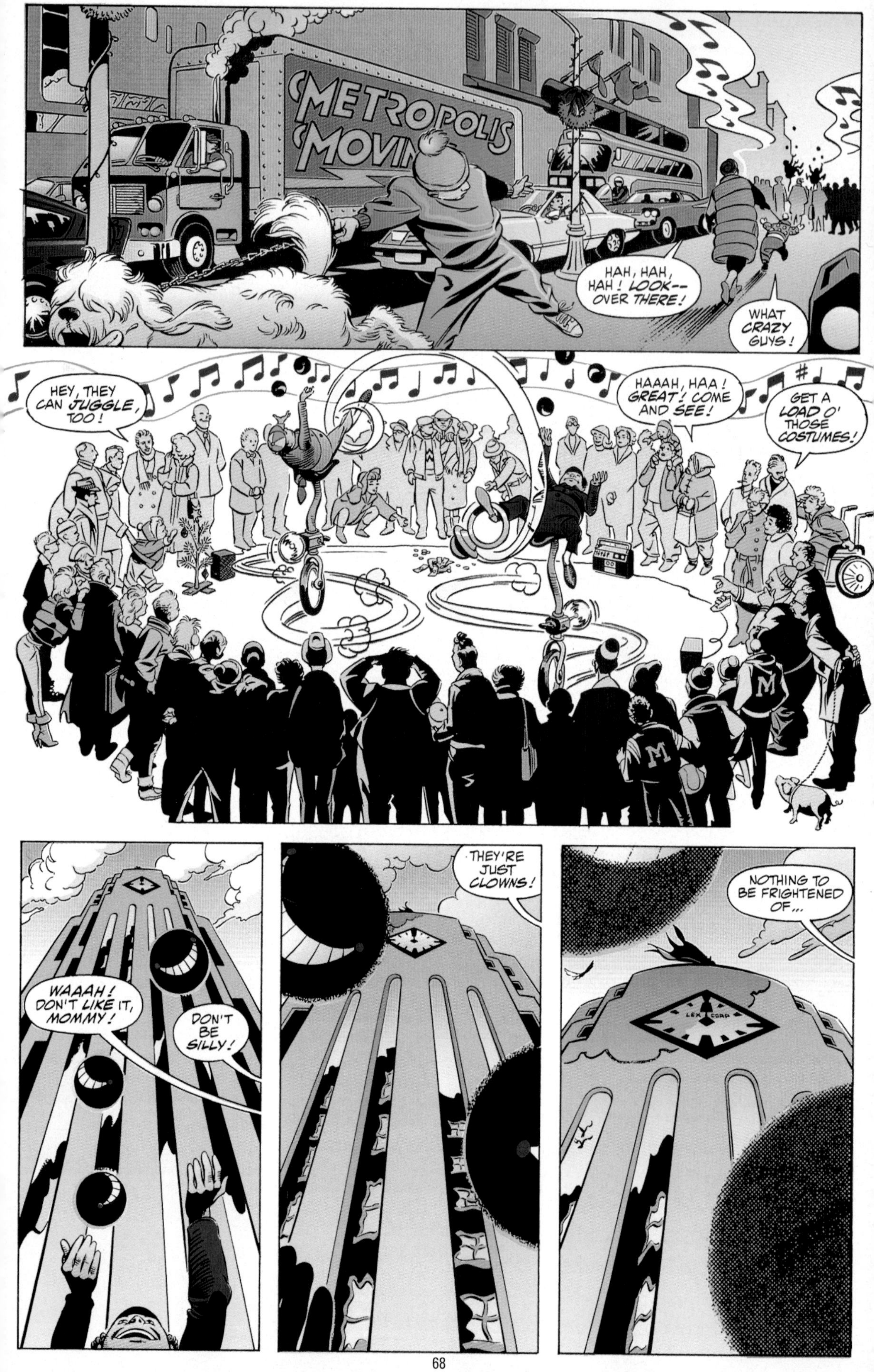
METROPOLIS MOVIN
HAH, HAH, HAH! LOOK-- OVER THERE!
WHAT CRAZY GUYS!
HEY, THEY CAN JUGGLE, TOO!
HAAAH, HAA! GREAT! COME AND SEE!
GET A LOAD O' THOSE COSTUMES!
WAAAH! DON'T LIKE IT, MOMMY!
DON'T BE SILLY!
THEY'RE JUST CLOWNS!
NOTHING TO BE FRIGHTENED OF...
LEX CORP

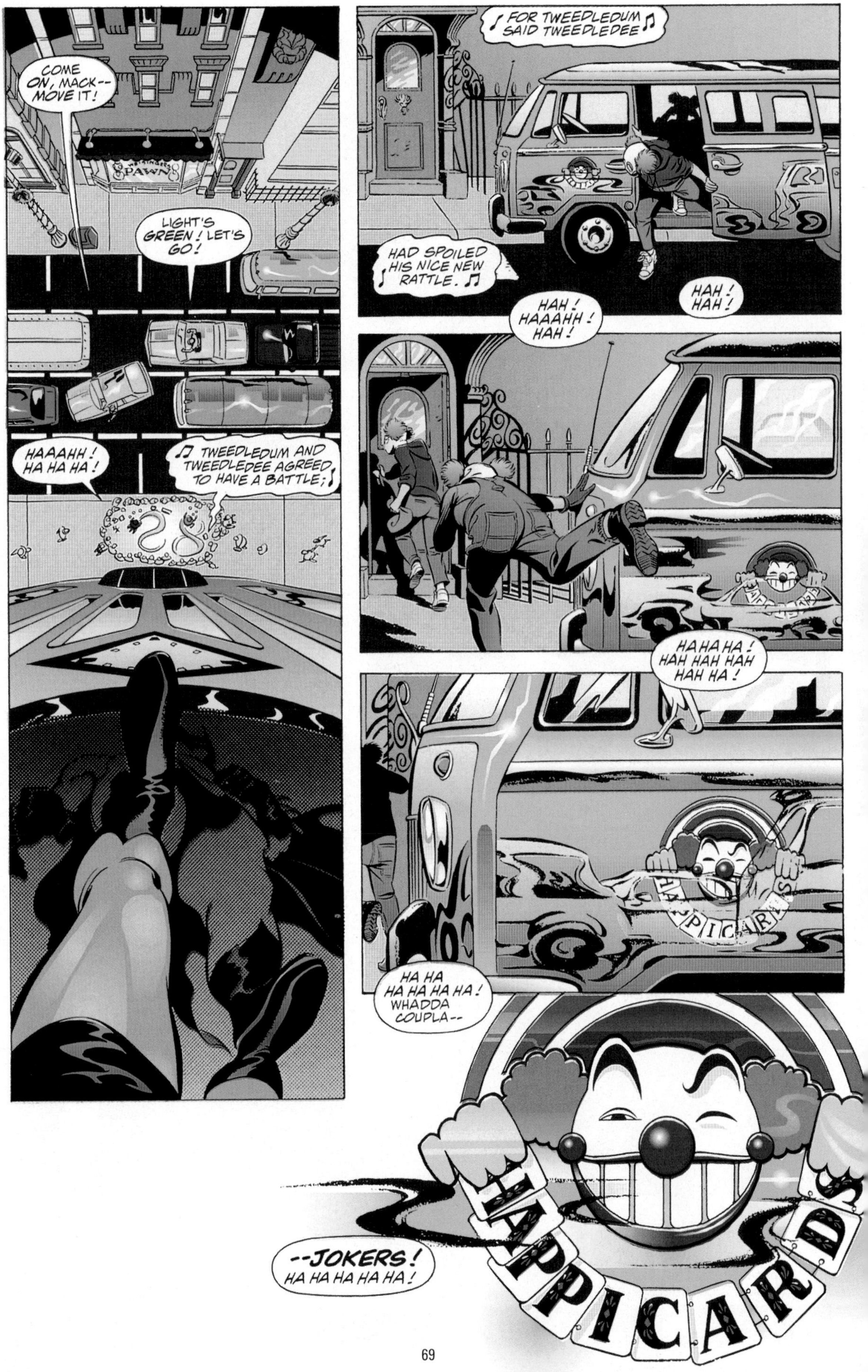
COME ON, MACK-- MOVE IT!
PAWN
LIGHT'S GREEN! LET'S GO!
HAAAHH! HA HA HA!
♫ TWEEDLEDUM AND TWEEDLEDEE AGREED TO HAVE A BATTLE; ♪
♪ FOR TWEEDLEDUM SAID TWEEDLEDEE ♫
HAD SPOILED HIS NICE NEW RATTLE. ♫
HAH! HAAAHH! HAH!
HAH! HAH!
HA HA HA! HAH HAH HAH HAH HA!
HA HA HA HA HA HA! WHADDA COUPLA--
--JOKERS! HA HA HA HA HA!
HAPPICARDS

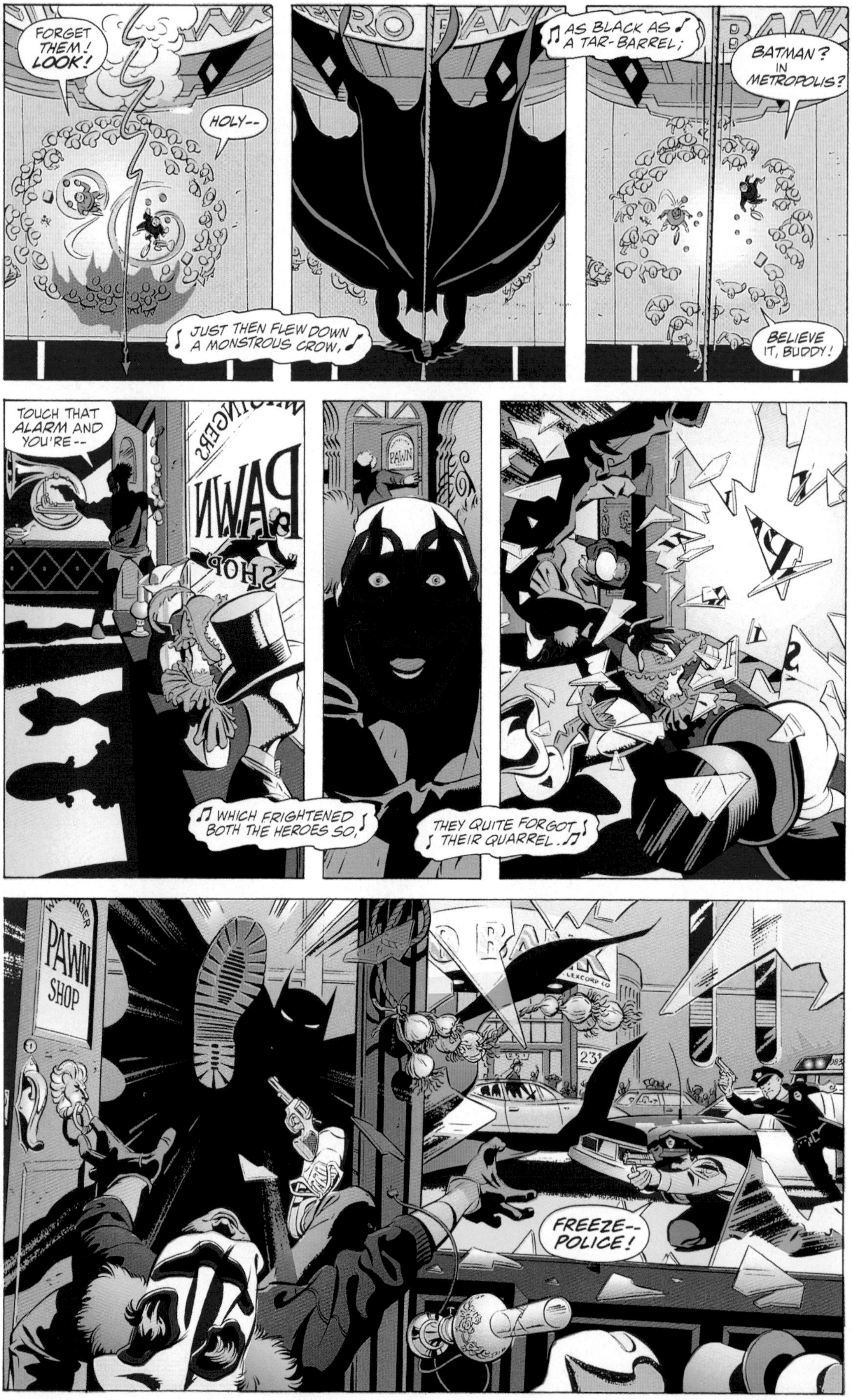
FORGET THEM! LOOK!
HOLY--
JUST THEN FLEW DOWN A MONSTROUS CROW,
AS BLACK AS A TAR-BARREL;
BATMAN? IN METROPOLIS?
BELIEVE IT, BUDDY!
TOUCH THAT ALARM AND YOU'RE--
PAWN SHOP
WHICH FRIGHTENED BOTH THE HEROES SO,
THEY QUITE FORGOT THEIR QUARREL.
PAWN SHOP
FREEZE-- POLICE!

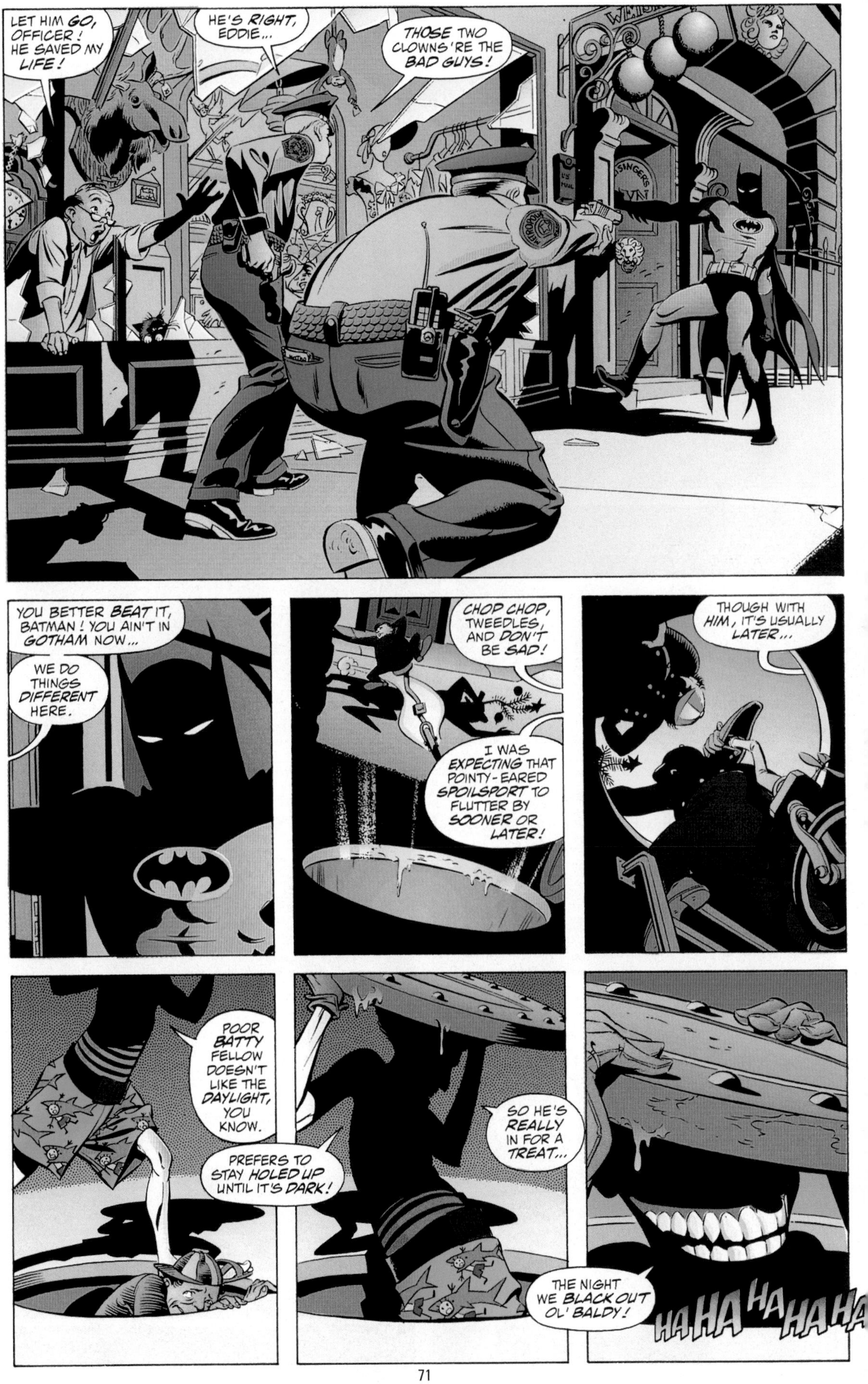
LET HIM GO, OFFICER! HE SAVED MY LIFE!
HE'S RIGHT, EDDIE...
THOSE TWO CLOWNS'RE THE BAD GUYS!
YOU BETTER BEAT IT, BATMAN! YOU AIN'T IN GOTHAM NOW...
WE DO THINGS DIFFERENT HERE.
CHOP CHOP, TWEEDLES, AND DON'T BE SAD!
I WAS EXPECTING THAT POINTY-EARED SPOILSPORT TO FLUTTER BY SOONER OR LATER!
THOUGH WITH HIM, IT'S USUALLY LATER...
POOR BATTY FELLOW DOESN'T LIKE THE DAYLIGHT, YOU KNOW.
PREFERS TO STAY HOLED UP UNTIL IT'S DARK!
SO HE'S REALLY IN FOR A TREAT...
THE NIGHT WE BLACK OUT OL' BALDY!
HA HA HA HA HA

...URGENT, CALLING ME *THIS* LATE!

WHAT? B-BUT THAT'S THE DAY AFTER *TOMORROW*! A-AND THEN *METROPOLIS*?

YES. YOU KNOW I HAVE NO CHOICE. BUT W-WHY THE *RUSH*?

BY *WHEN*? *CHRISTMAS*? MAXIMUM P-PUBLICITY... I SEE.

LOOK, I *CAN'T* TALK NOW--

HE'S COMING!

SHHH!

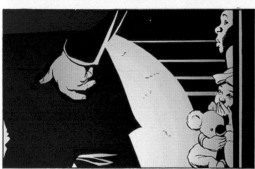

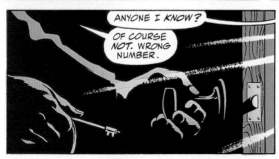

ANYONE I *KNOW*?

OF COURSE *NOT*. WRONG NUMBER.

NUISANCE. NOW, ABOUT YOUR, HEH, *ENCOUNTER GROUP*, SON...

I *TOLD* YOU. THEY'LL BE READY *SOON*. WE'VE--

HE SHUT THE DOOR, ANNIE...

ZACK, SOMEONE'S--

ANN? ZACHARY?

TH-THOUGHT I HEARD SOMEONE *UPSTAIRS*...

ME, *TOO*. THEN THE PHONE RANG...

WHAT ARE YOU TWO UP TO...?

YES. PHONE WOKE *ME*, TOO... THOUGHT I'D GET A *SANDWICH* TO HELP ME *SLEEP*.

WANT TO *SHARE* IT?

YES, *SIR*, REVEREND FULBRIGHT!

OH, YES, *PLEASE*!

OKAY. THEN BACK TO *BED* BEFORE YOU WAKE UP THE *REST* OF THE *DORM*...

SOMEONE IN THE *ATTIC*-- A *FINE* TALE...!

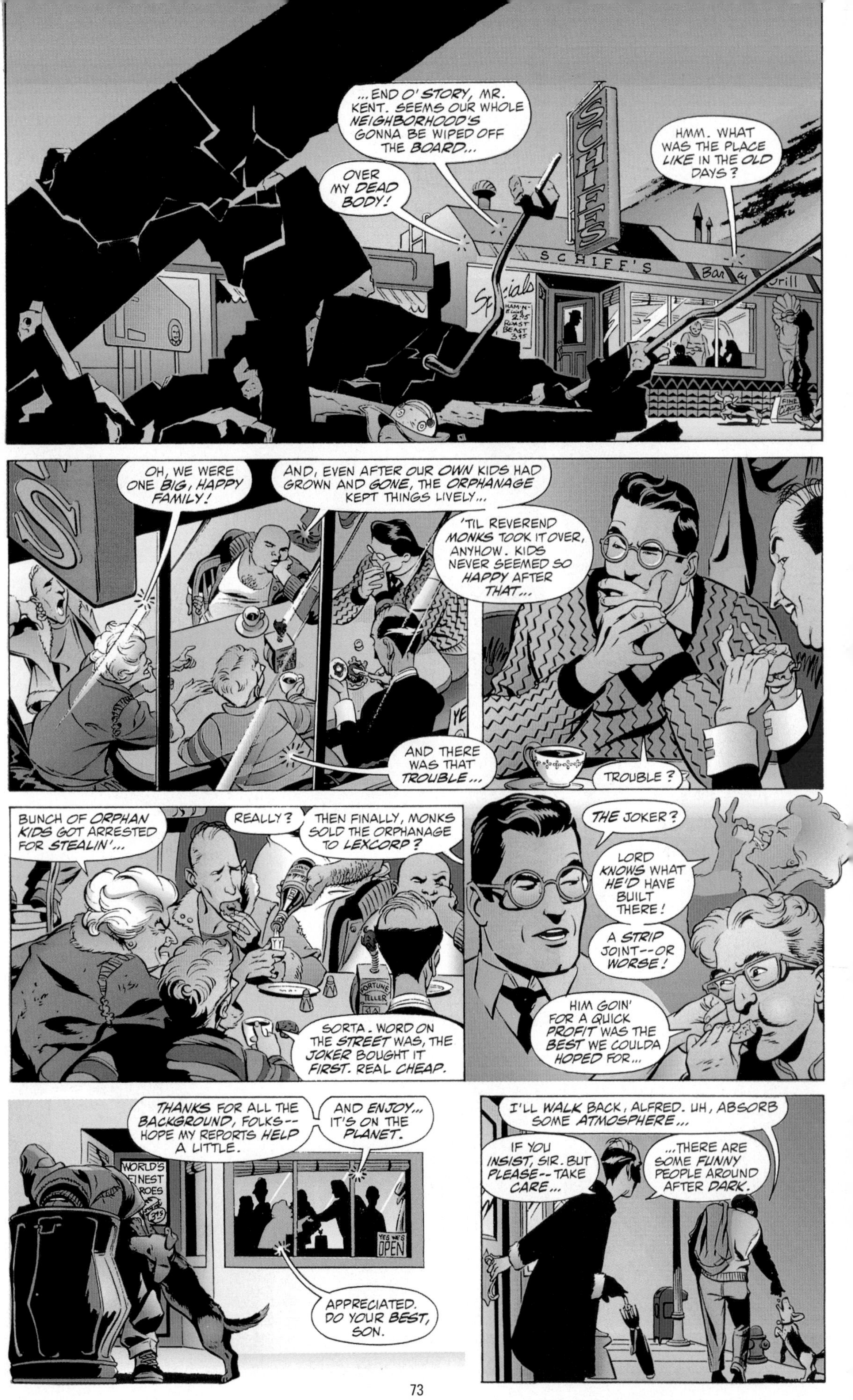
...END O' STORY, MR. KENT. SEEMS OUR WHOLE NEIGHBORHOOD'S GONNA BE WIPED OFF THE BOARD...
OVER MY DEAD BODY!
SCHIFFS
SCHIFF'S
Bar & Grill
HMM. WHAT WAS THE PLACE LIKE IN THE OLD DAYS?
OH, WE WERE ONE BIG, HAPPY FAMILY!
AND, EVEN AFTER OUR OWN KIDS HAD GROWN AND GONE, THE ORPHANAGE KEPT THINGS LIVELY...
'TIL REVEREND MONKS TOOK IT OVER, ANYHOW. KIDS NEVER SEEMED SO HAPPY AFTER THAT...
AND THERE WAS THAT TROUBLE...
TROUBLE?
BUNCH OF ORPHAN KIDS GOT ARRESTED FOR STEALIN'...
REALLY?
THEN FINALLY, MONKS SOLD THE ORPHANAGE TO LEXCORP?
SORTA. WORD ON THE STREET WAS, THE JOKER BOUGHT IT FIRST. REAL CHEAP.
FORTUNE TELLER
THE JOKER?
LORD KNOWS WHAT HE'D HAVE BUILT THERE!
A STRIP JOINT--OR WORSE!
HIM GOIN' FOR A QUICK PROFIT WAS THE BEST WE COULDA HOPED FOR...
THANKS FOR ALL THE BACKGROUND, FOLKS--HOPE MY REPORTS HELP A LITTLE.
AND ENJOY... IT'S ON THE PLANET.
YES WE'S OPEN
APPRECIATED. DO YOUR BEST, SON.
I'LL WALK BACK, ALFRED. UH, ABSORB SOME ATMOSPHERE...
IF YOU INSIST, SIR. BUT PLEASE--TAKE CARE...
...THERE ARE SOME FUNNY PEOPLE AROUND AFTER DARK.

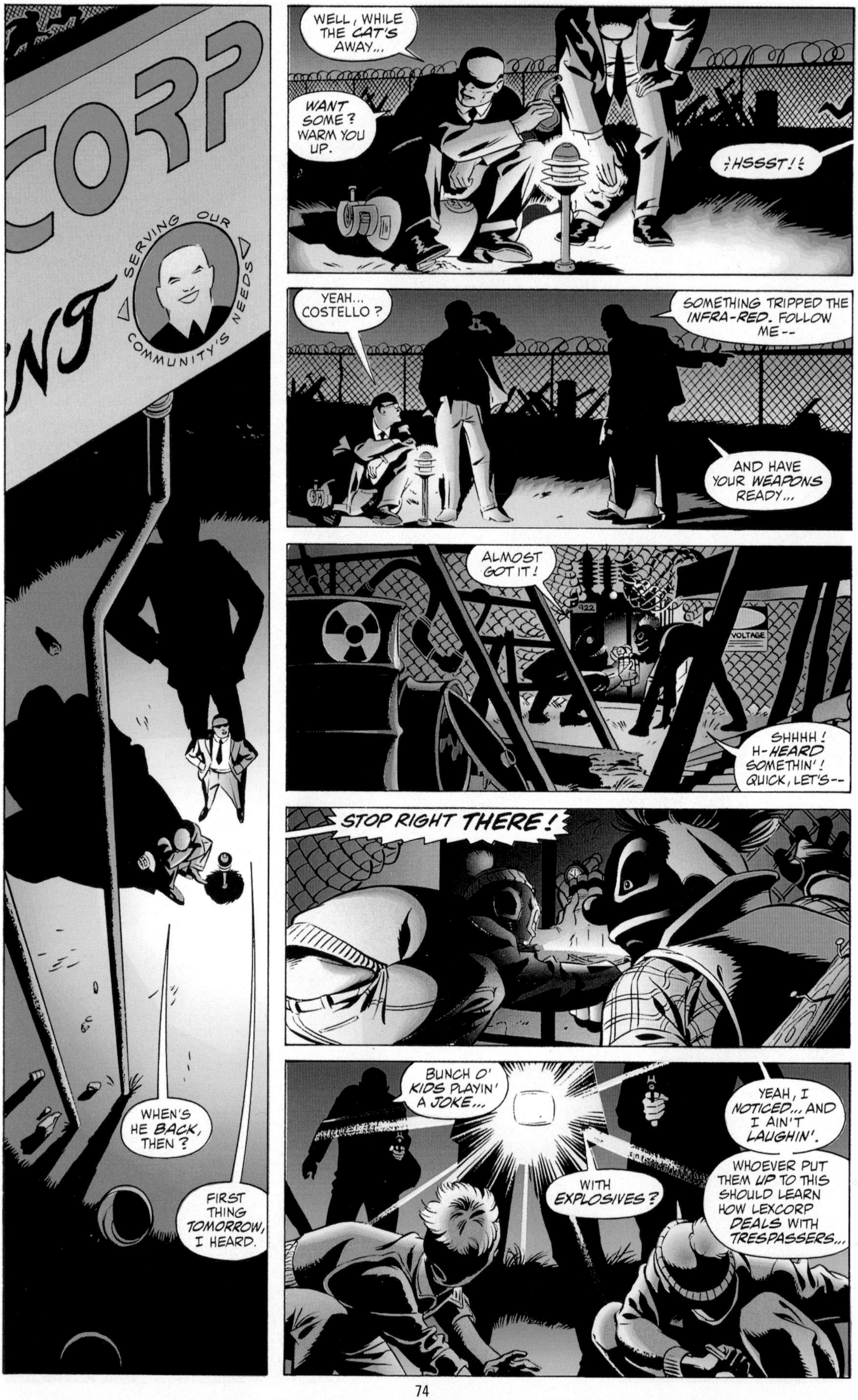
CORP
SERVING OUR COMMUNITY'S NEEDS
WHEN'S HE BACK, THEN?
FIRST THING TOMORROW, I HEARD.
WELL, WHILE THE CAT'S AWAY...
WANT SOME? WARM YOU UP.
¡HSSST!¡
YEAH... COSTELLO?
SOMETHING TRIPPED THE INFRA-RED. FOLLOW ME--
AND HAVE YOUR WEAPONS READY...
ALMOST GOT IT!
VOLTAGE
SHHHH! H-HEARD SOMETHIN'! QUICK, LET'S--
STOP RIGHT THERE!
BUNCH O' KIDS PLAYIN' A JOKE...
YEAH, I NOTICED... AND I AIN'T LAUGHIN'.
WITH EXPLOSIVES?
WHOEVER PUT THEM UP TO THIS SHOULD LEARN HOW LEXCORP DEALS WITH TRESPASSERS...

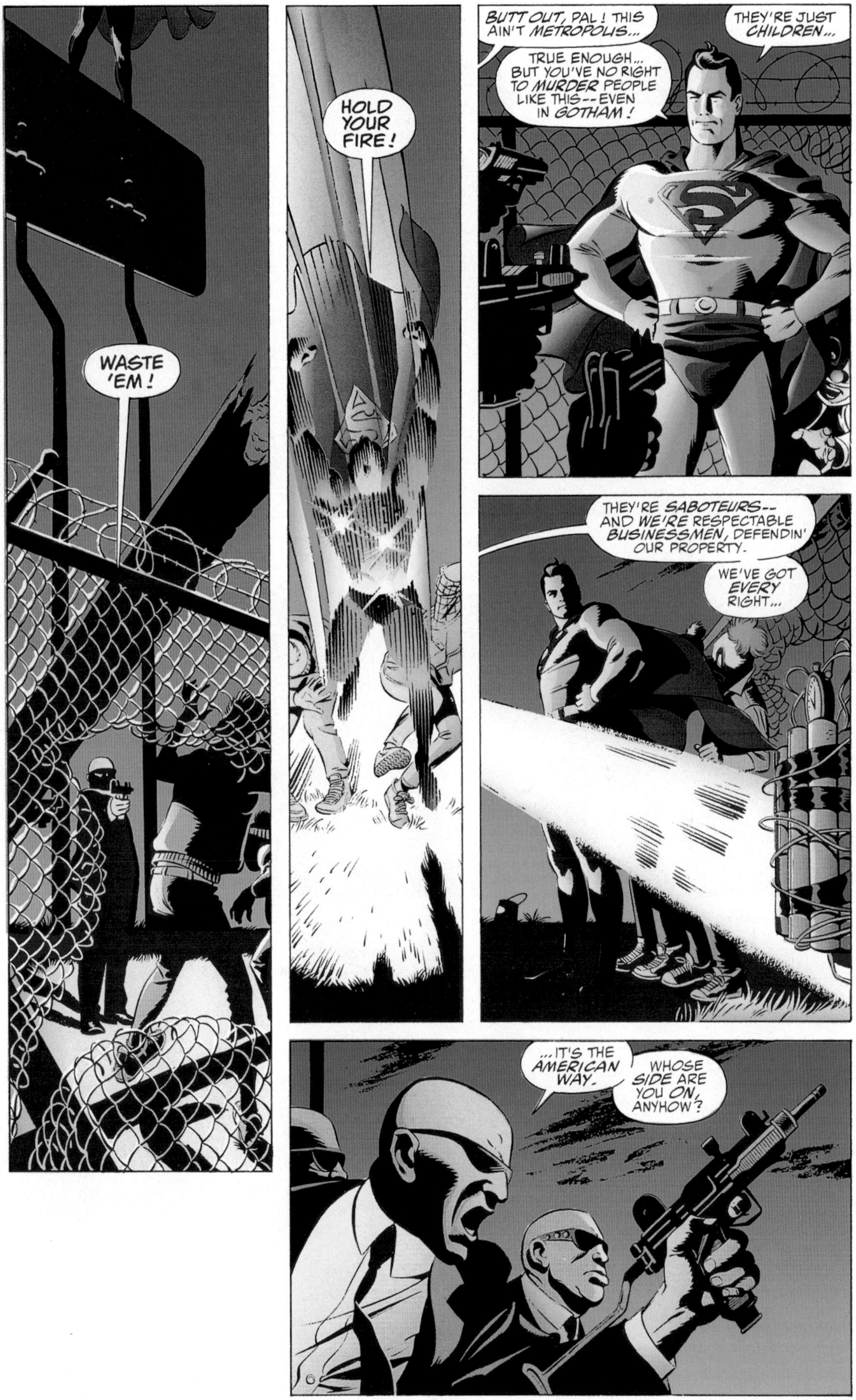
WASTE 'EM!
HOLD YOUR FIRE!
BUTT OUT, PAL! THIS AIN'T METROPOLIS...
TRUE ENOUGH... BUT YOU'VE NO RIGHT TO MURDER PEOPLE LIKE THIS-- EVEN IN GOTHAM!
THEY'RE JUST CHILDREN...
THEY'RE SABOTEURS-- AND WE'RE RESPECTABLE BUSINESSMEN, DEFENDIN' OUR PROPERTY.
WE'VE GOT EVERY RIGHT...
...IT'S THE AMERICAN WAY.
WHOSE SIDE ARE YOU ON, ANYHOW?

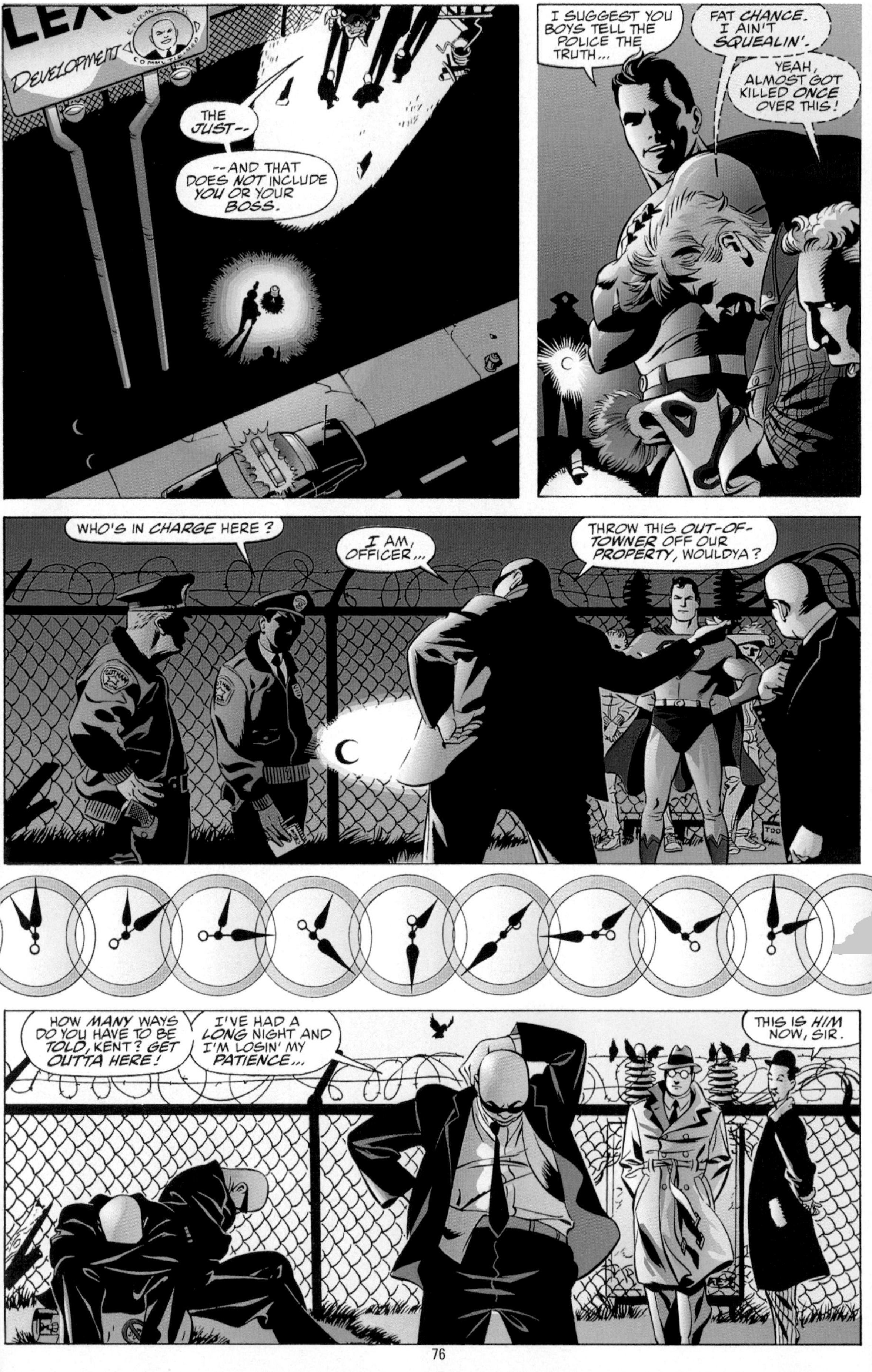
LEX
DEVELOPMENT
THE JUST--
--AND THAT DOES NOT INCLUDE YOU OR YOUR BOSS.
I SUGGEST YOU BOYS TELL THE POLICE THE TRUTH...
FAT CHANCE. I AIN'T SQUEALIN'.
YEAH, ALMOST GOT KILLED ONCE OVER THIS!
WHO'S IN CHARGE HERE?
I AM, OFFICER...
THROW THIS OUT-OF-TOWNER OFF OUR PROPERTY, WOULDYA?
HOW MANY WAYS DO YOU HAVE TO BE TOLD, KENT? GET OUTTA HERE!
I'VE HAD A LONG NIGHT AND I'M LOSIN' MY PATIENCE...
THIS IS HIM NOW, SIR.

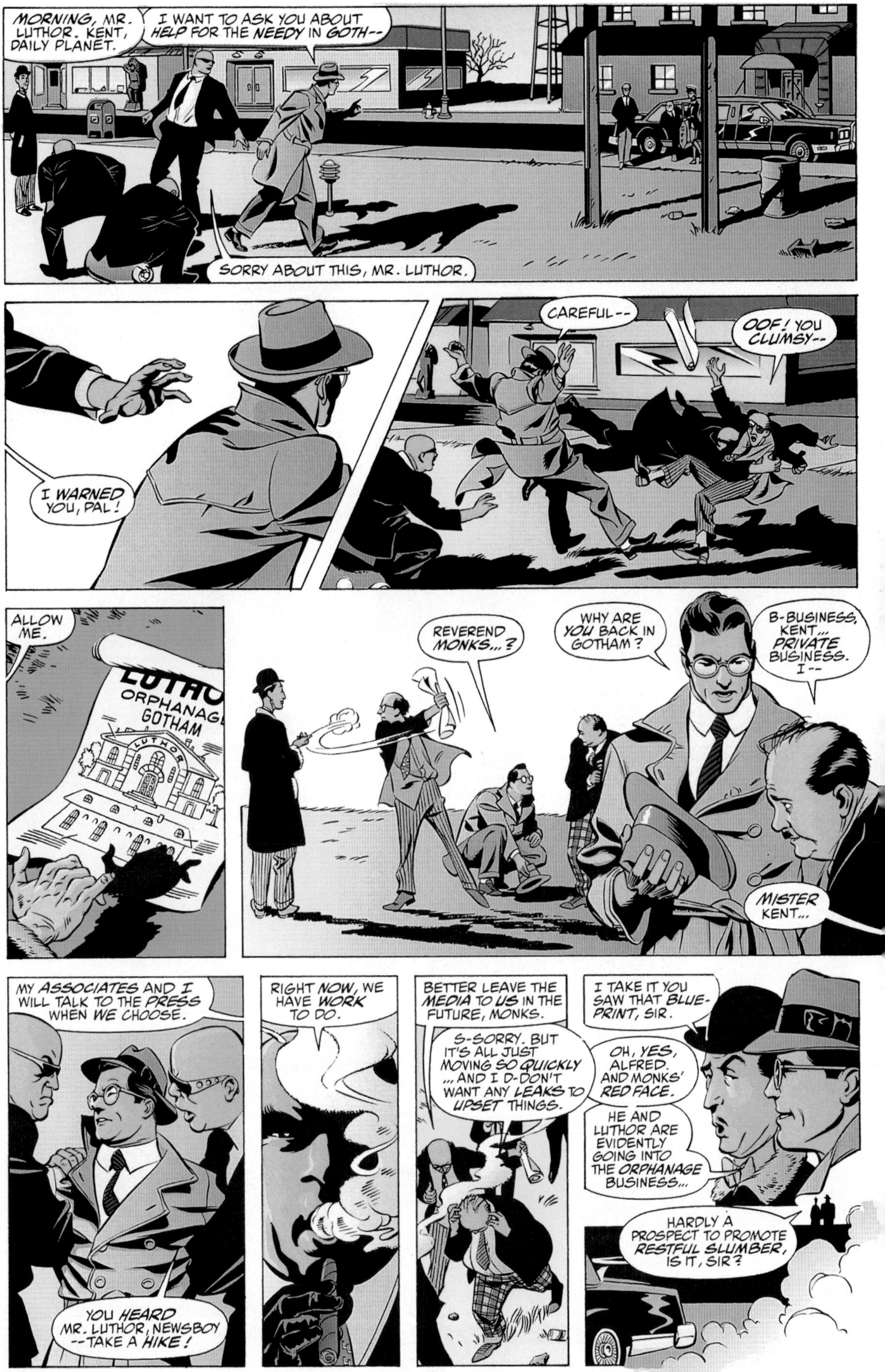
MORNING, MR. LUTHOR. KENT, DAILY PLANET.
I WANT TO ASK YOU ABOUT HELP FOR THE NEEDY IN GOTH--
SORRY ABOUT THIS, MR. LUTHOR.
I WARNED YOU, PAL!
CAREFUL--
OOF! YOU CLUMSY--
ALLOW ME.
LUTHOR ORPHANAGE GOTHAM
LUTHOR
REVEREND MONKS...?
WHY ARE YOU BACK IN GOTHAM?
B-BUSINESS, KENT... PRIVATE BUSINESS. I--
MISTER KENT...
MY ASSOCIATES AND I WILL TALK TO THE PRESS WHEN WE CHOOSE.
YOU HEARD MR. LUTHOR, NEWSBOY --TAKE A HIKE!
RIGHT NOW, WE HAVE WORK TO DO.
BETTER LEAVE THE MEDIA TO US IN THE FUTURE, MONKS.
S-SORRY. BUT IT'S ALL JUST MOVING SO QUICKLY ...AND I D-DON'T WANT ANY LEAKS TO UPSET THINGS.
I TAKE IT YOU SAW THAT BLUE-PRINT, SIR.
OH, YES, ALFRED. AND MONKS' RED FACE.
HE AND LUTHOR ARE EVIDENTLY GOING INTO THE ORPHANAGE BUSINESS...
HARDLY A PROSPECT TO PROMOTE RESTFUL SLUMBER, IS IT, SIR?

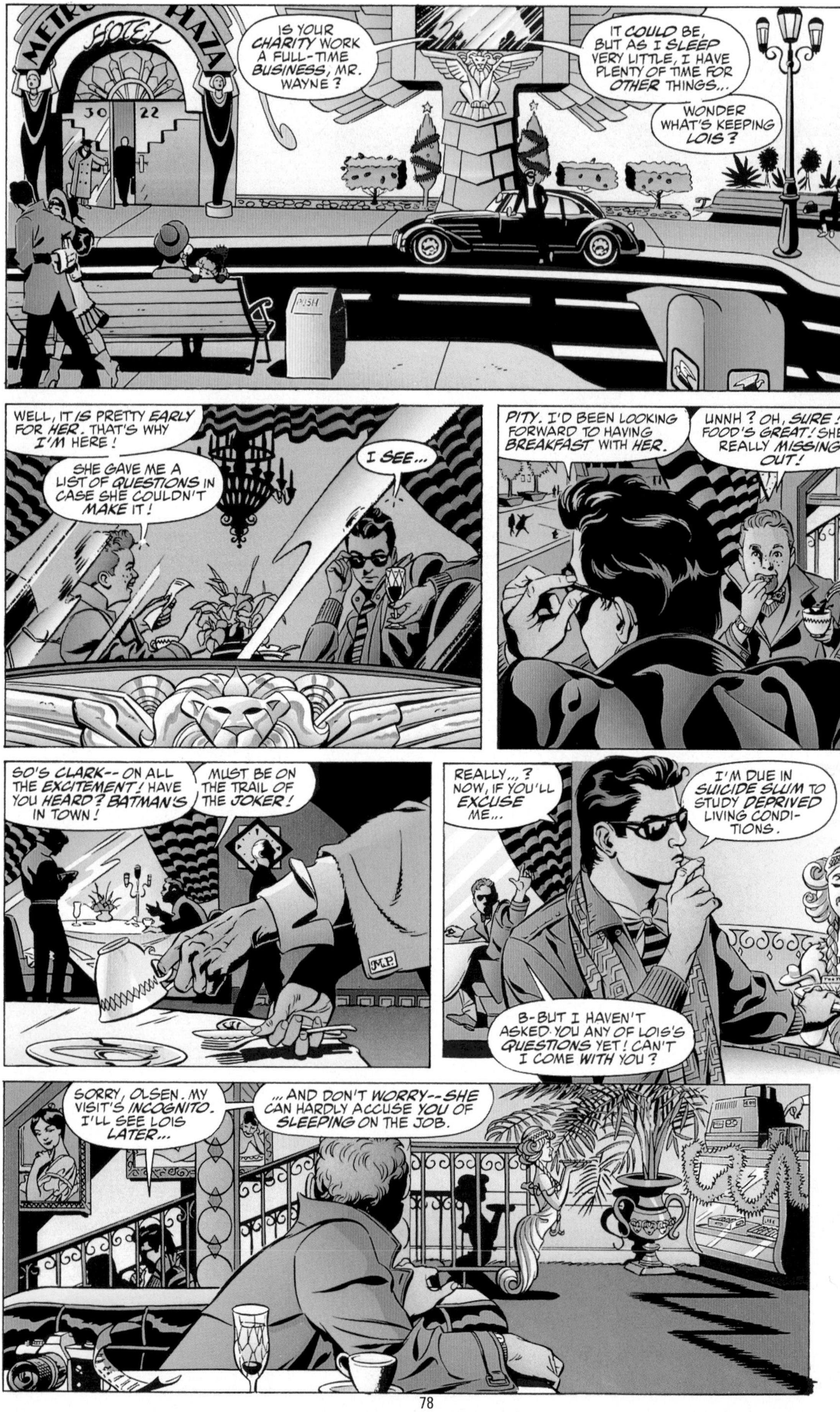

METROPOLIS PLAZA HOTEL
30 22
IS YOUR CHARITY WORK A FULL-TIME BUSINESS, MR. WAYNE?
IT COULD BE, BUT AS I SLEEP VERY LITTLE, I HAVE PLENTY OF TIME FOR OTHER THINGS...
WONDER WHAT'S KEEPING LOIS?
PUSH
WELL, IT IS PRETTY EARLY FOR HER. THAT'S WHY I'M HERE!
SHE GAVE ME A LIST OF QUESTIONS IN CASE SHE COULDN'T MAKE IT!
I SEE...
PITY. I'D BEEN LOOKING FORWARD TO HAVING BREAKFAST WITH HER.
UNNH? OH, SURE! FOOD'S GREAT! SHE'S REALLY MISSING OUT!
SO'S CLARK-- ON ALL THE EXCITEMENT! HAVE YOU HEARD? BATMAN'S IN TOWN!
MUST BE ON THE TRAIL OF THE JOKER!
M.P.
REALLY...? NOW, IF YOU'LL EXCUSE ME...
I'M DUE IN SUICIDE SLUM TO STUDY DEPRIVED LIVING CONDITIONS.
B-BUT I HAVEN'T ASKED YOU ANY OF LOIS'S QUESTIONS YET! CAN'T I COME WITH YOU?
SORRY, OLSEN. MY VISIT'S INCOGNITO. I'LL SEE LOIS LATER...
...AND DON'T WORRY--SHE CAN HARDLY ACCUSE YOU OF SLEEPING ON THE JOB.

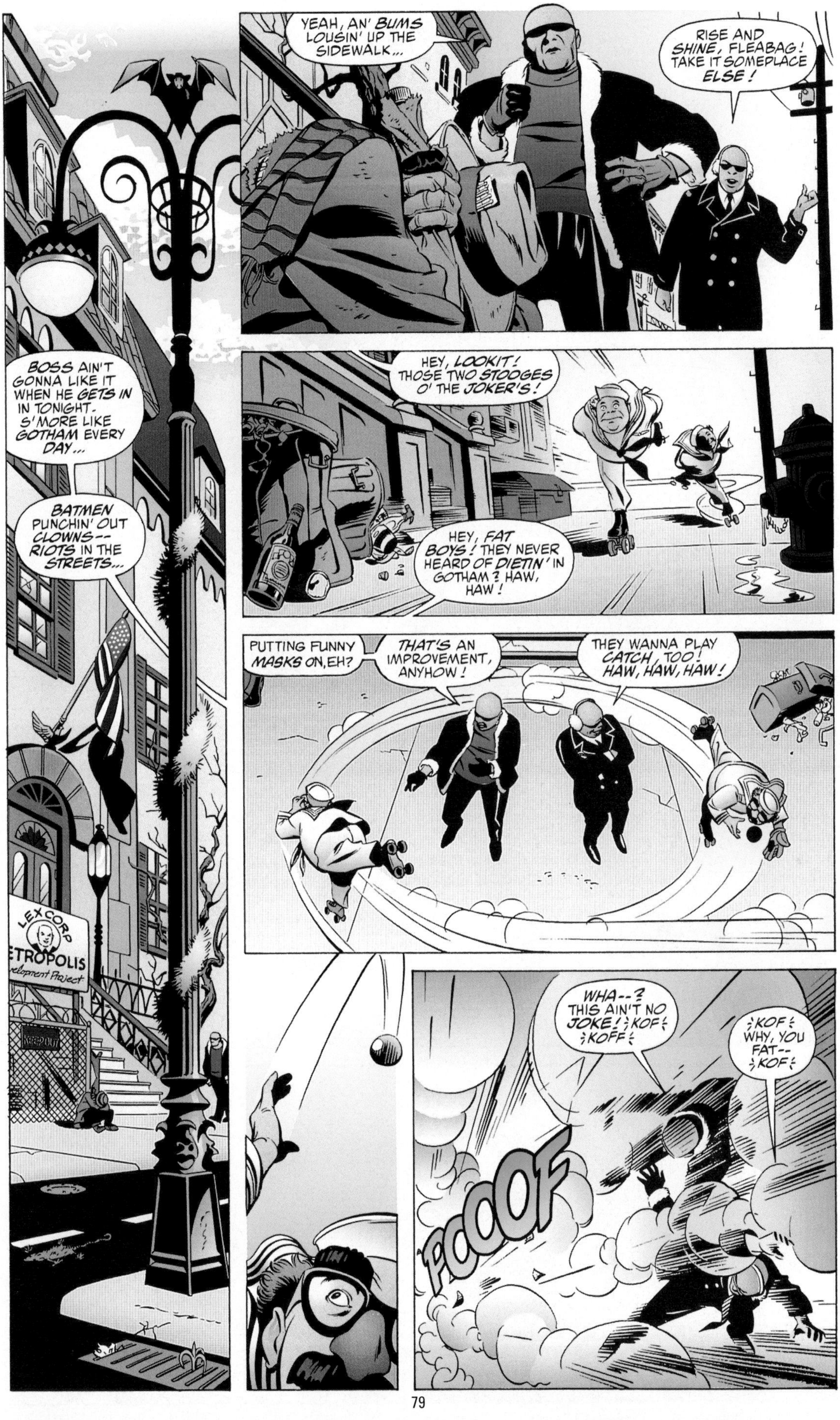

BOSS AIN'T GONNA LIKE IT WHEN HE GETS IN IN TONIGHT. S'MORE LIKE GOTHAM EVERY DAY...
BATMEN PUNCHIN' OUT CLOWNS-- RIOTS IN THE STREETS...
LEXCORP
ETROPOLIS
velopment Project
KEEP OUT
YEAH, AN' BUMS LOUSIN' UP THE SIDEWALK...
RISE AND SHINE, FLEABAG! TAKE IT SOMEPLACE ELSE!
HEY, LOOKIT! THOSE TWO STOOGES O' THE JOKER'S!
HEY, FAT BOYS! THEY NEVER HEARD OF DIETIN' IN GOTHAM? HAW, HAW!
PUTTING FUNNY MASKS ON, EH?
THAT'S AN IMPROVEMENT, ANYHOW!
THEY WANNA PLAY CATCH, TOO! HAW, HAW, HAW!
WHA--? THIS AIN'T NO JOKE! ¦KOF¦ ¦KOFF¦
¦KOF¦ WHY, YOU FAT-- ¦KOF¦
POOOF

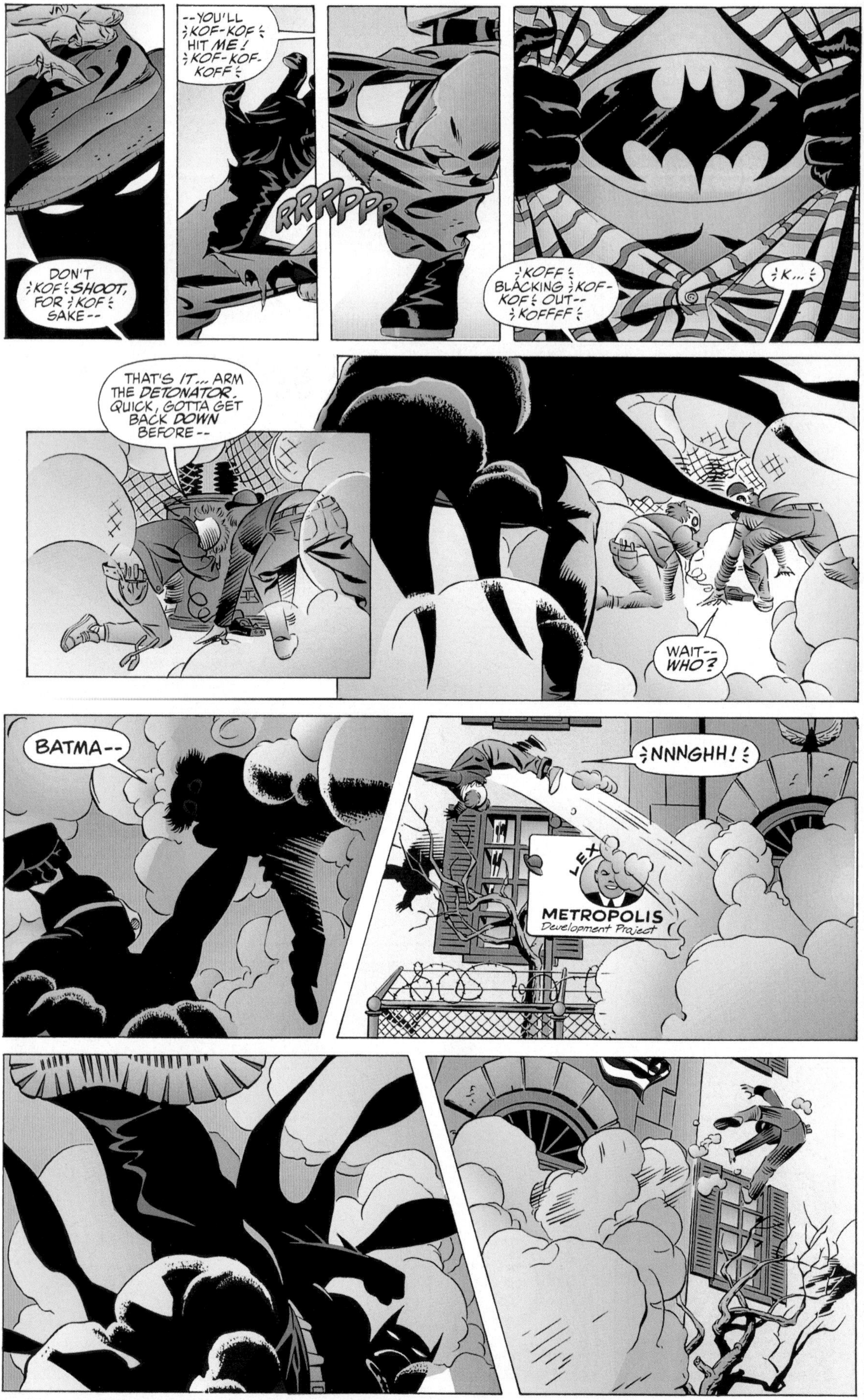

--YOU'LL KOF-KOF HIT ME! KOF-KOF-KOFF
DON'T KOF SHOOT, FOR KOF SAKE--
RRRPPP
KOFF BLACKING KOF-KOF OUT--KOFFFF
K...
THAT'S IT... ARM THE DETONATOR. QUICK, GOTTA GET BACK DOWN BEFORE--
WAIT--WHO?
BATMA--
NNNGHH!
LEX
METROPOLIS
Development Project

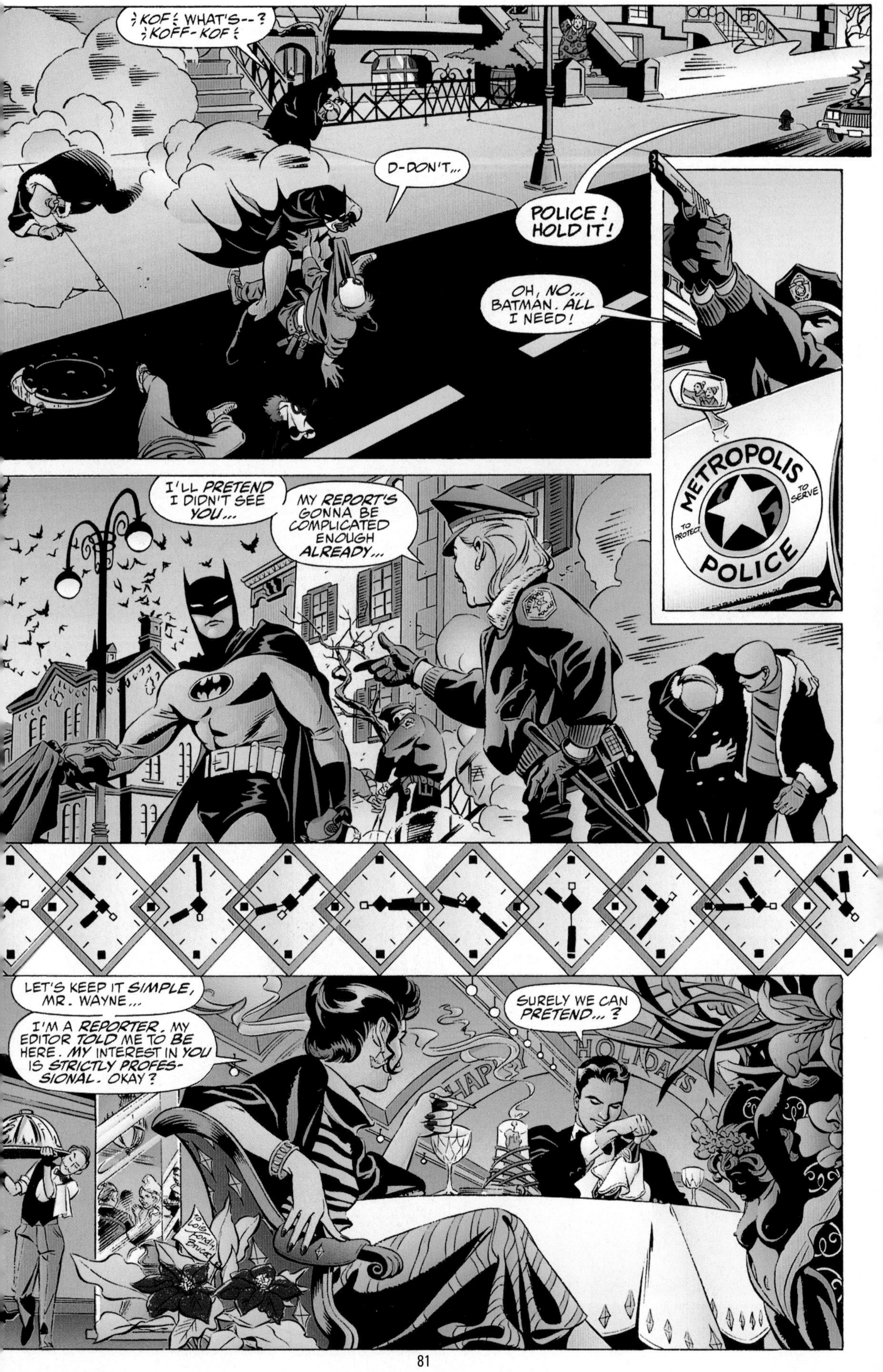
KOF WHAT'S--? KOFF-KOF
D-DON'T...
POLICE! HOLD IT!
OH, NO... BATMAN. ALL I NEED!
METROPOLIS POLICE
TO PROTECT TO SERVE
I'LL PRETEND I DIDN'T SEE YOU...
MY REPORT'S GONNA BE COMPLICATED ENOUGH ALREADY...
LET'S KEEP IT SIMPLE, MR. WAYNE...
I'M A REPORTER. MY EDITOR TOLD ME TO BE HERE. MY INTEREST IN YOU IS STRICTLY PROFESSIONAL. OKAY?
SURELY WE CAN PRETEND...?
HAPPY HOLIDAYS

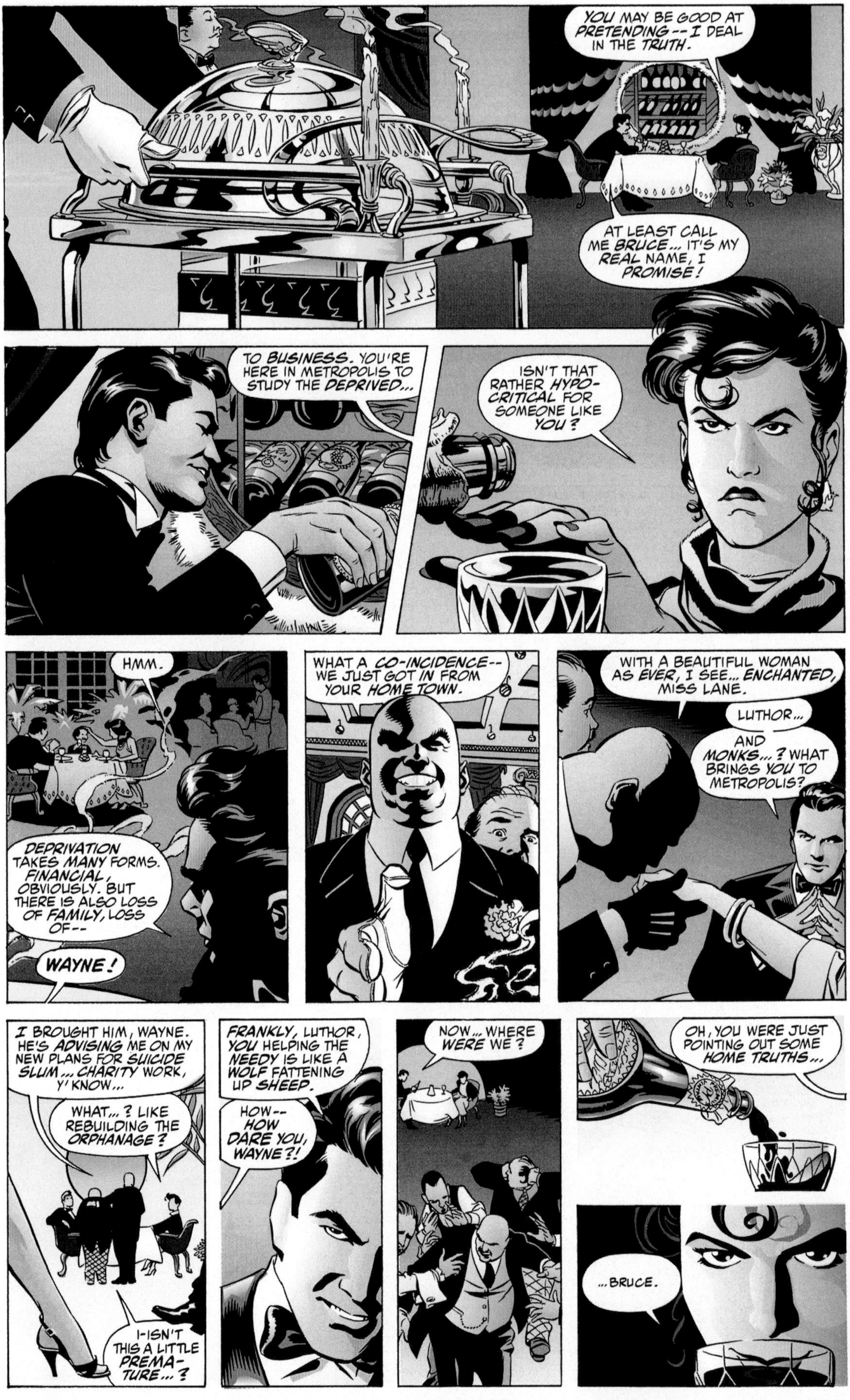
YOU MAY BE GOOD AT PRETENDING -- I DEAL IN THE TRUTH.
AT LEAST CALL ME BRUCE... IT'S MY REAL NAME, I PROMISE!
TO BUSINESS. YOU'RE HERE IN METROPOLIS TO STUDY THE DEPRIVED...
ISN'T THAT RATHER HYPO-CRITICAL FOR SOMEONE LIKE YOU?
HMM.
DEPRIVATION TAKES MANY FORMS. FINANCIAL, OBVIOUSLY. BUT THERE IS ALSO LOSS OF FAMILY, LOSS OF--
WAYNE!
WHAT A CO-INCIDENCE-- WE JUST GOT IN FROM YOUR HOME TOWN.
WITH A BEAUTIFUL WOMAN AS EVER, I SEE... ENCHANTED, MISS LANE.
LUTHOR...
AND MONKS...? WHAT BRINGS YOU TO METROPOLIS?
I BROUGHT HIM, WAYNE. HE'S ADVISING ME ON MY NEW PLANS FOR SUICIDE SLUM... CHARITY WORK, Y'KNOW...
WHAT...? LIKE REBUILDING THE ORPHANAGE?
I-ISN'T THIS A LITTLE PREMA-TURE...?
FRANKLY, LUTHOR, YOU HELPING THE NEEDY IS LIKE A WOLF FATTENING UP SHEEP.
HOW-- HOW DARE YOU, WAYNE?!
NOW... WHERE WERE WE?
OH, YOU WERE JUST POINTING OUT SOME HOME TRUTHS...
...BRUCE.

OH, I'LL ADMIT IT, COMMISSIONER-- I AM GLAD TO BE GOING HOME FOR CHRISTMAS...

WELL, METROPOLIS, ANYHOW.

UH, WHERE ARE WE NOW?

THAT'S CRIME ALLEY OVER THERE... WELL NAMED, AS YOU CAN SEE.

WHAT HAPPENED? ARSON?

YEAH. ODD CASE... MANAGER CATCHES SOMEONE PLANTING A FIRE-BOMB. GUY PUTS UP HIS HANDS--

--AND THE DAMN THING EXPLODES ANYWAY. FORENSIC FOUND REMAINS OF A REMOTE-CONTROL DEVICE.

I UNDERSTAND THE JOKER OWNS MOST OF THESE ¿AHEM¿ ESTAB-LISHMENTS, COM-MISSIONER...

WHO IN GOTHAM WOULD DARE CROSS HIM?

I HAVE MY SUSPICIONS. LET'S JUST SAY WE'RE LOOKING INTO OUT-OF-TOWN CONNECTIONS.

SPEAKING OF WHICH, DID YOU GET ONE OF THESE?

AH, THE PARTY.

Reverend Oliver Monks, M.D.
requests the pleasure of the company of
COMMISSIONER JAMES GORDON
at a grand
Christmas Party
to be held at MIDWAY ORPHANAGE
DECEMBER 24th AT 8.00 PM
SPECIAL GUEST: LEX LUTHOR
The children wi[ll perf]orm their version
of the classic ["ALICE"] stories.
R.S.V.P.
DRESS OPTIO[NAL]

NOT YET. THE STAR GUEST IS NO SURPRISE, THOUGH.

HMM... DIDN'T REALIZE MONKS WAS A DOCTOR. INTERESTING...

WELL, THANKS FOR THE TOUR, COMMIS-SIONER GORDON.

IF YOU'LL EXCUSE ME, I'VE SOME, UH, URGENT CALLS TO MAKE BEFORE I LEAVE FOR HOME...

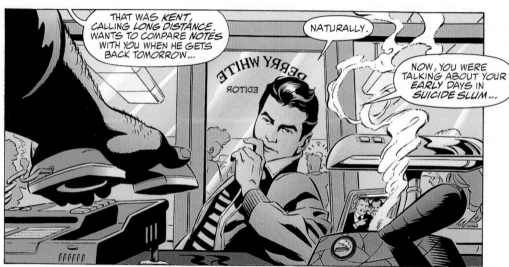

THAT WAS *KENT*, CALLING LONG DISTANCE. WANTS TO COMPARE *NOTES* WITH YOU WHEN HE GETS BACK TOMORROW...

DERRY WHITE EDITOR

NATURALLY.

NOW, YOU WERE TALKING ABOUT YOUR *EARLY DAYS* IN *SUICIDE SLUM*...

A *WORLD AWAY*... *LEX LUTHOR* AND I WERE *FRIENDS* BACK *THEN*.

MY PARENTS DIDN'T *LIKE* ME PLAYING WITH THE *ORPHANAGE* KIDS...

...SAID THEY WERE A *BAD INFLU-ENCE*.

IRONIC, CONSIDERING HOW *LUTHOR* TURNED OUT, AFTER *HIS FOLKS'* DEATH...

STILL, *WYLIE* FINALLY DRAGGED THE ORPHANAGE THROUGH THE *MUD*, TOO.

THE *ROBBERIES*, YOU MEAN, AND THE LITTLE *GIRL* ... THE *DECOY*.

YES. HER *DEATH* DREW ATTENTION TO THE *ORPHANAGE* AND, INEVITABLY, TO *WYLIE* HIMSELF...

BUT THEY NEVER FOUND THE *MONEY*. WYLIE TOLD THEM NOTH--

NOW I *THINK* OF IT, HE WOULD'VE BEEN A *DEAD RINGER* FOR MONKS !

HAVE TO *ASK* MONKS ABOUT IT TOMORROW NIGHT. WILL *YOU* BE THERE, WAYNE ?

SAAAY... THERE'S A *CONNECTION* I NEVER *MADE* BEFORE.

I REMEMBER A *KID* VISITING THE *ORPHANAGE* FOR WYLIE'S BIRTHDAY PARTY ONCE... HIS *NEPHEW* OR SOMETHING.

MAYBE. IF MY *RESEARCH* GOES TO PLAN.

THANKS FOR ALL YOUR *TIME*, MR. *WHITE*...

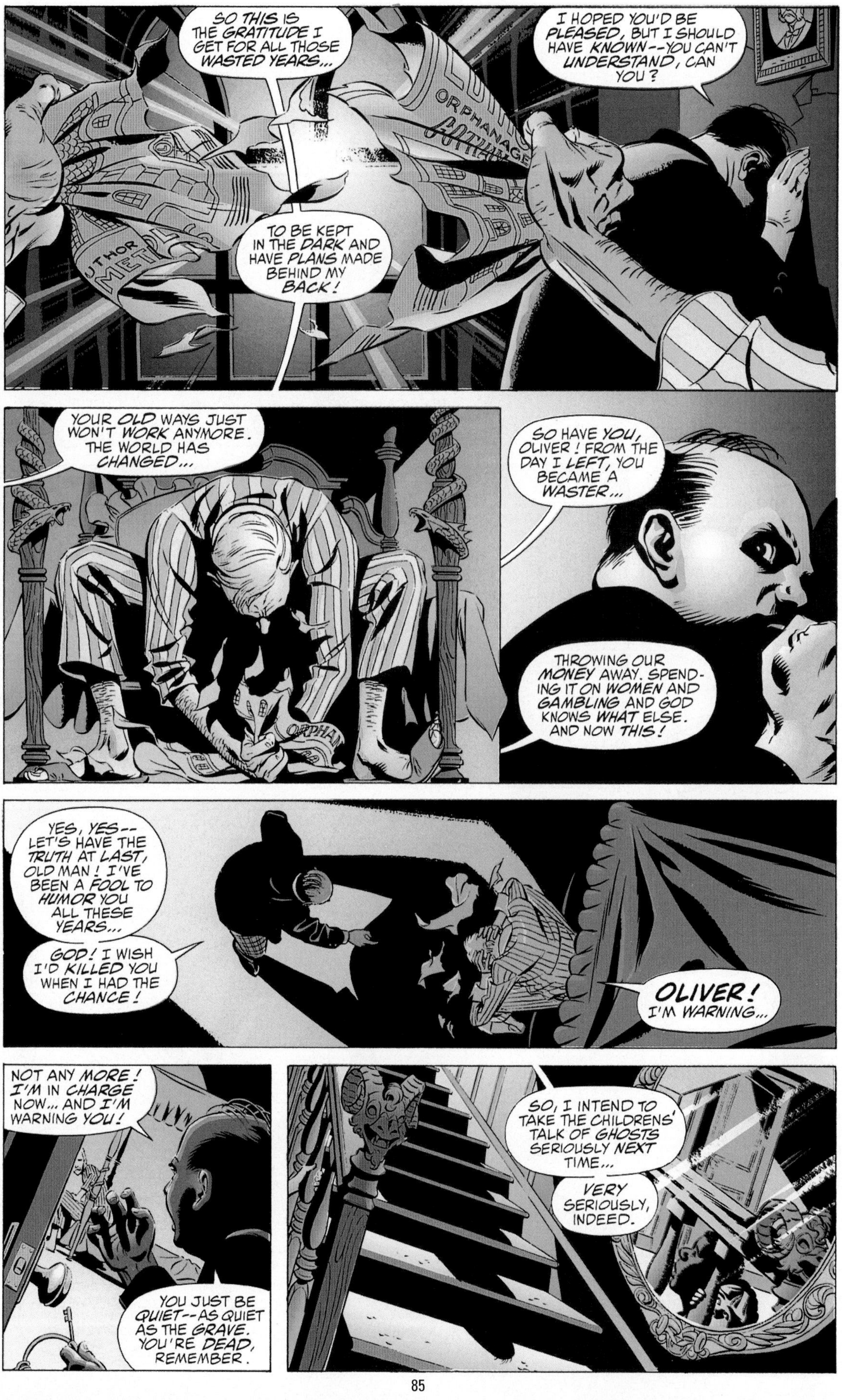
SO THIS IS THE GRATITUDE I GET FOR ALL THOSE WASTED YEARS...
TO BE KEPT IN THE DARK AND HAVE PLANS MADE BEHIND MY BACK!
I HOPED YOU'D BE PLEASED, BUT I SHOULD HAVE KNOWN--YOU CAN'T UNDERSTAND, CAN YOU?
ORPHANAGE
YOUR OLD WAYS JUST WON'T WORK ANYMORE. THE WORLD HAS CHANGED...
SO HAVE YOU, OLIVER! FROM THE DAY I LEFT, YOU BECAME A WASTER...
THROWING OUR MONEY AWAY. SPENDING IT ON WOMEN AND GAMBLING AND GOD KNOWS WHAT ELSE. AND NOW THIS!
YES, YES-- LET'S HAVE THE TRUTH AT LAST, OLD MAN! I'VE BEEN A FOOL TO HUMOR YOU ALL THESE YEARS...
GOD! I WISH I'D KILLED YOU WHEN I HAD THE CHANCE!
OLIVER! I'M WARNING...
NOT ANY MORE! I'M IN CHARGE NOW... AND I'M WARNING YOU!
YOU JUST BE QUIET--AS QUIET AS THE GRAVE. YOU'RE DEAD, REMEMBER.
SO, I INTEND TO TAKE THE CHILDRENS' TALK OF GHOSTS SERIOUSLY NEXT TIME...
VERY SERIOUSLY, INDEED.

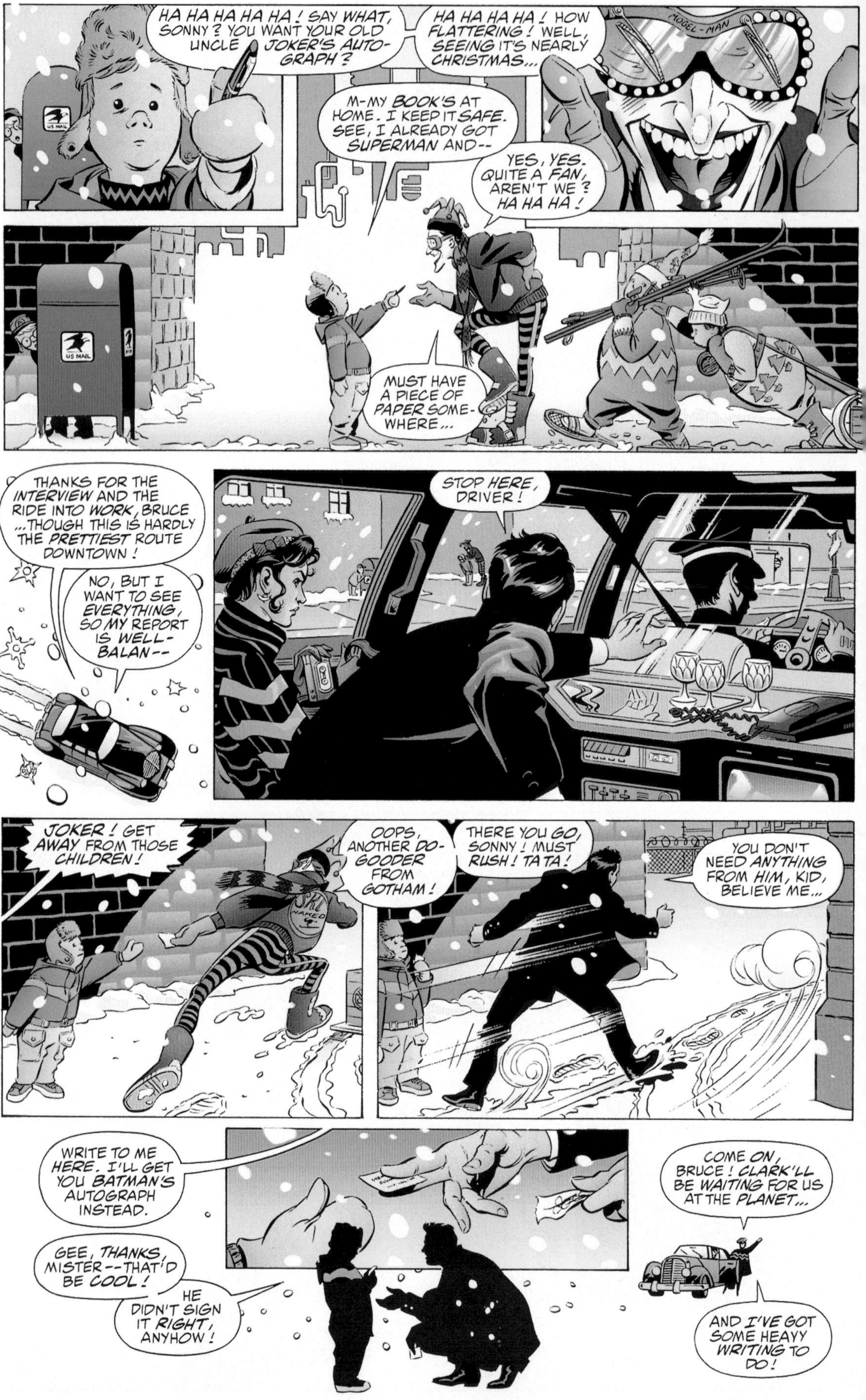
HA HA HA HA HA! SAY WHAT, SONNY? YOU WANT YOUR OLD UNCLE JOKER'S AUTOGRAPH?
HA HA HA HA! HOW FLATTERING! WELL, SEEING IT'S NEARLY CHRISTMAS...
MOGEL-MAN
US MAIL
M-MY BOOK'S AT HOME. I KEEP IT SAFE. SEE, I ALREADY GOT SUPERMAN AND--
YES, YES. QUITE A FAN, AREN'T WE? HA HA HA!
US MAIL
MUST HAVE A PIECE OF PAPER SOMEWHERE...
THANKS FOR THE INTERVIEW AND THE RIDE INTO WORK, BRUCE ...THOUGH THIS IS HARDLY THE PRETTIEST ROUTE DOWNTOWN!
NO, BUT I WANT TO SEE EVERYTHING, SO MY REPORT IS WELL-BALAN--
STOP HERE, DRIVER!
JOKER! GET AWAY FROM THOSE CHILDREN!
OOPS, ANOTHER DO-GOODER FROM GOTHAM!
THERE YOU GO, SONNY! MUST RUSH! TA TA!
YOU DON'T NEED ANYTHING FROM HIM, KID, BELIEVE ME...
WRITE TO ME HERE. I'LL GET YOU BATMAN'S AUTOGRAPH INSTEAD.
GEE, THANKS, MISTER--THAT'D BE COOL!
HE DIDN'T SIGN IT RIGHT, ANYHOW!
COME ON, BRUCE! CLARK'LL BE WAITING FOR US AT THE PLANET...
AND I'VE GOT SOME HEAVY WRITING TO DO!

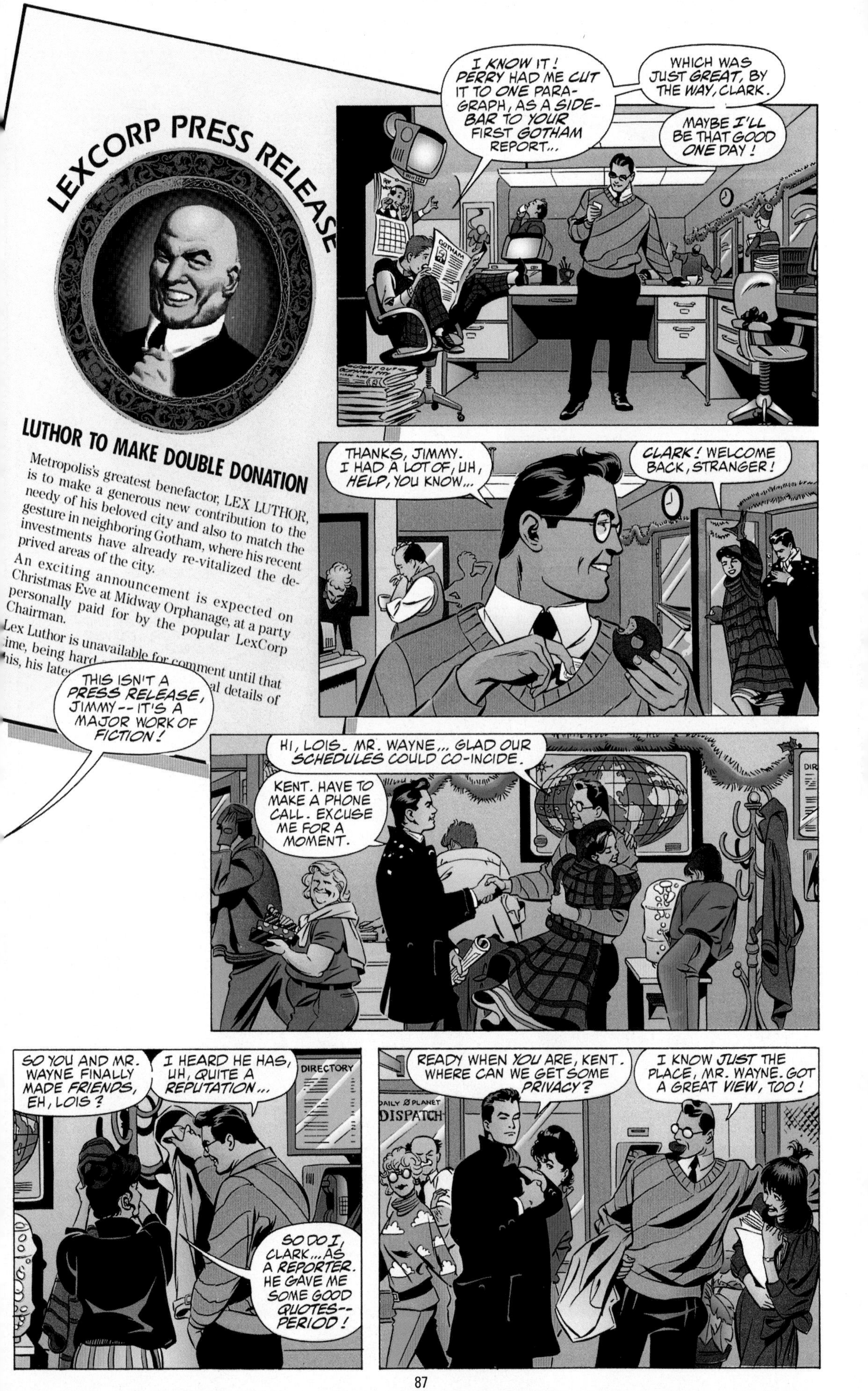

LEXCORP PRESS RELEASE
LUTHOR TO MAKE DOUBLE DONATION
Metropolis's greatest benefactor, LEX LUTHOR, is to make a generous new contribution to the needy of his beloved city and also to match the gesture in neighboring Gotham, where his recent investments have already re-vitalized the deprived areas of the city.
An exciting announcement is expected on Christmas Eve at Midway Orphanage, at a party personally paid for by the popular LexCorp Chairman.
Lex Luthor is unavailable for comment until that
THIS ISN'T A PRESS RELEASE, JIMMY -- IT'S A MAJOR WORK OF FICTION!
I KNOW IT! PERRY HAD ME CUT IT TO ONE PARAGRAPH, AS A SIDEBAR TO YOUR FIRST GOTHAM REPORT...
WHICH WAS JUST GREAT, BY THE WAY, CLARK.
MAYBE I'LL BE THAT GOOD ONE DAY!
THANKS, JIMMY. I HAD A LOT OF, UH, HELP, YOU KNOW...
CLARK! WELCOME BACK, STRANGER!
HI, LOIS. MR. WAYNE... GLAD OUR SCHEDULES COULD CO-INCIDE.
KENT. HAVE TO MAKE A PHONE CALL. EXCUSE ME FOR A MOMENT.
SO YOU AND MR. WAYNE FINALLY MADE FRIENDS, EH, LOIS?
I HEARD HE HAS, UH, QUITE A REPUTATION...
DIRECTORY
SO DO I, CLARK... AS A REPORTER. HE GAVE ME SOME GOOD QUOTES-- PERIOD!
DAILY PLANET DISPATCH
READY WHEN YOU ARE, KENT. WHERE CAN WE GET SOME PRIVACY?
I KNOW JUST THE PLACE, MR. WAYNE. GOT A GREAT VIEW, TOO!

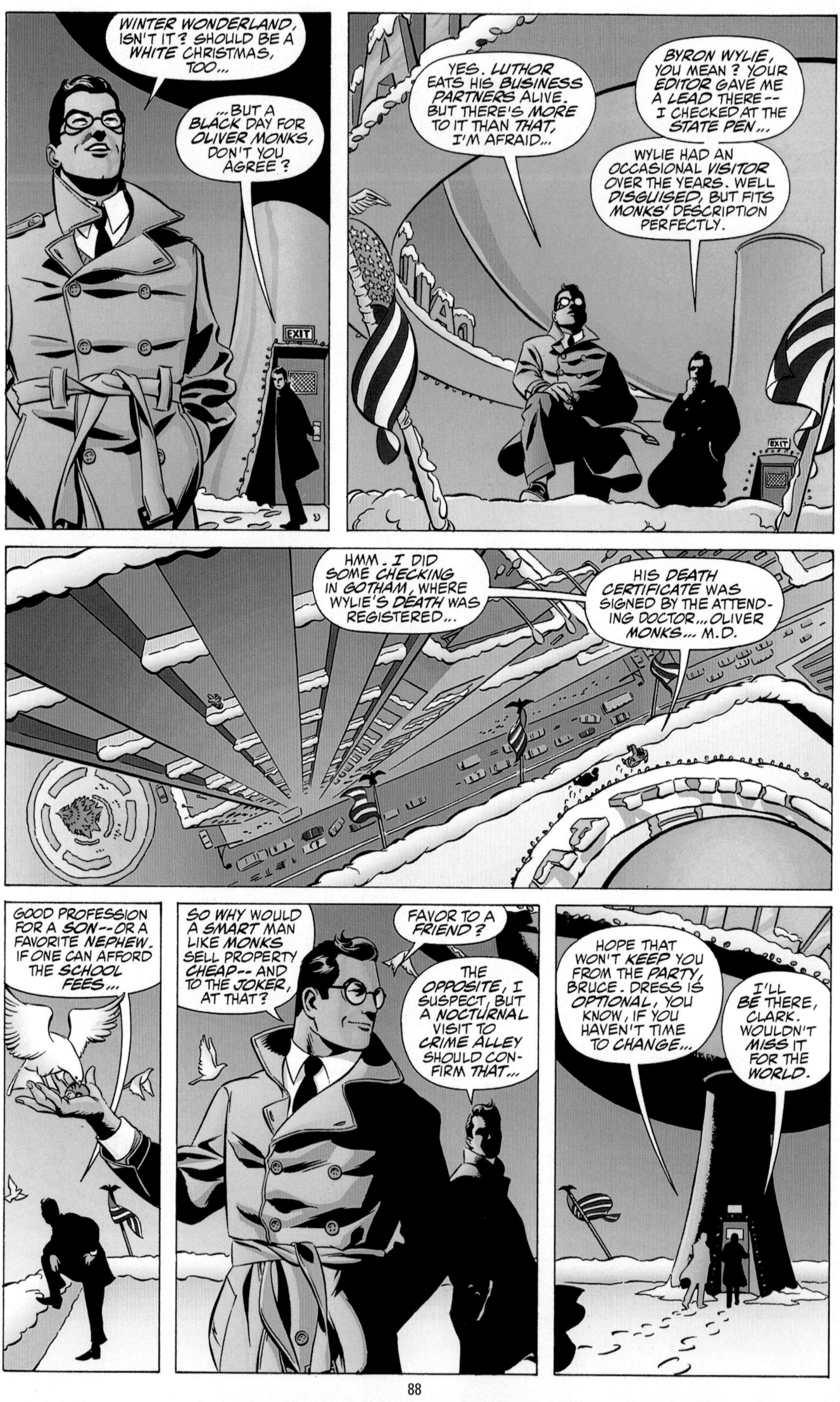
WINTER WONDERLAND, ISN'T IT? SHOULD BE A WHITE CHRISTMAS, TOO...
...BUT A BLACK DAY FOR OLIVER MONKS, DON'T YOU AGREE?
EXIT
YES. LUTHOR EATS HIS BUSINESS PARTNERS ALIVE. BUT THERE'S MORE TO IT THAN THAT, I'M AFRAID...
BYRON WYLIE, YOU MEAN? YOUR EDITOR GAVE ME A LEAD THERE-- I CHECKED AT THE STATE PEN...
WYLIE HAD AN OCCASIONAL VISITOR OVER THE YEARS. WELL DISGUISED, BUT FITS MONKS' DESCRIPTION PERFECTLY.
EXIT
HMM. I DID SOME CHECKING IN GOTHAM, WHERE WYLIE'S DEATH WAS REGISTERED...
HIS DEATH CERTIFICATE WAS SIGNED BY THE ATTENDING DOCTOR... OLIVER MONKS... M.D.
GOOD PROFESSION FOR A SON--OR A FAVORITE NEPHEW. IF ONE CAN AFFORD THE SCHOOL FEES...
SO WHY WOULD A SMART MAN LIKE MONKS SELL PROPERTY CHEAP-- AND TO THE JOKER, AT THAT?
FAVOR TO A FRIEND?
THE OPPOSITE, I SUSPECT, BUT A NOCTURNAL VISIT TO CRIME ALLEY SHOULD CONFIRM THAT...
HOPE THAT WON'T KEEP YOU FROM THE PARTY, BRUCE. DRESS IS OPTIONAL, YOU KNOW, IF YOU HAVEN'T TIME TO CHANGE...
I'LL BE THERE, CLARK. WOULDN'T MISS IT FOR THE WORLD.

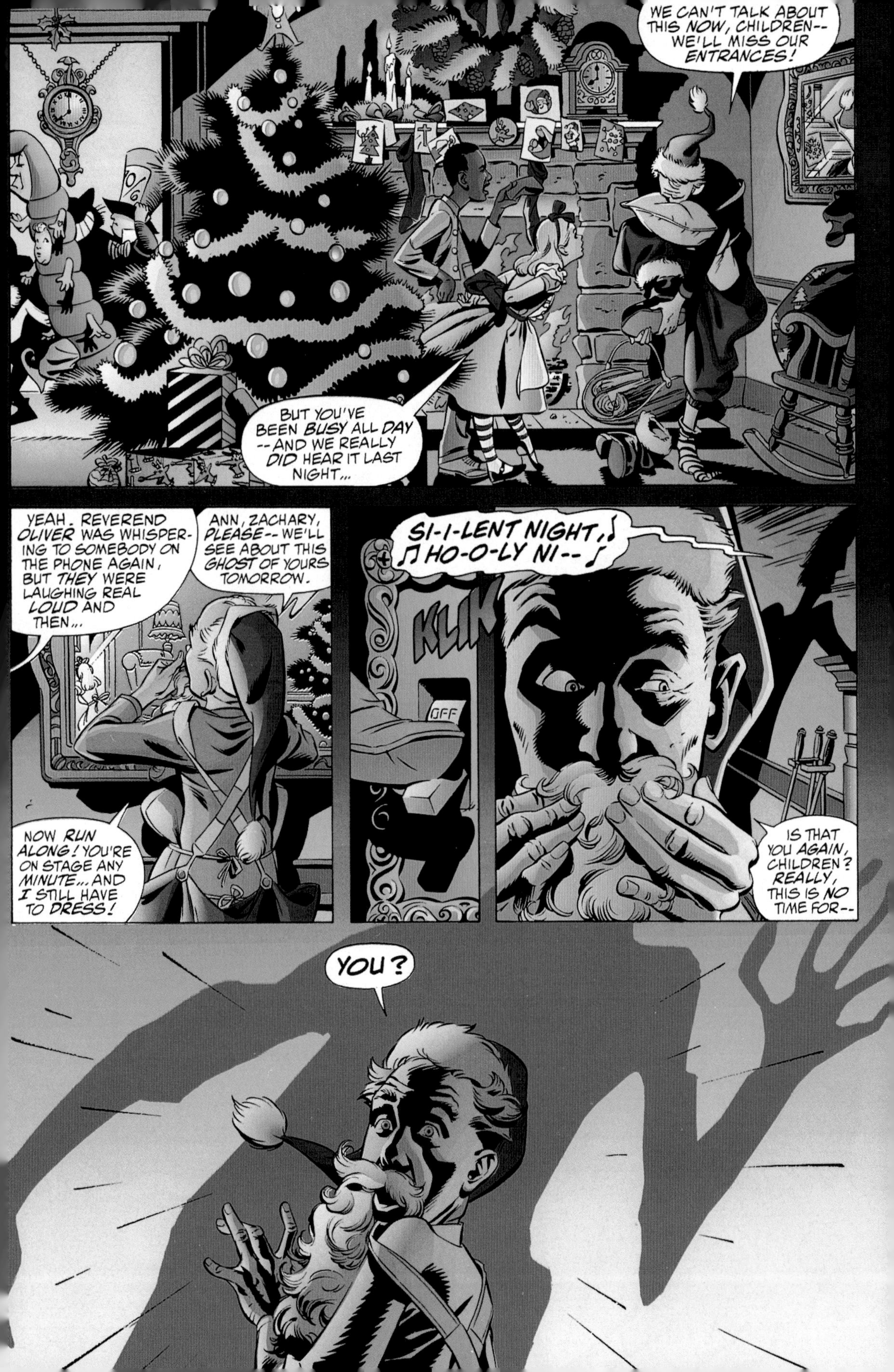
WE CAN'T TALK ABOUT THIS NOW, CHILDREN-- WE'LL MISS OUR ENTRANCES!
BUT YOU'VE BEEN BUSY ALL DAY --AND WE REALLY DID HEAR IT LAST NIGHT...
YEAH. REVEREND OLIVER WAS WHISPERING TO SOMEBODY ON THE PHONE AGAIN, BUT THEY WERE LAUGHING REAL LOUD AND THEN...
ANN, ZACHARY, PLEASE-- WE'LL SEE ABOUT THIS GHOST OF YOURS TOMORROW.
NOW RUN ALONG! YOU'RE ON STAGE ANY MINUTE... AND I STILL HAVE TO DRESS!
SI-I-LENT NIGHT, HO-O-LY NI--
KLIK
OFF
IS THAT YOU AGAIN, CHILDREN? REALLY, THIS IS NO TIME FOR--
YOU?

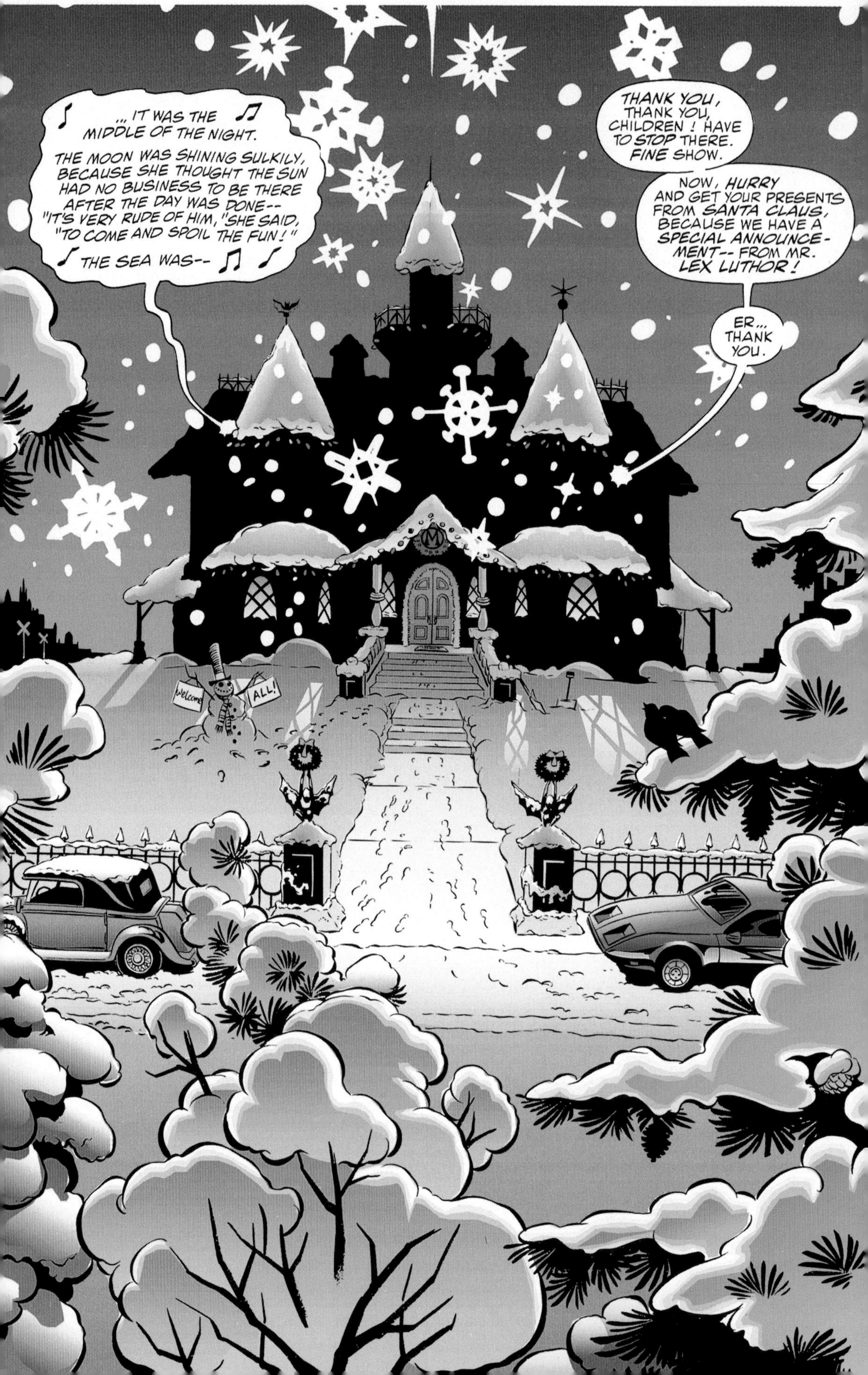
♪ ... IT WAS THE ♫ MIDDLE OF THE NIGHT.
THE MOON WAS SHINING SULKILY, BECAUSE SHE THOUGHT THE SUN HAD NO BUSINESS TO BE THERE AFTER THE DAY WAS DONE-- "IT'S VERY RUDE OF HIM," SHE SAID, "TO COME AND SPOIL THE FUN!"
♪ THE SEA WAS-- ♫ ♪
THANK YOU, THANK YOU, CHILDREN! HAVE TO STOP THERE. FINE SHOW.
NOW, HURRY AND GET YOUR PRESENTS FROM SANTA CLAUS, BECAUSE WE HAVE A SPECIAL ANNOUNCEMENT-- FROM MR. LEX LUTHOR!
ER... THANK YOU.
Welcome
ALL!

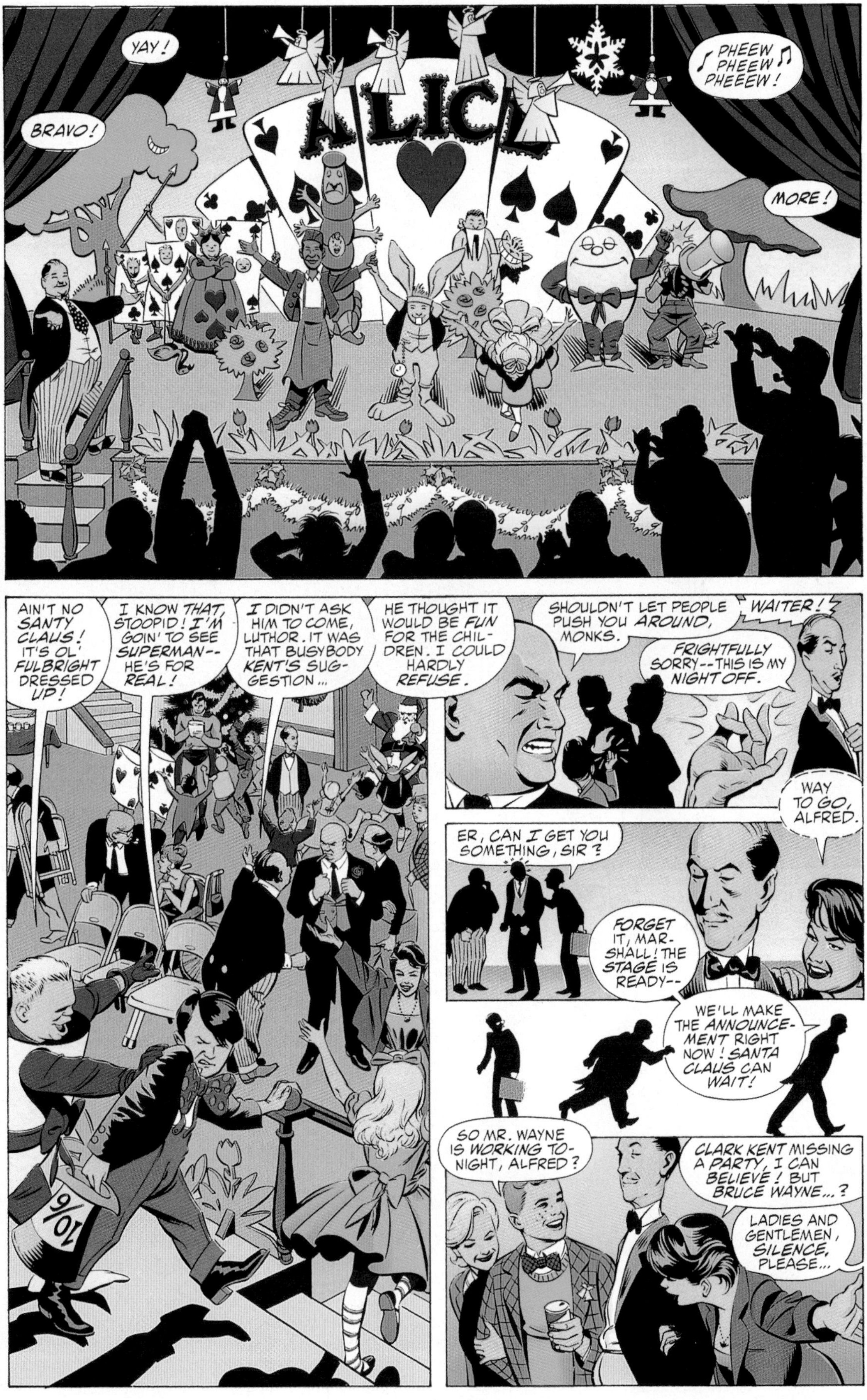
YAY!
BRAVO!
PHEEW PHEEW PHEEEW!
MORE!
ALIC
AIN'T NO SANTY CLAUS! IT'S OL' FULBRIGHT DRESSED UP!
I KNOW THAT, STOOPID! I'M GOIN' TO SEE SUPERMAN-- HE'S FOR REAL!
I DIDN'T ASK HIM TO COME, LUTHOR. IT WAS THAT BUSYBODY KENT'S SUGGESTION...
HE THOUGHT IT WOULD BE FUN FOR THE CHILDREN. I COULD HARDLY REFUSE.
10/6
SHOULDN'T LET PEOPLE PUSH YOU AROUND, MONKS.
WAITER!
FRIGHTFULLY SORRY--THIS IS MY NIGHT OFF.
WAY TO GO, ALFRED.
ER, CAN I GET YOU SOMETHING, SIR?
FORGET IT, MARSHALL! THE STAGE IS READY--
WE'LL MAKE THE ANNOUNCEMENT RIGHT NOW! SANTA CLAUS CAN WAIT!
SO MR. WAYNE IS WORKING TONIGHT, ALFRED?
CLARK KENT MISSING A PARTY, I CAN BELIEVE! BUT BRUCE WAYNE...?
LADIES AND GENTLEMEN, SILENCE, PLEASE...

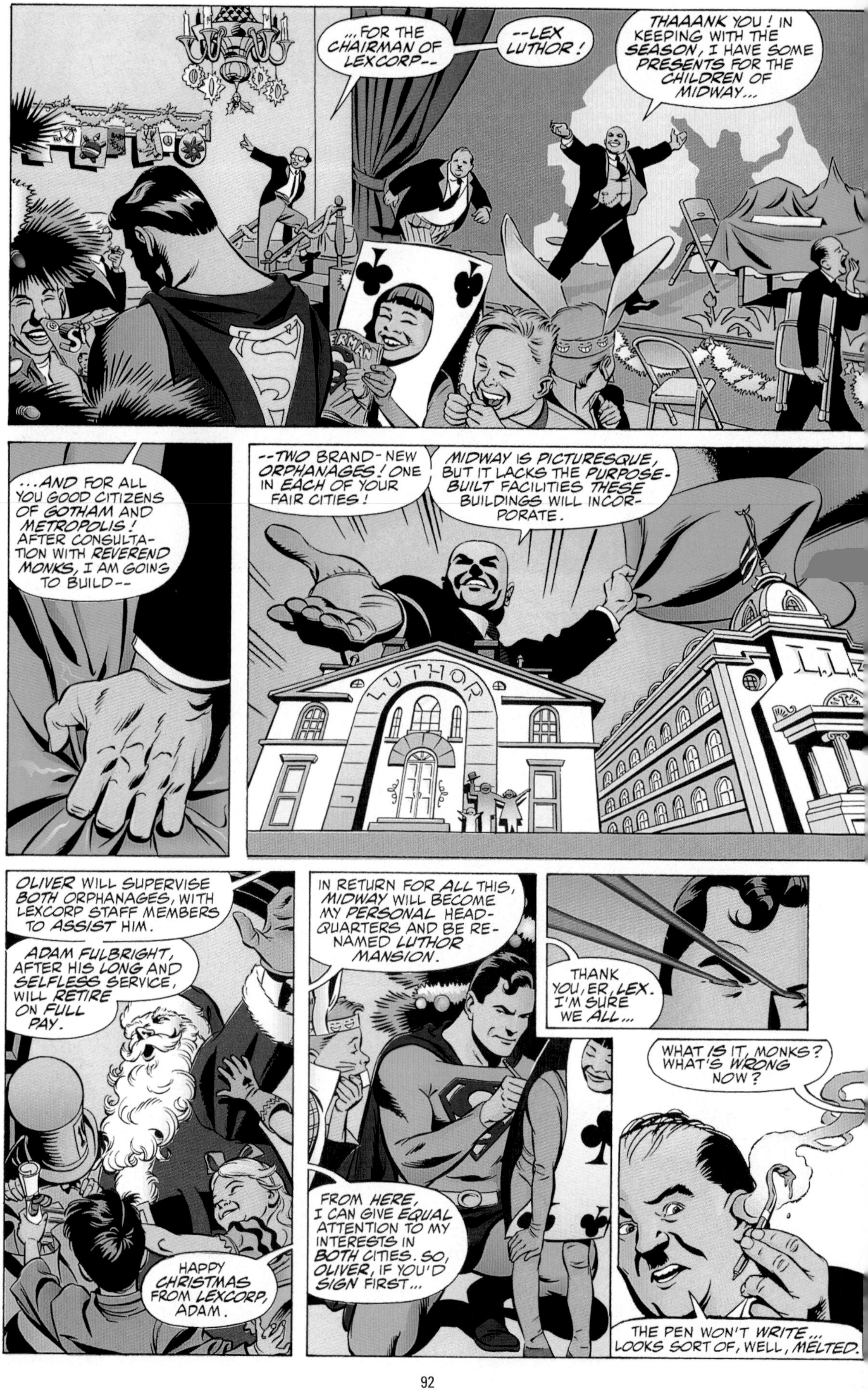
...FOR THE CHAIRMAN OF LEXCORP--
--LEX LUTHOR!
THAAANK YOU! IN KEEPING WITH THE SEASON, I HAVE SOME PRESENTS FOR THE CHILDREN OF MIDWAY...
...AND FOR ALL YOU GOOD CITIZENS OF GOTHAM AND METROPOLIS! AFTER CONSULTATION WITH REVEREND MONKS, I AM GOING TO BUILD--
--TWO BRAND-NEW ORPHANAGES! ONE IN EACH OF YOUR FAIR CITIES!
MIDWAY IS PICTURESQUE, BUT IT LACKS THE PURPOSE-BUILT FACILITIES THESE BUILDINGS WILL INCORPORATE.
LUTHOR
OLIVER WILL SUPERVISE BOTH ORPHANAGES, WITH LEXCORP STAFF MEMBERS TO ASSIST HIM.
ADAM FULBRIGHT, AFTER HIS LONG AND SELFLESS SERVICE, WILL RETIRE ON FULL PAY.
HAPPY CHRISTMAS FROM LEXCORP, ADAM.
IN RETURN FOR ALL THIS, MIDWAY WILL BECOME MY PERSONAL HEADQUARTERS AND BE RENAMED LUTHOR MANSION.
FROM HERE, I CAN GIVE EQUAL ATTENTION TO MY INTERESTS IN BOTH CITIES. SO, OLIVER, IF YOU'D SIGN FIRST...
THANK YOU, ER, LEX. I'M SURE WE ALL...
WHAT IS IT, MONKS? WHAT'S WRONG NOW?
THE PEN WON'T WRITE... LOOKS SORT OF, WELL, MELTED.

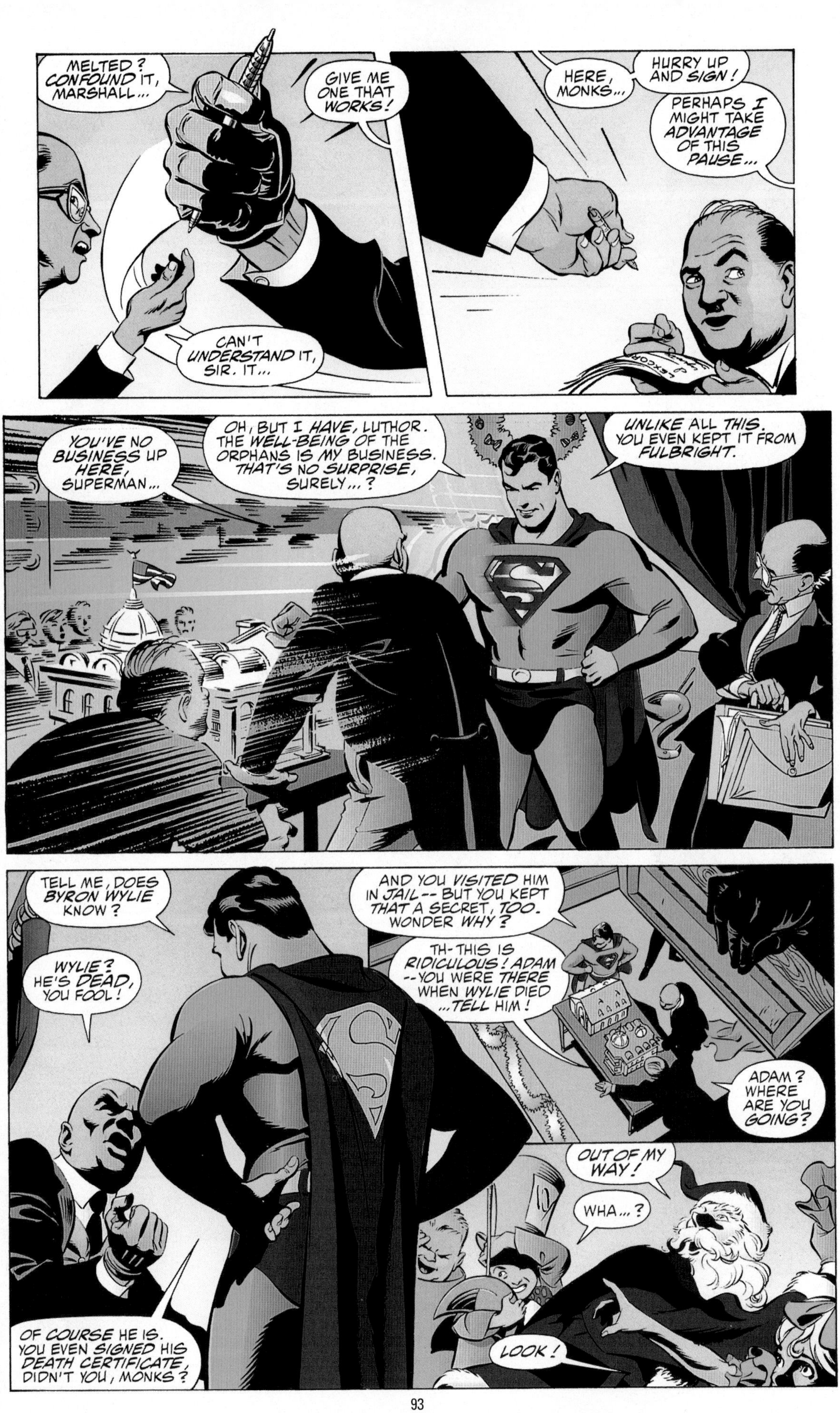
MELTED? CONFOUND IT, MARSHALL...
GIVE ME ONE THAT WORKS!
CAN'T UNDERSTAND IT, SIR. IT...
HERE, MONKS...
HURRY UP AND SIGN!
PERHAPS I MIGHT TAKE ADVANTAGE OF THIS PAUSE...
YOU'VE NO BUSINESS UP HERE, SUPERMAN...
OH, BUT I HAVE, LUTHOR. THE WELL-BEING OF THE ORPHANS IS MY BUSINESS. THAT'S NO SURPRISE, SURELY...?
UNLIKE ALL THIS. YOU EVEN KEPT IT FROM FULBRIGHT.
TELL ME, DOES BYRON WYLIE KNOW?
WYLIE? HE'S DEAD, YOU FOOL!
AND YOU VISITED HIM IN JAIL-- BUT YOU KEPT THAT A SECRET, TOO. WONDER WHY?
TH-THIS IS RIDICULOUS! ADAM --YOU WERE THERE WHEN WYLIE DIED ...TELL HIM!
ADAM? WHERE ARE YOU GOING?
OUT OF MY WAY!
WHA...?
OF COURSE HE IS. YOU EVEN SIGNED HIS DEATH CERTIFICATE, DIDN'T YOU, MONKS?
LOOK!

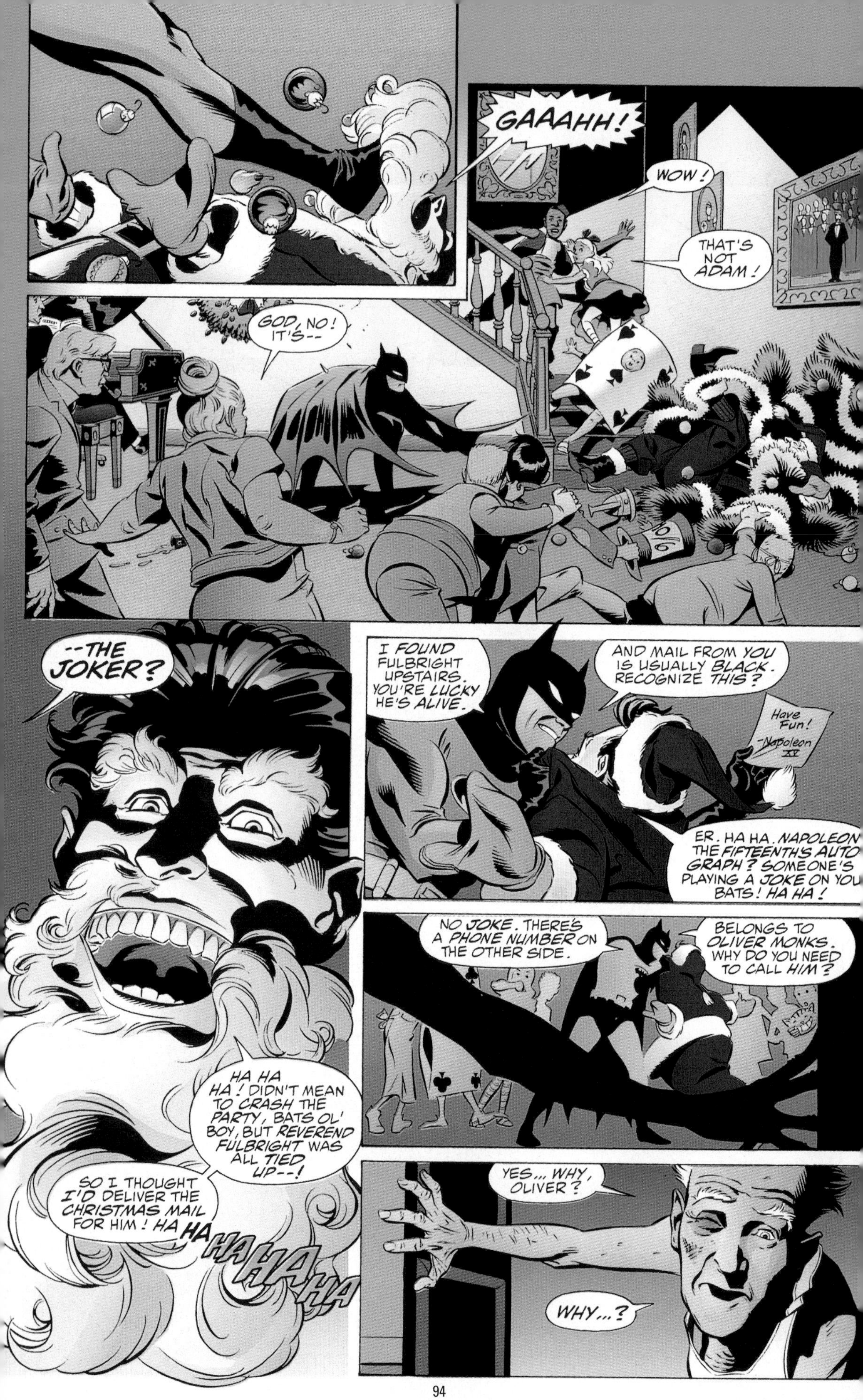

GAAAHH!
WOW!
THAT'S NOT ADAM!
GOD, NO! IT'S--
--THE JOKER?
HA HA HA! DIDN'T MEAN TO CRASH THE PARTY, BATS OL' BOY, BUT REVEREND FULBRIGHT WAS ALL TIED UP--!
SO I THOUGHT I'D DELIVER THE CHRISTMAS MAIL FOR HIM! HA HA HA HA HA HA
I FOUND FULBRIGHT UPSTAIRS. YOU'RE LUCKY HE'S ALIVE.
AND MAIL FROM YOU IS USUALLY BLACK. RECOGNIZE THIS?
Have Fun! -Napoleon XV
ER. HA HA. NAPOLEON THE FIFTEENTH'S AUTOGRAPH? SOMEONE'S PLAYING A JOKE ON YOU BATS! HA HA!
NO JOKE. THERE'S A PHONE NUMBER ON THE OTHER SIDE.
BELONGS TO OLIVER MONKS. WHY DO YOU NEED TO CALL HIM?
YES... WHY, OLIVER?
WHY...?

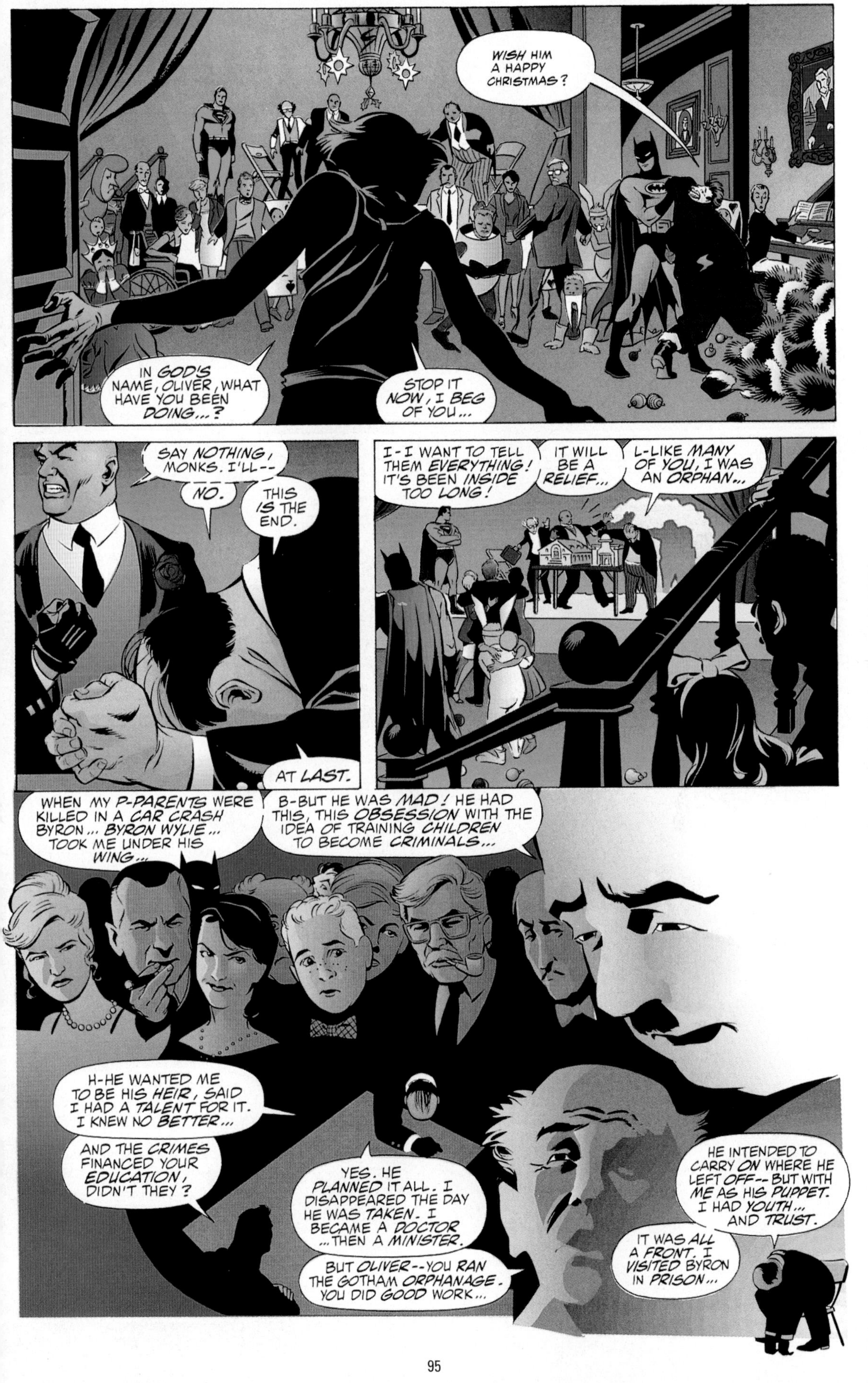
WISH HIM A HAPPY CHRISTMAS?
IN GOD'S NAME, OLIVER, WHAT HAVE YOU BEEN DOING...?
STOP IT NOW, I BEG OF YOU...
SAY NOTHING, MONKS. I'LL--
NO.
THIS IS THE END.
AT LAST.
I-I WANT TO TELL THEM EVERYTHING! IT'S BEEN INSIDE TOO LONG!
IT WILL BE A RELIEF...
L-LIKE MANY OF YOU, I WAS AN ORPHAN...
WHEN MY P-PARENTS WERE KILLED IN A CAR CRASH BYRON... BYRON WYLIE... TOOK ME UNDER HIS WING...
B-BUT HE WAS MAD! HE HAD THIS, THIS OBSESSION WITH THE IDEA OF TRAINING CHILDREN TO BECOME CRIMINALS...
H-HE WANTED ME TO BE HIS HEIR, SAID I HAD A TALENT FOR IT. I KNEW NO BETTER...
AND THE CRIMES FINANCED YOUR EDUCATION, DIDN'T THEY?
YES. HE PLANNED IT ALL. I DISAPPEARED THE DAY HE WAS TAKEN. I BECAME A DOCTOR ...THEN A MINISTER.
BUT OLIVER--YOU RAN THE GOTHAM ORPHANAGE. YOU DID GOOD WORK...
HE INTENDED TO CARRY ON WHERE HE LEFT OFF-- BUT WITH ME AS HIS PUPPET. I HAD YOUTH... AND TRUST.
IT WAS ALL A FRONT. I VISITED BYRON IN PRISON...

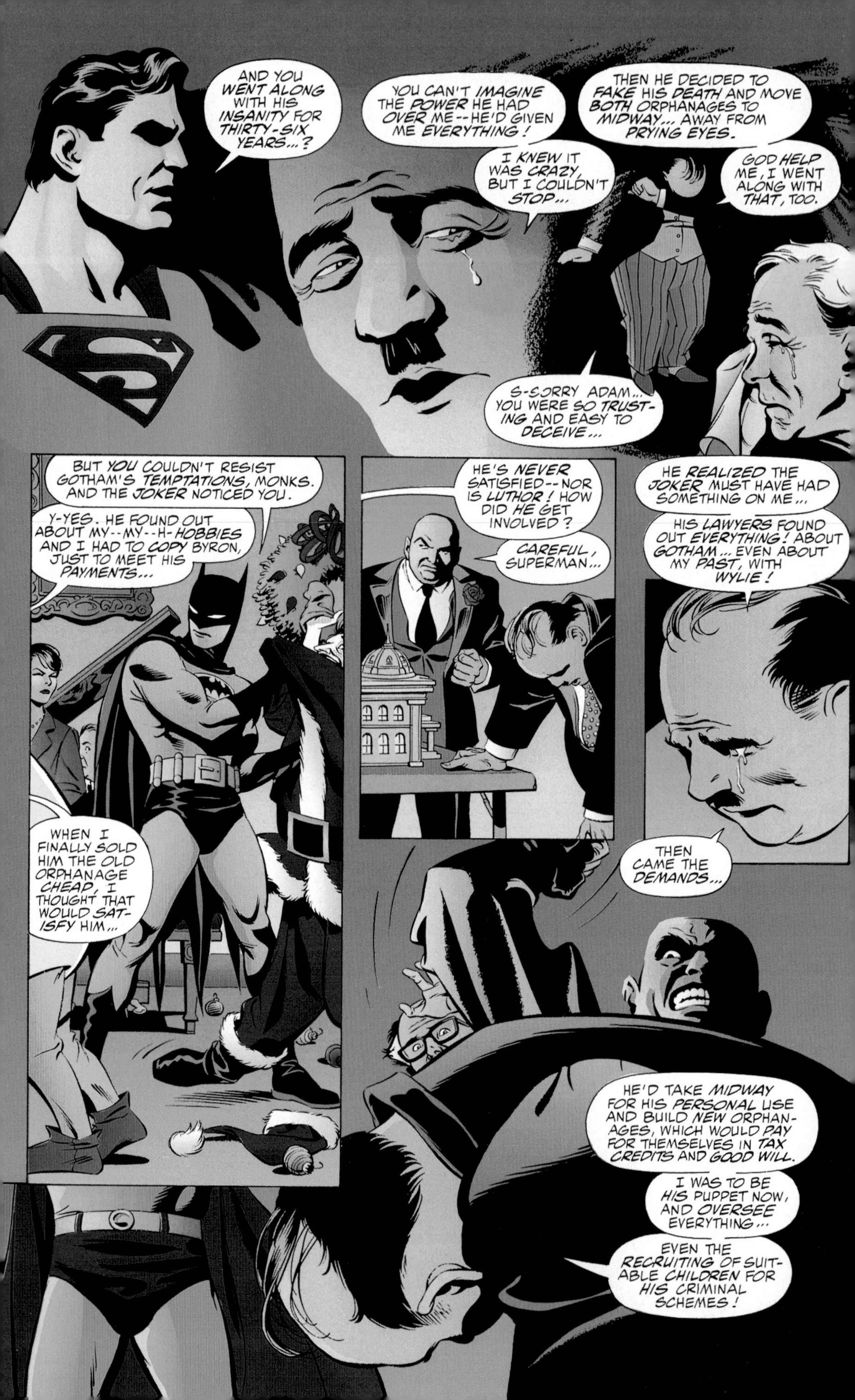

AND YOU WENT ALONG WITH HIS INSANITY FOR THIRTY-SIX YEARS...?
YOU CAN'T IMAGINE THE POWER HE HAD OVER ME--HE'D GIVEN ME EVERYTHING!
I KNEW IT WAS CRAZY, BUT I COULDN'T STOP...
THEN HE DECIDED TO FAKE HIS DEATH AND MOVE BOTH ORPHANAGES TO MIDWAY... AWAY FROM PRYING EYES.
GOD HELP ME, I WENT ALONG WITH THAT, TOO.
S-SORRY ADAM... YOU WERE SO TRUSTING AND EASY TO DECEIVE...
BUT YOU COULDN'T RESIST GOTHAM'S TEMPTATIONS, MONKS. AND THE JOKER NOTICED YOU.
Y-YES. HE FOUND OUT ABOUT MY--MY--H-HOBBIES AND I HAD TO COPY BYRON, JUST TO MEET HIS PAYMENTS...
WHEN I FINALLY SOLD HIM THE OLD ORPHANAGE CHEAP, I THOUGHT THAT WOULD SATISFY HIM...
HE'S NEVER SATISFIED--NOR IS LUTHOR! HOW DID HE GET INVOLVED?
CAREFUL, SUPERMAN...
HE REALIZED THE JOKER MUST HAVE HAD SOMETHING ON ME...
HIS LAWYERS FOUND OUT EVERYTHING! ABOUT GOTHAM... EVEN ABOUT MY PAST, WITH WYLIE!
THEN CAME THE DEMANDS...
HE'D TAKE MIDWAY FOR HIS PERSONAL USE AND BUILD NEW ORPHANAGES, WHICH WOULD PAY FOR THEMSELVES IN TAX CREDITS AND GOOD WILL.
I WAS TO BE HIS PUPPET NOW, AND OVERSEE EVERYTHING...
EVEN THE RECRUITING OF SUITABLE CHILDREN FOR HIS CRIMINAL SCHEMES!

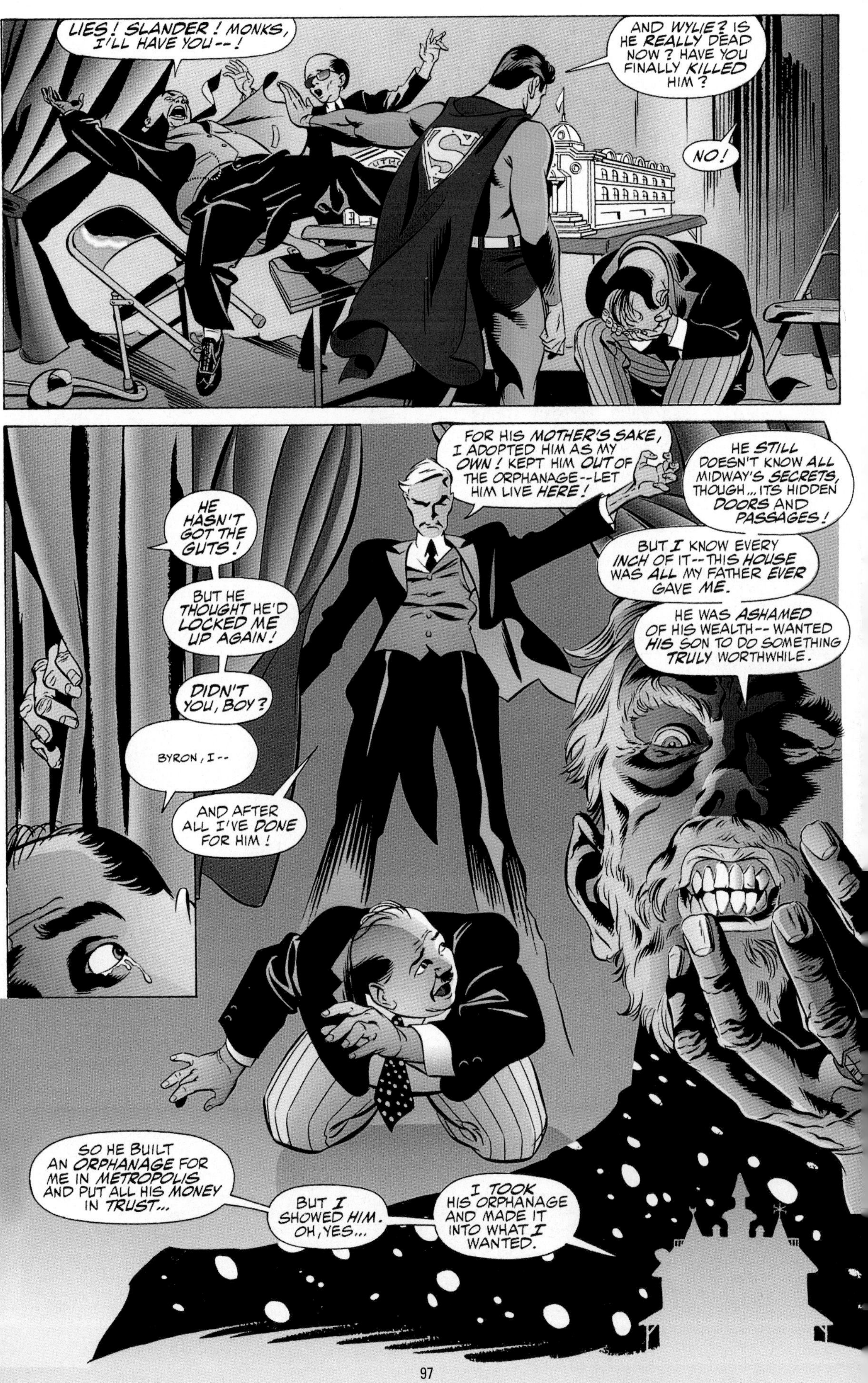

LIES! SLANDER! MONKS, I'LL HAVE YOU--!
AND WYLIE? IS HE REALLY DEAD NOW? HAVE YOU FINALLY KILLED HIM?
NO!
FOR HIS MOTHER'S SAKE, I ADOPTED HIM AS MY OWN! KEPT HIM OUT OF THE ORPHANAGE--LET HIM LIVE HERE!
HE HASN'T GOT THE GUTS!
BUT HE THOUGHT HE'D LOCKED ME UP AGAIN!
DIDN'T YOU, BOY?
BYRON, I--
AND AFTER ALL I'VE DONE FOR HIM!
HE STILL DOESN'T KNOW ALL MIDWAY'S SECRETS, THOUGH... ITS HIDDEN DOORS AND PASSAGES!
BUT I KNOW EVERY INCH OF IT--THIS HOUSE WAS ALL MY FATHER EVER GAVE ME.
HE WAS ASHAMED OF HIS WEALTH--WANTED HIS SON TO DO SOMETHING TRULY WORTHWHILE.
SO HE BUILT AN ORPHANAGE FOR ME IN METROPOLIS AND PUT ALL HIS MONEY IN TRUST...
BUT I SHOWED HIM. OH, YES...
I TOOK HIS ORPHANAGE AND MADE IT INTO WHAT I WANTED.

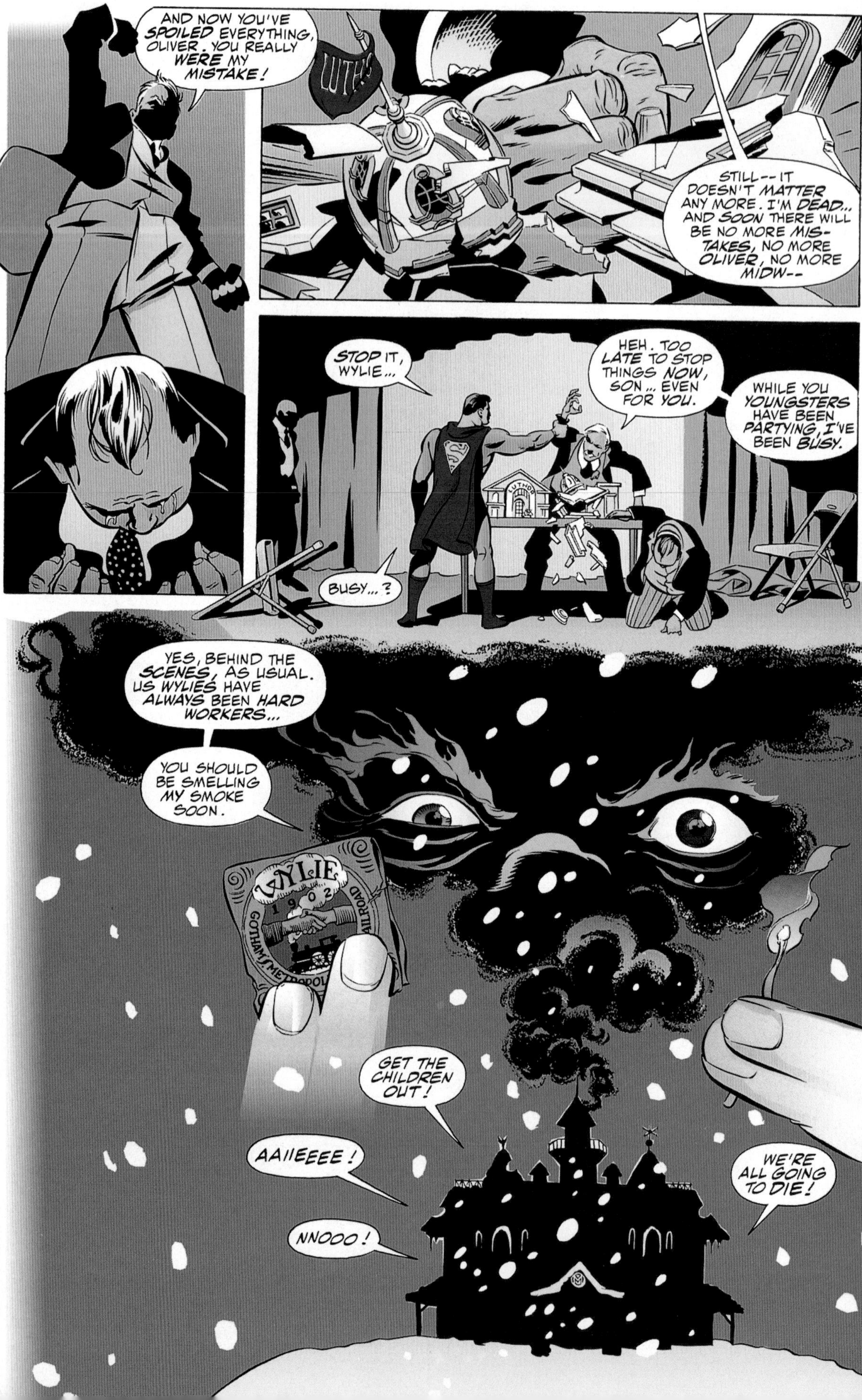

AND NOW YOU'VE SPOILED EVERYTHING, OLIVER. YOU REALLY WERE MY MISTAKE!
LUTH
STILL-- IT DOESN'T MATTER ANY MORE. I'M DEAD... AND SOON THERE WILL BE NO MORE MIS-TAKES, NO MORE OLIVER, NO MORE MIDW--
STOP IT, WYLIE...
HEH. TOO LATE TO STOP THINGS NOW, SON... EVEN FOR YOU.
WHILE YOU YOUNGSTERS HAVE BEEN PARTYING, I'VE BEEN BUSY.
LUTHOR
BUSY...?
YES, BEHIND THE SCENES, AS USUAL. US WYLIES HAVE ALWAYS BEEN HARD WORKERS...
YOU SHOULD BE SMELLING MY SMOKE SOON.
WYLIE
1902
GOTHAM'S METROPOL RAILROAD
GET THE CHILDREN OUT!
AAIIEEEE!
NNOOO!
WE'RE ALL GOING TO DIE!

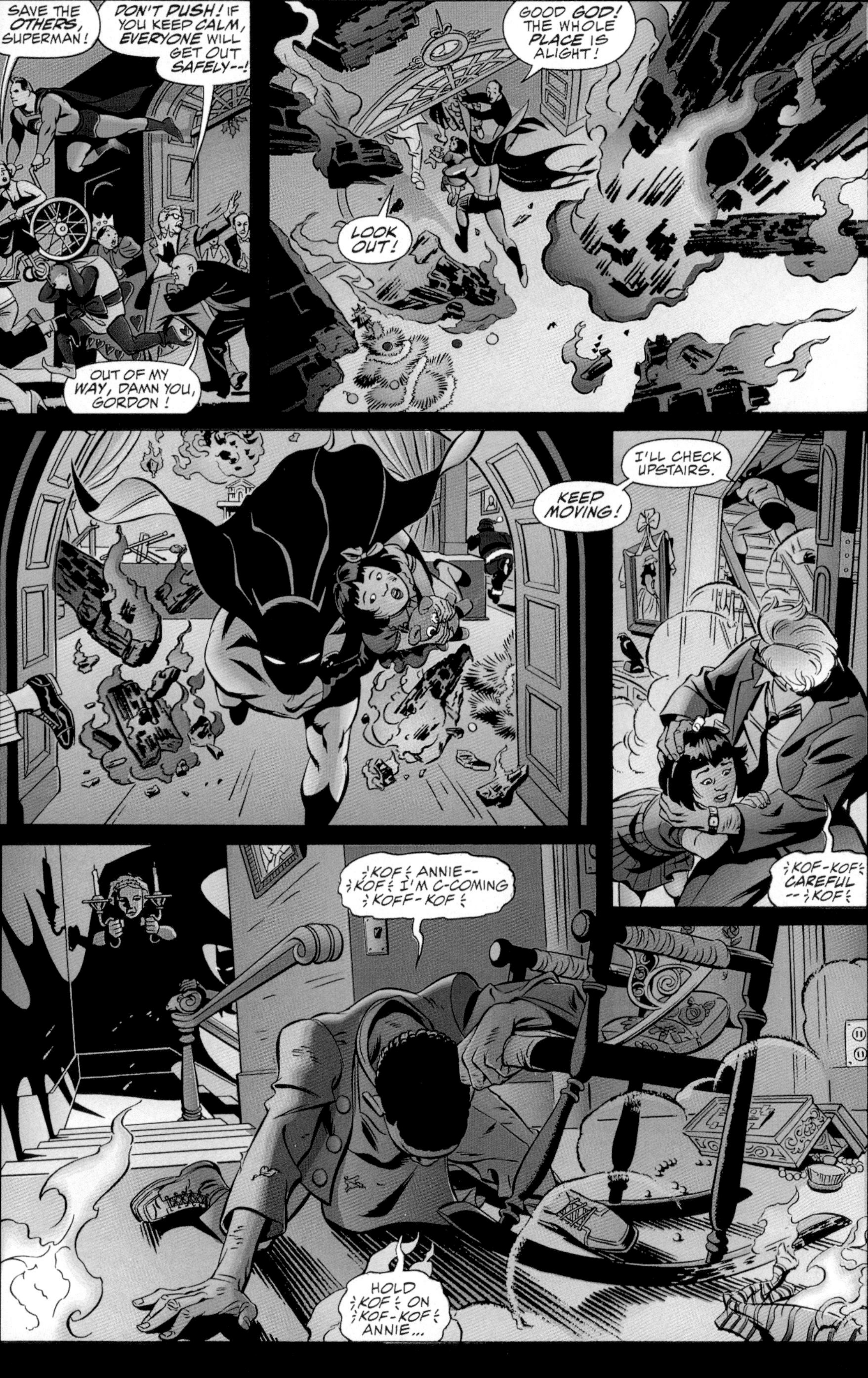
SAVE THE OTHERS, SUPERMAN!
DON'T PUSH! IF YOU KEEP CALM, EVERYONE WILL GET OUT SAFELY--!
OUT OF MY WAY, DAMN YOU, GORDON!
GOOD GOD! THE WHOLE PLACE IS ALIGHT!
LOOK OUT!
I'LL CHECK UPSTAIRS.
KEEP MOVING!
¦KOF-KOF¦ CAREFUL --¦KOF¦
¦KOF¦ ANNIE-- ¦KOF¦ I'M C-COMING ¦KOFF-KOF¦
HOLD ¦KOF¦ ON ¦KOF-KOF¦ ANNIE...

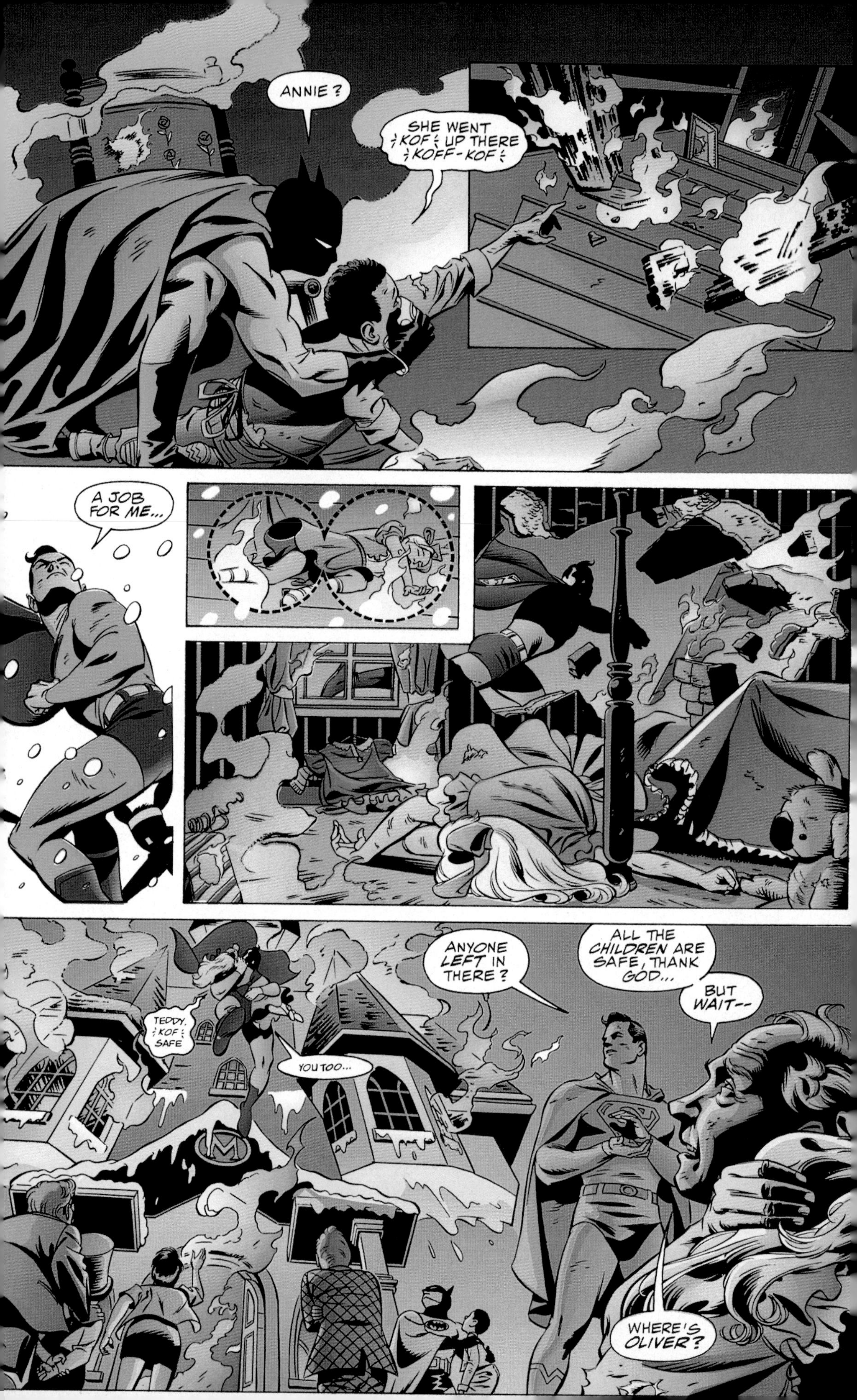
ANNIE?
SHE WENT ¦KOF¦ UP THERE ¦KOFF-KOF¦
A JOB FOR ME...
ANYONE LEFT IN THERE?
ALL THE CHILDREN ARE SAFE, THANK GOD...
BUT WAIT--
TEDDY. ¦KOF¦ SAFE
YOU TOO...
WHERE'S OLIVER?

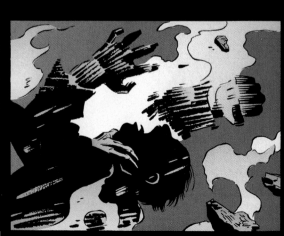

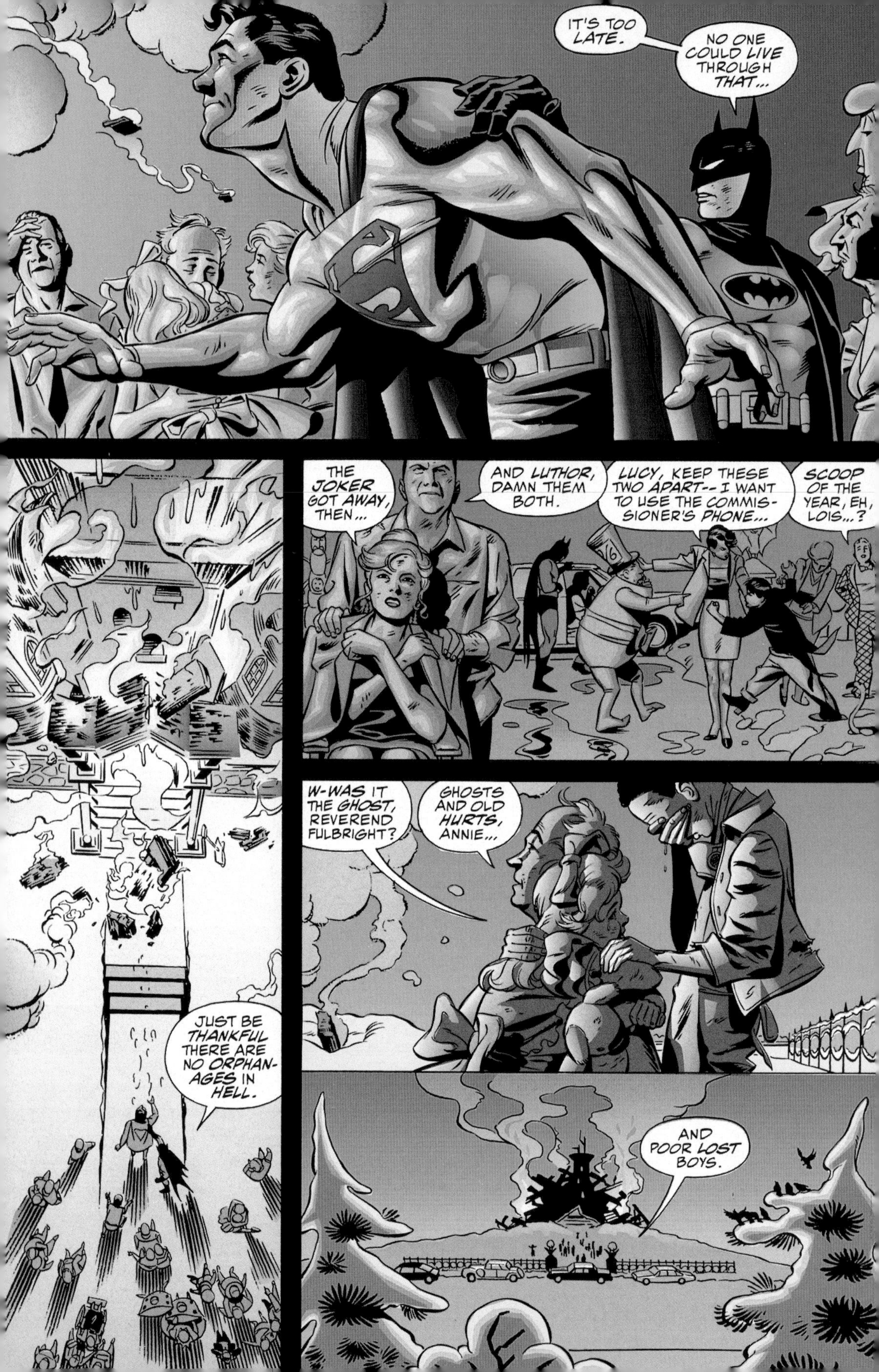
IT'S TOO LATE.
NO ONE COULD LIVE THROUGH THAT...
THE JOKER GOT AWAY, THEN...
AND LUTHOR, DAMN THEM BOTH.
LUCY, KEEP THESE TWO APART-- I WANT TO USE THE COMMISSIONER'S PHONE...
SCOOP OF THE YEAR, EH, LOIS...?
W-WAS IT THE GHOST, REVEREND FULBRIGHT?
GHOSTS AND OLD HURTS, ANNIE...
JUST BE THANKFUL THERE ARE NO ORPHANAGES IN HELL.
AND POOR LOST BOYS.

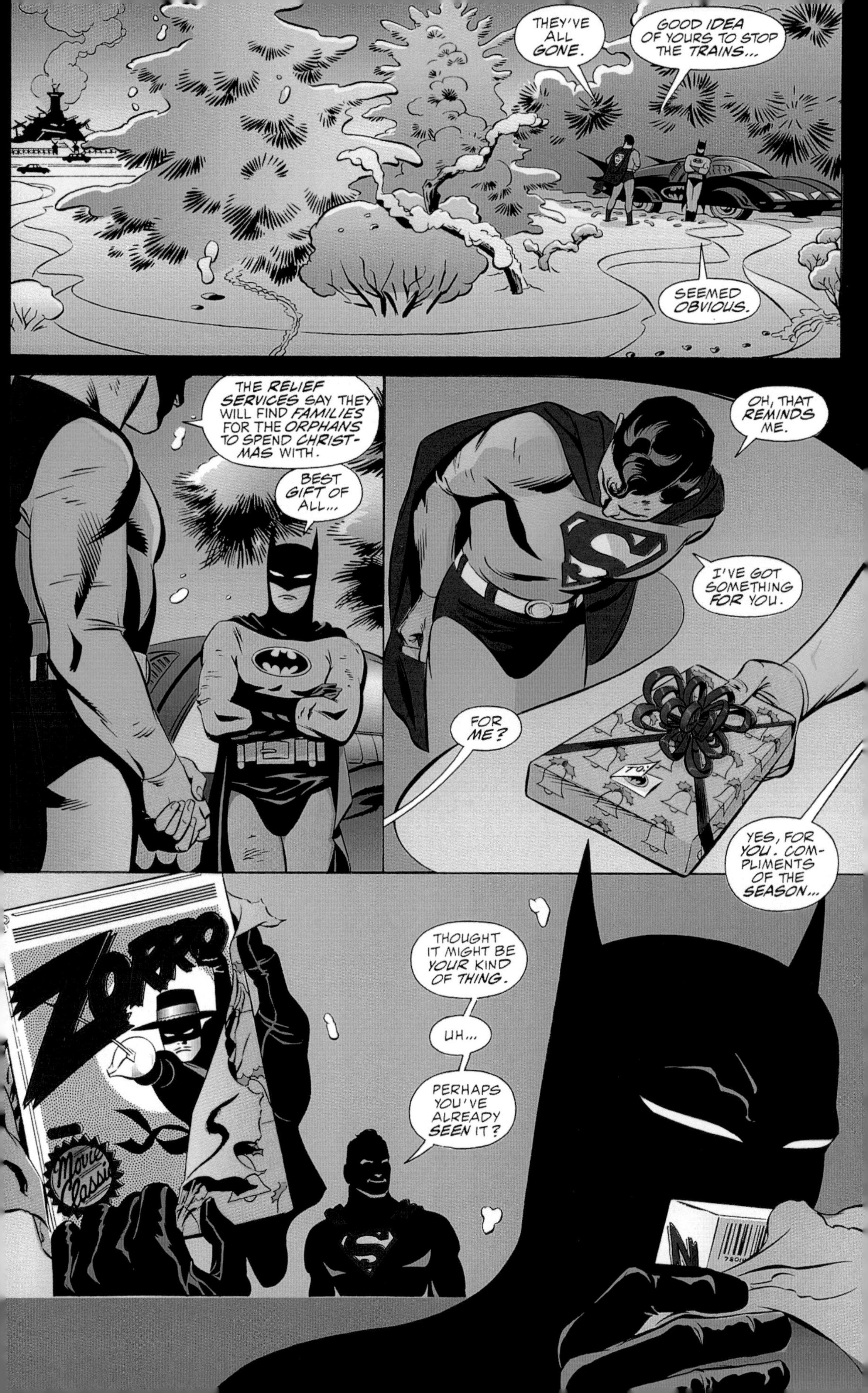
THEY'VE ALL GONE.
GOOD IDEA OF YOURS TO STOP THE TRAINS...
SEEMED OBVIOUS.
THE RELIEF SERVICES SAY THEY WILL FIND FAMILIES FOR THE ORPHANS TO SPEND CHRIST-MAS WITH.
BEST GIFT OF ALL...
OH, THAT REMINDS ME.
I'VE GOT SOMETHING FOR YOU.
FOR ME?
TO:
YES, FOR YOU. COM-PLIMENTS OF THE SEASON...
ZORRO
Movie Classic
THOUGHT IT MIGHT BE YOUR KIND OF THING.
UH...
PERHAPS YOU'VE ALREADY SEEN IT?

YES.

I HAVE.

UH... WELL....

SHOULD, UH, BRING BACK SOME MEMORIES, ANYWAY...

HAS ALREADY.

YOU KNOW, YOU'D BE WELCOME TO SPEND THE HOLIDAYS AT *WAYNE MANOR*, IF --

THANKS, BUT I'LL BE SPENDING CHRISTMAS WITH *FRIENDS*.

OH, FRIENDS IN *METROPOLIS*, I MEAN...

WELL, ANYWAY, HAPPY *HOLIDAYS*, BRUCE.

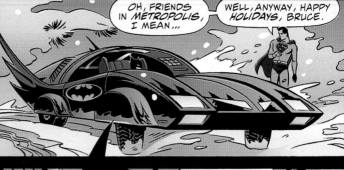

CRIME *NEVER* TAKES A HOLIDAY, CLARK.

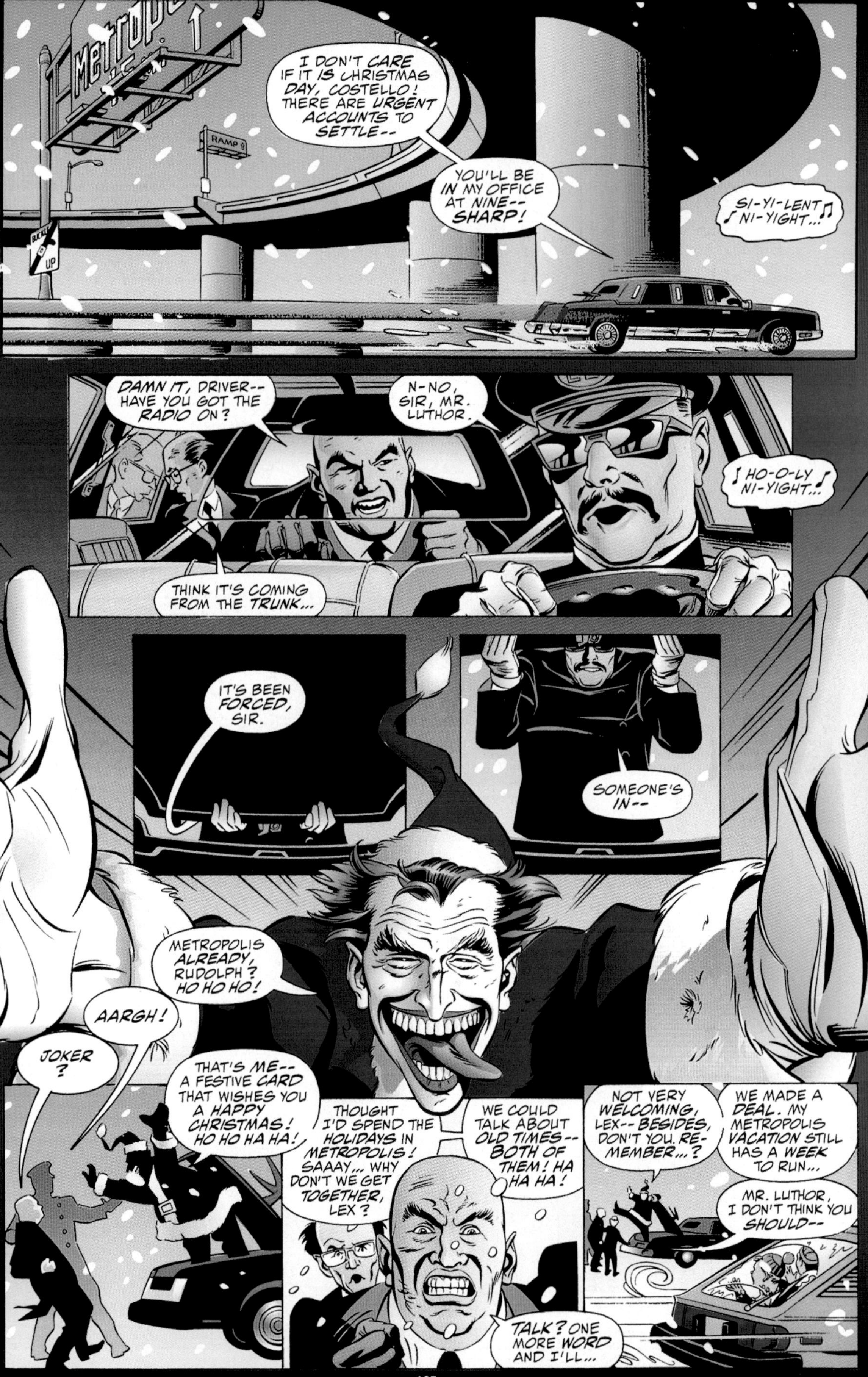
I DON'T CARE IF IT IS CHRISTMAS DAY, COSTELLO! THERE ARE URGENT ACCOUNTS TO SETTLE--
YOU'LL BE IN MY OFFICE AT NINE--SHARP!
SI-YI-LENT ♪ NI-YIGHT... ♫
DAMN IT, DRIVER--HAVE YOU GOT THE RADIO ON?
N-NO, SIR, MR. LUTHOR.
♪ HO-O-LY NI-YIGHT... ♪
THINK IT'S COMING FROM THE TRUNK...
IT'S BEEN FORCED, SIR.
SOMEONE'S IN--
METROPOLIS ALREADY, RUDOLPH? HO HO HO!
AARGH!
JOKER?
THAT'S ME--A FESTIVE CARD THAT WISHES YOU A HAPPY CHRISTMAS! HO HO HA HA!
THOUGHT I'D SPEND THE HOLIDAYS IN METROPOLIS! SAAAY... WHY DON'T WE GET TOGETHER, LEX?
WE COULD TALK ABOUT OLD TIMES--BOTH OF THEM! HA HA HA!
TALK? ONE MORE WORD AND I'LL...
NOT VERY WELCOMING, LEX--BESIDES, DON'T YOU. RE-MEMBER...?
WE MADE A DEAL. MY METROPOLIS VACATION STILL HAS A WEEK TO RUN...
MR. LUTHOR, I DON'T THINK YOU SHOULD--

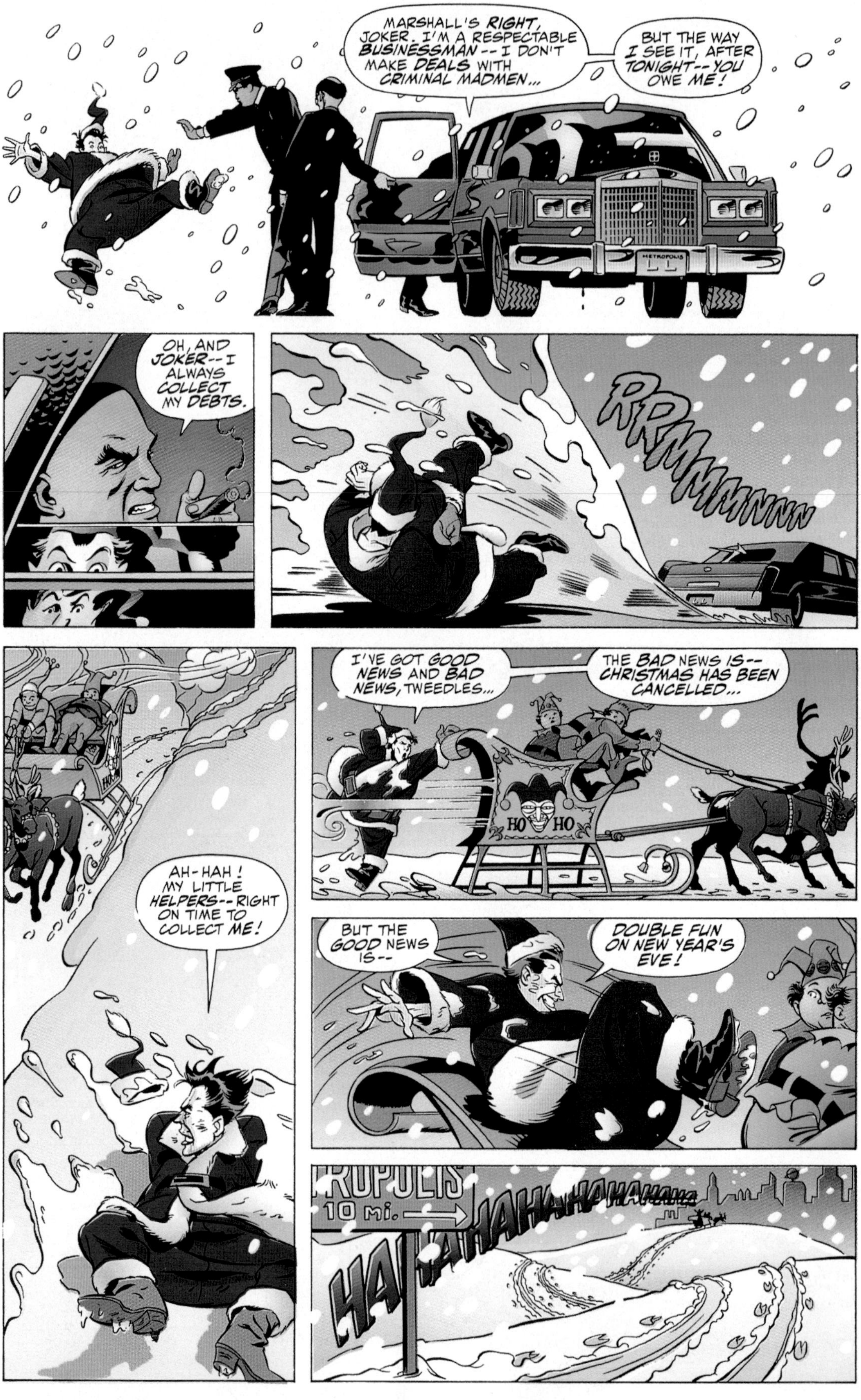
MARSHALL'S RIGHT, JOKER. I'M A RESPECTABLE BUSINESSMAN -- I DON'T MAKE DEALS WITH CRIMINAL MADMEN...
BUT THE WAY I SEE IT, AFTER TONIGHT -- YOU OWE ME!
METROPOLIS
LL
OH, AND JOKER -- I ALWAYS COLLECT MY DEBTS.
RRMMMMNNN
AH-HAH! MY LITTLE HELPERS -- RIGHT ON TIME TO COLLECT ME!
I'VE GOT GOOD NEWS AND BAD NEWS, TWEEDLES...
THE BAD NEWS IS -- CHRISTMAS HAS BEEN CANCELLED...
HO HO
BUT THE GOOD NEWS IS --
DOUBLE FUN ON NEW YEAR'S EVE!
TROPOLIS
10 mi.
HAHAHAHAHAHAHAHAHA

BOOK THREE

WORLDS AT WAR

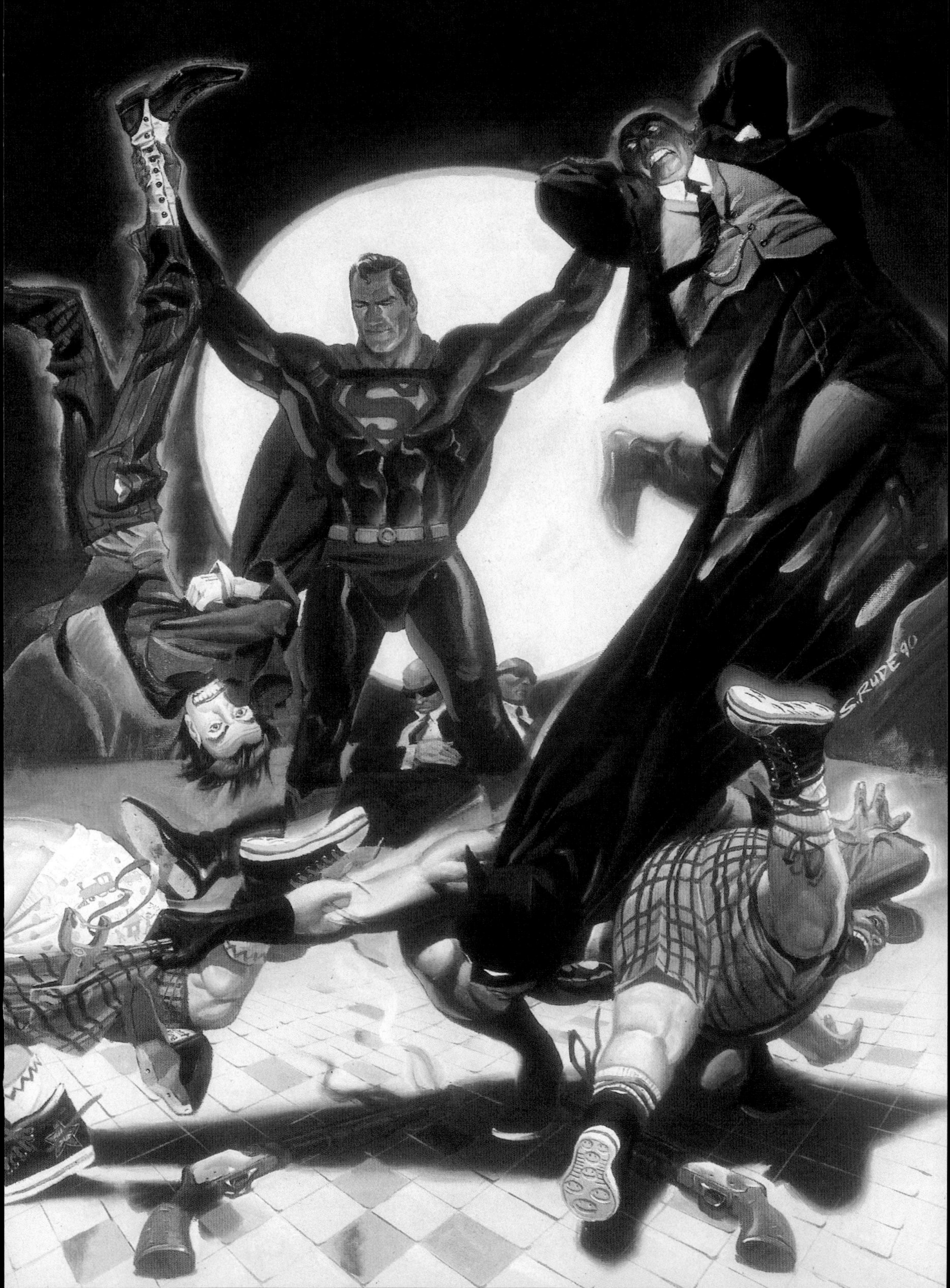
S.RUDE '90

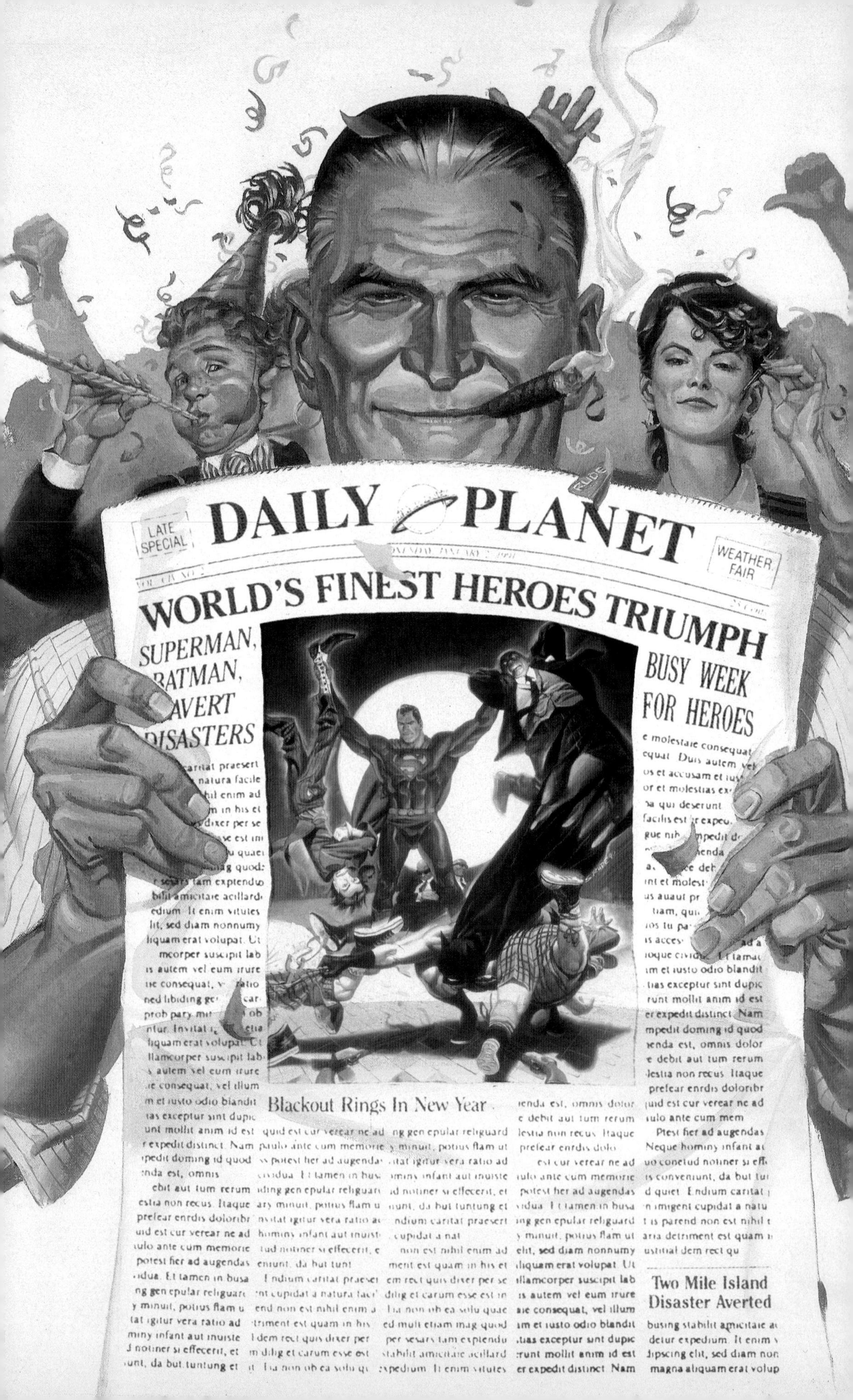
DAILY PLANET
LATE SPECIAL
WEATHER FAIR
WORLD'S FINEST HEROES TRIUMPH
SUPERMAN,
AVERT
BUSY WEEK FOR HEROES
Blackout Rings In New Year
Two Mile Island Disaster Averted

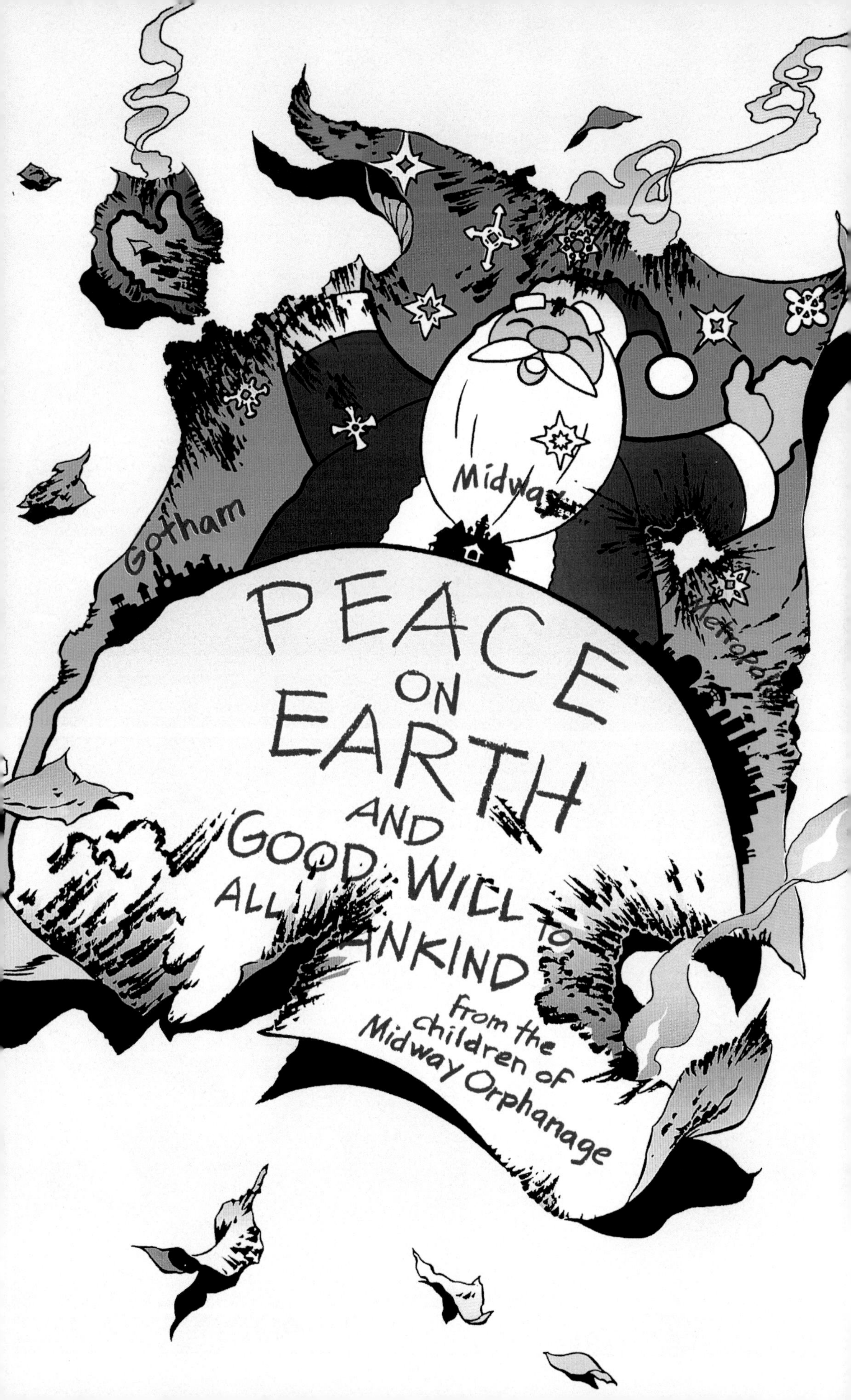
Gotham
PEACE
ON
EARTH
AND
GOOD WILL TO
ALL
ANKIND
from the
children of
Midway Orphanage

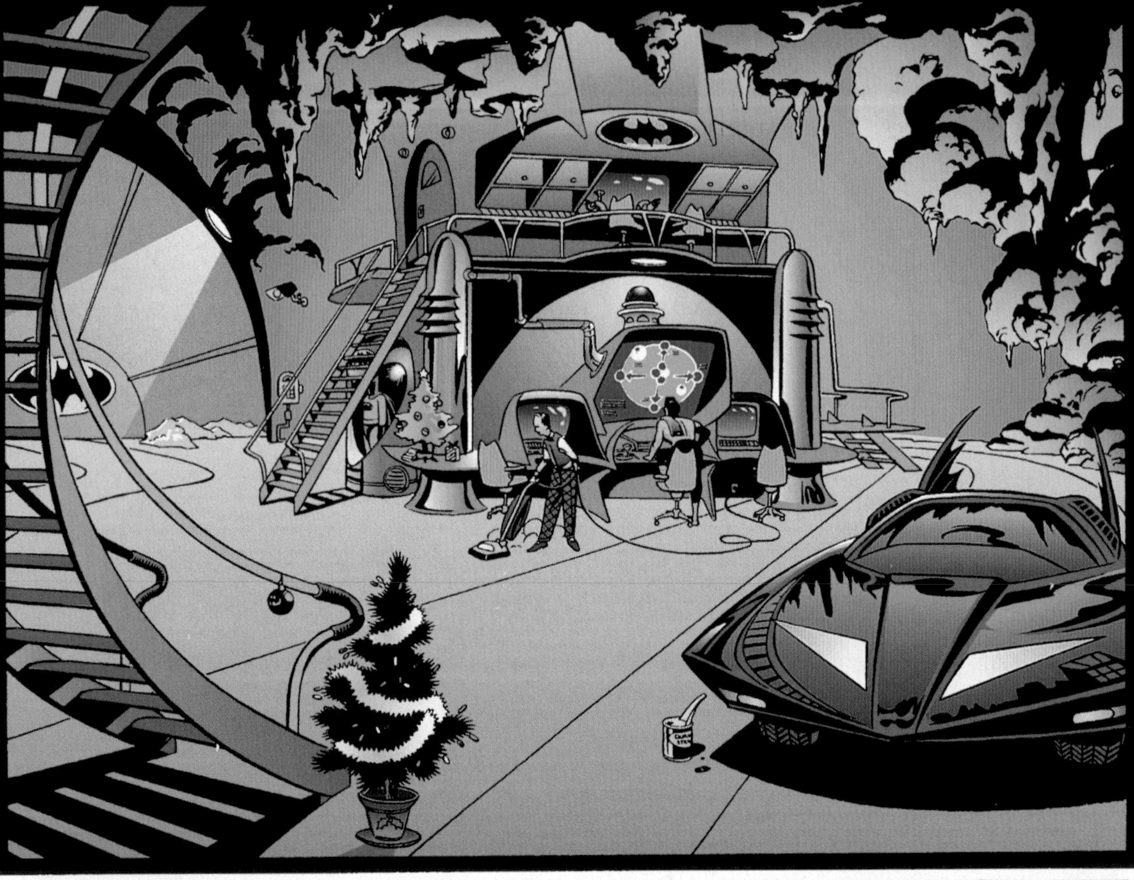

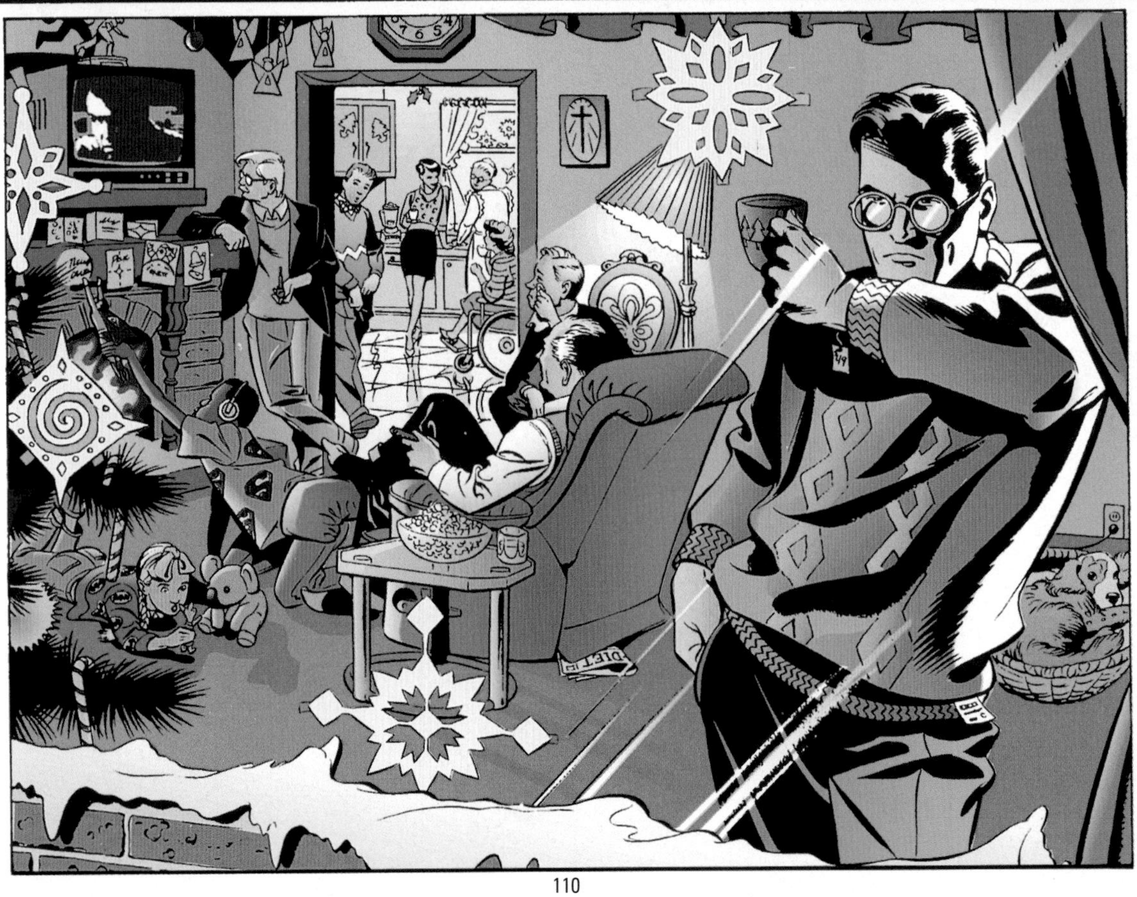

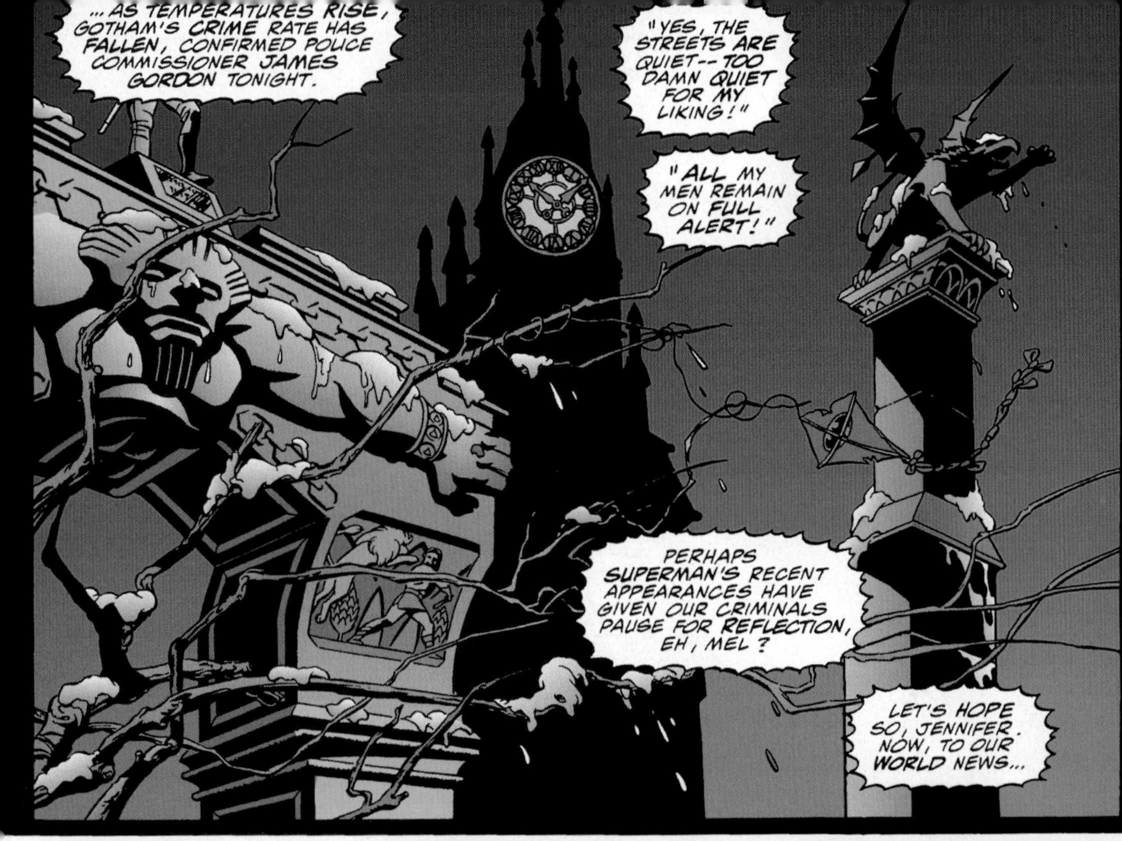
...AS TEMPERATURES RISE, GOTHAM'S CRIME RATE HAS FALLEN, CONFIRMED POLICE COMMISSIONER JAMES GORDON TONIGHT.
"YES, THE STREETS ARE QUIET--TOO DAMN QUIET FOR MY LIKING!"
"ALL MY MEN REMAIN ON FULL ALERT!"
PERHAPS SUPERMAN'S RECENT APPEARANCES HAVE GIVEN OUR CRIMINALS PAUSE FOR REFLECTION, EH, MEL?
LET'S HOPE SO, JENNIFER. NOW, TO OUR WORLD NEWS...

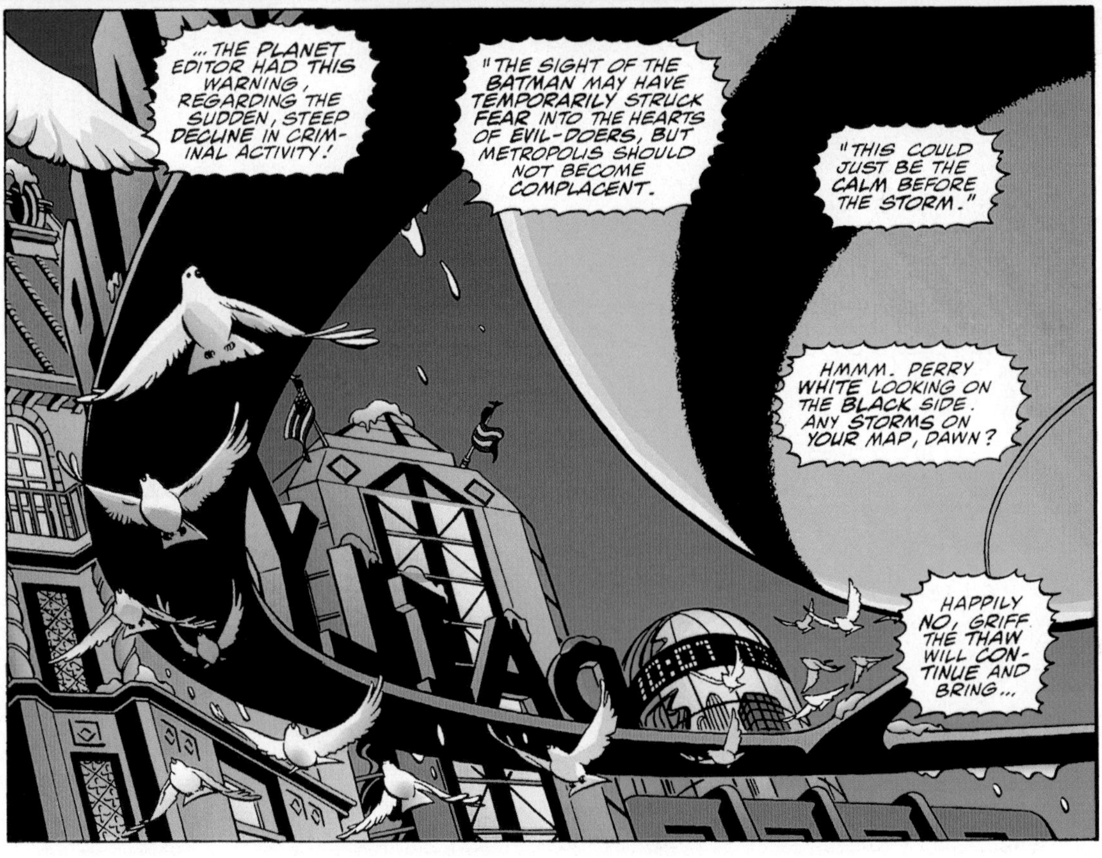
...THE PLANET EDITOR HAD THIS WARNING, REGARDING THE SUDDEN, STEEP DECLINE IN CRIMINAL ACTIVITY!
"THE SIGHT OF THE BATMAN MAY HAVE TEMPORARILY STRUCK FEAR INTO THE HEARTS OF EVIL-DOERS, BUT METROPOLIS SHOULD NOT BECOME COMPLACENT.
"THIS COULD JUST BE THE CALM BEFORE THE STORM."
HMMM. PERRY WHITE LOOKING ON THE BLACK SIDE. ANY STORMS ON YOUR MAP, DAWN?
HAPPILY NO, GRIFF. THE THAW WILL CONTINUE AND BRING...

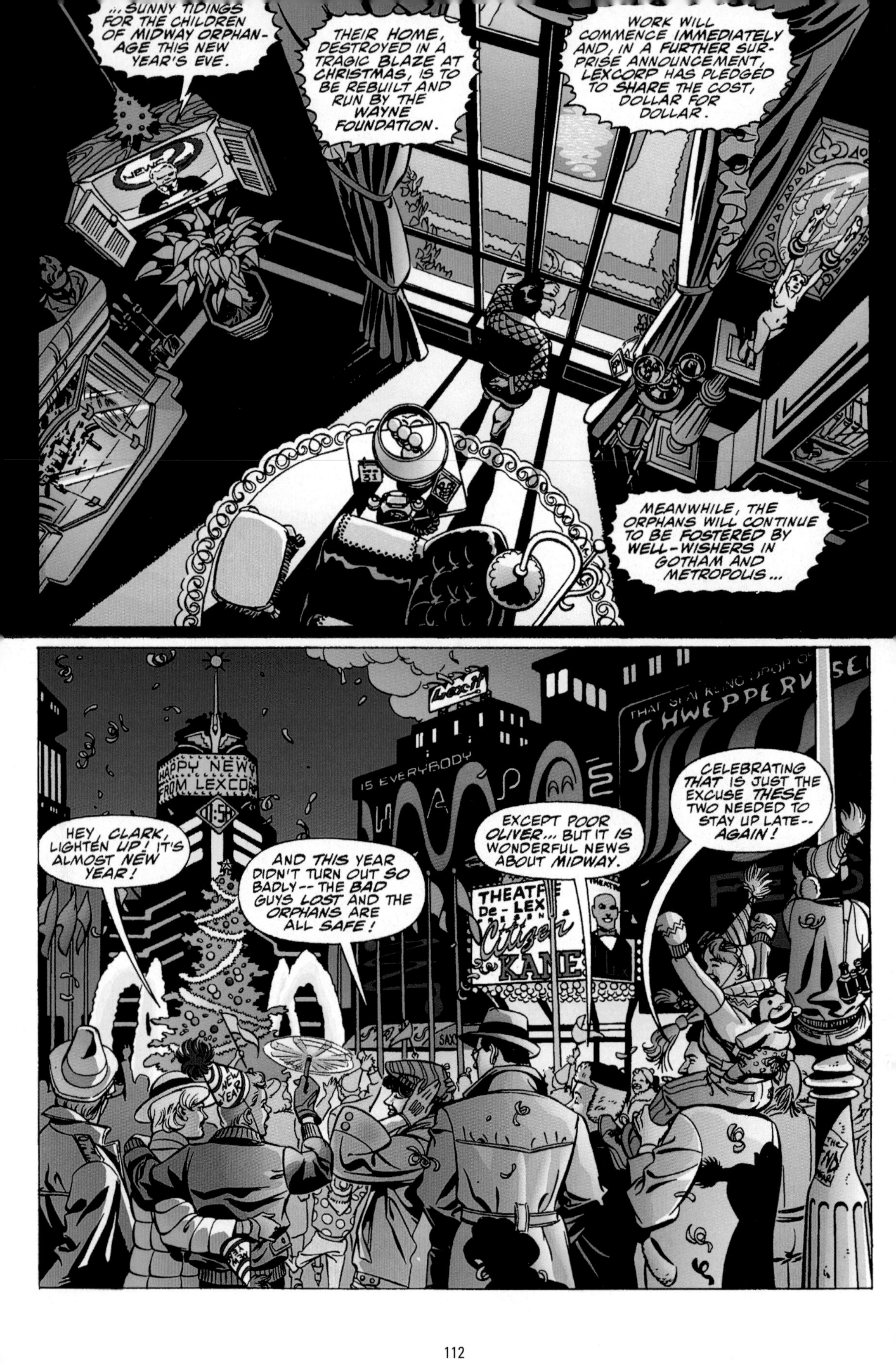
...SUNNY TIDINGS FOR THE CHILDREN OF MIDWAY ORPHANAGE THIS NEW YEAR'S EVE.
THEIR HOME, DESTROYED IN A TRAGIC BLAZE AT CHRISTMAS, IS TO BE REBUILT AND RUN BY THE WAYNE FOUNDATION.
WORK WILL COMMENCE IMMEDIATELY AND, IN A FURTHER SURPRISE ANNOUNCEMENT, LEXCORP HAS PLEDGED TO SHARE THE COST, DOLLAR FOR DOLLAR.
MEANWHILE, THE ORPHANS WILL CONTINUE TO BE FOSTERED BY WELL-WISHERS IN GOTHAM AND METROPOLIS...
IS EVERYBODY
Citizen
KANE
HEY, CLARK, LIGHTEN UP! IT'S ALMOST NEW YEAR!
AND THIS YEAR DIDN'T TURN OUT SO BADLY-- THE BAD GUYS LOST AND THE ORPHANS ARE ALL SAFE!
EXCEPT POOR OLIVER... BUT IT IS WONDERFUL NEWS ABOUT MIDWAY.
CELEBRATING THAT IS JUST THE EXCUSE THESE TWO NEEDED TO STAY UP LATE-- AGAIN!

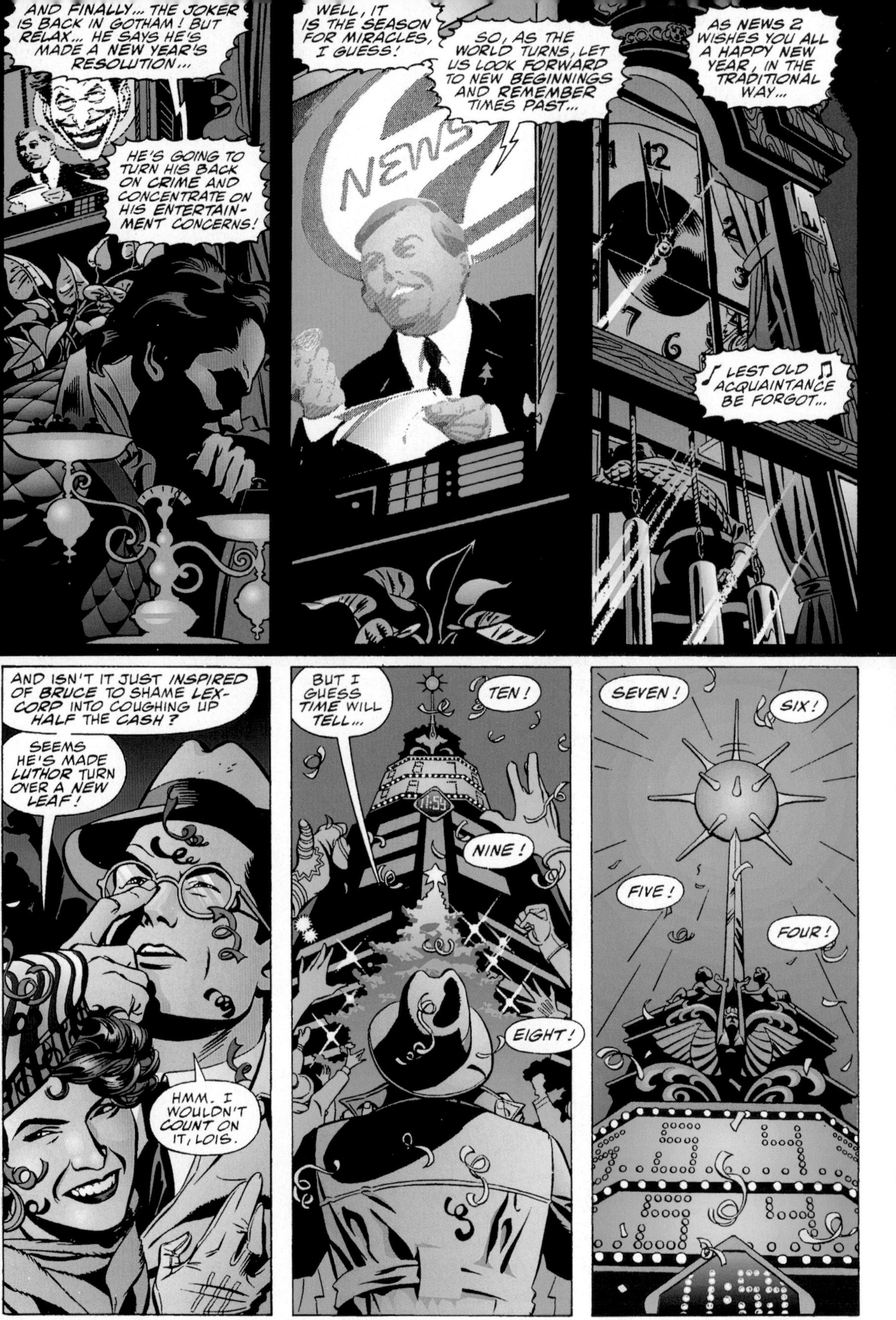
AND FINALLY... THE JOKER IS BACK IN GOTHAM! BUT RELAX... HE SAYS HE'S MADE A NEW YEAR'S RESOLUTION...
HE'S GOING TO TURN HIS BACK ON CRIME AND CONCENTRATE ON HIS ENTERTAINMENT CONCERNS!
WELL, IT IS THE SEASON FOR MIRACLES, I GUESS!
SO, AS THE WORLD TURNS, LET US LOOK FORWARD TO NEW BEGINNINGS AND REMEMBER TIMES PAST...
NEWS
AS NEWS 2 WISHES YOU ALL A HAPPY NEW YEAR, IN THE TRADITIONAL WAY...
♪ LEST OLD ♫ ACQUAINTANCE BE FORGOT...
AND ISN'T IT JUST INSPIRED OF BRUCE TO SHAME LEXCORP INTO COUGHING UP HALF THE CASH?
SEEMS HE'S MADE LUTHOR TURN OVER A NEW LEAF!
HMM. I WOULDN'T COUNT ON IT, LOIS.
BUT I GUESS TIME WILL TELL...
TEN!
11:59
NINE!
EIGHT!
SEVEN!
SIX!
FIVE!
FOUR!

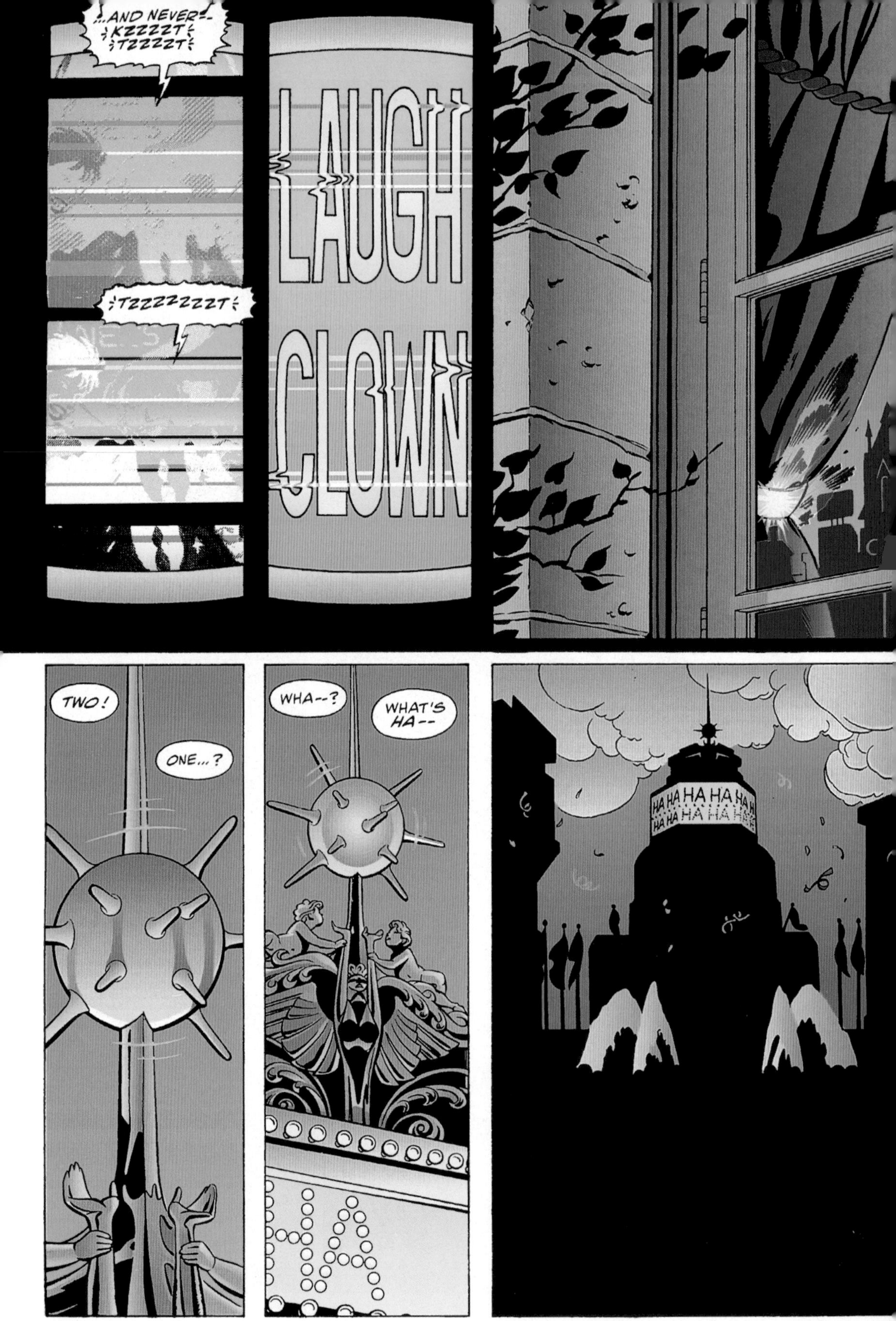

...AND NEVER--
KZZZZT
TZZZZZT
LAUGH
CLOWN
TZZZZZZZZT
TWO!
ONE...?
WHA--?
WHAT'S HA--
HA HA HA HA HA H
HA HA HA HA HA HA
HA

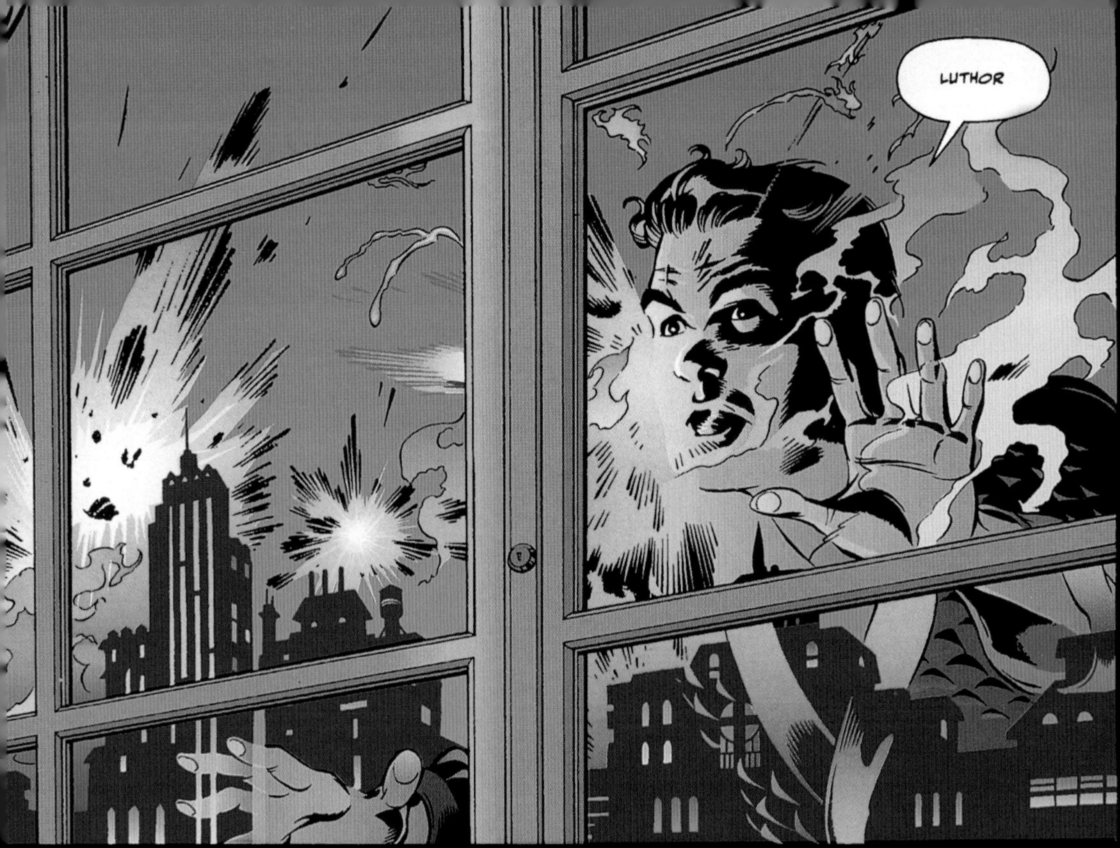
LUTHOR

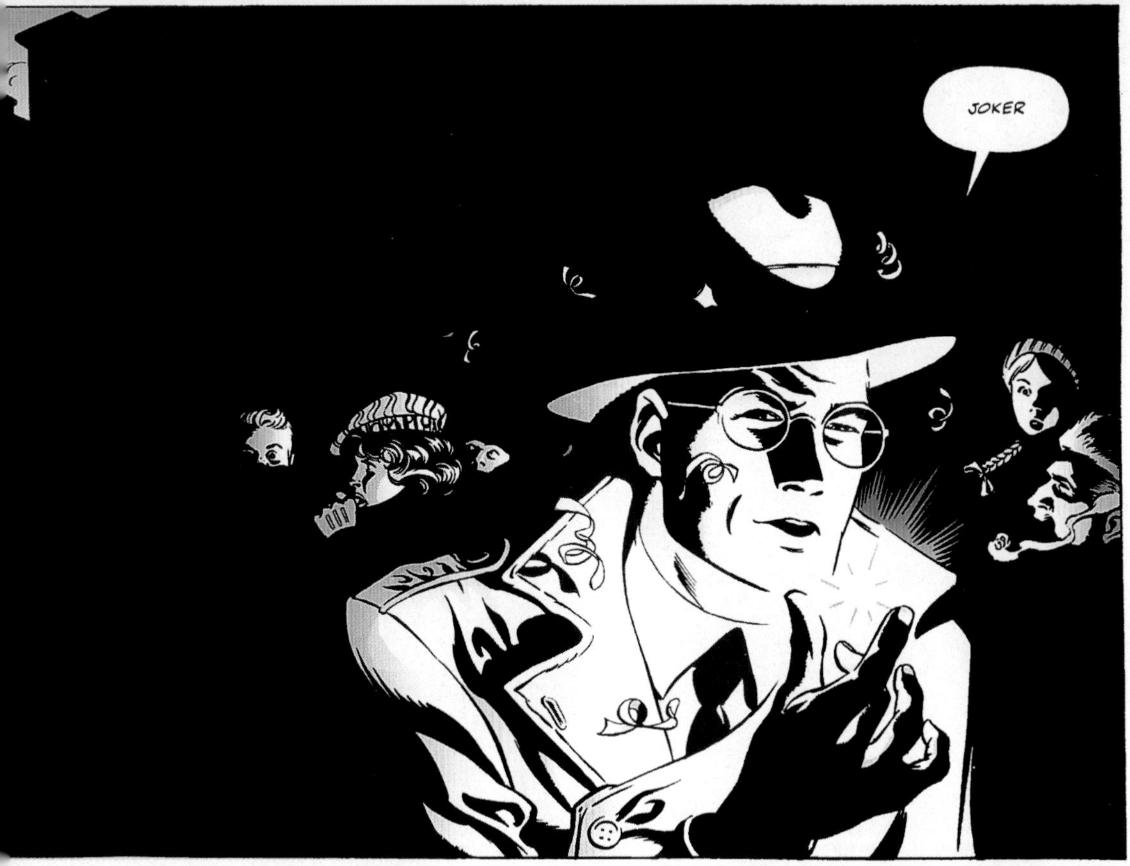
JOKER

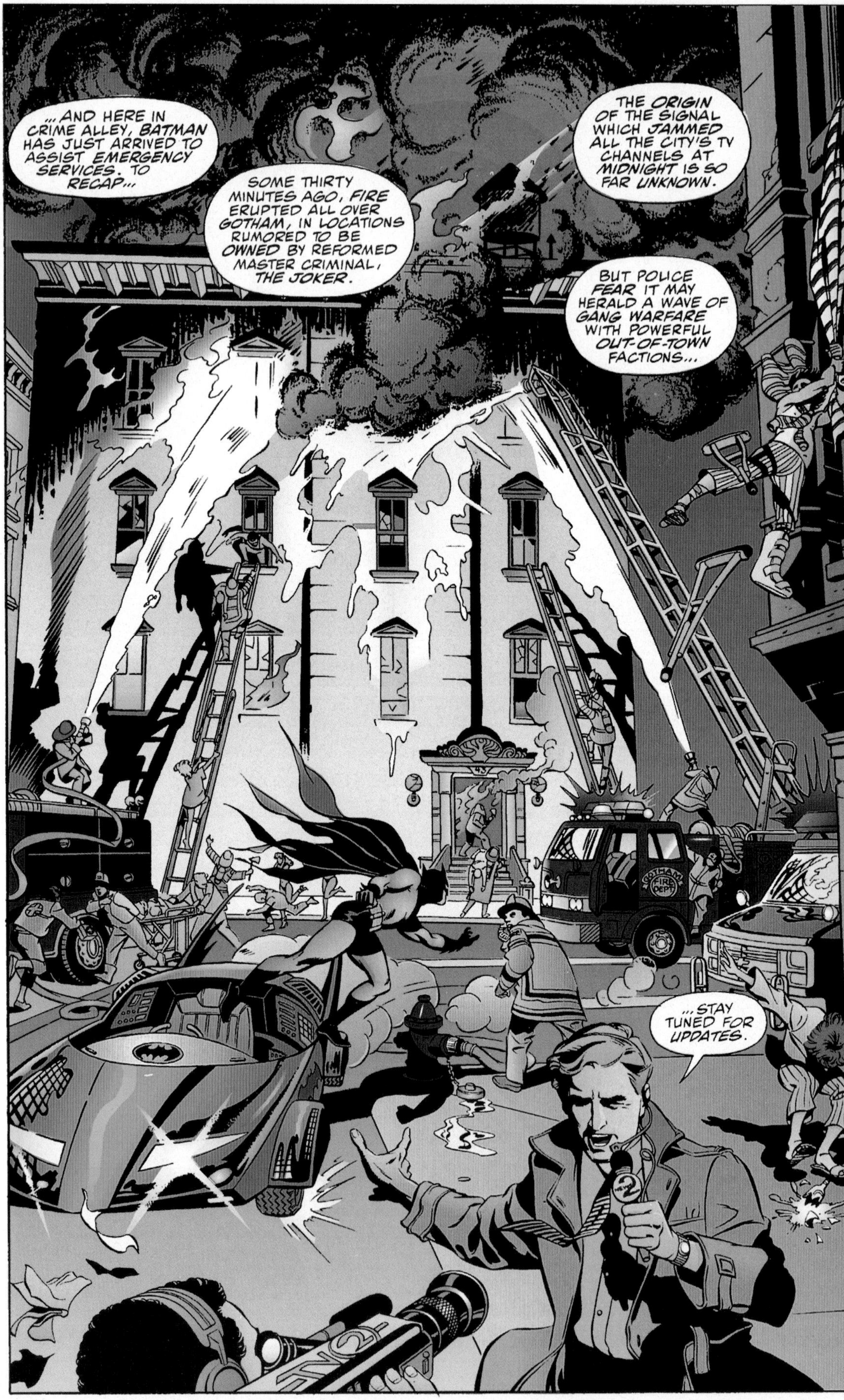
...AND HERE IN CRIME ALLEY, BATMAN HAS JUST ARRIVED TO ASSIST EMERGENCY SERVICES. TO RECAP...
SOME THIRTY MINUTES AGO, FIRE ERUPTED ALL OVER GOTHAM, IN LOCATIONS RUMORED TO BE OWNED BY REFORMED MASTER CRIMINAL, THE JOKER.
THE ORIGIN OF THE SIGNAL WHICH JAMMED ALL THE CITY'S TV CHANNELS AT MIDNIGHT IS SO FAR UNKNOWN.
BUT POLICE FEAR IT MAY HERALD A WAVE OF GANG WARFARE WITH POWERFUL OUT-OF-TOWN FACTIONS...
...STAY TUNED FOR UPDATES.
GOTHAM FIRE DEPT

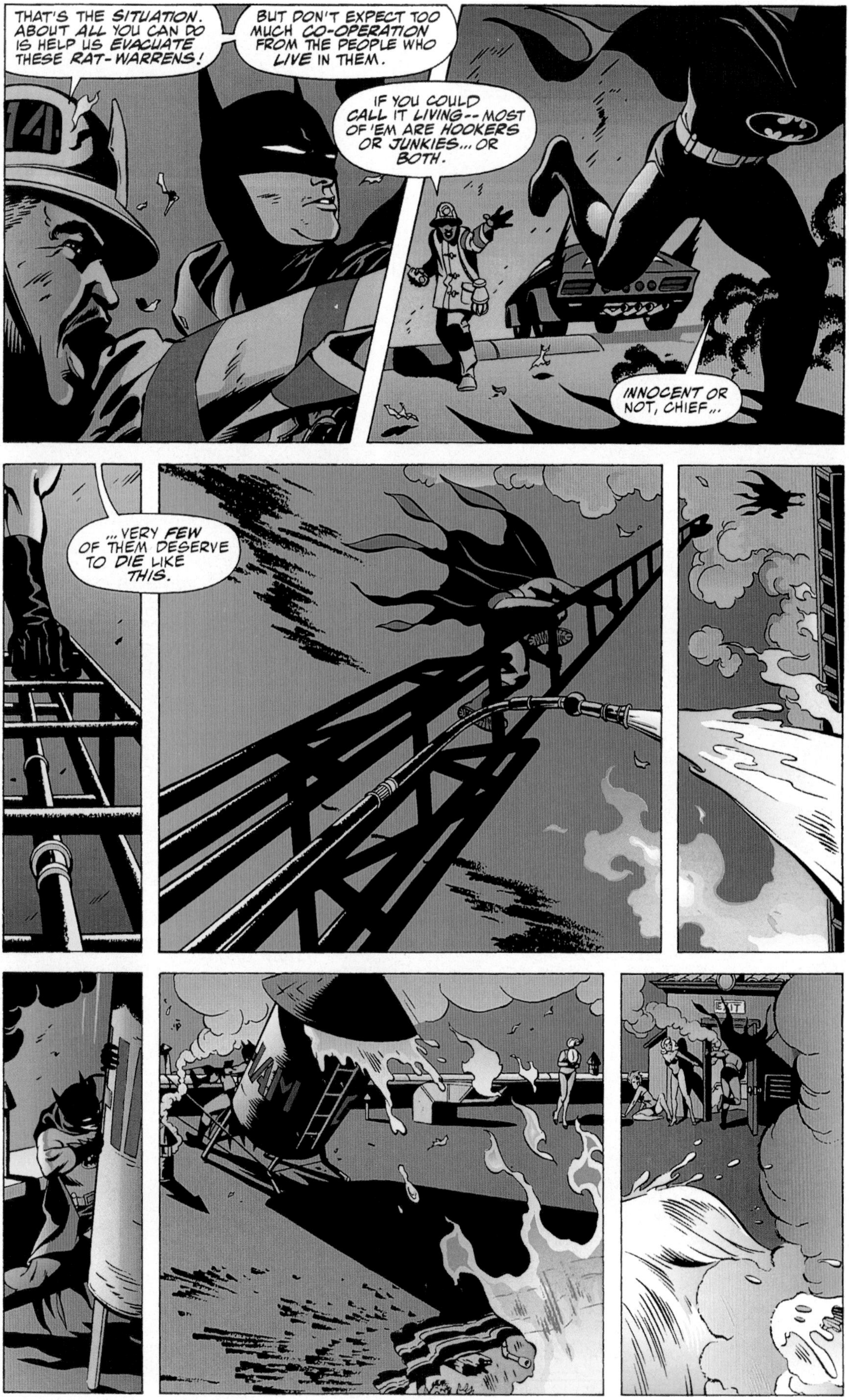
THAT'S THE SITUATION. ABOUT ALL YOU CAN DO IS HELP US EVACUATE THESE RAT-WARRENS!
BUT DON'T EXPECT TOO MUCH CO-OPERATION FROM THE PEOPLE WHO LIVE IN THEM.
IF YOU COULD CALL IT LIVING-- MOST OF 'EM ARE HOOKERS OR JUNKIES... OR BOTH.
INNOCENT OR NOT, CHIEF...
...VERY FEW OF THEM DESERVE TO DIE LIKE THIS.
EXIT

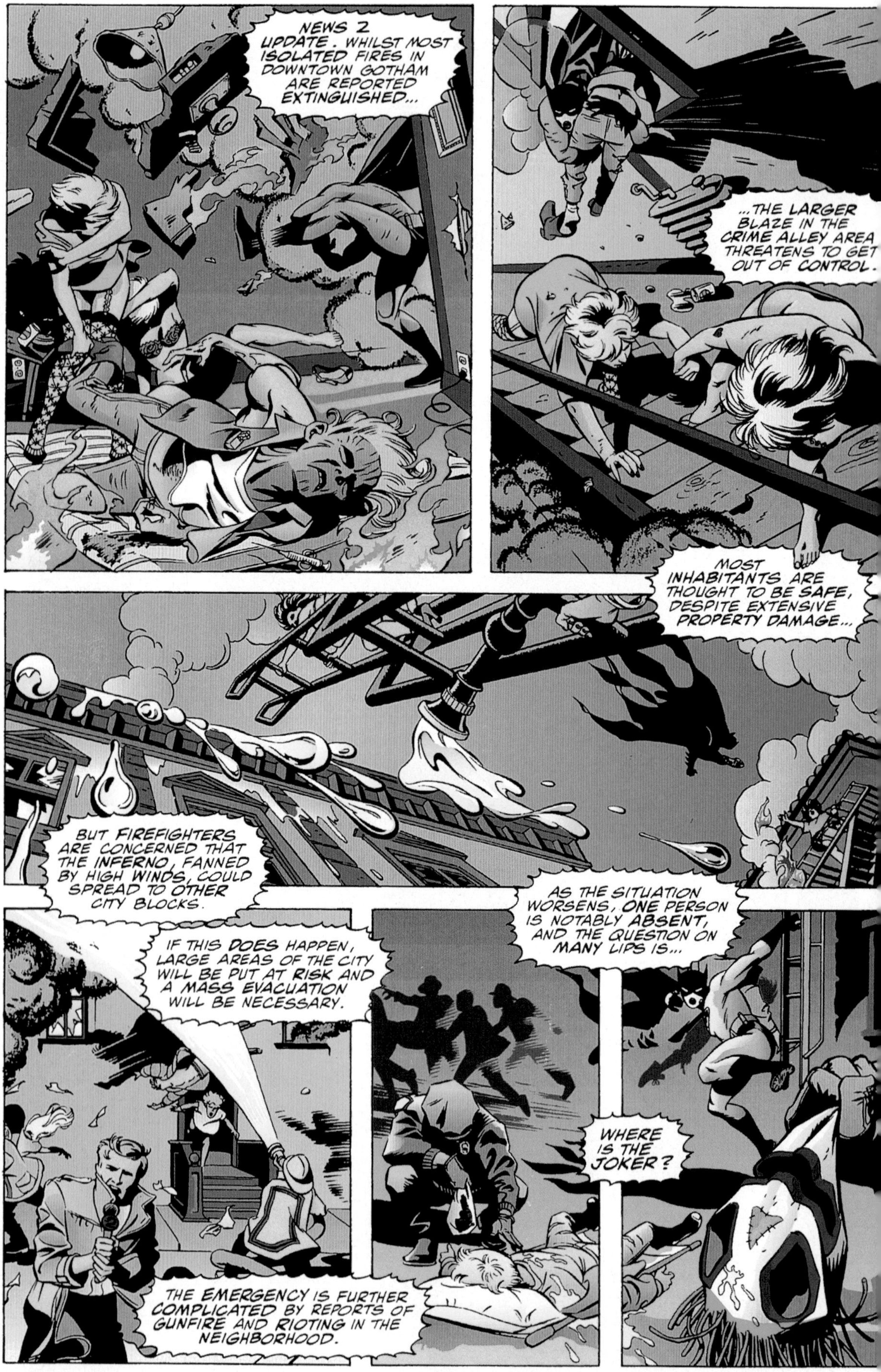
NEWS 2 UPDATE. WHILST MOST ISOLATED FIRES IN DOWNTOWN GOTHAM ARE REPORTED EXTINGUISHED...
...THE LARGER BLAZE IN THE CRIME ALLEY AREA THREATENS TO GET OUT OF CONTROL.
MOST INHABITANTS ARE THOUGHT TO BE SAFE, DESPITE EXTENSIVE PROPERTY DAMAGE...
BUT FIREFIGHTERS ARE CONCERNED THAT THE INFERNO, FANNED BY HIGH WINDS, COULD SPREAD TO OTHER CITY BLOCKS.
IF THIS DOES HAPPEN, LARGE AREAS OF THE CITY WILL BE PUT AT RISK AND A MASS EVACUATION WILL BE NECESSARY.
THE EMERGENCY IS FURTHER COMPLICATED BY REPORTS OF GUNFIRE AND RIOTING IN THE NEIGHBORHOOD.
AS THE SITUATION WORSENS, ONE PERSON IS NOTABLY ABSENT, AND THE QUESTION ON MANY LIPS IS...
WHERE IS THE JOKER?

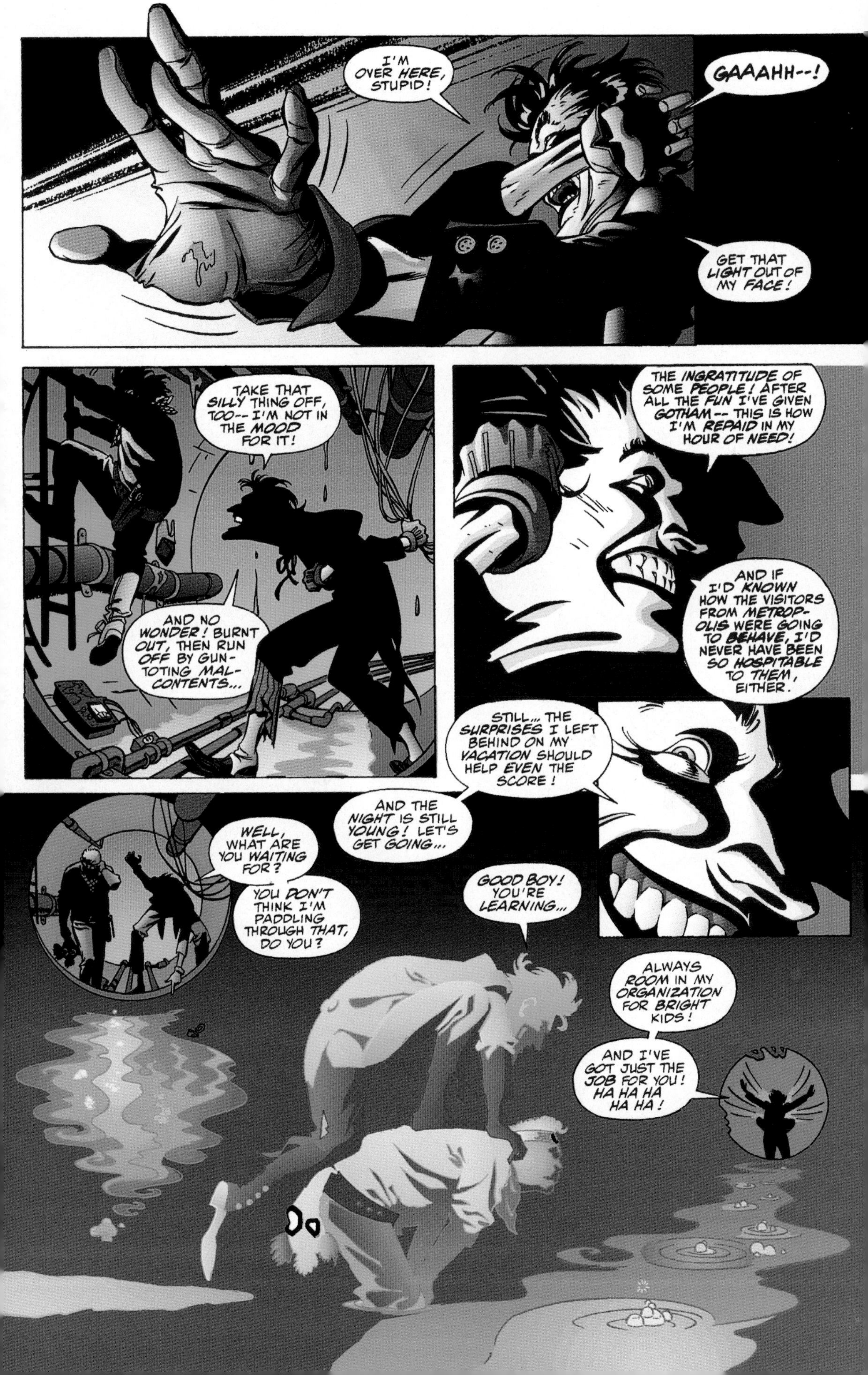
I'M OVER HERE, STUPID!
GAAAHH--!
GET THAT LIGHT OUT OF MY FACE!
TAKE THAT SILLY THING OFF, TOO-- I'M NOT IN THE MOOD FOR IT!
AND NO WONDER! BURNT OUT, THEN RUN OFF BY GUN-TOTING MAL-CONTENTS...
THE INGRATITUDE OF SOME PEOPLE! AFTER ALL THE FUN I'VE GIVEN GOTHAM -- THIS IS HOW I'M REPAID IN MY HOUR OF NEED!
AND IF I'D KNOWN HOW THE VISITORS FROM METROP-OLIS WERE GOING TO BEHAVE, I'D NEVER HAVE BEEN SO HOSPITABLE TO THEM, EITHER.
STILL... THE SURPRISES I LEFT BEHIND ON MY VACATION SHOULD HELP EVEN THE SCORE!
AND THE NIGHT IS STILL YOUNG! LET'S GET GOING...
WELL, WHAT ARE YOU WAITING FOR?
YOU DON'T THINK I'M PADDLING THROUGH THAT, DO YOU?
GOOD BOY! YOU'RE LEARNING...
ALWAYS ROOM IN MY ORGANIZATION FOR BRIGHT KIDS!
AND I'VE GOT JUST THE JOB FOR YOU! HA HA HA HA HA!

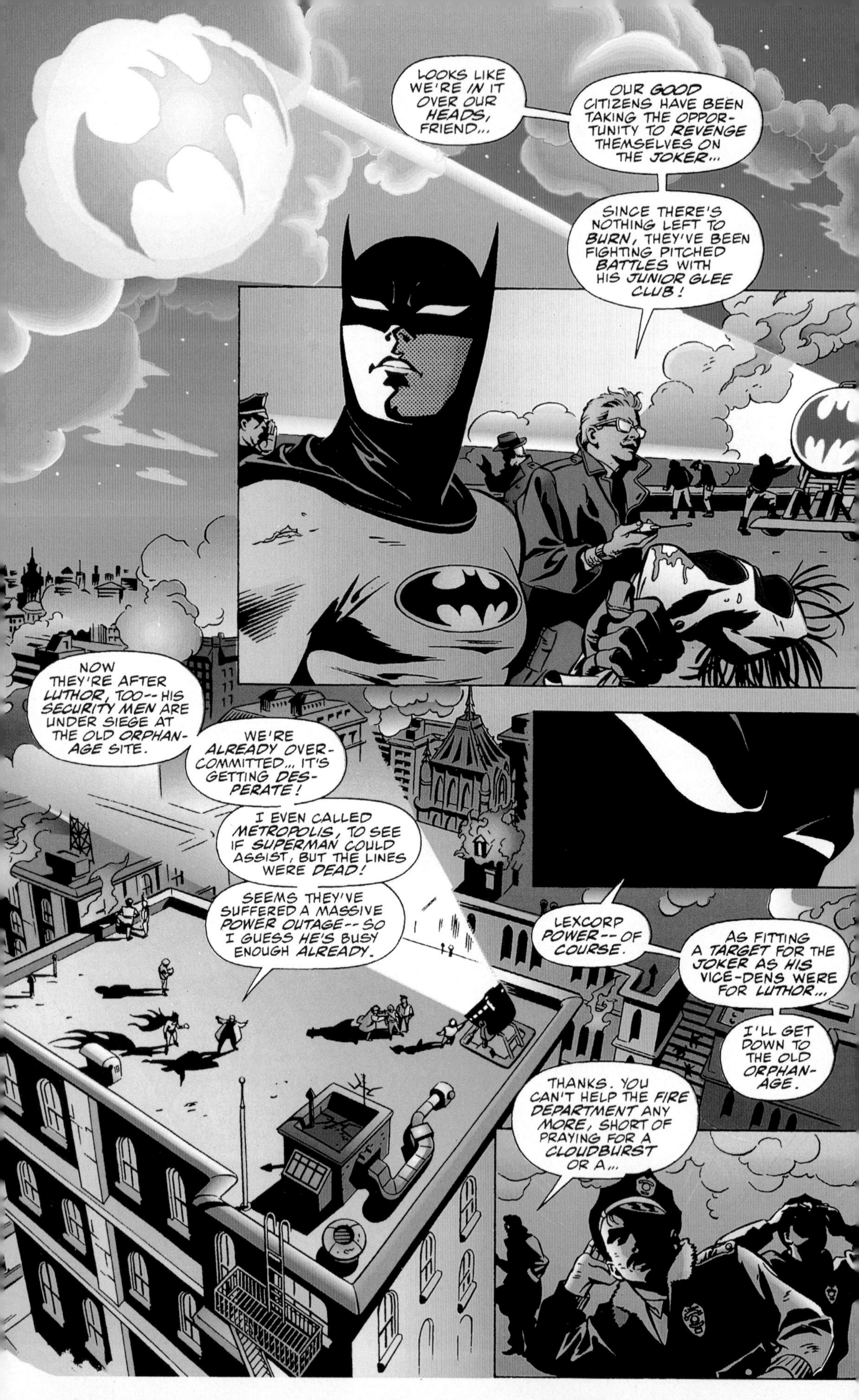
LOOKS LIKE WE'RE IN IT OVER OUR HEADS, FRIEND...
OUR GOOD CITIZENS HAVE BEEN TAKING THE OPPORTUNITY TO REVENGE THEMSELVES ON THE JOKER...
SINCE THERE'S NOTHING LEFT TO BURN, THEY'VE BEEN FIGHTING PITCHED BATTLES WITH HIS JUNIOR GLEE CLUB!
NOW THEY'RE AFTER LUTHOR, TOO-- HIS SECURITY MEN ARE UNDER SIEGE AT THE OLD ORPHANAGE SITE.
WE'RE ALREADY OVER-COMMITTED... IT'S GETTING DESPERATE!
I EVEN CALLED METROPOLIS, TO SEE IF SUPERMAN COULD ASSIST, BUT THE LINES WERE DEAD!
SEEMS THEY'VE SUFFERED A MASSIVE POWER OUTAGE-- SO I GUESS HE'S BUSY ENOUGH ALREADY.
LEXCORP POWER-- OF COURSE.
AS FITTING A TARGET FOR THE JOKER AS HIS VICE-DENS WERE FOR LUTHOR...
I'LL GET DOWN TO THE OLD ORPHANAGE.
THANKS. YOU CAN'T HELP THE FIRE DEPARTMENT ANY MORE, SHORT OF PRAYING FOR A CLOUDBURST OR A...

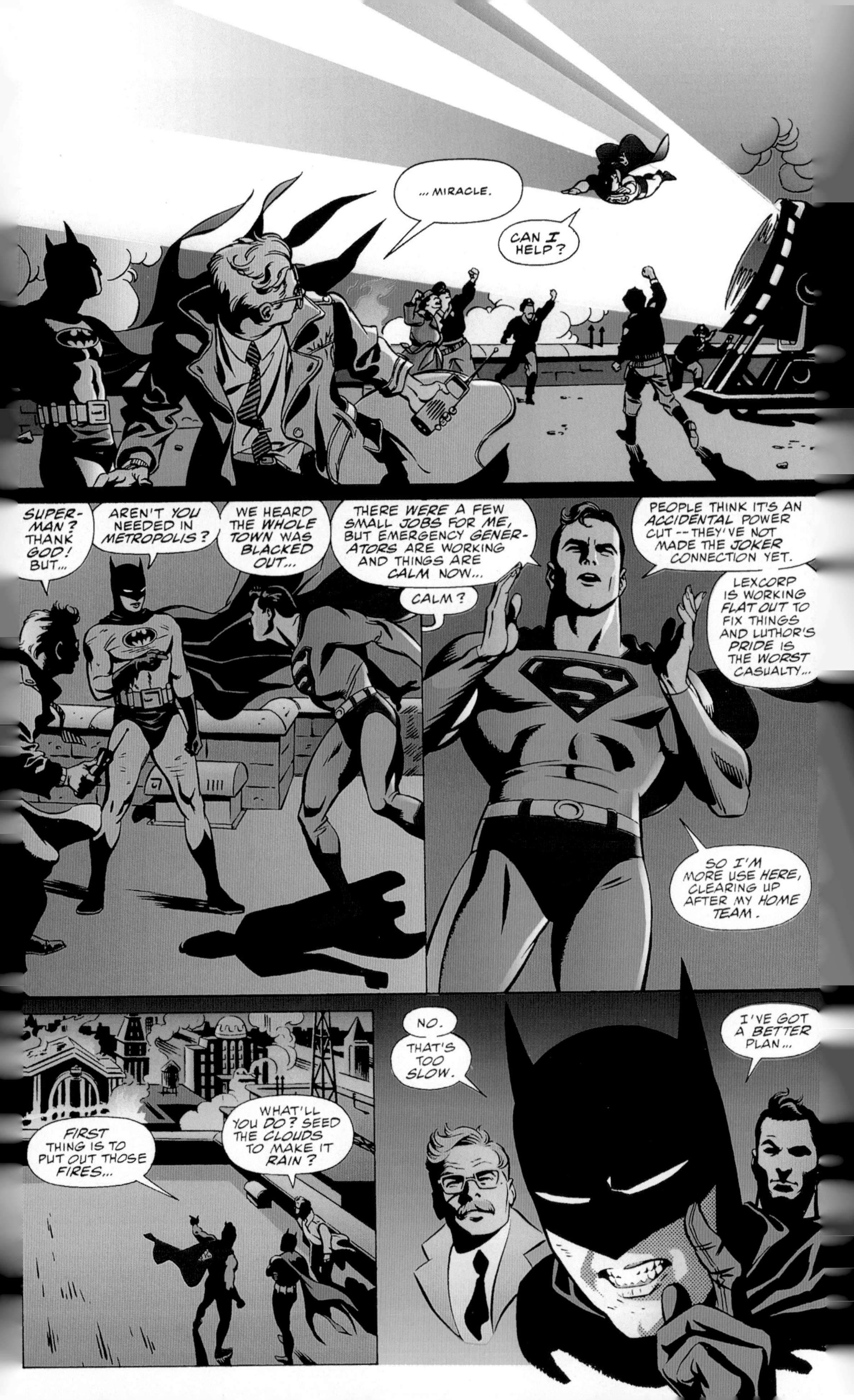
...MIRACLE.
CAN I HELP?
SUPER-MAN? THANK GOD! BUT...
AREN'T YOU NEEDED IN METROPOLIS?
WE HEARD THE WHOLE TOWN WAS BLACKED OUT...
THERE WERE A FEW SMALL JOBS FOR ME, BUT EMERGENCY GENER-ATORS ARE WORKING AND THINGS ARE CALM NOW...
CALM?
PEOPLE THINK IT'S AN ACCIDENTAL POWER CUT -- THEY'VE NOT MADE THE JOKER CONNECTION YET.
LEXCORP IS WORKING FLAT OUT TO FIX THINGS AND LUTHOR'S PRIDE IS THE WORST CASUALTY...
SO I'M MORE USE HERE, CLEARING UP AFTER MY HOME TEAM.
FIRST THING IS TO PUT OUT THOSE FIRES...
WHAT'LL YOU DO? SEED THE CLOUDS TO MAKE IT RAIN?
NO.
THAT'S TOO SLOW.
I'VE GOT A BETTER PLAN...

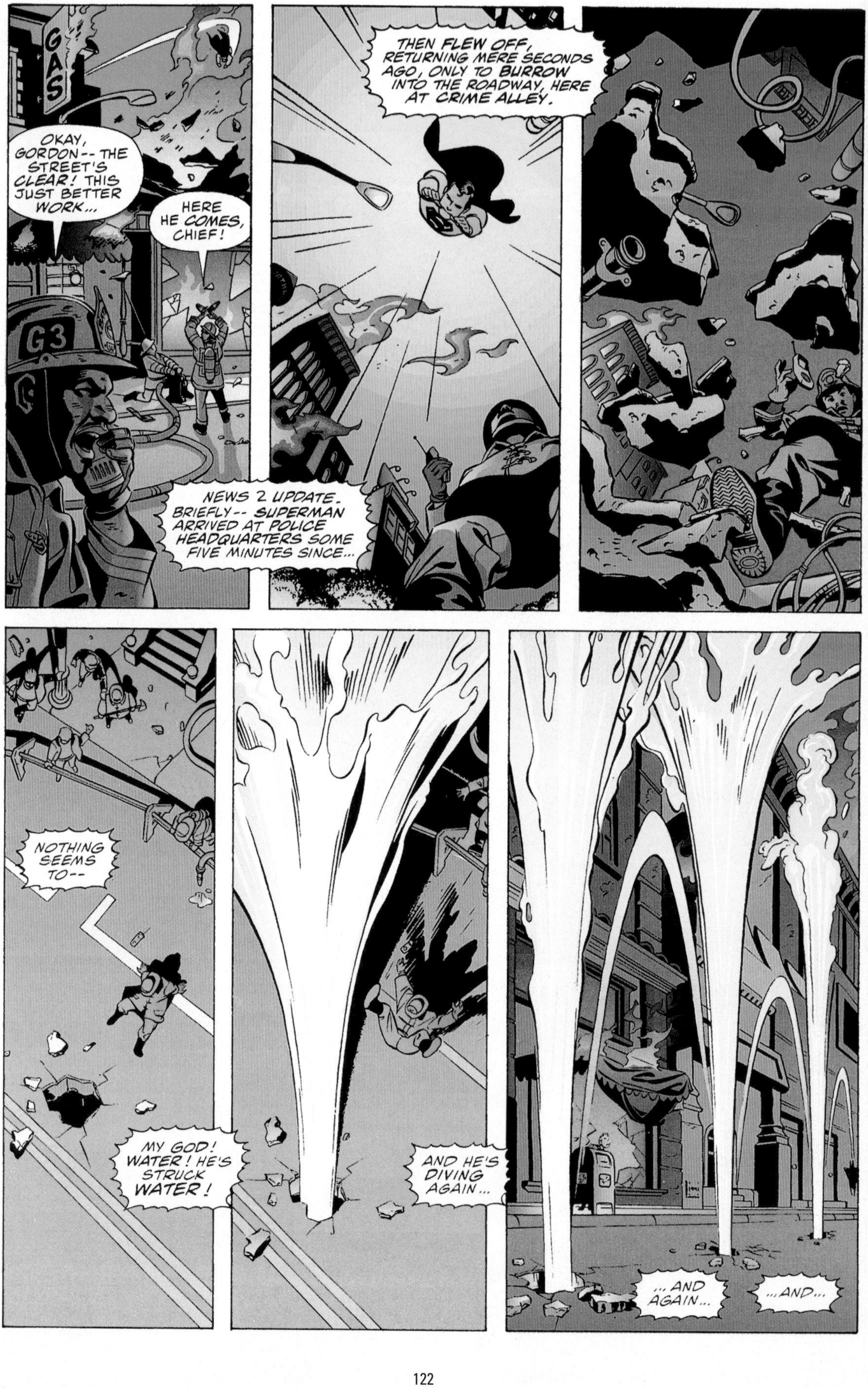
OKAY, GORDON-- THE STREET'S CLEAR! THIS JUST BETTER WORK...
HERE HE COMES, CHIEF!
G3
GAS
THEN FLEW OFF, RETURNING MERE SECONDS AGO, ONLY TO BURROW INTO THE ROADWAY, HERE AT CRIME ALLEY.
NEWS 2 UPDATE. BRIEFLY-- SUPERMAN ARRIVED AT POLICE HEADQUARTERS SOME FIVE MINUTES SINCE...
NOTHING SEEMS TO--
MY GOD! WATER! HE'S STRUCK WATER!
AND HE'S DIVING AGAIN...
...AND AGAIN...
...AND...

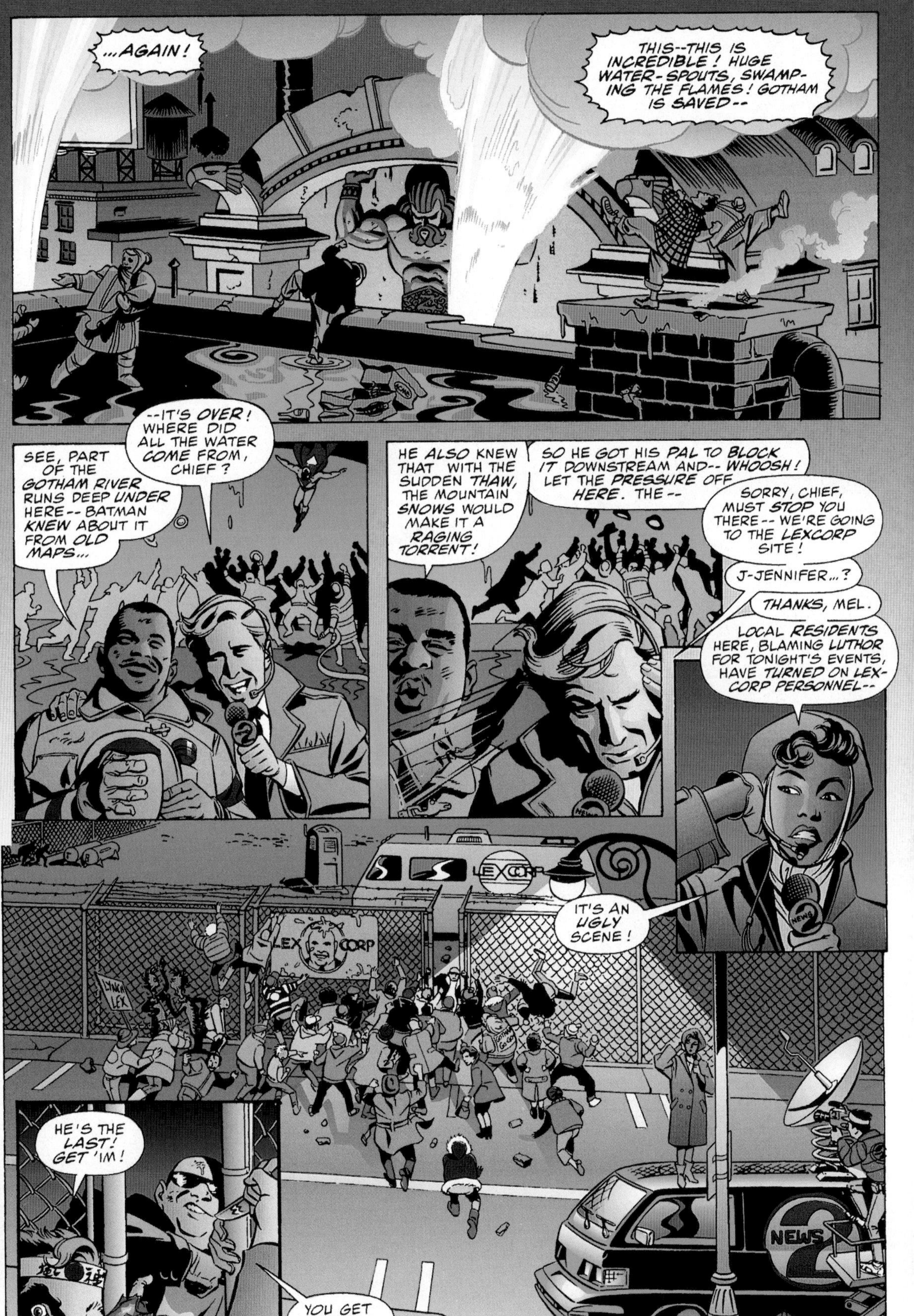
...AGAIN!
THIS--THIS IS INCREDIBLE! HUGE WATER-SPOUTS, SWAMPING THE FLAMES! GOTHAM IS SAVED--
--IT'S OVER! WHERE DID ALL THE WATER COME FROM, CHIEF?
SEE, PART OF THE GOTHAM RIVER RUNS DEEP UNDER HERE-- BATMAN KNEW ABOUT IT FROM OLD MAPS...
HE ALSO KNEW THAT WITH THE SUDDEN THAW, THE MOUNTAIN SNOWS WOULD MAKE IT A RAGING TORRENT!
SO HE GOT HIS PAL TO BLOCK IT DOWNSTREAM AND-- WHOOSH! LET THE PRESSURE OFF HERE. THE--
SORRY, CHIEF, MUST STOP YOU THERE-- WE'RE GOING TO THE LEXCORP SITE!
J-JENNIFER...?
THANKS, MEL.
LOCAL RESIDENTS HERE, BLAMING LUTHOR FOR TONIGHT'S EVENTS, HAVE TURNED ON LEXCORP PERSONNEL--
IT'S AN UGLY SCENE!
LEXCORP
HE'S THE LAST! GET 'IM!
YOU GET THIS, BIG-MOUTH--
NEWS 2

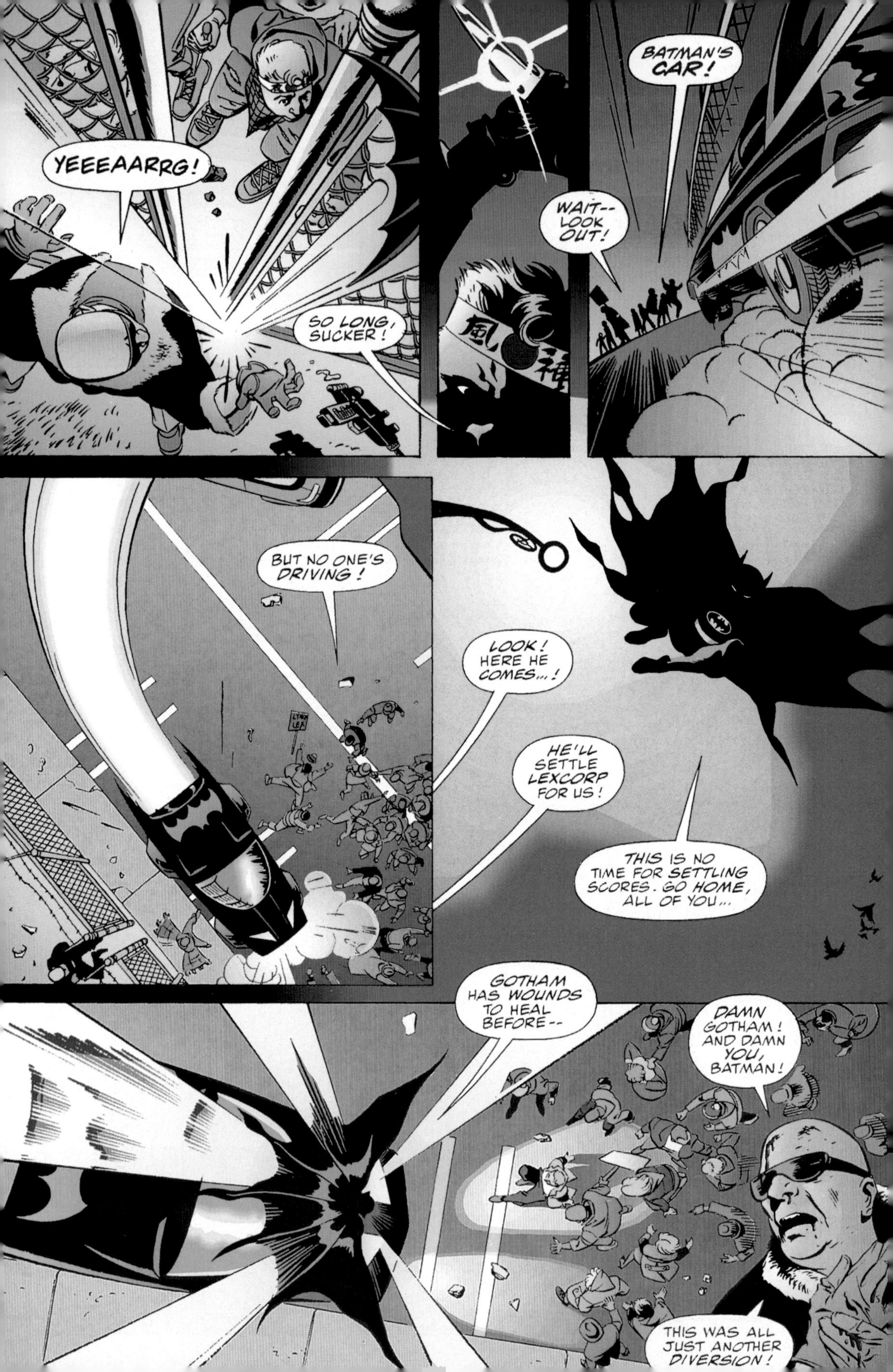
YEEEAARRG!
SO LONG, SUCKER!
WAIT-- LOOK OUT!
BATMAN'S CAR!
BUT NO ONE'S DRIVING!
LOOK! HERE HE COMES...!
HE'LL SETTLE LEXCORP FOR US!
THIS IS NO TIME FOR SETTLING SCORES. GO HOME, ALL OF YOU...
GOTHAM HAS WOUNDS TO HEAL BEFORE--
DAMN GOTHAM! AND DAMN YOU, BATMAN!
THIS WAS ALL JUST ANOTHER DIVERSION!

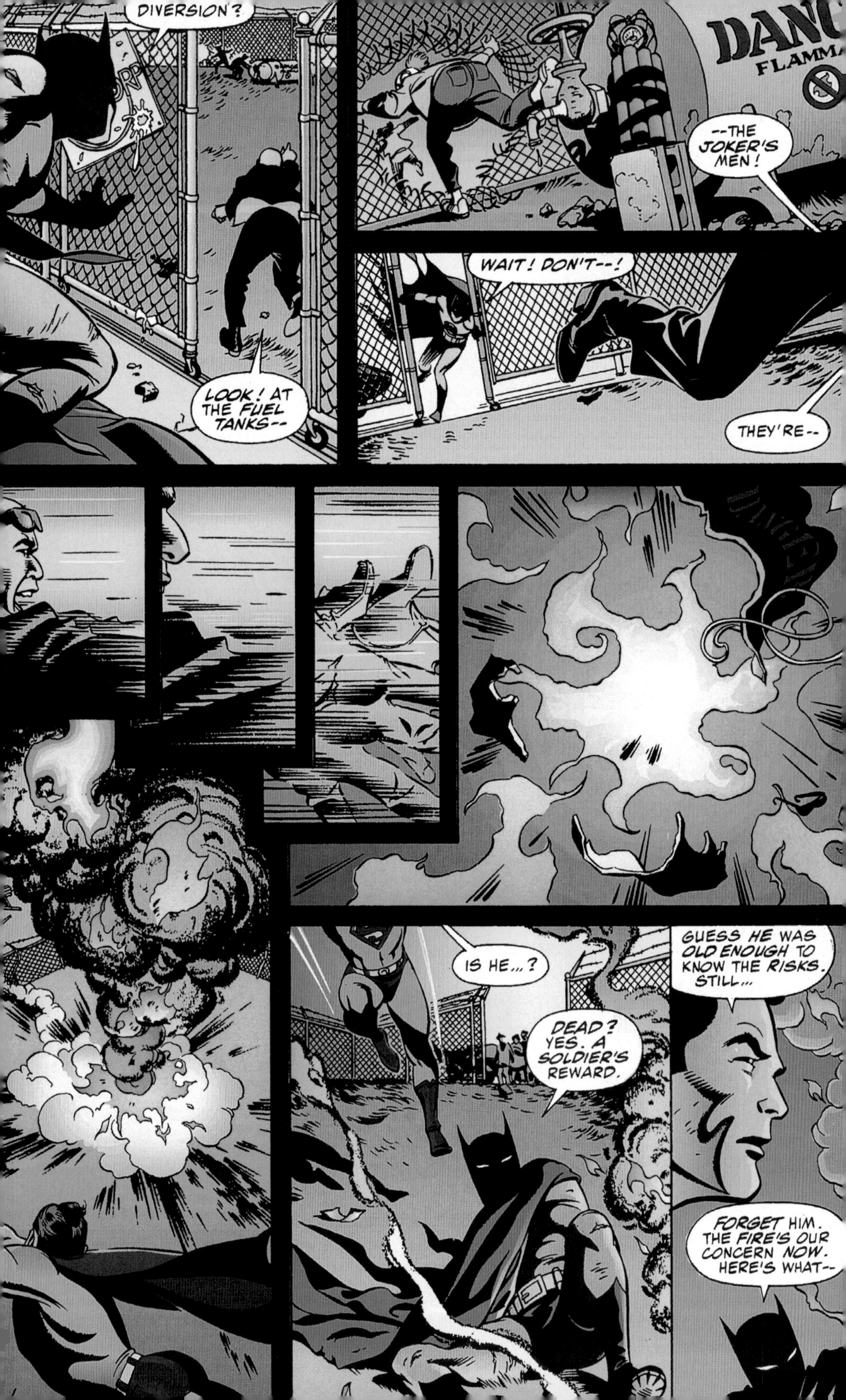
DIVERSION?
LOOK! AT THE FUEL TANKS--
--THE JOKER'S MEN!
WAIT! DON'T--!
THEY'RE--
IS HE...?
DEAD? YES. A SOLDIER'S REWARD.
GUESS HE WAS OLD ENOUGH TO KNOW THE RISKS. STILL...
FORGET HIM. THE FIRE'S OUR CONCERN NOW. HERE'S WHAT--

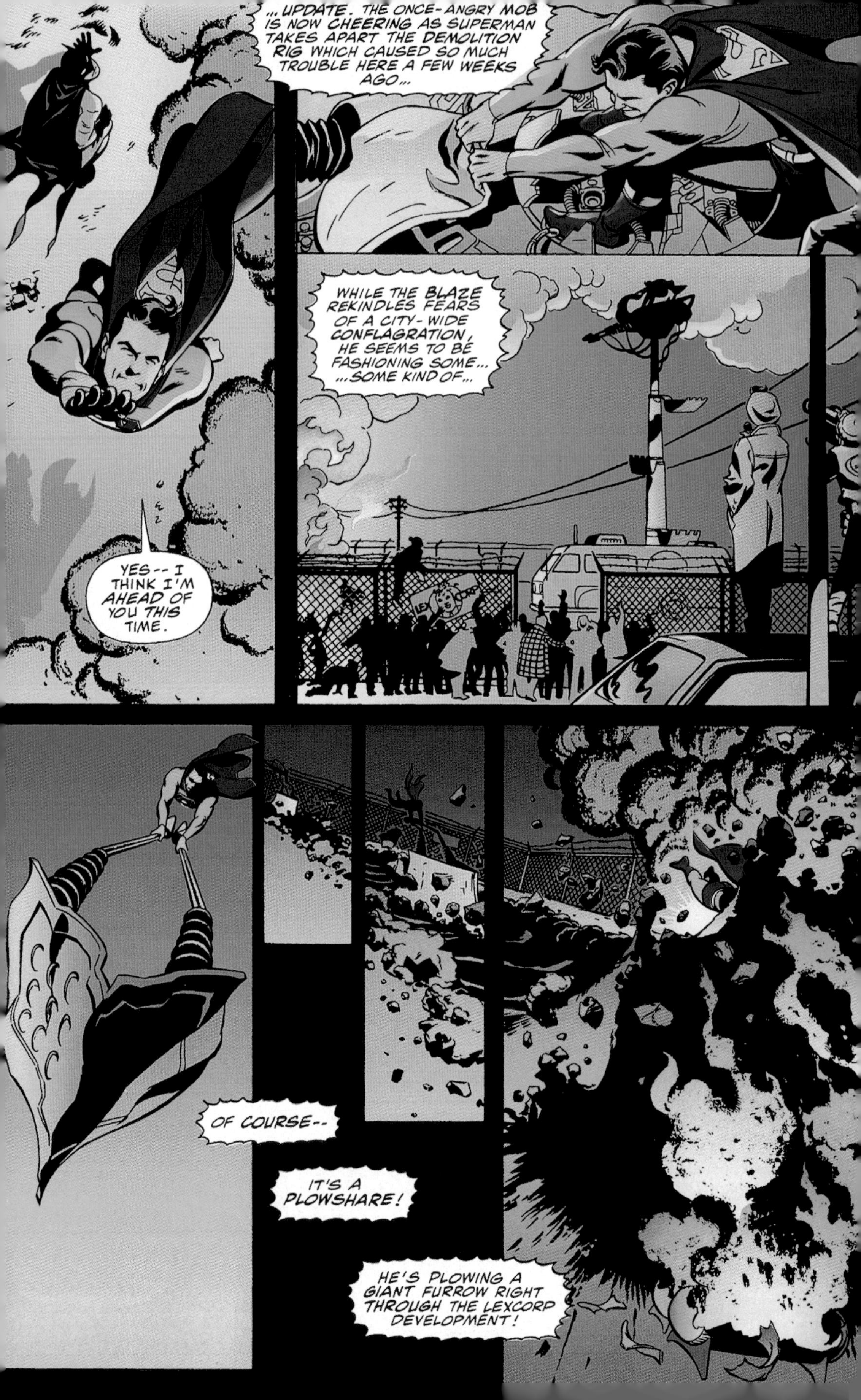
...UPDATE. THE ONCE-ANGRY MOB IS NOW CHEERING AS SUPERMAN TAKES APART THE DEMOLITION RIG WHICH CAUSED SO MUCH TROUBLE HERE A FEW WEEKS AGO...
YES-- I THINK I'M AHEAD OF YOU THIS TIME.
WHILE THE BLAZE REKINDLES FEARS OF A CITY-WIDE CONFLAGRATION, HE SEEMS TO BE FASHIONING SOME... ...SOME KIND OF...
OF COURSE--
IT'S A PLOWSHARE!
HE'S PLOWING A GIANT FURROW RIGHT THROUGH THE LEXCORP DEVELOPMENT!

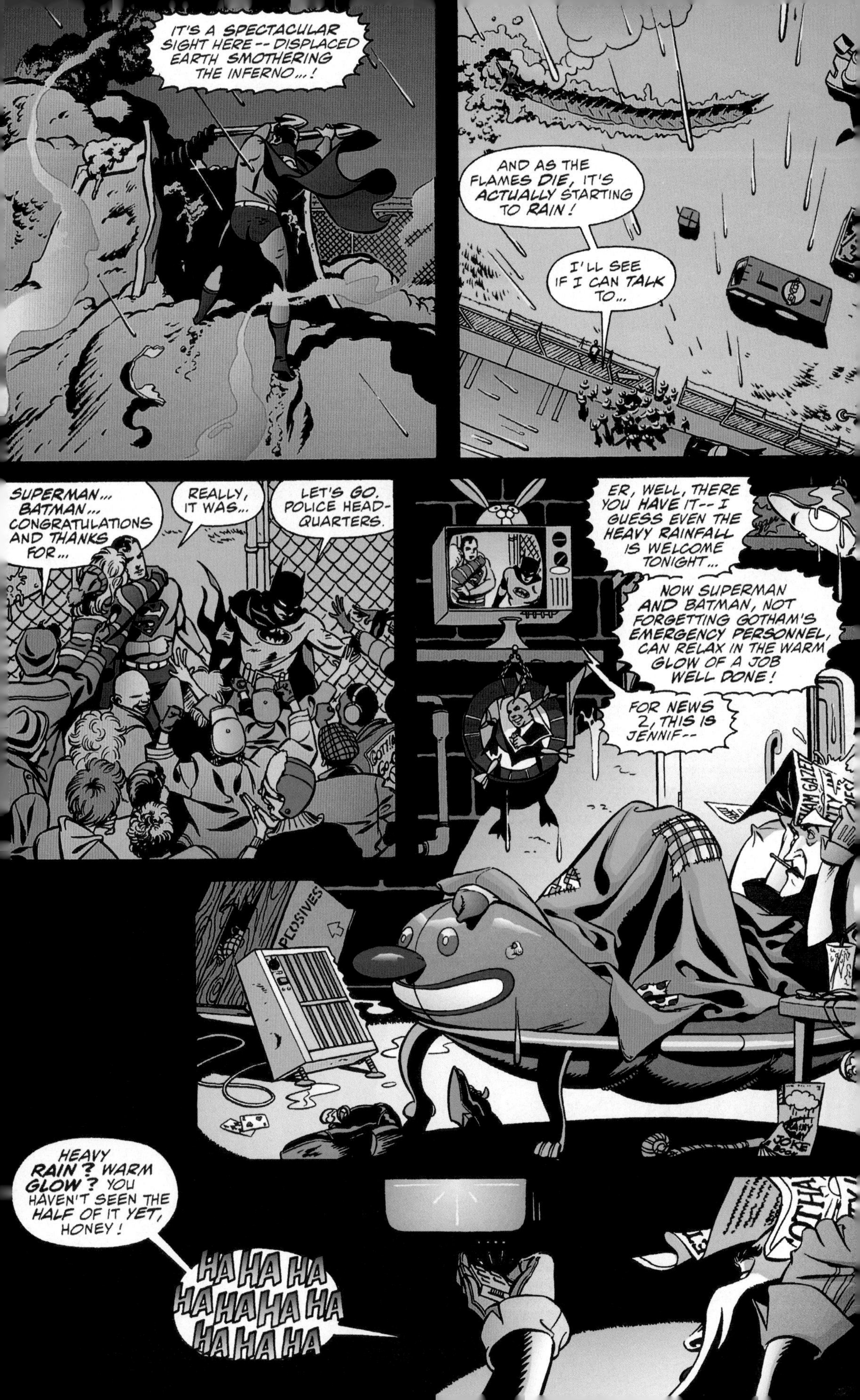
IT'S A SPECTACULAR SIGHT HERE -- DISPLACED EARTH SMOTHERING THE INFERNO...!
AND AS THE FLAMES DIE, IT'S ACTUALLY STARTING TO RAIN!
I'LL SEE IF I CAN TALK TO...
SUPERMAN... BATMAN... CONGRATULATIONS AND THANKS FOR...
REALLY, IT WAS...
LET'S GO. POLICE HEAD-QUARTERS.
ER, WELL, THERE YOU HAVE IT-- I GUESS EVEN THE HEAVY RAINFALL IS WELCOME TONIGHT...
NOW SUPERMAN AND BATMAN, NOT FORGETTING GOTHAM'S EMERGENCY PERSONNEL, CAN RELAX IN THE WARM GLOW OF A JOB WELL DONE!
FOR NEWS 2, THIS IS JENNIF--
HEAVY RAIN? WARM GLOW? YOU HAVEN'T SEEN THE HALF OF IT YET, HONEY!
HA HA HA HA HA HA HA HA HA HA HA HA

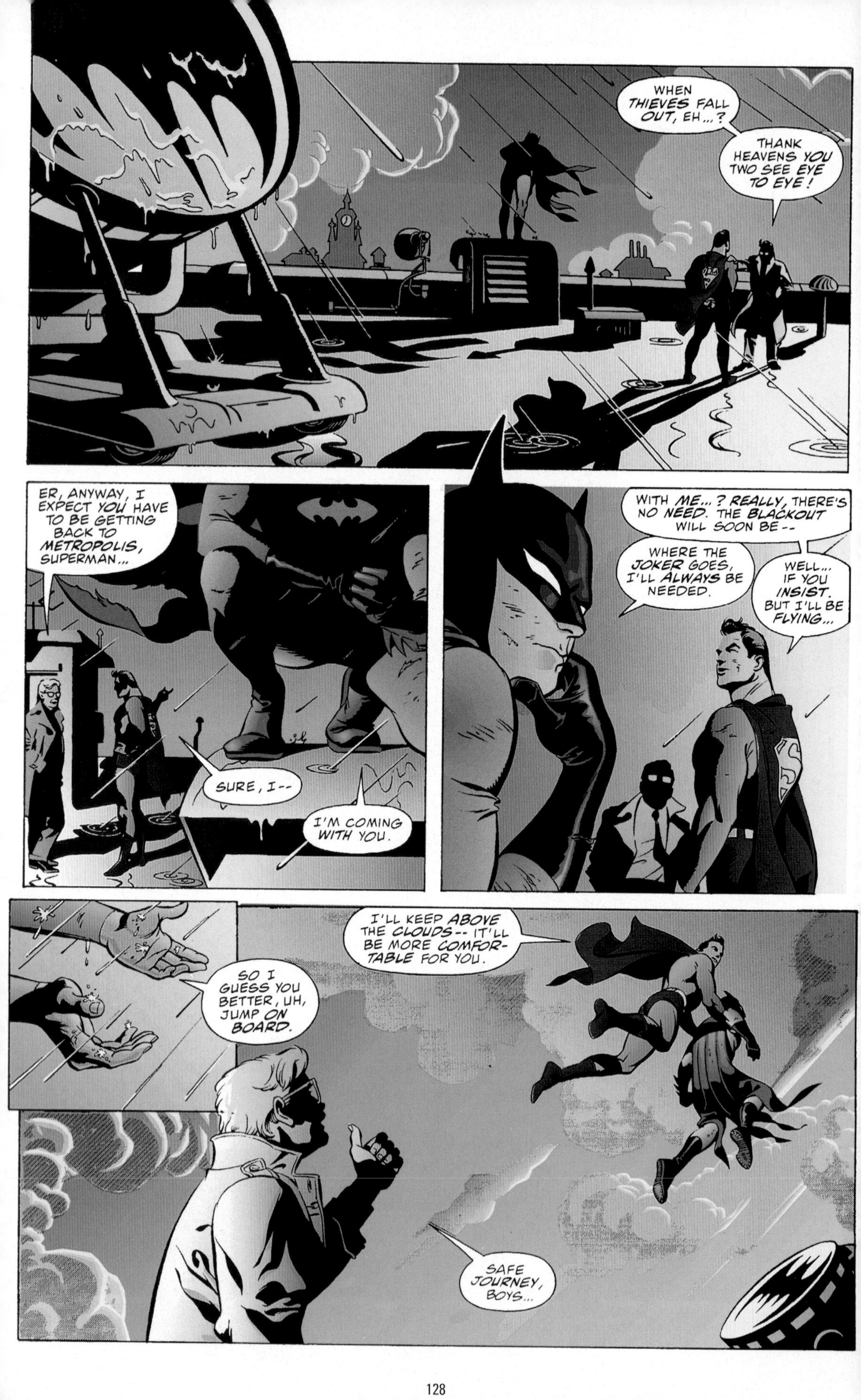
WHEN THIEVES FALL OUT, EH...?
THANK HEAVENS YOU TWO SEE EYE TO EYE!
ER, ANYWAY, I EXPECT YOU HAVE TO BE GETTING BACK TO METROPOLIS, SUPERMAN...
SURE, I--
I'M COMING WITH YOU.
WITH ME...? REALLY, THERE'S NO NEED. THE BLACKOUT WILL SOON BE--
WHERE THE JOKER GOES, I'LL ALWAYS BE NEEDED.
WELL... IF YOU INSIST. BUT I'LL BE FLYING...
SO I GUESS YOU BETTER, UH, JUMP ON BOARD.
I'LL KEEP ABOVE THE CLOUDS-- IT'LL BE MORE COMFORTABLE FOR YOU.
SAFE JOURNEY, BOYS...

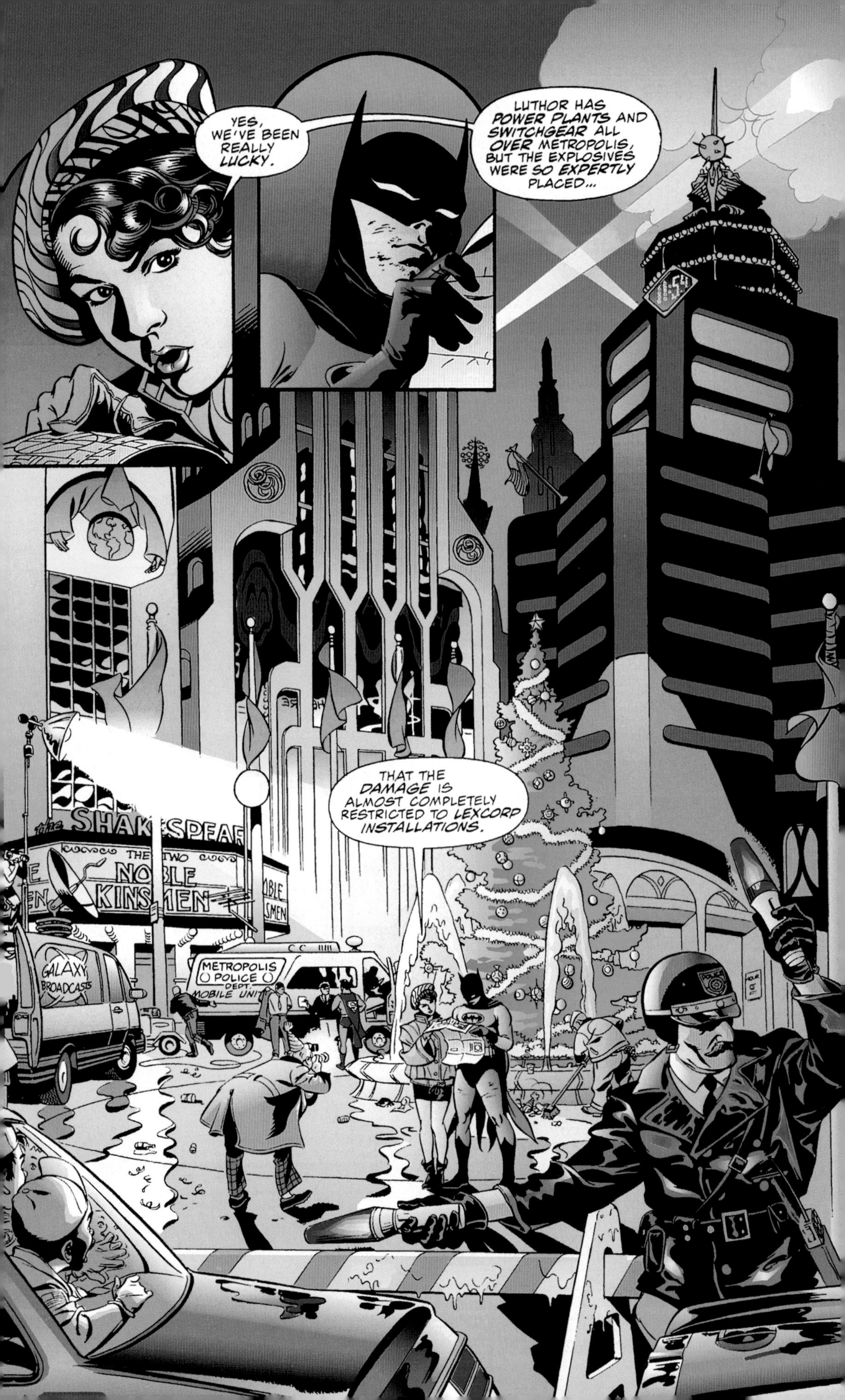
YES, WE'VE BEEN REALLY LUCKY.
LUTHOR HAS POWER PLANTS AND SWITCHGEAR ALL OVER METROPOLIS, BUT THE EXPLOSIVES WERE SO EXPERTLY PLACED...
THAT THE DAMAGE IS ALMOST COMPLETELY RESTRICTED TO LEXCORP INSTALLATIONS.
the SHAKESPEAR
THE TWO NOBLE KINSMEN
GALAXY BROADCASTS
METROPOLIS POLICE DEPT. MOBILE UNIT

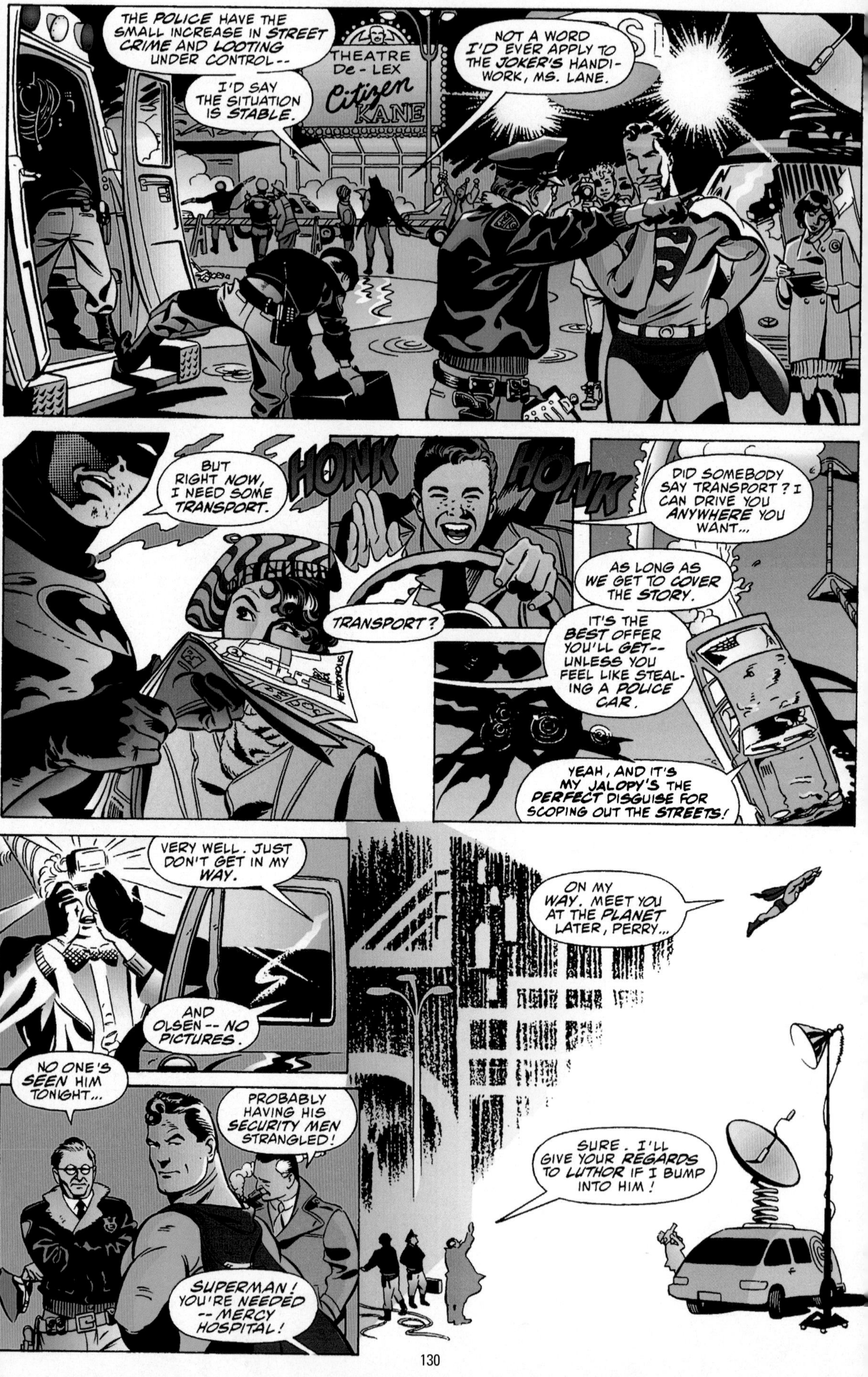
THE POLICE HAVE THE SMALL INCREASE IN STREET CRIME AND LOOTING UNDER CONTROL--
THEATRE De-LEX
Citizen KANE
I'D SAY THE SITUATION IS STABLE.
NOT A WORD I'D EVER APPLY TO THE JOKER'S HANDIWORK, MS. LANE.
BUT RIGHT NOW, I NEED SOME TRANSPORT.
HONK
HONK
METROPOLIS
TRANSPORT?
DID SOMEBODY SAY TRANSPORT? I CAN DRIVE YOU ANYWHERE YOU WANT...
AS LONG AS WE GET TO COVER THE STORY.
IT'S THE BEST OFFER YOU'LL GET-- UNLESS YOU FEEL LIKE STEALING A POLICE CAR.
YEAH, AND IT'S MY JALOPY'S THE PERFECT DISGUISE FOR SCOPING OUT THE STREETS!
VERY WELL. JUST DON'T GET IN MY WAY.
AND OLSEN -- NO PICTURES.
NO ONE'S SEEN HIM TONIGHT...
PROBABLY HAVING HIS SECURITY MEN STRANGLED!
SUPERMAN! YOU'RE NEEDED -- MERCY HOSPITAL!
ON MY WAY. MEET YOU AT THE PLANET LATER, PERRY...
SURE. I'LL GIVE YOUR REGARDS TO LUTHOR IF I BUMP INTO HIM!

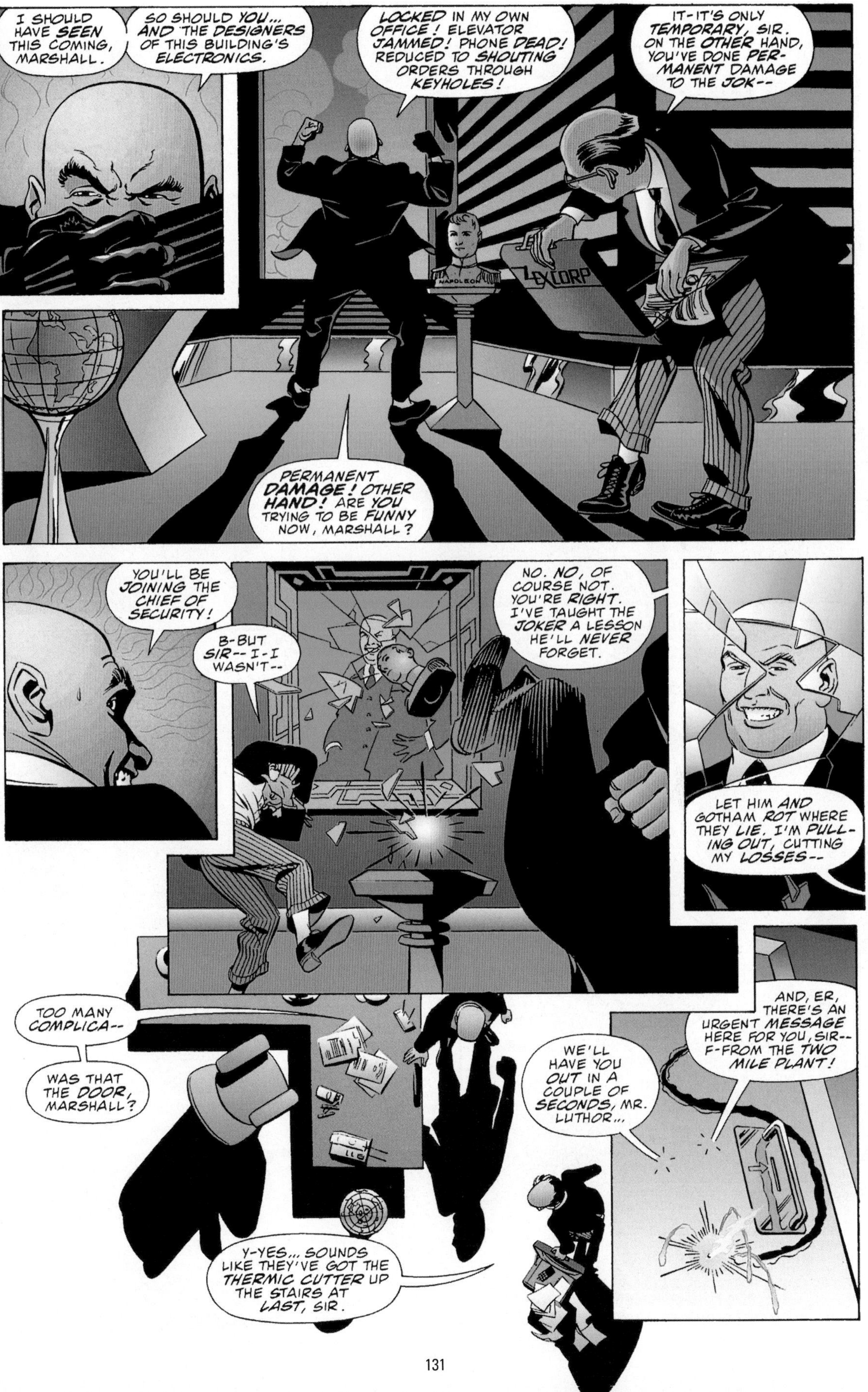
I SHOULD HAVE SEEN THIS COMING, MARSHALL.
SO SHOULD YOU... AND THE DESIGNERS OF THIS BUILDING'S ELECTRONICS.
LOCKED IN MY OWN OFFICE! ELEVATOR JAMMED! PHONE DEAD! REDUCED TO SHOUTING ORDERS THROUGH KEYHOLES!
IT-IT'S ONLY TEMPORARY, SIR. ON THE OTHER HAND, YOU'VE DONE PERMANENT DAMAGE TO THE JOK--
NAPOLEON
LEXCORP
PERMANENT DAMAGE! OTHER HAND! ARE YOU TRYING TO BE FUNNY NOW, MARSHALL?
YOU'LL BE JOINING THE CHIEF OF SECURITY!
B-BUT SIR-- I-I WASN'T--
NO. NO, OF COURSE NOT. YOU'RE RIGHT. I'VE TAUGHT THE JOKER A LESSON HE'LL NEVER FORGET.
LET HIM AND GOTHAM ROT WHERE THEY LIE. I'M PULLING OUT, CUTTING MY LOSSES--
TOO MANY COMPLICA--
WAS THAT THE DOOR, MARSHALL?
WE'LL HAVE YOU OUT IN A COUPLE OF SECONDS, MR. LUTHOR...
AND, ER, THERE'S AN URGENT MESSAGE HERE FOR YOU, SIR-- F-FROM THE TWO MILE PLANT!
Y-YES... SOUNDS LIKE THEY'VE GOT THE THERMIC CUTTER UP THE STAIRS AT LAST, SIR.

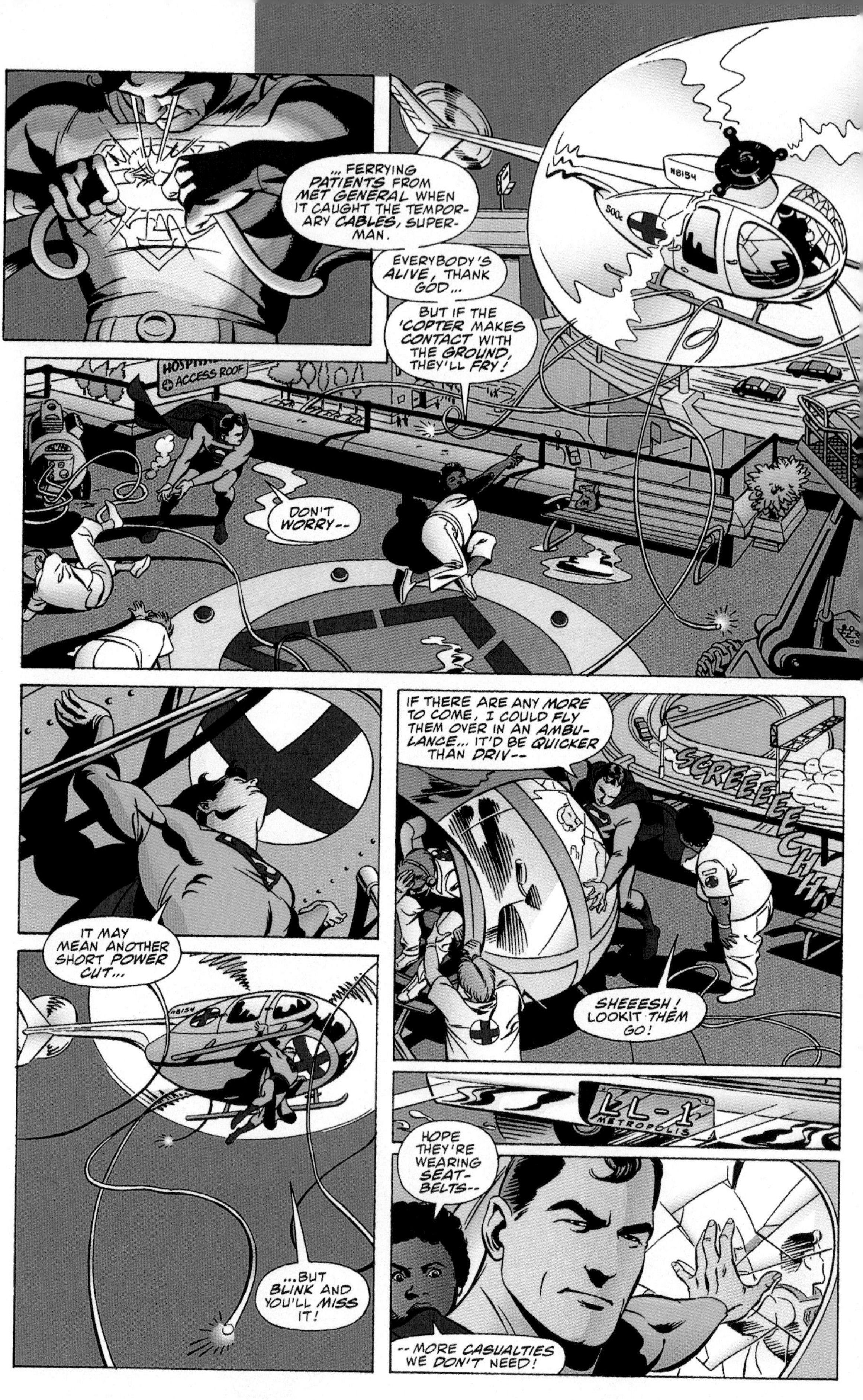
...FERRYING PATIENTS FROM MET GENERAL WHEN IT CAUGHT THE TEMPORARY CABLES, SUPERMAN.
N8154
EVERYBODY'S ALIVE, THANK GOD...
BUT IF THE 'COPTER MAKES CONTACT WITH THE GROUND, THEY'LL FRY!
ACCESS ROOF
DON'T WORRY--
IT MAY MEAN ANOTHER SHORT POWER CUT...
...BUT BLINK AND YOU'LL MISS IT!
IF THERE ARE ANY MORE TO COME, I COULD FLY THEM OVER IN AN AMBULANCE... IT'D BE QUICKER THAN DRIV--
SCREEEEECH
SHEEESH! LOOKIT THEM GO!
LL-1
METROPOLIS
HOPE THEY'RE WEARING SEAT-BELTS--
--MORE CASUALTIES WE DON'T NEED!

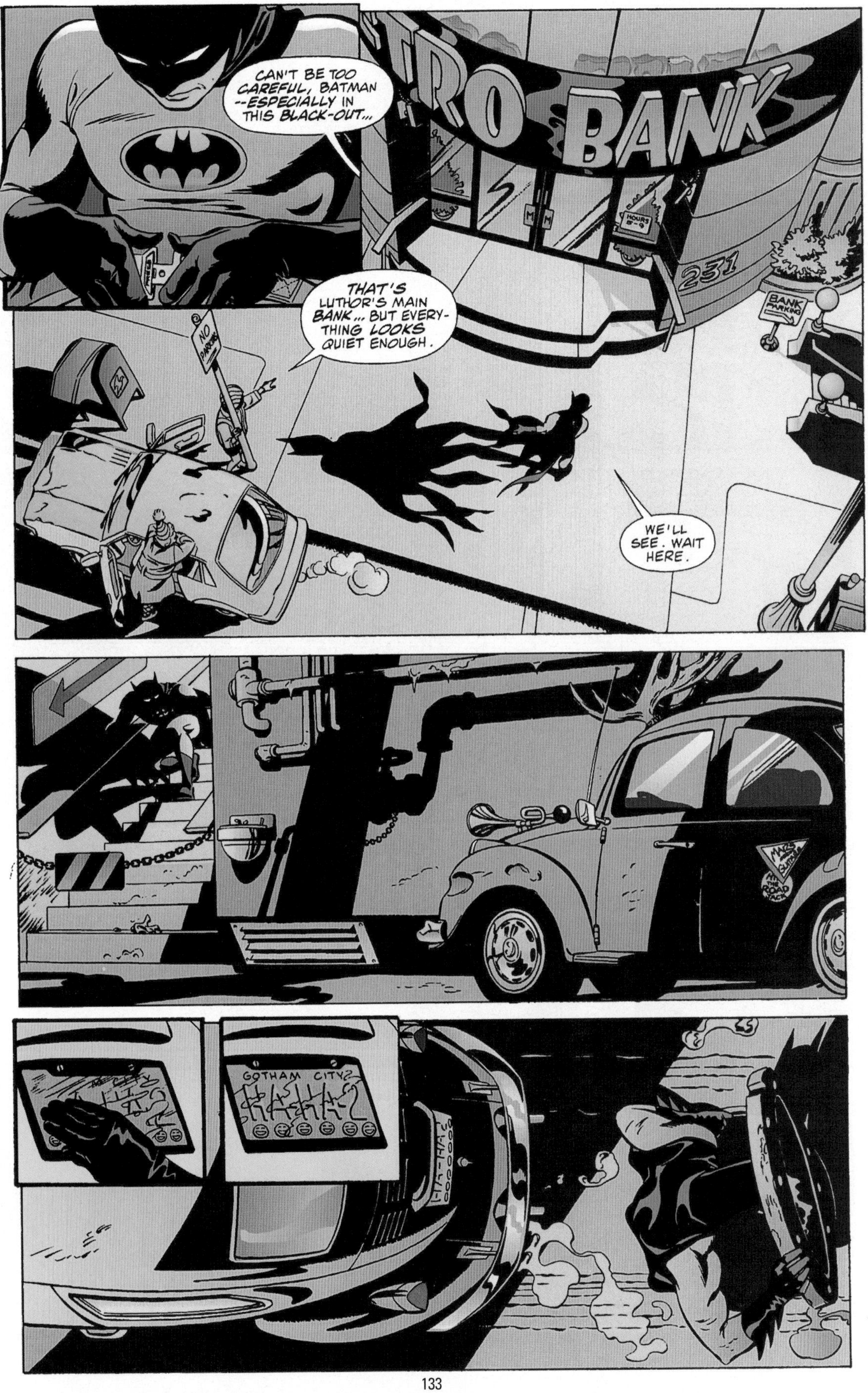
CAN'T BE TOO CAREFUL, BATMAN --ESPECIALLY IN THIS BLACK-OUT...
TRO BANK
231
NO PARKING
BANK PARKING
THAT'S LUTHOR'S MAIN BANK... BUT EVERY-THING LOOKS QUIET ENOUGH.
WE'LL SEE. WAIT HERE.
GOTHAM CITY

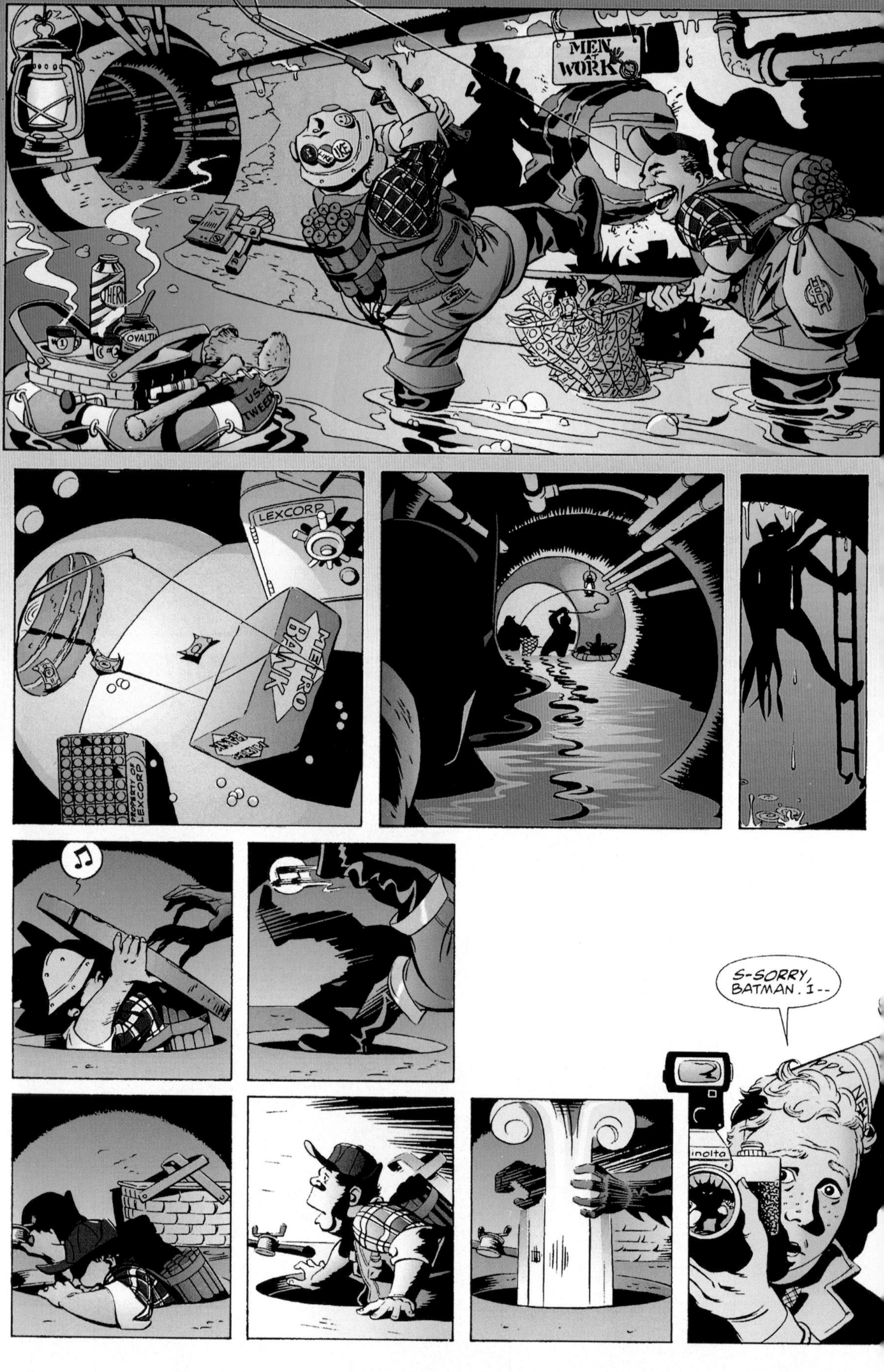
MEN AT WORK
USS TWEED
LEXCORP
METRO BANK
PROPERTY OF LEXCORP
S-SORRY, BATMAN. I--

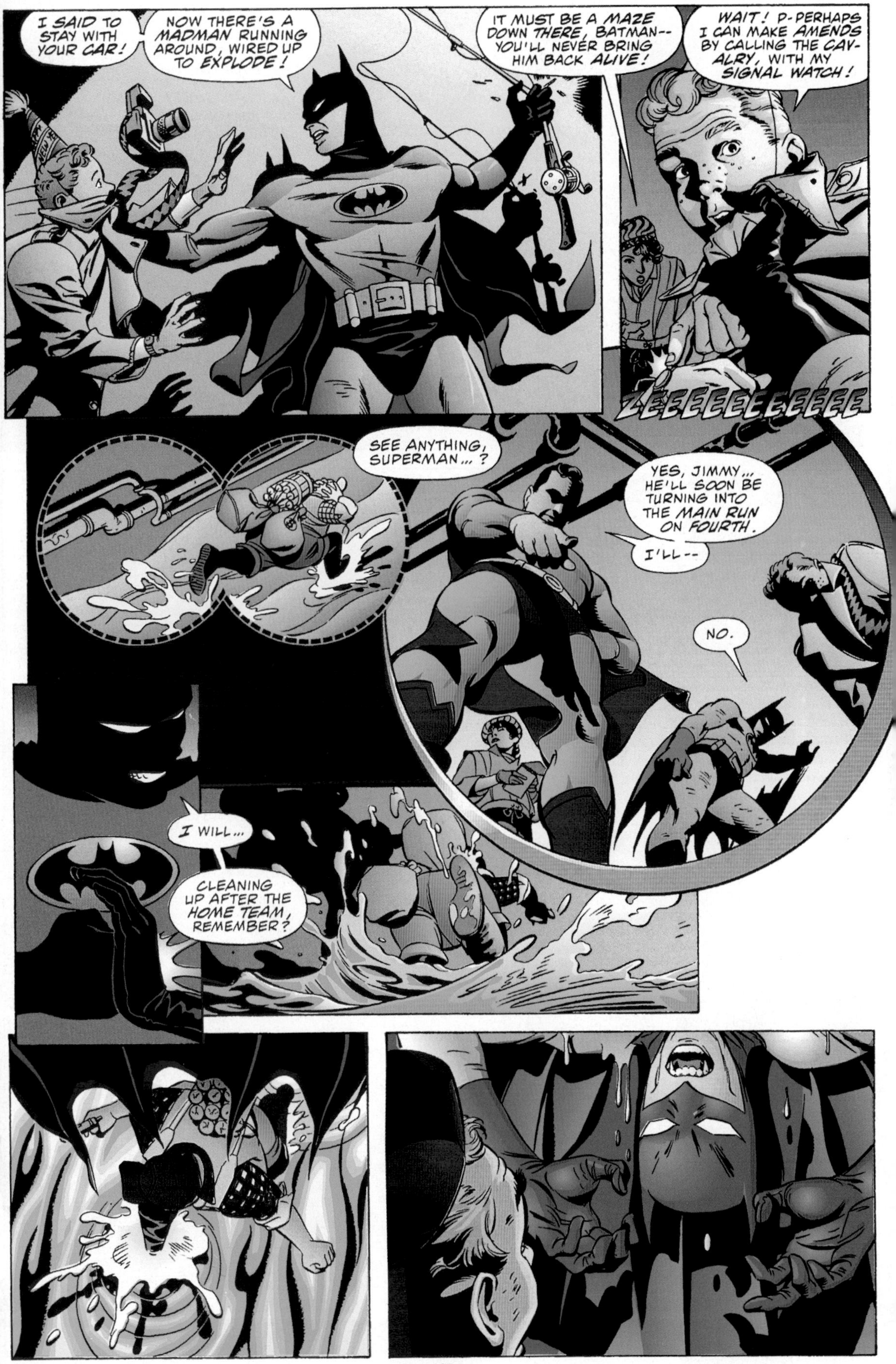

I SAID TO STAY WITH YOUR CAR!
NOW THERE'S A MADMAN RUNNING AROUND, WIRED UP TO EXPLODE!
IT MUST BE A MAZE DOWN THERE, BATMAN-- YOU'LL NEVER BRING HIM BACK ALIVE!
WAIT! P-PERHAPS I CAN MAKE AMENDS BY CALLING THE CAV-ALRY, WITH MY SIGNAL WATCH!
ZEEEEEEEEEEEE
SEE ANYTHING, SUPERMAN...?
YES, JIMMY... HE'LL SOON BE TURNING INTO THE MAIN RUN ON FOURTH.
I'LL--
NO.
I WILL...
CLEANING UP AFTER THE HOME TEAM, REMEMBER?

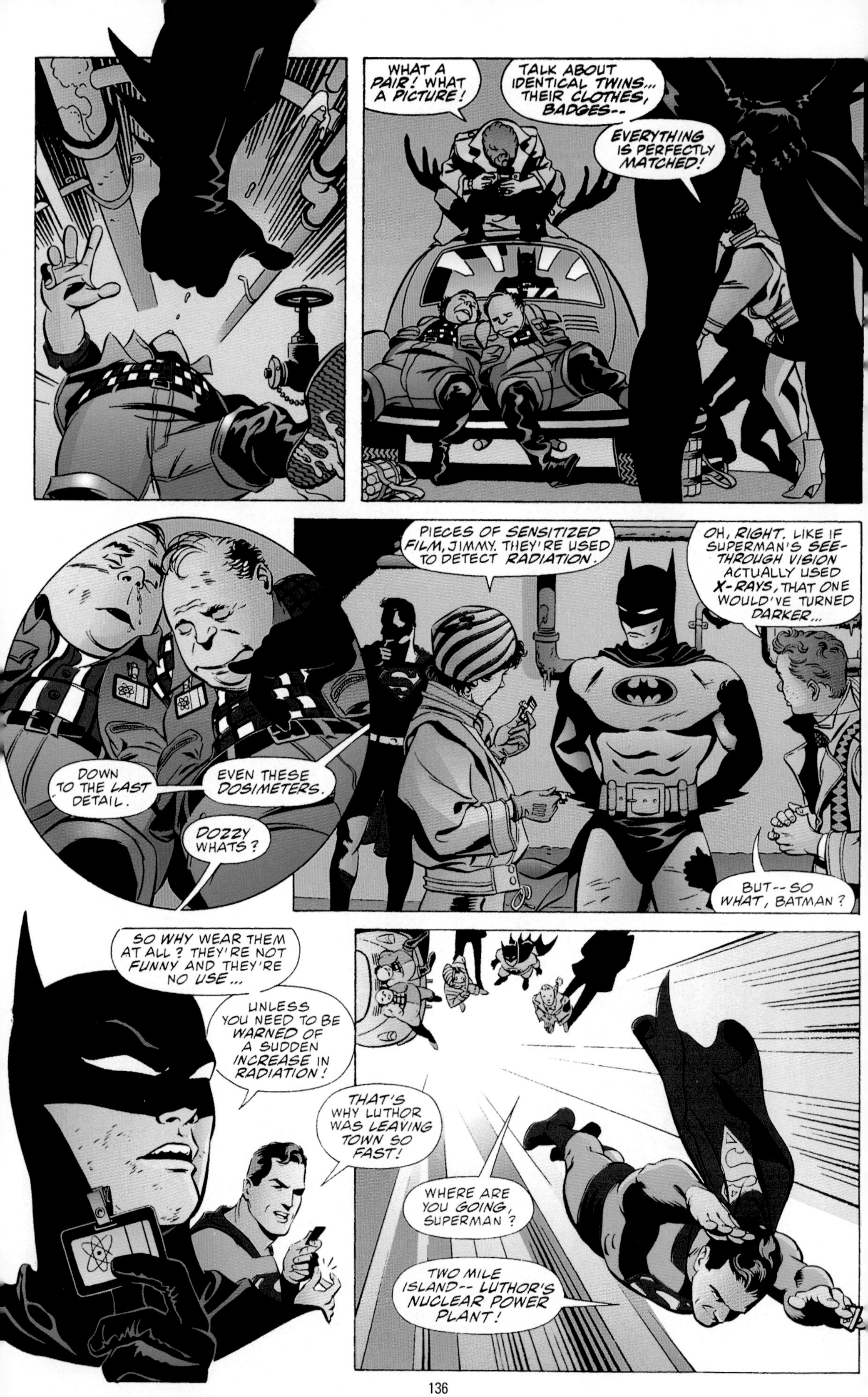
WHAT A PAIR! WHAT A PICTURE!
TALK ABOUT IDENTICAL TWINS... THEIR CLOTHES, BADGES--
EVERYTHING IS PERFECTLY MATCHED!
DOWN TO THE LAST DETAIL.
EVEN THESE DOSIMETERS.
DOZZY WHATS?
PIECES OF SENSITIZED FILM, JIMMY. THEY'RE USED TO DETECT RADIATION.
OH, RIGHT. LIKE IF SUPERMAN'S SEE-THROUGH VISION ACTUALLY USED X-RAYS, THAT ONE WOULD'VE TURNED DARKER...
BUT--SO WHAT, BATMAN?
SO WHY WEAR THEM AT ALL? THEY'RE NOT FUNNY AND THEY'RE NO USE...
UNLESS YOU NEED TO BE WARNED OF A SUDDEN INCREASE IN RADIATION!
THAT'S WHY LUTHOR WAS LEAVING TOWN SO FAST!
WHERE ARE YOU GOING, SUPERMAN?
TWO MILE ISLAND-- LUTHOR'S NUCLEAR POWER PLANT!

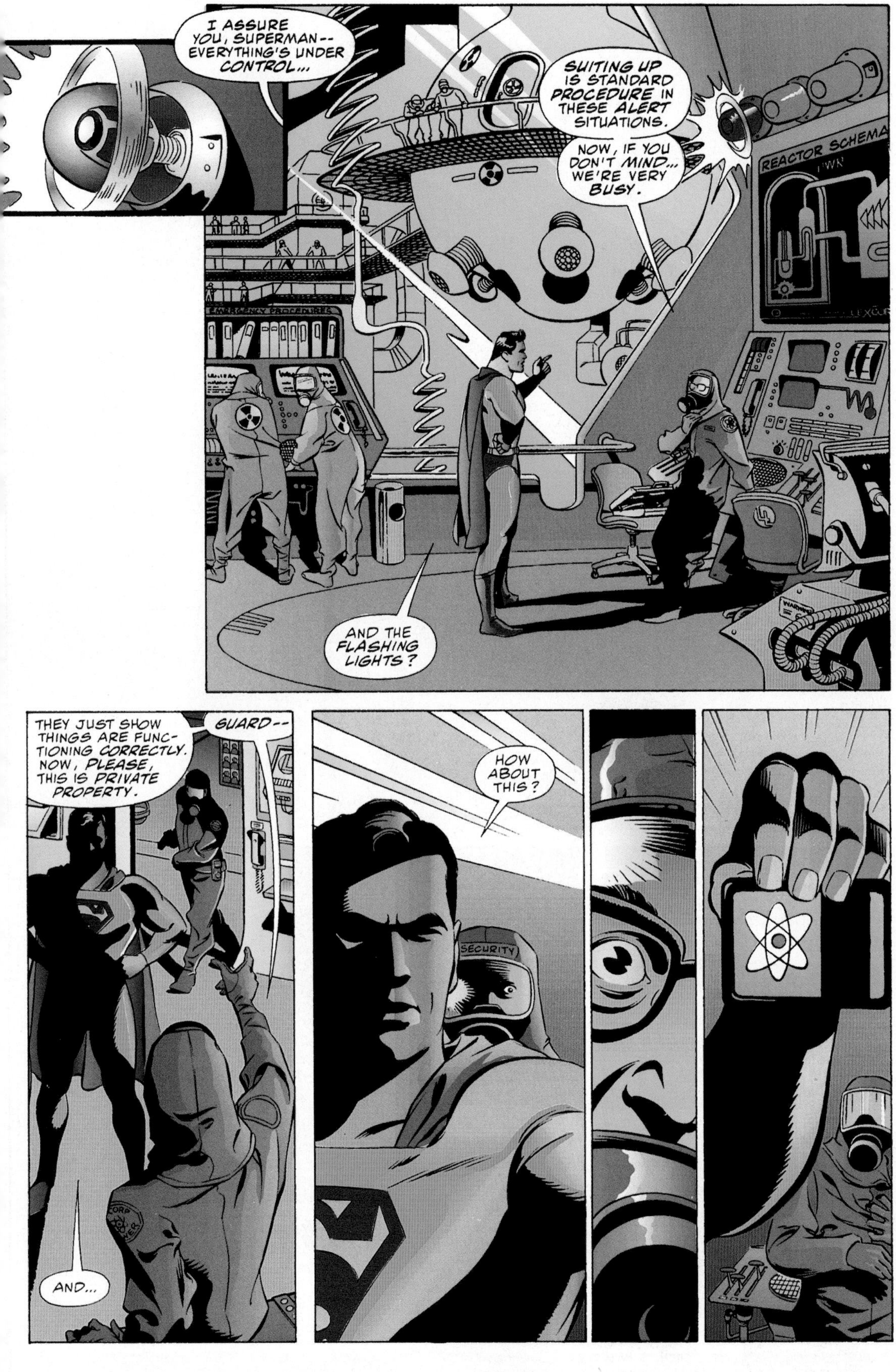
I ASSURE YOU, SUPERMAN-- EVERYTHING'S UNDER CONTROL...
SUITING UP IS STANDARD PROCEDURE IN THESE ALERT SITUATIONS.
NOW, IF YOU DON'T MIND... WE'RE VERY BUSY.
AND THE FLASHING LIGHTS?
THEY JUST SHOW THINGS ARE FUNCTIONING CORRECTLY. NOW, PLEASE, THIS IS PRIVATE PROPERTY.
GUARD--
AND...
HOW ABOUT THIS?
SECURITY

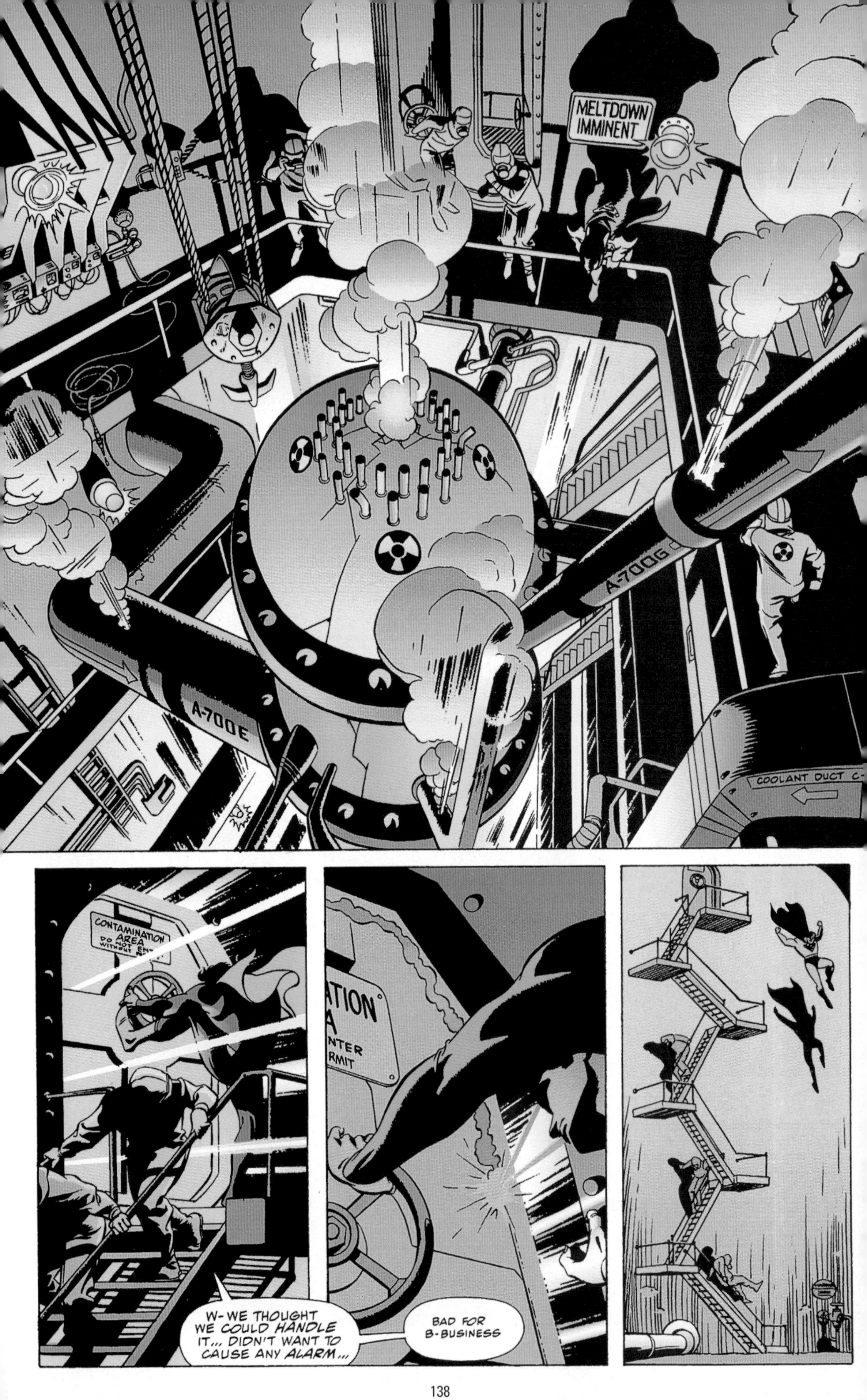
MELTDOWN IMMINENT
A-700G
A-700E
COOLANT DUCT C-
CONTAMINATION AREA
W-WE THOUGHT WE COULD HANDLE IT... DIDN'T WANT TO CAUSE ANY ALARM...
BAD FOR B-BUSINESS

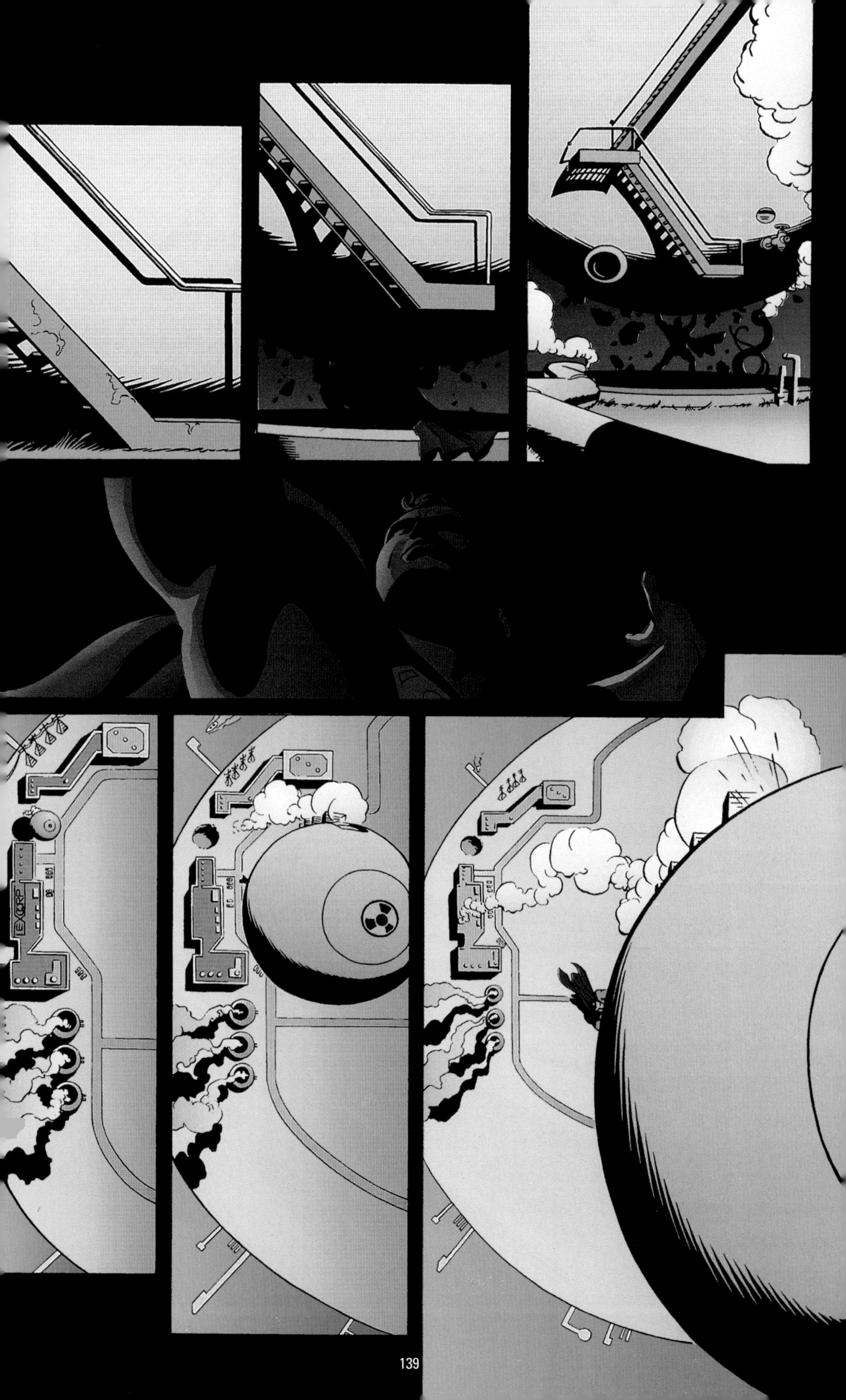
LEXCORP

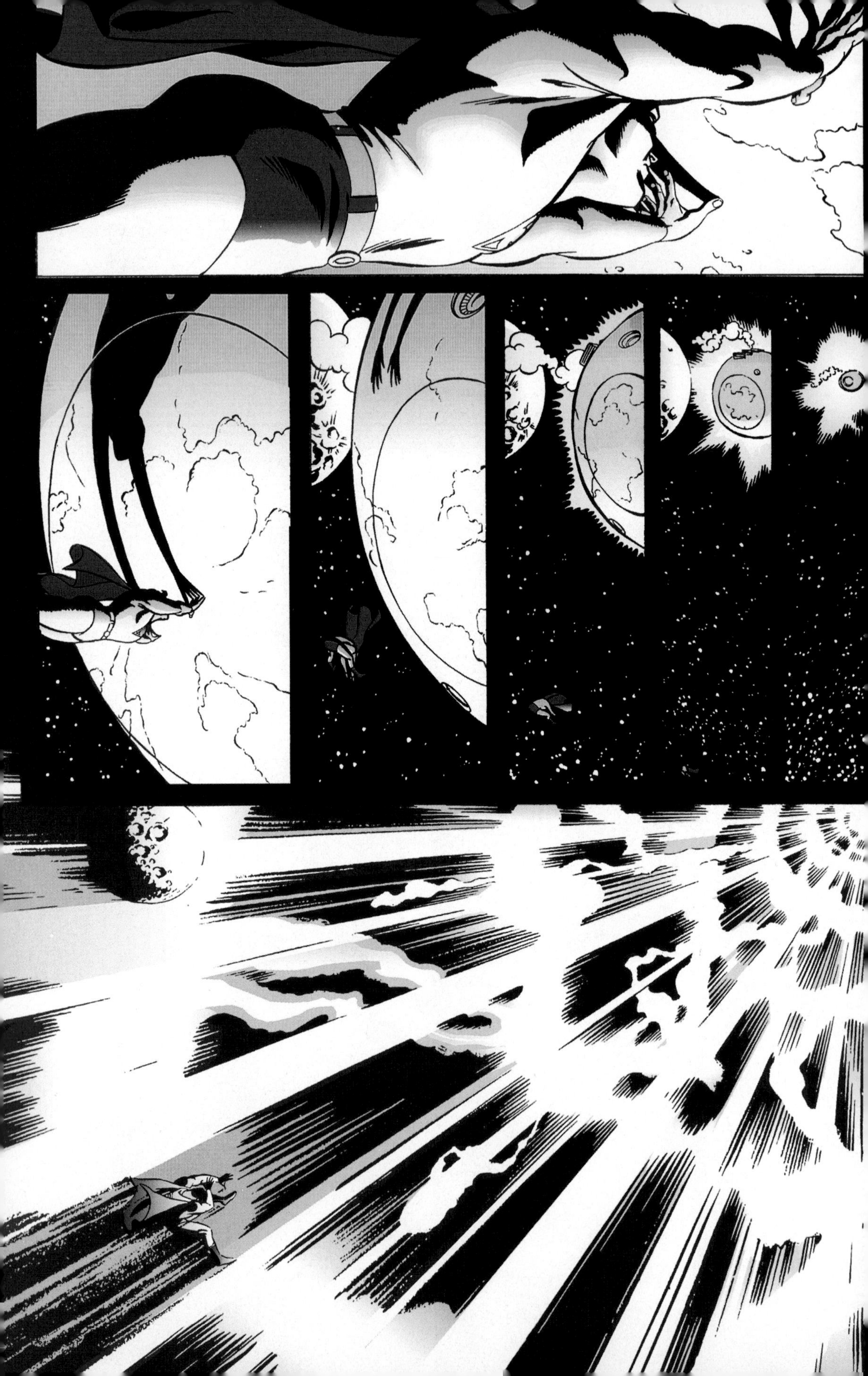

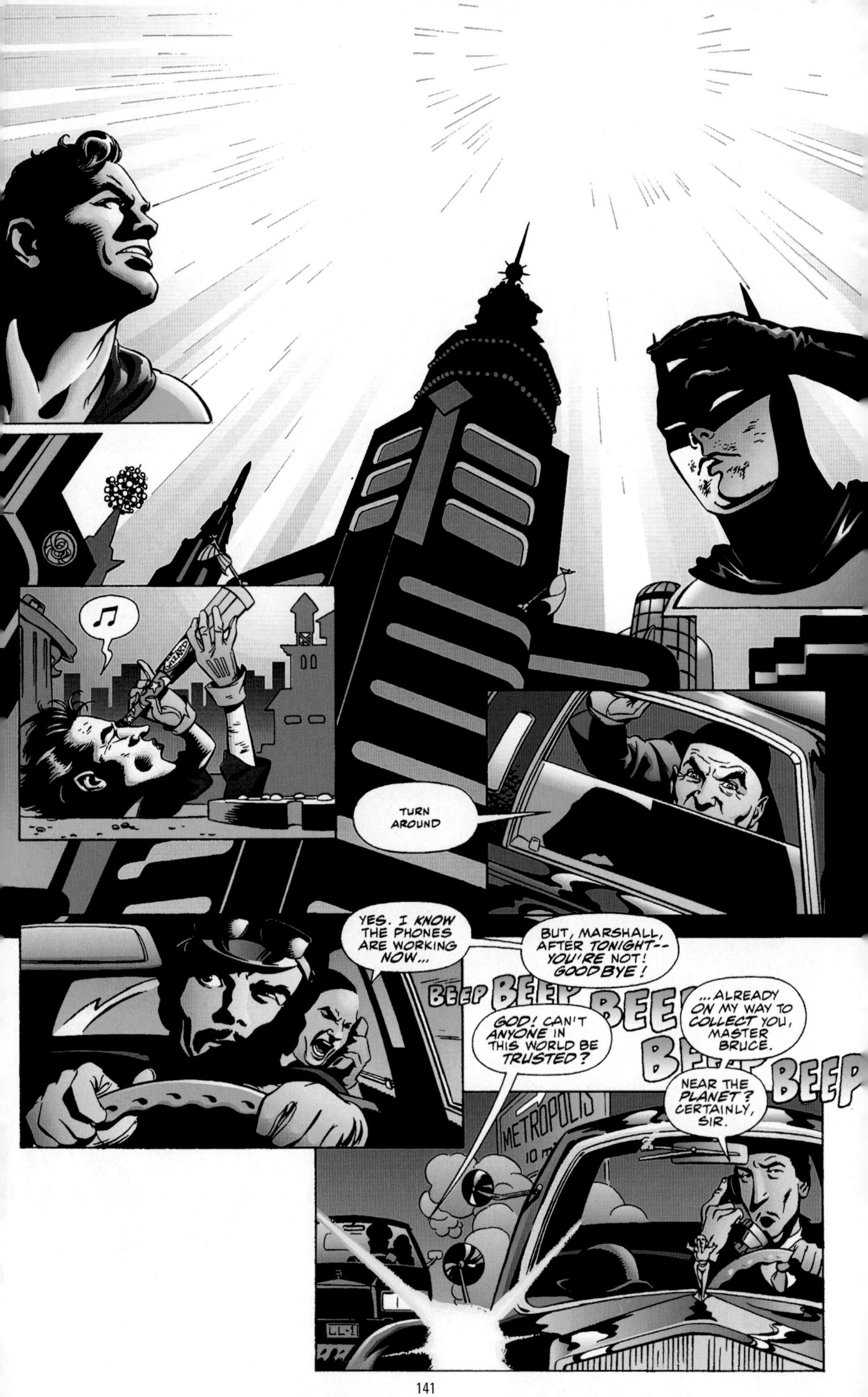

♫
TURN AROUND
YES. I KNOW THE PHONES ARE WORKING NOW...
BUT, MARSHALL, AFTER TONIGHT-- YOU'RE NOT! GOODBYE!
BEEP BEEP BEEP BEEP BEEP
GOD! CAN'T ANYONE IN THIS WORLD BE TRUSTED?
...ALREADY ON MY WAY TO COLLECT YOU, MASTER BRUCE.
NEAR THE PLANET? CERTAINLY, SIR.
METROPOLIS
LL-1

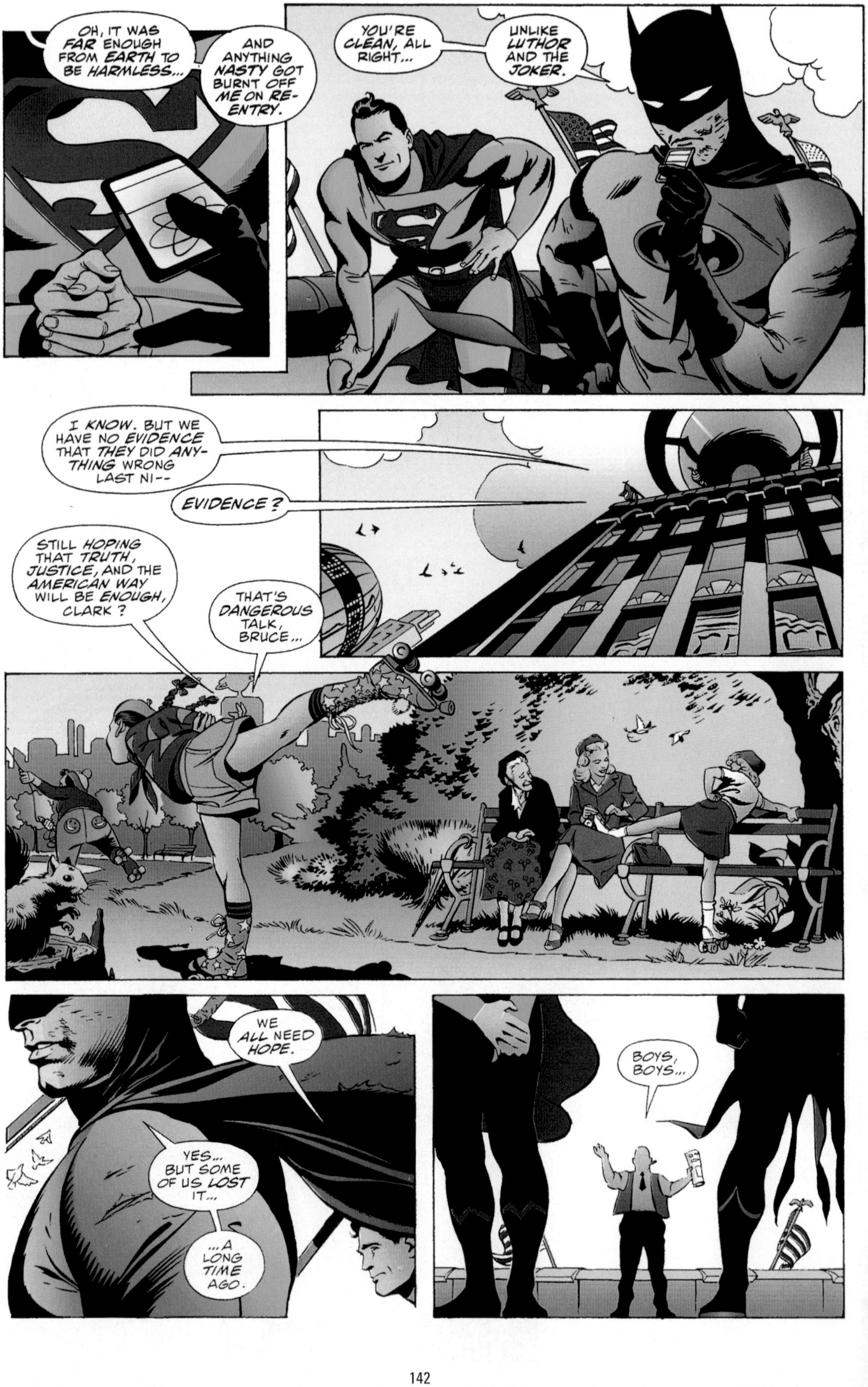
OH, IT WAS FAR ENOUGH FROM EARTH TO BE HARMLESS...
AND ANYTHING NASTY GOT BURNT OFF ME ON RE-ENTRY.
YOU'RE CLEAN, ALL RIGHT...
UNLIKE LUTHOR AND THE JOKER.
I KNOW. BUT WE HAVE NO EVIDENCE THAT THEY DID ANYTHING WRONG LAST NI--
EVIDENCE?
STILL HOPING THAT TRUTH, JUSTICE, AND THE AMERICAN WAY WILL BE ENOUGH, CLARK?
THAT'S DANGEROUS TALK, BRUCE...
WE ALL NEED HOPE.
YES... BUT SOME OF US LOST IT...
...A LONG TIME AGO.
BOYS, BOYS...

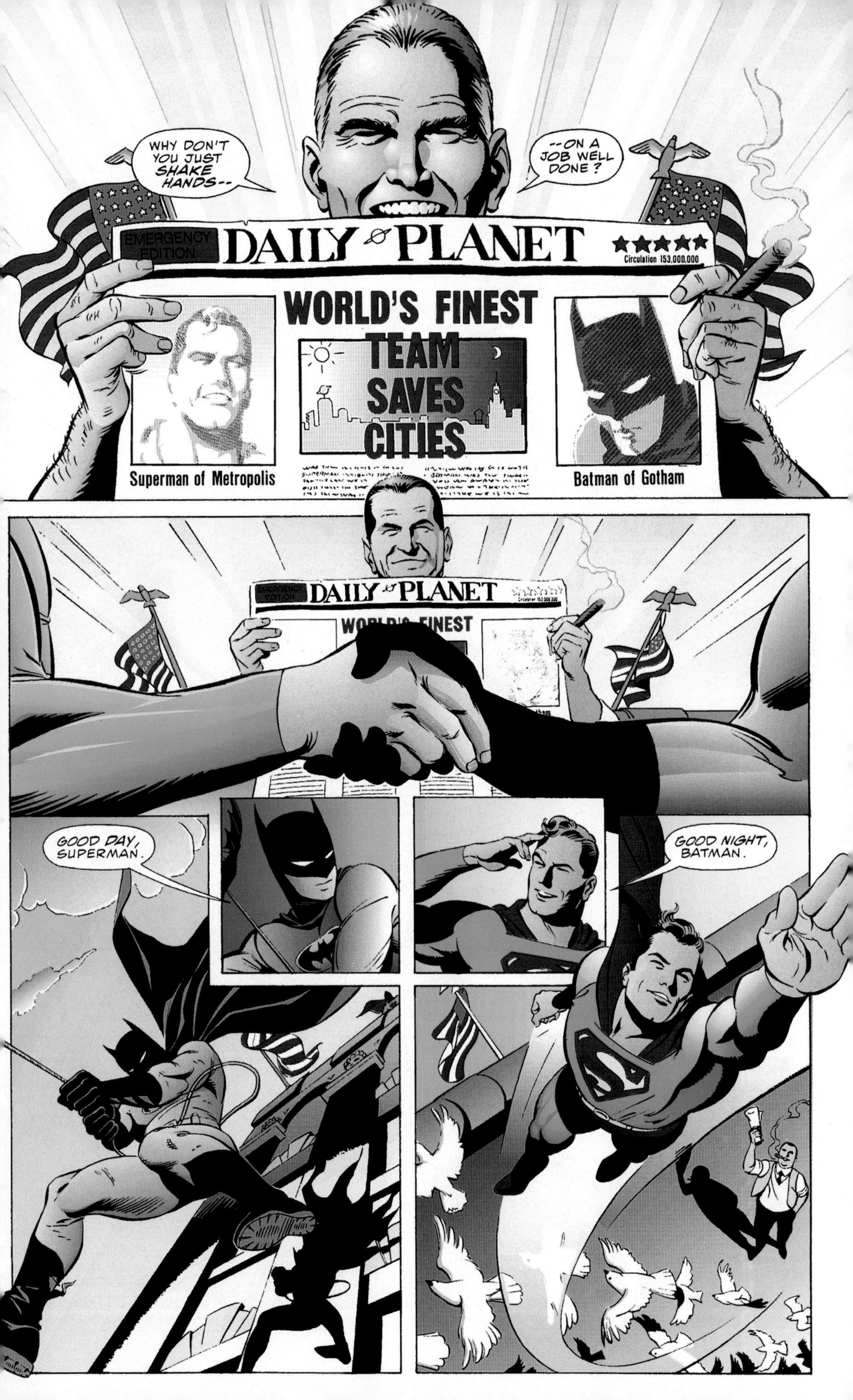
WHY DON'T YOU JUST SHAKE HANDS--
--ON A JOB WELL DONE?
EMERGENCY EDITION
DAILY PLANET
Circulation 153,000,000
WORLD'S FINEST
TEAM SAVES CITIES
Superman of Metropolis
Batman of Gotham
GOOD DAY, SUPERMAN.
GOOD NIGHT, BATMAN.

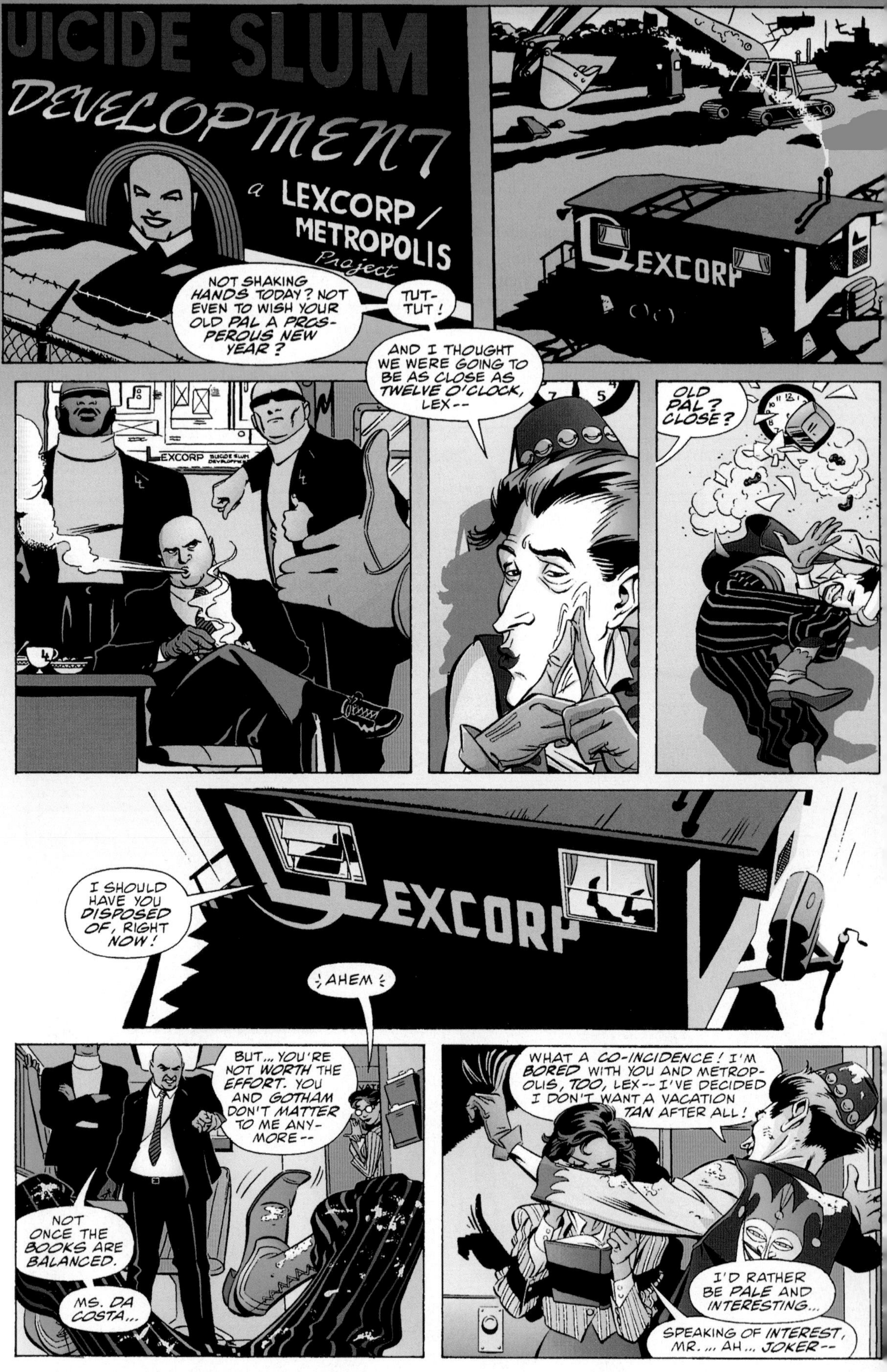
UICIDE SLUM
DEVELOPMENT
a LEXCORP/ METROPOLIS Project
LEXCORP
NOT SHAKING HANDS TODAY? NOT EVEN TO WISH YOUR OLD PAL A PROS-PEROUS NEW YEAR?
TUT-TUT!
AND I THOUGHT WE WERE GOING TO BE AS CLOSE AS TWELVE O'CLOCK, LEX--
LEXCORP SUICIDE SLUM DEVELOPMENT
OLD PAL? CLOSE?
I SHOULD HAVE YOU DISPOSED OF, RIGHT NOW!
LEXCORP
AHEM
BUT... YOU'RE NOT WORTH THE EFFORT. YOU AND GOTHAM DON'T MATTER TO ME ANY-MORE--
NOT ONCE THE BOOKS ARE BALANCED.
MS. DA COSTA...
WHAT A CO-INCIDENCE! I'M BORED WITH YOU AND METROP-OLIS, TOO, LEX-- I'VE DECIDED I DON'T WANT A VACATION TAN AFTER ALL!
I'D RATHER BE PALE AND INTERESTING...
SPEAKING OF INTEREST, MR. ... AH... JOKER--

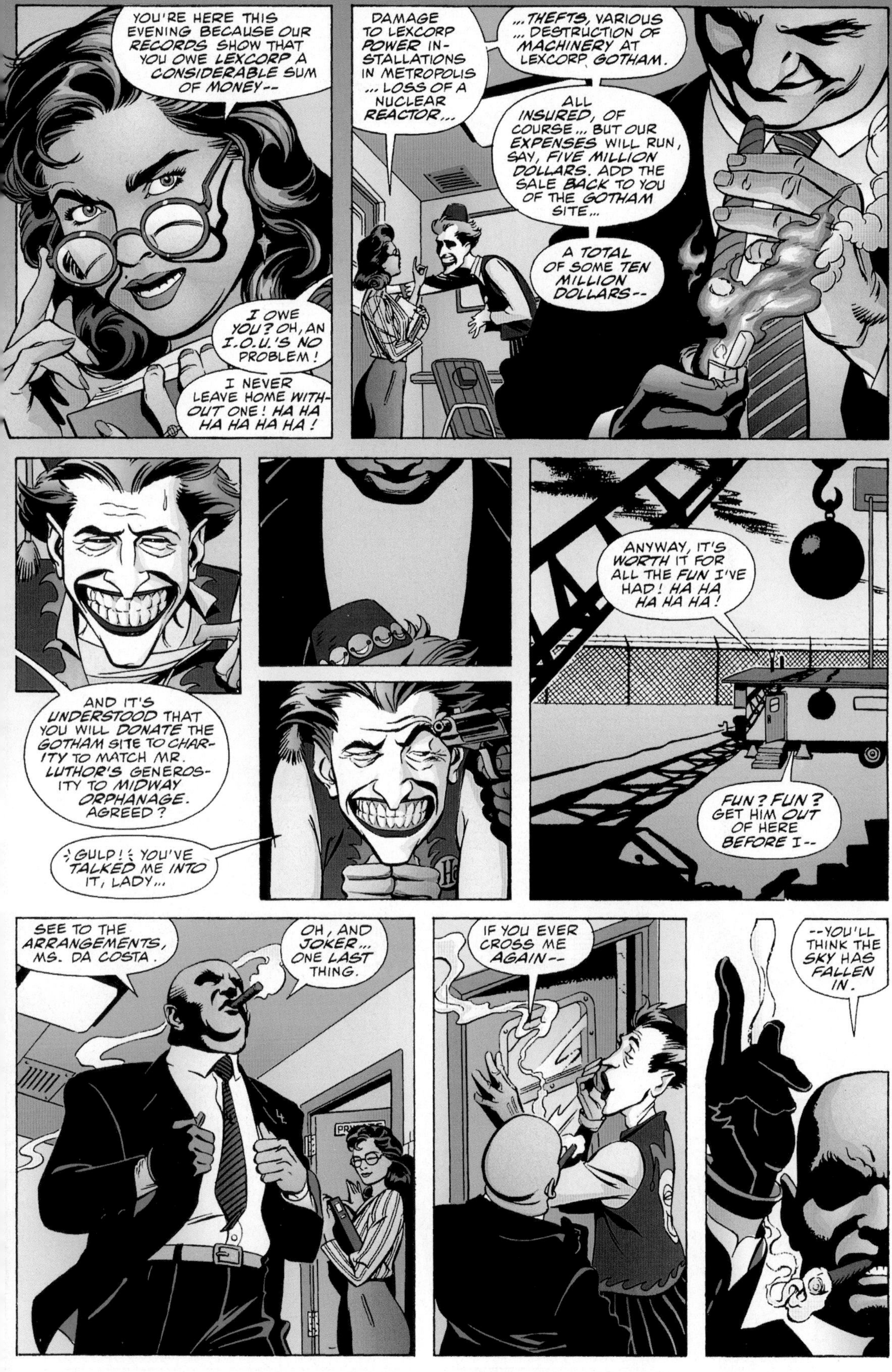
YOU'RE HERE THIS EVENING BECAUSE OUR RECORDS SHOW THAT YOU OWE LEXCORP A CONSIDERABLE SUM OF MONEY--
I OWE YOU? OH, AN I.O.U.'S NO PROBLEM!
I NEVER LEAVE HOME WITH-OUT ONE! HA HA HA HA HA HA!
DAMAGE TO LEXCORP POWER IN-STALLATIONS IN METROPOLIS ... LOSS OF A NUCLEAR REACTOR...
...THEFTS, VARIOUS ... DESTRUCTION OF MACHINERY AT LEXCORP GOTHAM.
ALL INSURED, OF COURSE... BUT OUR EXPENSES WILL RUN, SAY, FIVE MILLION DOLLARS. ADD THE SALE BACK TO YOU OF THE GOTHAM SITE...
A TOTAL OF SOME TEN MILLION DOLLARS--
AND IT'S UNDERSTOOD THAT YOU WILL DONATE THE GOTHAM SITE TO CHAR-ITY TO MATCH MR. LUTHOR'S GENEROS-ITY TO MIDWAY ORPHANAGE. AGREED?
GULP! YOU'VE TALKED ME INTO IT, LADY...
ANYWAY, IT'S WORTH IT FOR ALL THE FUN I'VE HAD! HA HA HA HA HA!
FUN? FUN? GET HIM OUT OF HERE BEFORE I--
SEE TO THE ARRANGEMENTS, MS. DA COSTA.
OH, AND JOKER... ONE LAST THING.
IF YOU EVER CROSS ME AGAIN--
--YOU'LL THINK THE SKY HAS FALLEN IN.

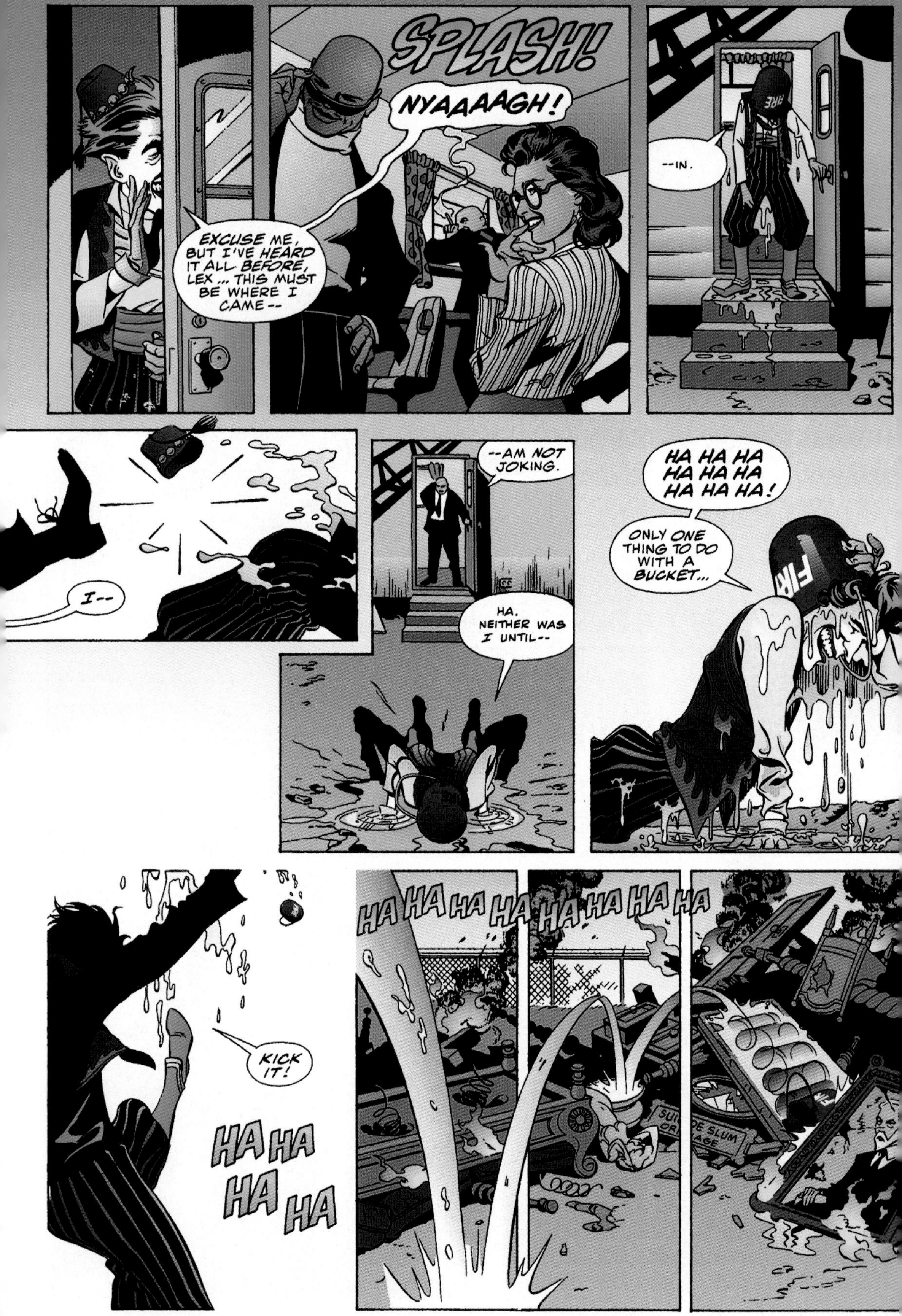

EXCUSE ME, BUT I'VE HEARD IT ALL BEFORE, LEX ... THIS MUST BE WHERE I CAME--
SPLASH!
NYAAAAGH!
--IN.
I--
--AM NOT JOKING.
HA. NEITHER WAS I UNTIL--
HA HA HA HA HA HA HA HA HA!
ONLY ONE THING TO DO WITH A BUCKET...
KICK IT!
HA HA HA HA
HA HA HA HA HA HA HA HA

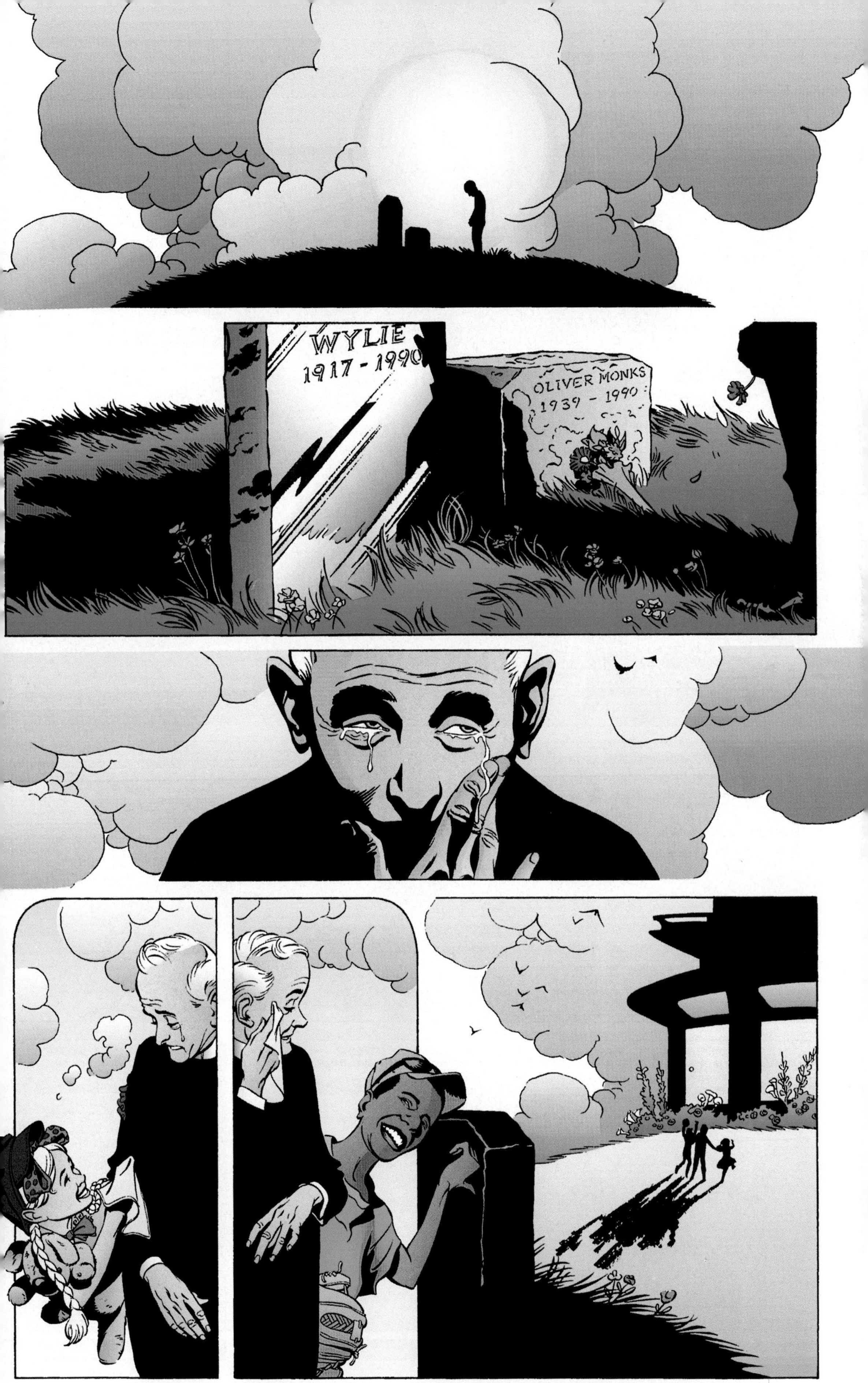
WYLIE
1917 - 1990
OLIVER MONKS
1939 - 1990

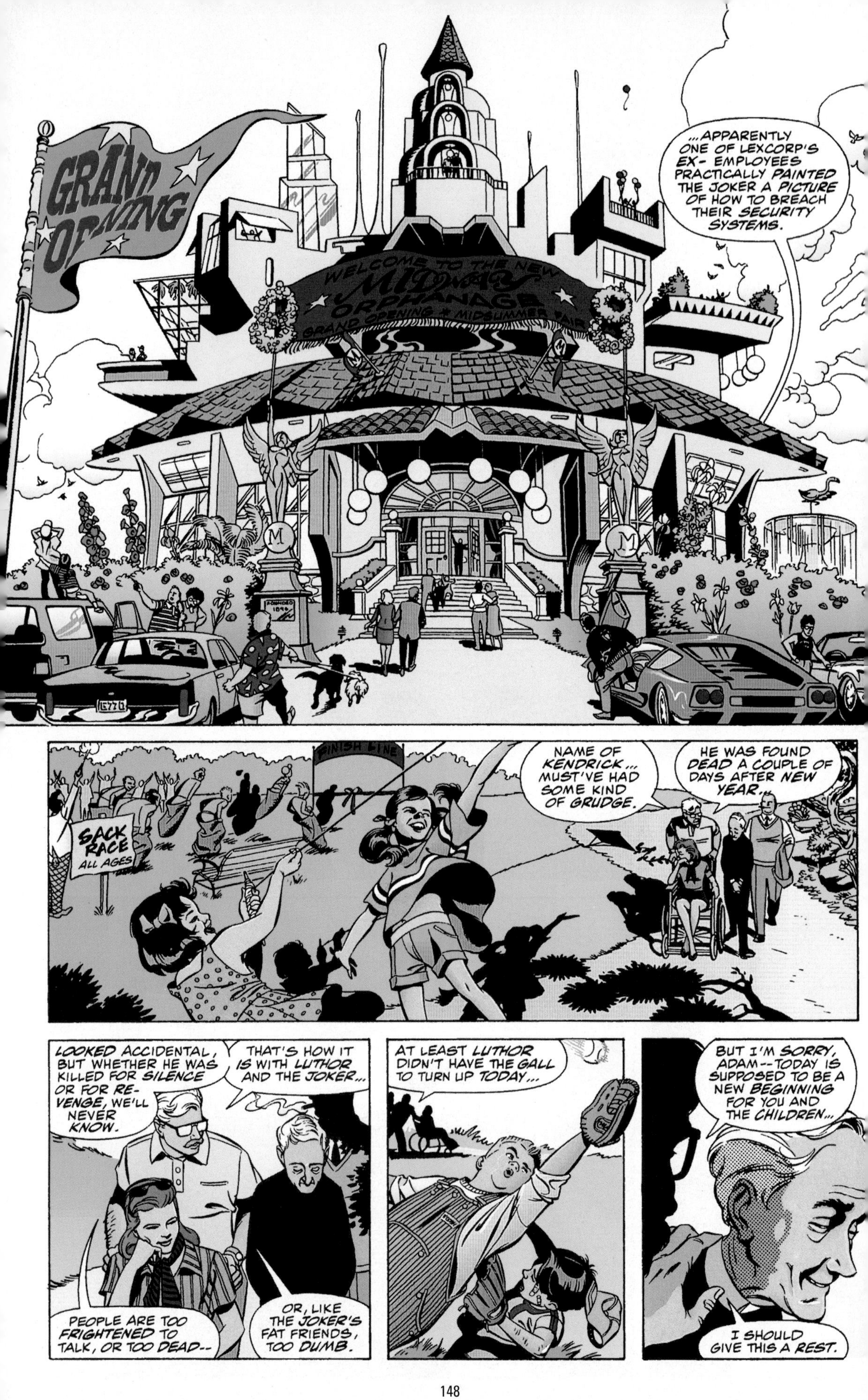
GRAND OPENING
WELCOME TO THE NEW MIDWAY ORPHANAGE
GRAND OPENING + MIDSUMMER FAIR
...APPARENTLY ONE OF LEXCORP'S EX-EMPLOYEES PRACTICALLY PAINTED THE JOKER A PICTURE OF HOW TO BREACH THEIR SECURITY SYSTEMS.
FINISH LINE
SACK RACE ALL AGES
NAME OF KENDRICK... MUST'VE HAD SOME KIND OF GRUDGE.
HE WAS FOUND DEAD A COUPLE OF DAYS AFTER NEW YEAR...
LOOKED ACCIDENTAL, BUT WHETHER HE WAS KILLED FOR SILENCE OR FOR REVENGE, WE'LL NEVER KNOW.
THAT'S HOW IT IS WITH LUTHOR AND THE JOKER...
PEOPLE ARE TOO FRIGHTENED TO TALK, OR TOO DEAD--
OR, LIKE THE JOKER'S FAT FRIENDS, TOO DUMB.
AT LEAST LUTHOR DIDN'T HAVE THE GALL TO TURN UP TODAY...
BUT I'M SORRY, ADAM--TODAY IS SUPPOSED TO BE A NEW BEGINNING FOR YOU AND THE CHILDREN...
I SHOULD GIVE THIS A REST.

OH, THAT'S ALL RIGHT, COMMISSIONER... WE CAN ALL *LEARN* FROM THE PAST. IT'S ONLY *DANGEROUS* WHEN WE GET *OBSESSED* BY IT.

I--I MUST *CON-FESS* THAT I STARTED TO LOOK FURTHER INTO THOSE AWFUL REVELA-TIONS ABOUT *BYRON WYLIE* AND POOR *OLIVER*...

I DISCOVERED IN SOME OLD *NEWSPAPER FILES* THAT WYLIE WAS ONCE, ER, *ROMANTICALLY INVOLVED* WITH OLIVER'S *MOTHER*...

B-BUT WHEN I STARTED TO WON-DER IF *OLIVER* MIGHT *REALLY* HAVE BEEN HIS *SON*, I DECIDED *ENOUGH* WAS *ENOUGH*.

AFTER FIFTY YEARS, THE *TRUTH* BECOMES FADED... ONLY YELLOWED *IDEALS* AND BRITTLE *EMOTIONS* REMAIN.

I JUST FEEL SO *SORRY* FOR *OLIVER*.

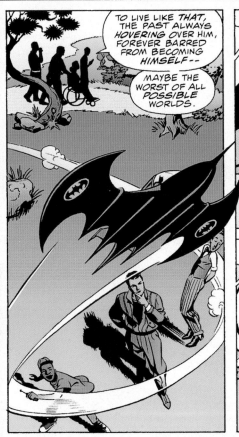

TO LIVE LIKE *THAT*, THE PAST ALWAYS *HOVERING* OVER HIM, FOREVER *BARRED* FROM BECOMING *HIMSELF*--

MAYBE THE *WORST* OF ALL POSSIBLE WORLDS.

MAYBE...

... BUT IT'S SOME CONSOLA-TION THAT YOUR SUGGESTION TO NAME THE NEW *ADVENTURE PLAYGROUND* ON THE OLD *GOTHAM ORPHANAGE* SITE AFTER HIM WAS *ADOPTED*.

AT LEAST *FUTURE* GENERA-TIONS WILL LINK HIS NAME WITH *CHILDHOOD FUN*...

NOT A BAD LEGACY...

HEY, IS *THAT* THE *TIME*? EXCUSE ME-- I'VE GOT A *DEAD-LINE*! MY COLUMN'S DUE...

NO *TIME* FOR *FUN* WHEN YOU'VE GOT A *PLANET* TO WORRY ABOUT, EH, PERRY?

PERRY'S PLANET

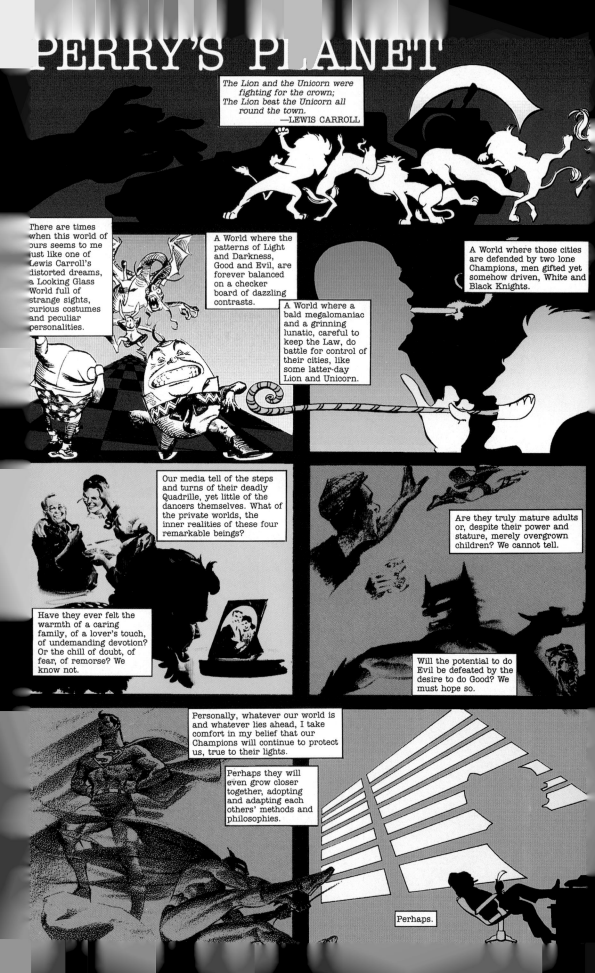

*The Lion and the Unicorn were
fighting for the crown;
The Lion beat the Unicorn all
round the town.*
—LEWIS CARROLL

There are times when this world of ours seems to me just like one of Lewis Carroll's distorted dreams, a Looking Glass World full of strange sights, curious costumes and peculiar personalities.

A World where the patterns of Light and Darkness, Good and Evil, are forever balanced on a checker board of dazzling contrasts.

A World where a bald megalomaniac and a grinning lunatic, careful to keep the Law, do battle for control of their cities, like some latter-day Lion and Unicorn.

A World where those cities are defended by two lone Champions, men gifted yet somehow driven, White and Black Knights.

Our media tell of the steps and turns of their deadly Quadrille, yet little of the dancers themselves. What of the private worlds, the inner realities of these four remarkable beings?

Have they ever felt the warmth of a caring family, of a lover's touch, of undemanding devotion? Or the chill of doubt, of fear, of remorse? We know not.

Are they truly mature adults or, despite their power and stature, merely overgrown children? We cannot tell.

Will the potential to do Evil be defeated by the desire to do Good? We must hope so.

Personally, whatever our world is and whatever lies ahead, I take comfort in my belief that our Champions will continue to protect us, true to their lights.

Perhaps they will even grow closer together, adopting and adapting each others' methods and philosophies.

Perhaps.

Or perhaps they must simply reflect what is obvious to anyone who cares to look through a window.
LUTHOR
SUPERMAN?
LEXCORP
BAH!

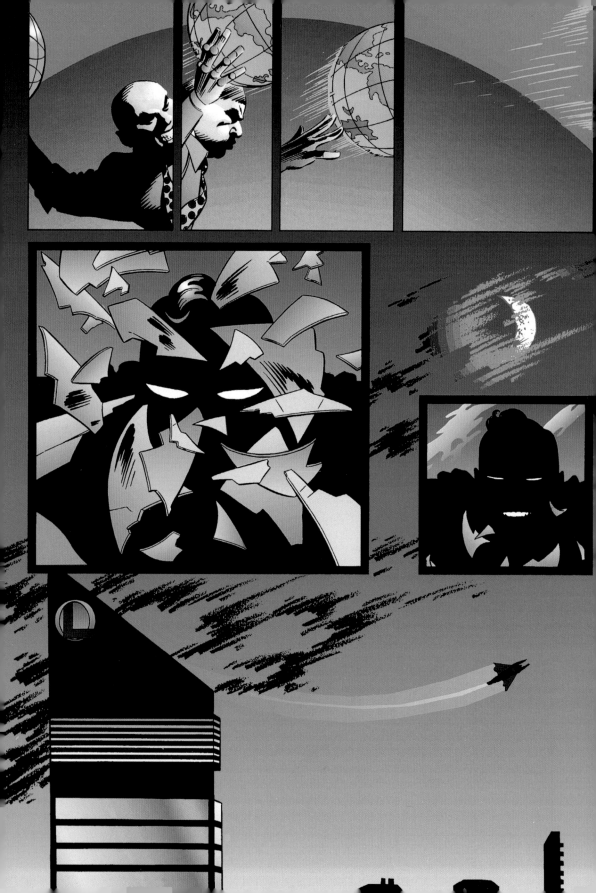

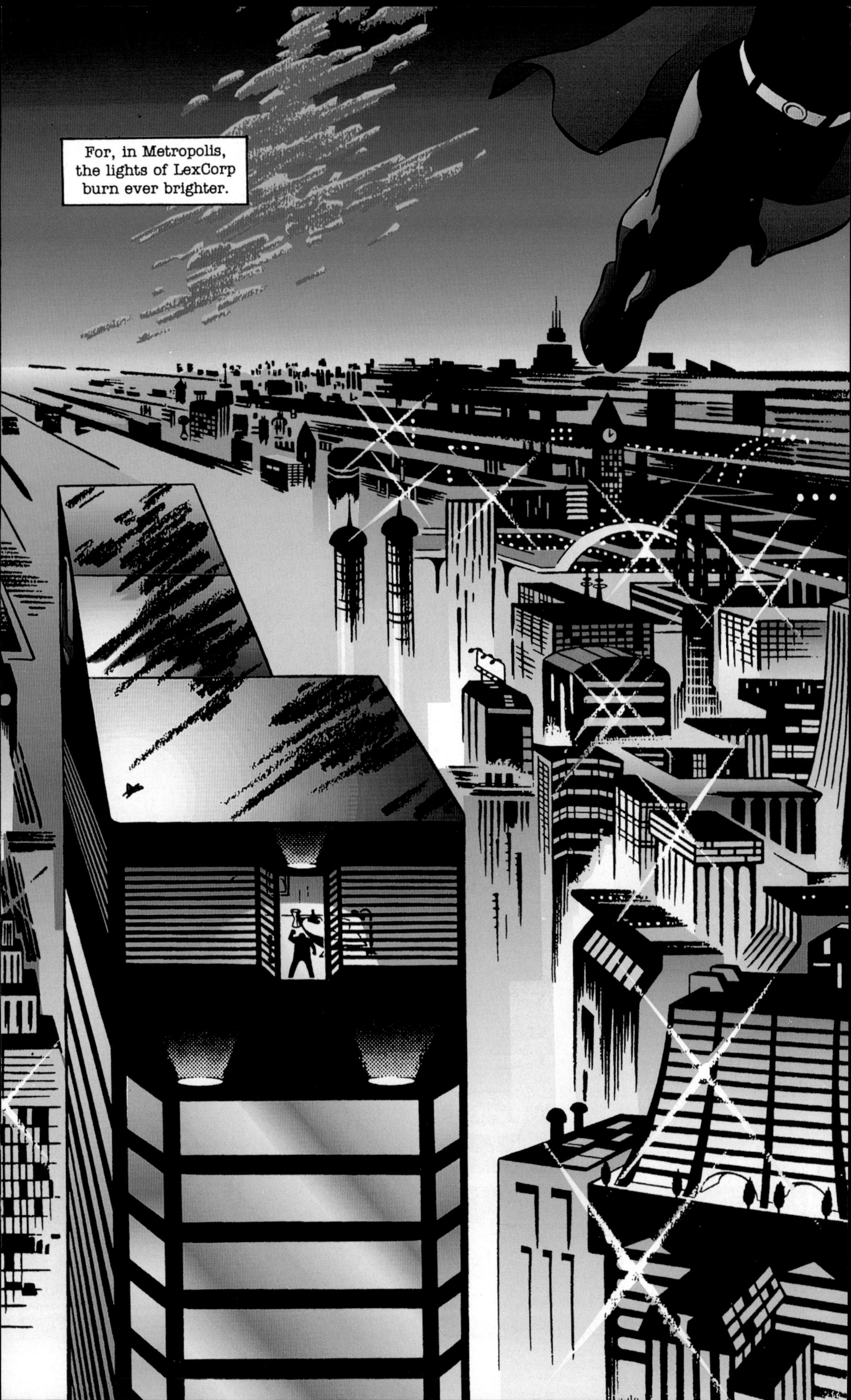
For, in Metropolis, the lights of LexCorp burn ever brighter.

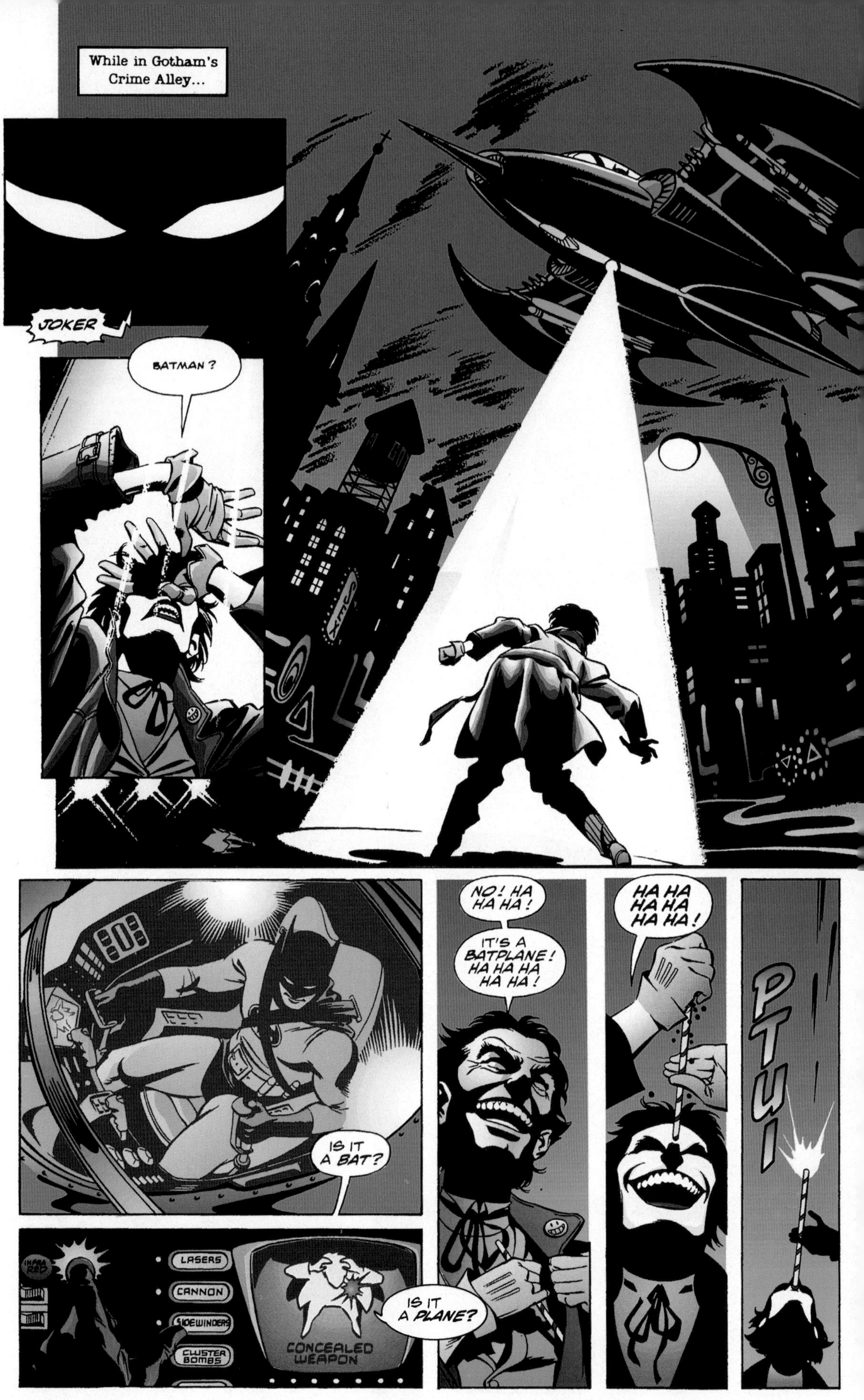
While in Gotham's Crime Alley...
JOKER
BATMAN?
IS IT A BAT?
INFRA RED
LASERS
CANNON
SIDEWINDERS
CLUSTER BOMBS
CONCEALED WEAPON
IS IT A PLANE?
NO! HA HA HA!
IT'S A BATPLANE! HA HA HA HA HA!
HA HA HA HA HA HA!
PTUI

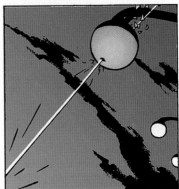

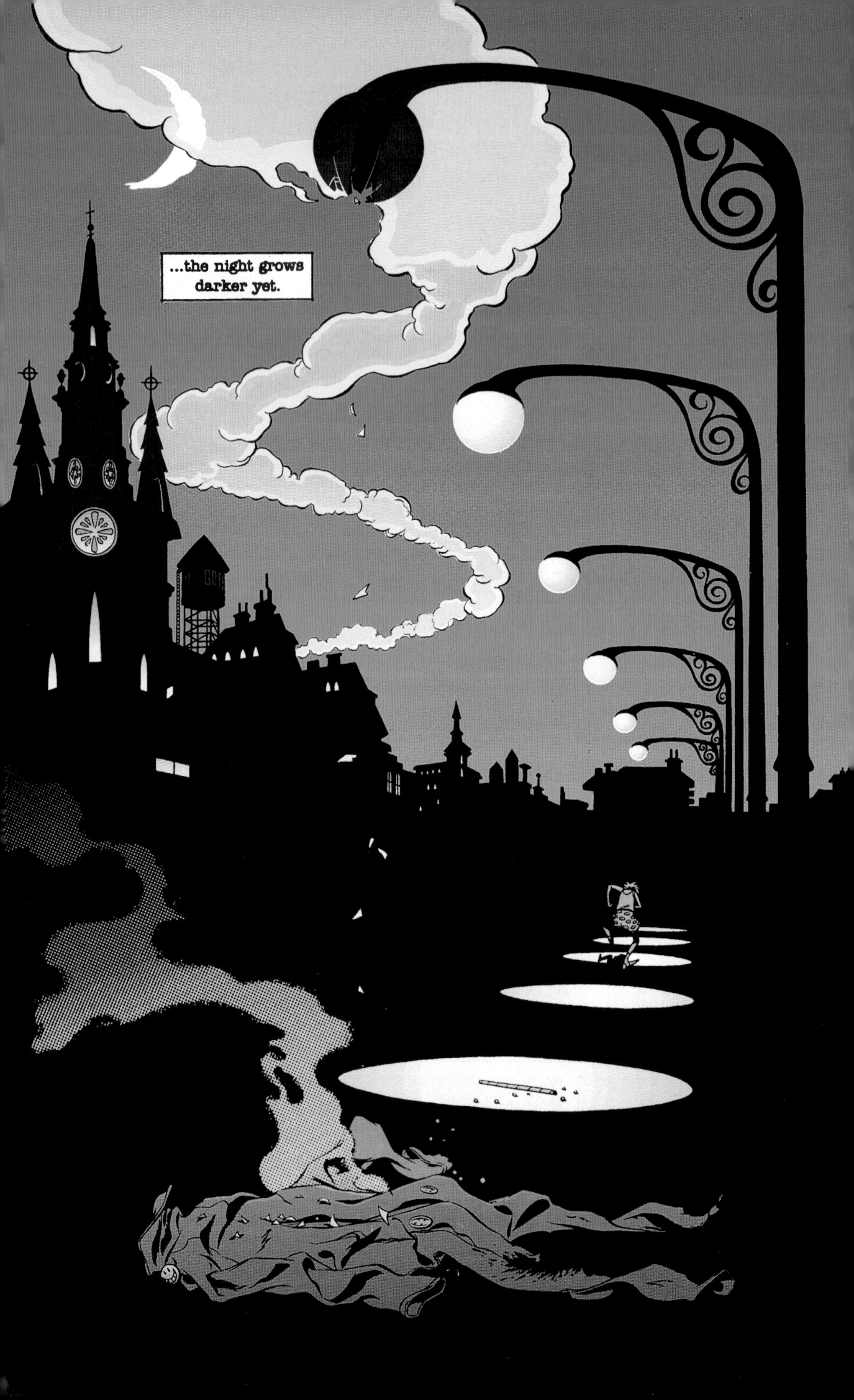
...the night grows
darker yet.

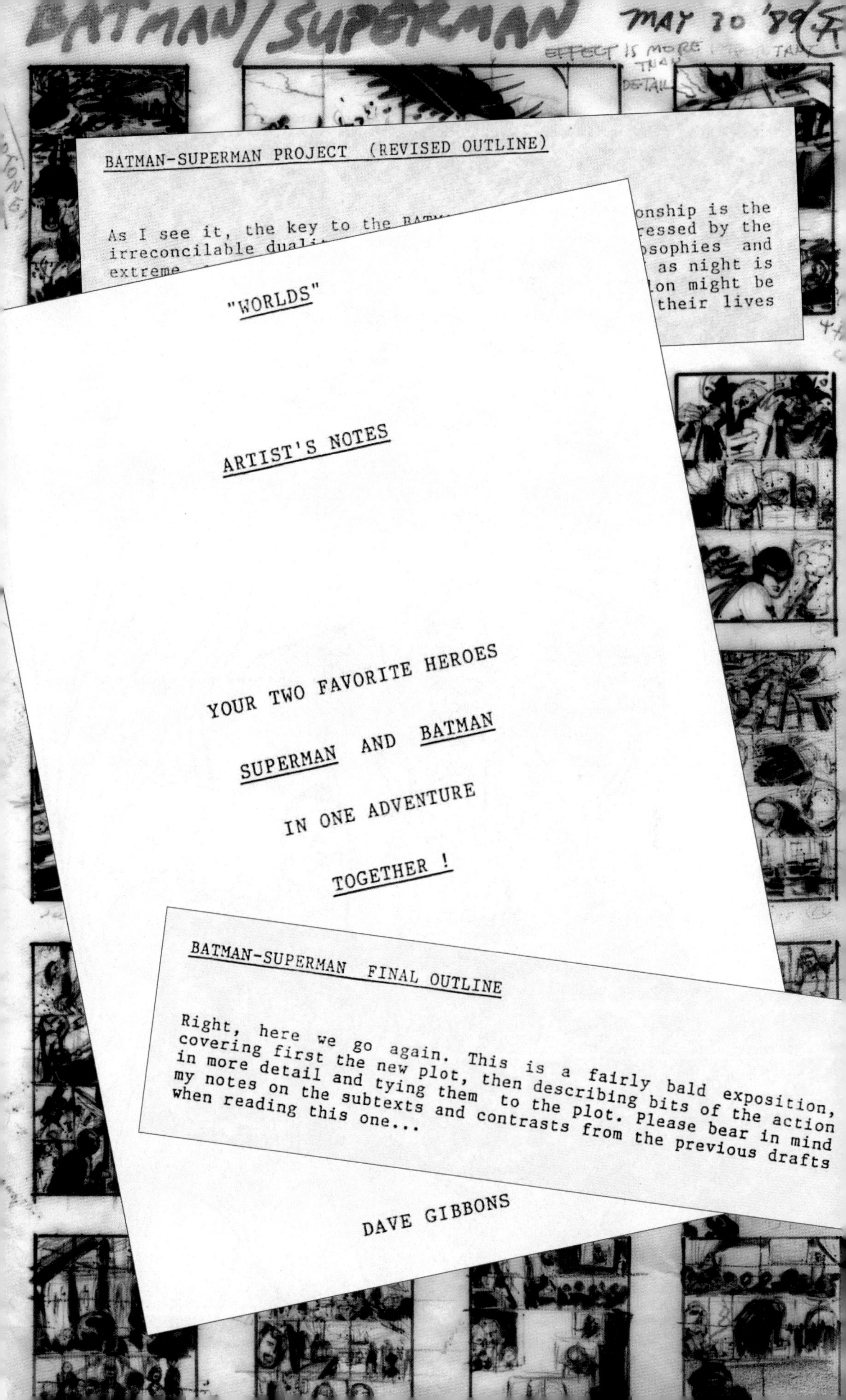

BATMAN/SUPERMAN
MAY 30 '89
EFFECT IS MORE IMPORTANT THAN DETAIL

BATMAN-SUPERMAN PROJECT (REVISED OUTLINE)

As I see it, the key to the BATM... onship is the irreconcilable duali... ressed by the ... osophies and extreme ... as night is ... lon might be ... their lives

"WORLDS"

ARTIST'S NOTES

YOUR TWO FAVORITE HEROES

SUPERMAN AND BATMAN

IN ONE ADVENTURE

TOGETHER !

DAVE GIBBONS

BATMAN-SUPERMAN FINAL OUTLINE

Right, here we go again. This is a fairly bald exposition, covering first the new plot, then describing bits of the action in more detail and tying them to the plot. Please bear in mind my notes on the subtexts and contrasts from the previous drafts when reading this one...

As you'll notice, I've been quite detailed and specific in my picture descriptions, but I'd like to STRESS that I don't want you to feel restricted or intimidated by this. Inevitably I've been visualizing the pictures very clearly as I've written them and have included everything that I felt necessary to communicate my vision. One of the particularly attractive things about this project is the fact that YOU'RE drawing it, so however you feel like improvising is just fine with me!

Having said that, I thought I'd include some more visual thoughts here and, in particular, character and location descriptions that I didn't want to clutter the individual picture descriptions up with.

I hope I'm not belaboring the obvious too much if I mention again that the main things to bring out are the visual CONTRASTS of the scenes. I've tried to contrast SILENT and WORDY scenes (although in the succeeding Books this will disappear as the worlds become more intermingled) to accentuate the theme, and similarly I've played LIGHT scenes against DARK scenes.

The times of day are important here, too, as we contrast DAY against NIGHT, DUSK against DAWN etc. Similarly, SUPERMAN's colorful brightness is played off against BATMAN's muted darkness, and the JOKER's bony gaudiness is contrasted with LUTHOR's squat soberness.

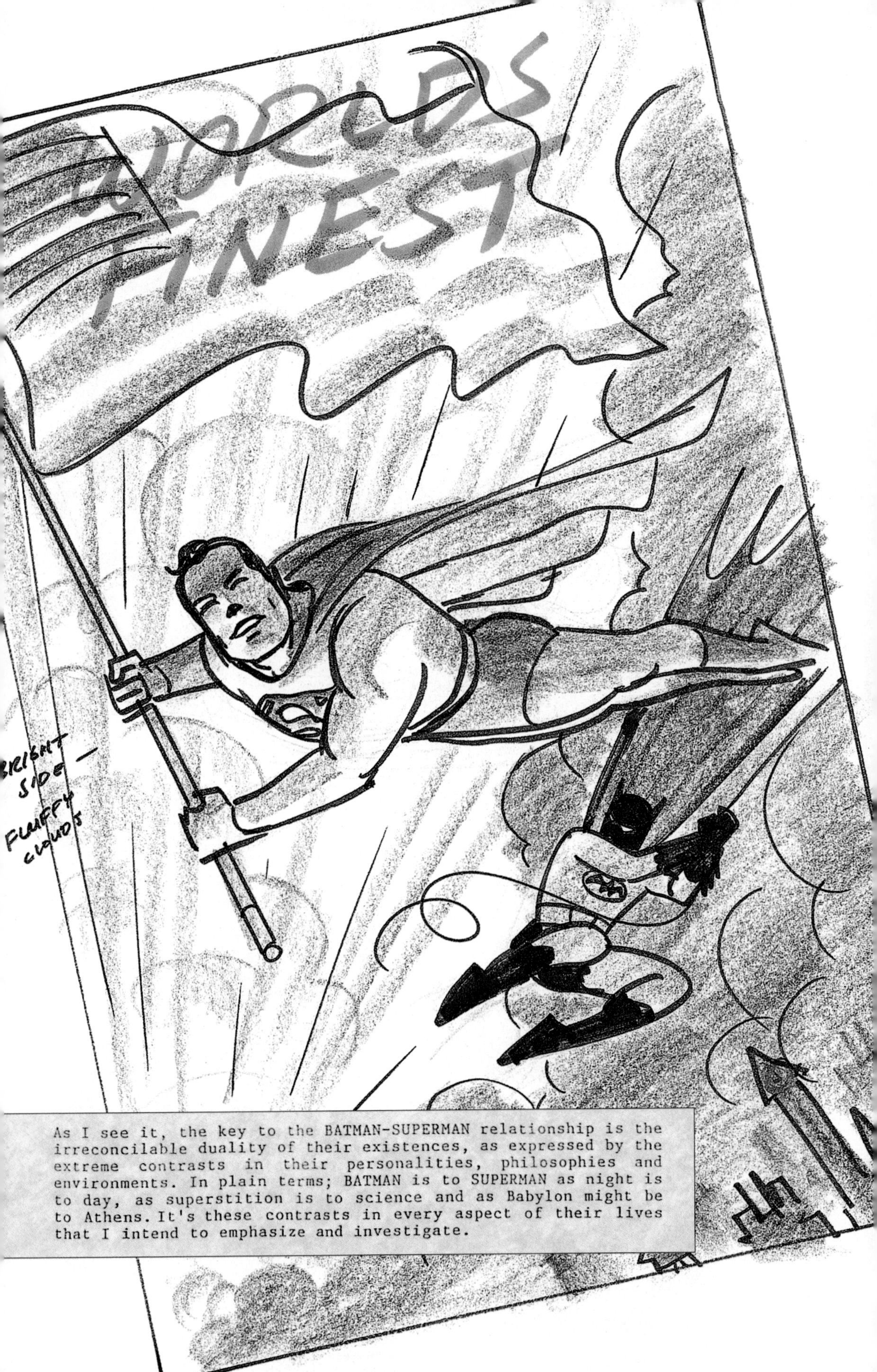
WORLDS FINEST
BRIGHT SIDE — FLUFFY CLOUDS

As I see it, the key to the BATMAN-SUPERMAN relationship is the irreconcilable duality of their existences, as expressed by the extreme contrasts in their personalities, philosophies and environments. In plain terms; BATMAN is to SUPERMAN as night is to day, as superstition is to science and as Babylon might be to Athens. It's these contrasts in every aspect of their lives that I intend to emphasize and investigate.

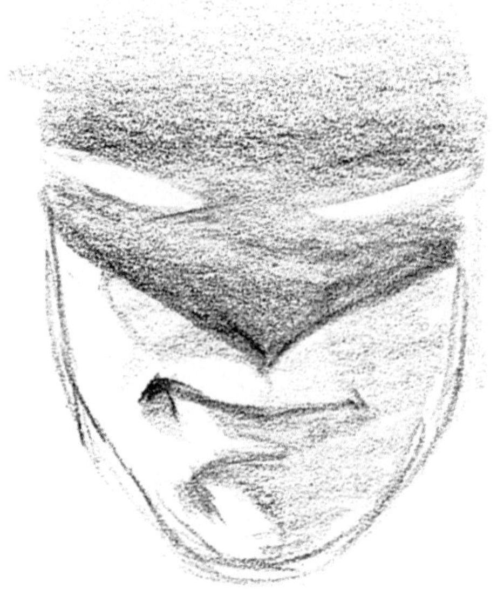

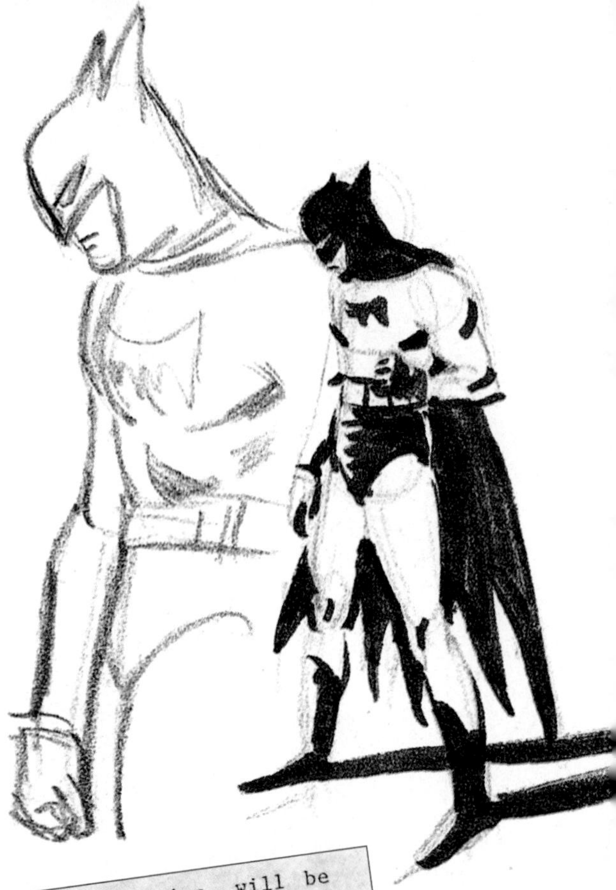

The overall mood of the piece, almost by definition, will be lighter than, say, DARK KNIGHT but darker than MAN OF STEEL. A kind of hard-boiled melodrama, a larger than life film noir. Our heroes have a semi-mythical gravitas and presence; the Fleischer SUPERMAN and Sprang BATMAN writ large.

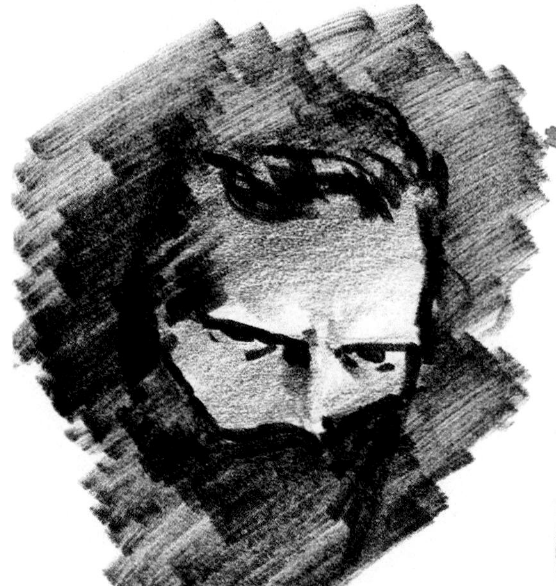

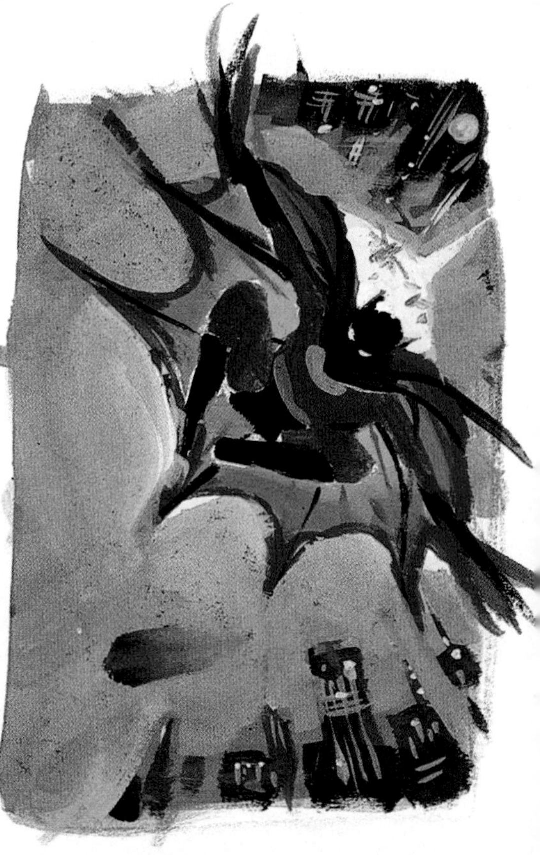

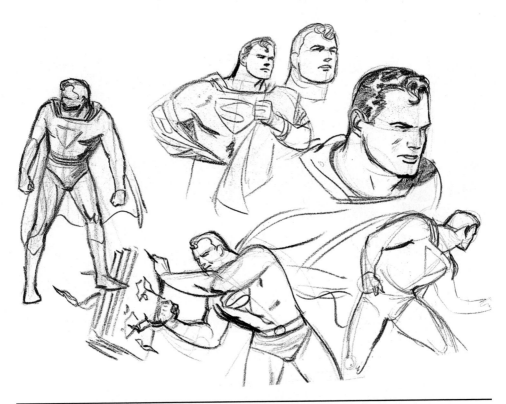

NOTES & SKETCHES

BY STEVE RUDE

Drawing these three issues of WORLD'S FINEST was the hardest job I ever did. I saw it as my one chance at doing Superman and Batman — the two biggest icons in the world of comics books — and I had to make it count.

I knew from the outset that my interpretations of these characters would be different from the other artists who'd drawn them. I wanted to bring them back to their original versions. Superman, in particular. The version that Siegel and Shuster created; the one depicted in the great Fleischer cartoons of the '40s. *That* was the version I believed in. I also read a great book by George Lowther from 1942.[*] It gave me the feel for Superman's character that I was looking for. Most memorable was the scene at a country fair where Clark Kent tries to save his dad's life. As for Batman, I would draw the very first version of him from the cover of DETECTIVE COMICS #27, from 1939, the year after Superman first appeared.

Some folks at DC felt that Superman needed to be updated and that my Batman was unrecognizable. I eventually gave in on Batman, but with Superman, I wouldn't budge. That was the version I wanted to draw, and according to early fan response, they were as whooped up about it as I was. (I would like to thank Darren McNeil and Mark Evanier for their valuable assistance in providing model sheets from the Fleischer Superman cartoons and other Golden Age reference material.)

Working with Dave Gibbons, known to most as a top-rate artist himself, was a real pleasure. Not only was he the easiest-going guy in the world, but he didn't mind being woken up at two o'clock in the morning to hear my latest ravings. What a guy!

When I finally finished with all three issues, I felt like I just emerged from a cave. I wondered if humanity still endured.

In no short time I was asked by Jenette Kahn if I'd be interested in doing a *second* WORLD'S FINEST series. "Give me a couple of years to recover," I muttered.

Still recovering...
Steve Rude
Sometime in 1992

[*] *The Adventures of Superman*, published by Random House.

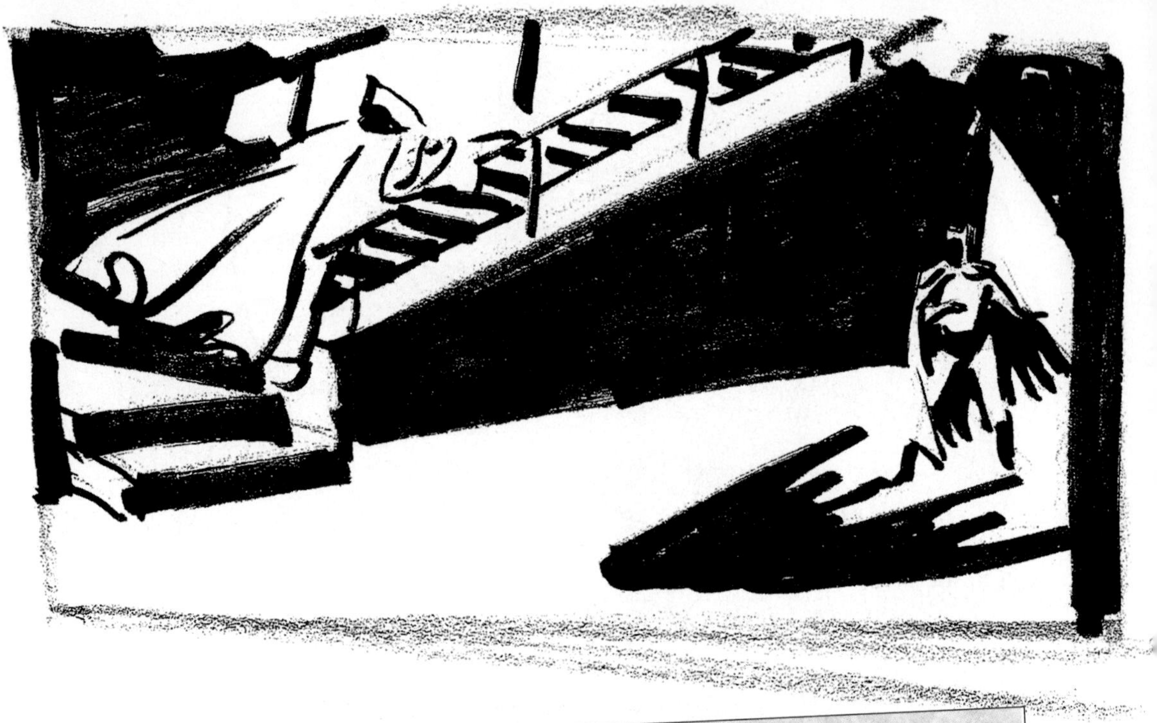

BATMAN has seen his parents gunned down - he knows for sure that they are dead. Only vengeance remains to him.

SUPERMAN, on the other hand, has only discovered the circumstances of his parents' death later and has always seemed to entertain the possibility that, somewhere out there, they (or their ghosts, holograms, or recorded personalities) still exist. Though, intellectually, he might deny it, some part of him still lives in hope.

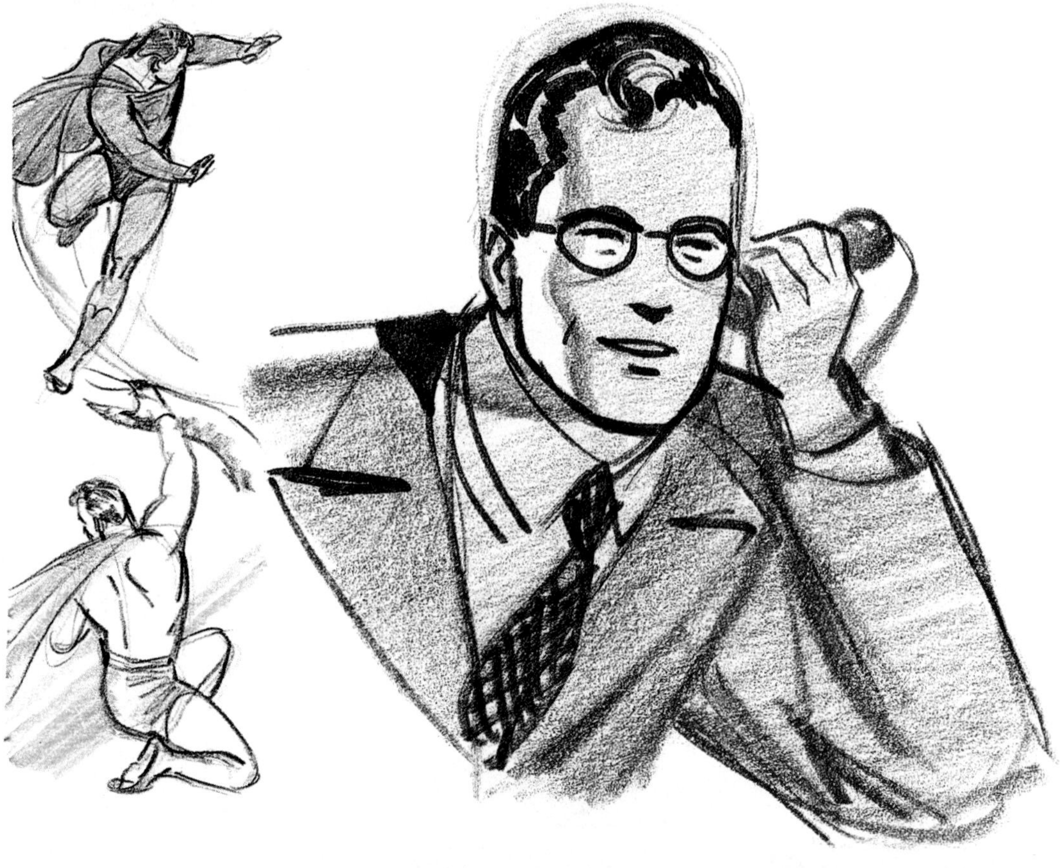

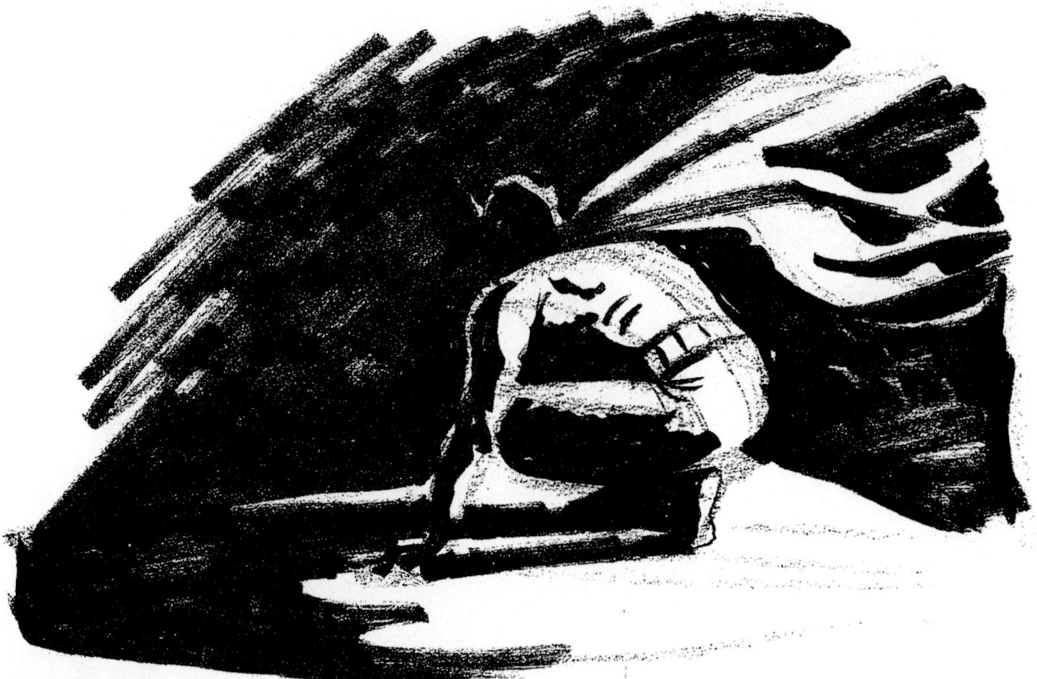

Two orphan boys, then, one consumed with dark vengeance and the other illuminated with glimmering hope.

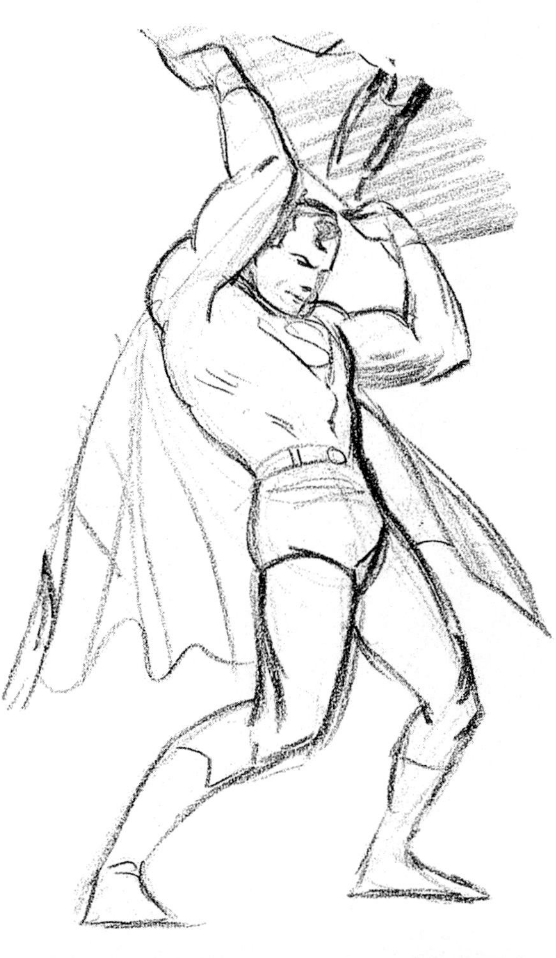

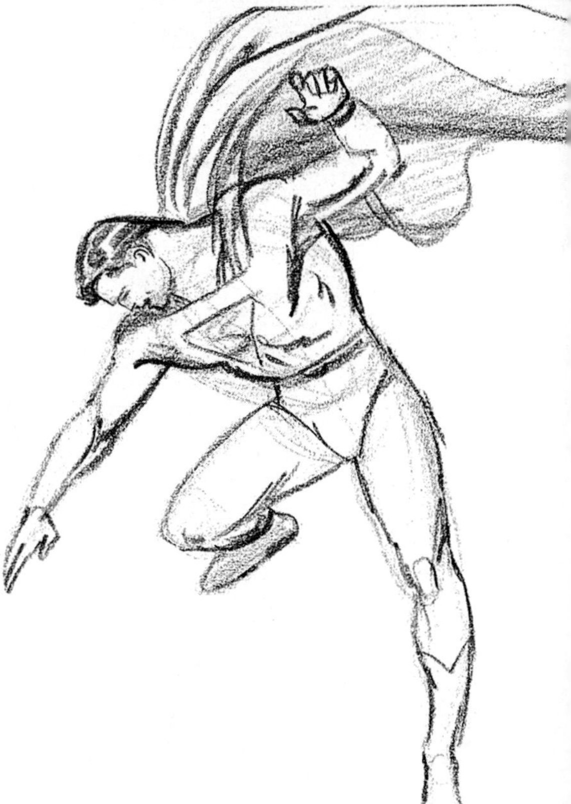

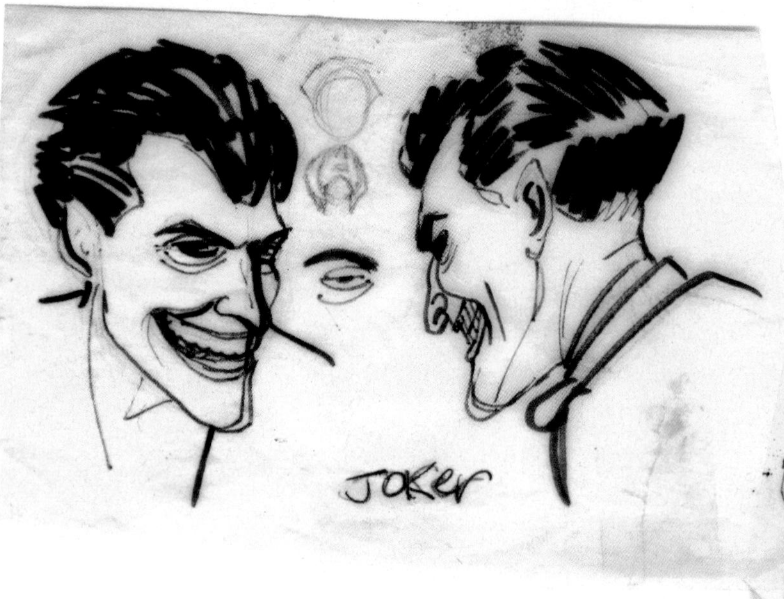
JOKer

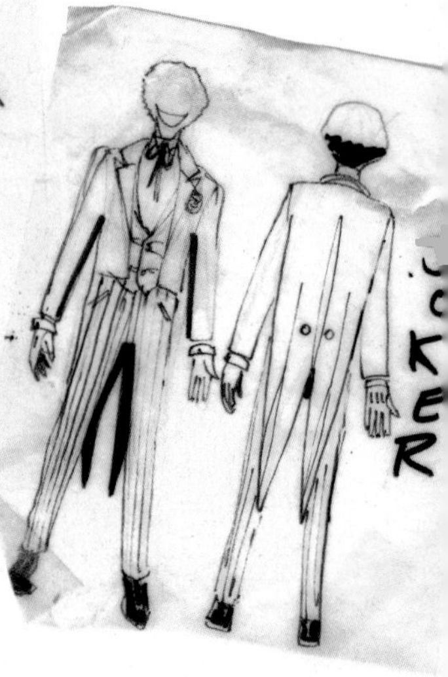
KER

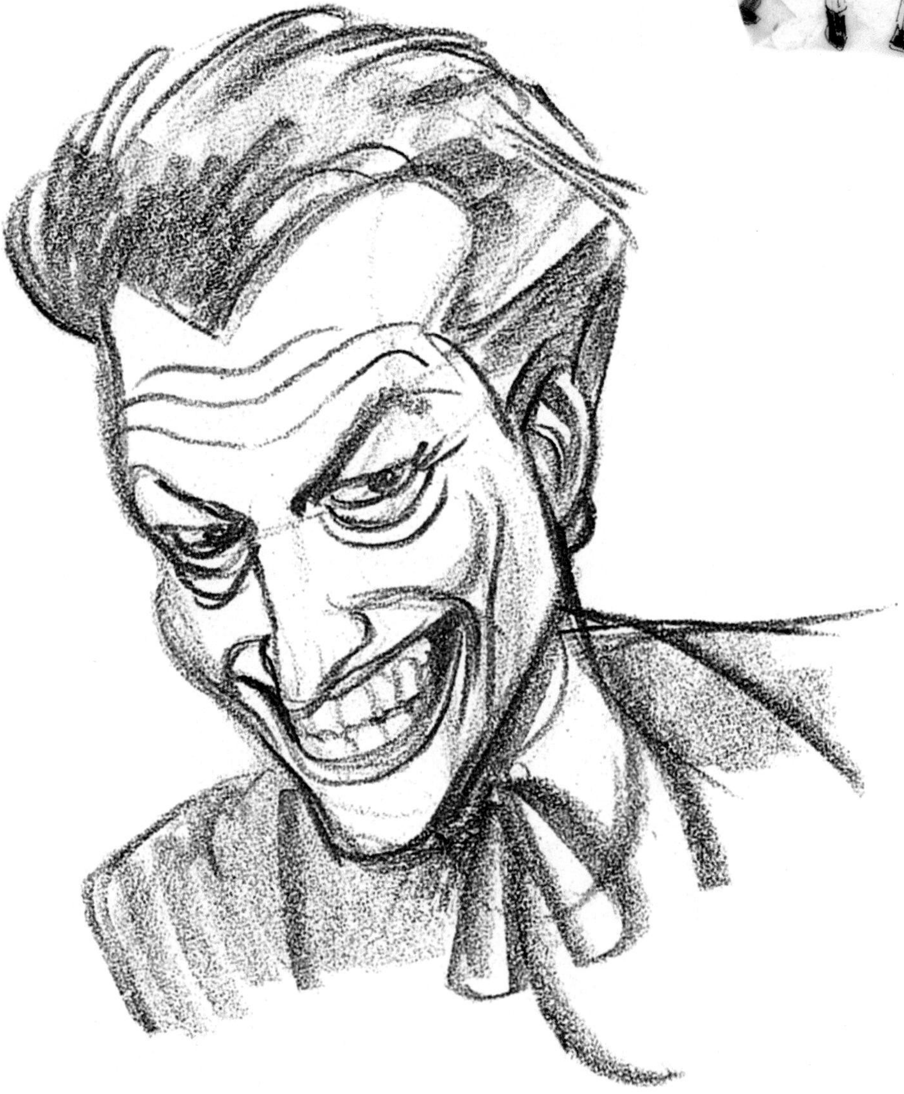

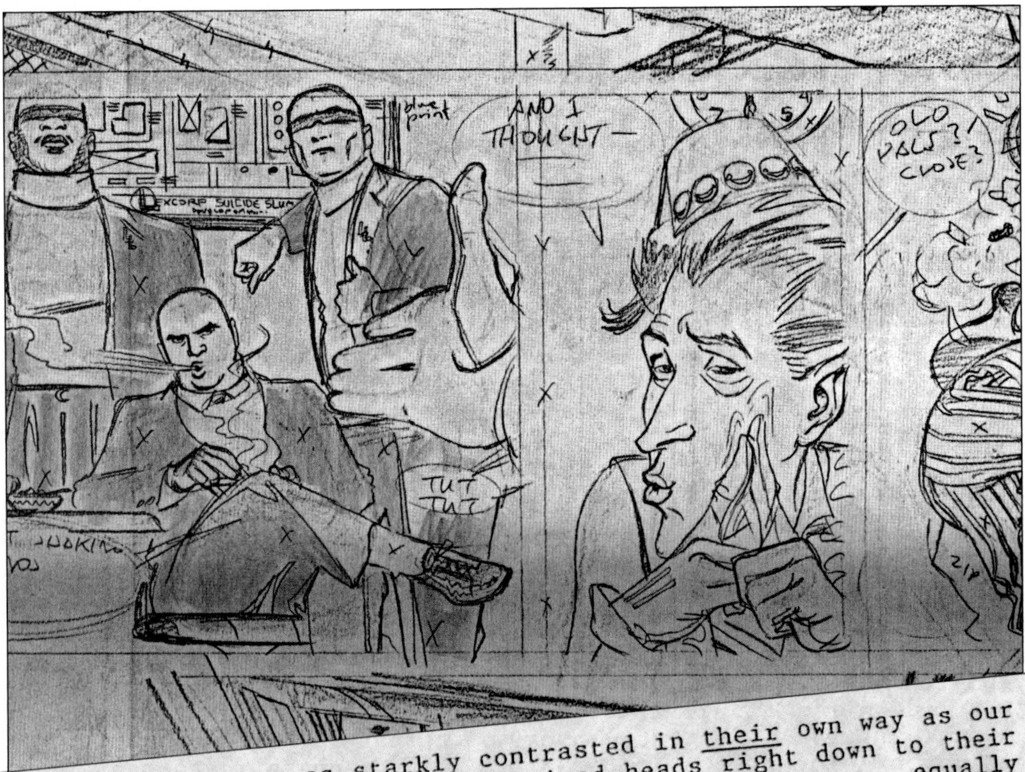
blue print
LEXCORP SUICIDE SLUM
AND I THOUGHT—
OLD PALS?! CLOSE?
TUT TUT

Our villains are as starkly contrasted in <u>their</u> own way as our heroes, from their bald/green haired heads right down to their black business shoes/purple spats. They are equally uncomfortable with each other: a bit like a medieval fool and a king, the one knowing just how far to go with a joke and the other just how far to tolerate the joke.

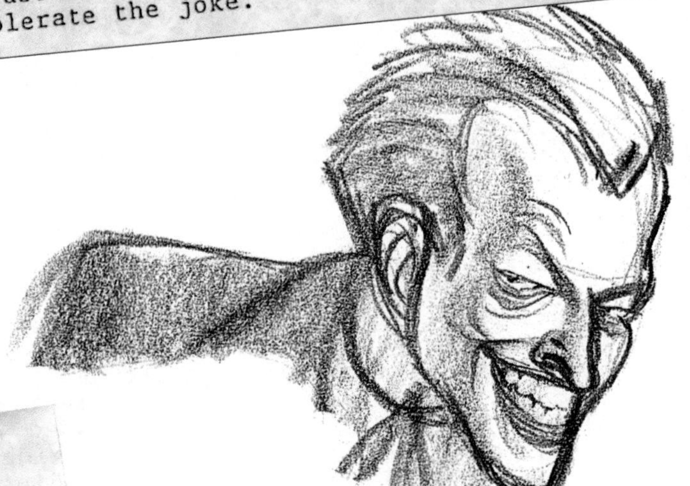

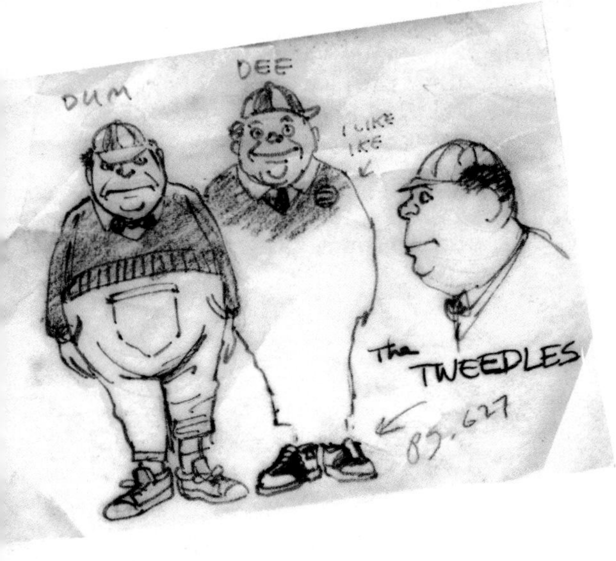
DUM
DEE
The TWEEDLES
85.627

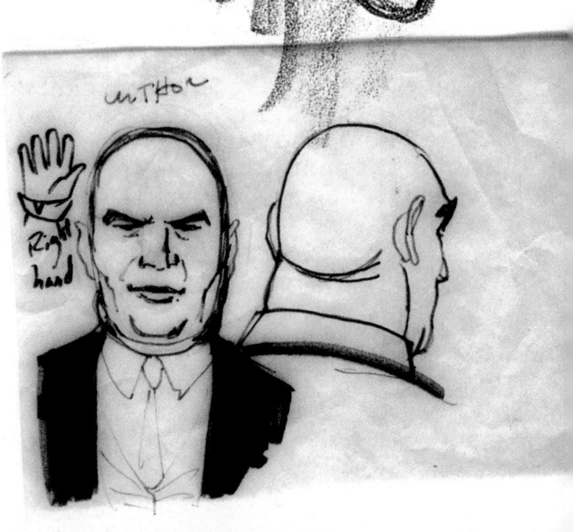
Right hand

As for the new locations, it's just the three orphanages, which I picture as follows:

SUICIDE SLUM ORPHANAGE: as we establish in the script, was founded in 1939 though the building may be even older than that. It stands on a busy street in Metropolis, in an area which has been fairly well developed since its notorious slum days. Luthor has recently bought up all the other buildings on the block where it stands and plans to build some grandiose complex on it. At the moment the block consists of some boarded up buildings, some in the process of demolition and some empty lots. There are lots of construction and demolition machines around and chain-link fencing to secure the various areas. The orphanage itself stands quite isolated, most of the neighboring buildings already having been levelled.

GOTHAM ORPHANAGE: a more dilapidated and older building than its counterpart in Metropolis, in a very seedy part of Gotham, close to the Crime Alley area. The block it stands on has not been modernized at all and consists mainly of low rent rooming houses. There is a paint factory, as featured in the script, and maybe a laundry, a liquor store and a cheap restaurant or two. Not a very pleasant neighborhood and ripe for the wrecking ball. The building style of this Orphanage should make it clearly different from the Suicide Slum one, to avoid any possibility of confusion.

MIDWAY ORPHANAGE: the script refers to this as having been built by Wylie's father, so it should be late 19th century, a typically rambling, spooky, isolated mansion. It has a multitude of steeply sloping roofs with myriad chimney stacks, windows etc. and has porches and outbuildings at its base. Inside is a large entrance hall which gives onto the main hall of the place.

The main hall is the setting for quite a bit of the action so I'll describe it in more detail: it's got the floor area of a good-sized ballroom and has a modestly sized 'stage' at one end. On this stage, to the right, is a small lectern, such as you'd find in a lecture theater. At the rear of the stage is a rear-projection movie screen and behind that (unseen until the climax of Book Two) is the recessed projection area. At the opposite end of the hall is the wide entrance door and, on either side of it, staircases leading upwards to a gallery. This gallery runs along the back of the hall, and has corridors leading off it to either side giving access to other rooms. Underneath the gallery, centrally sited above the entrance is a large clock. At least one side of the hall should have large diamond paned windows so that we can tell the time of day. The hall is panelled in dark wood and the stairs and gallery have ornate, heavy wooden balustrades.

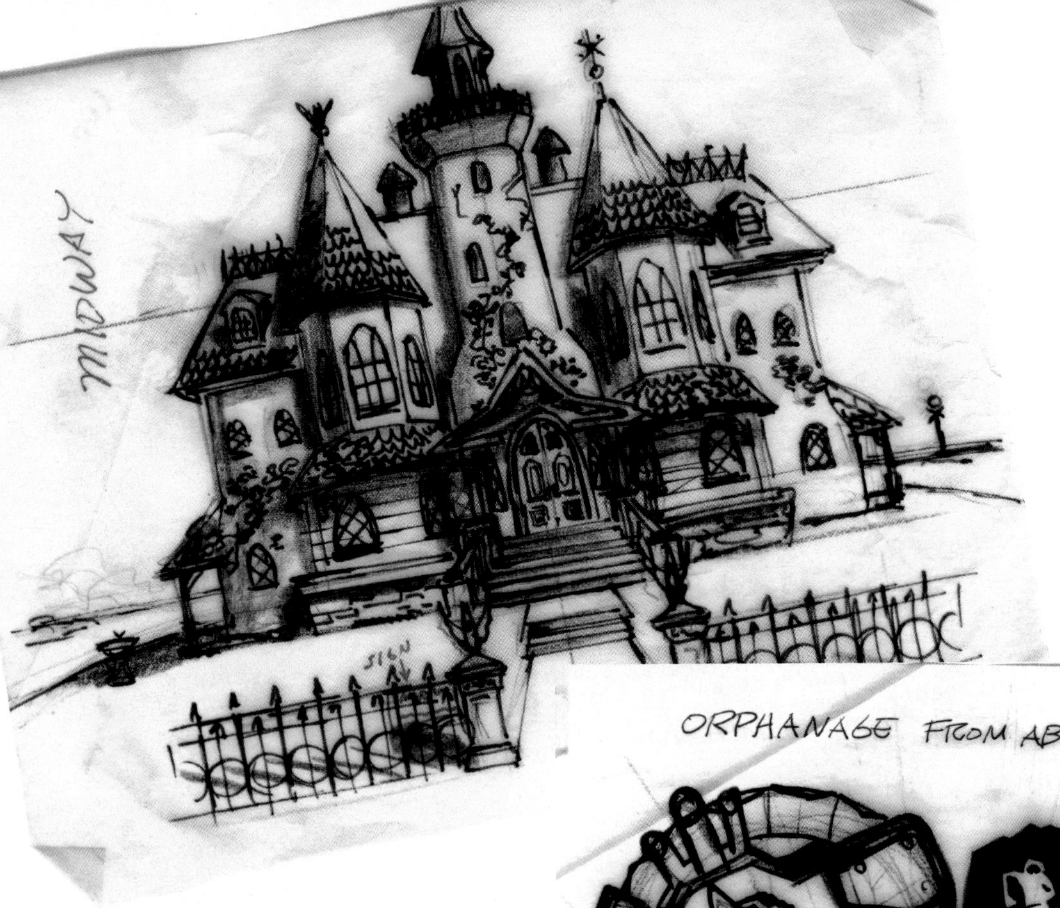
MIDWAY
SIGN

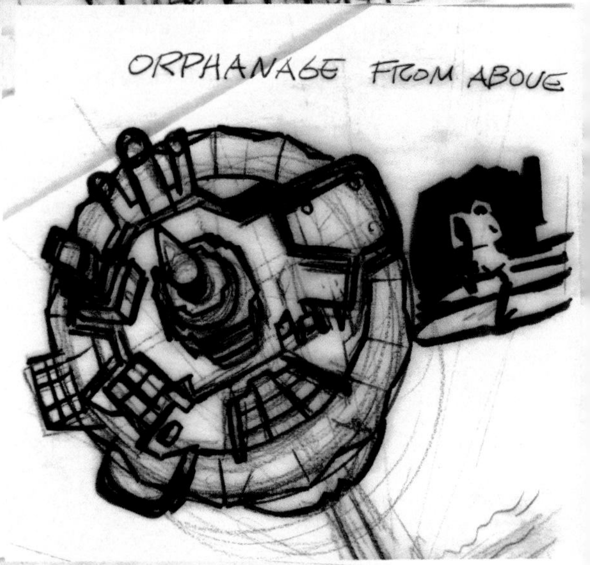
ORPHANAGE FROM ABOVE

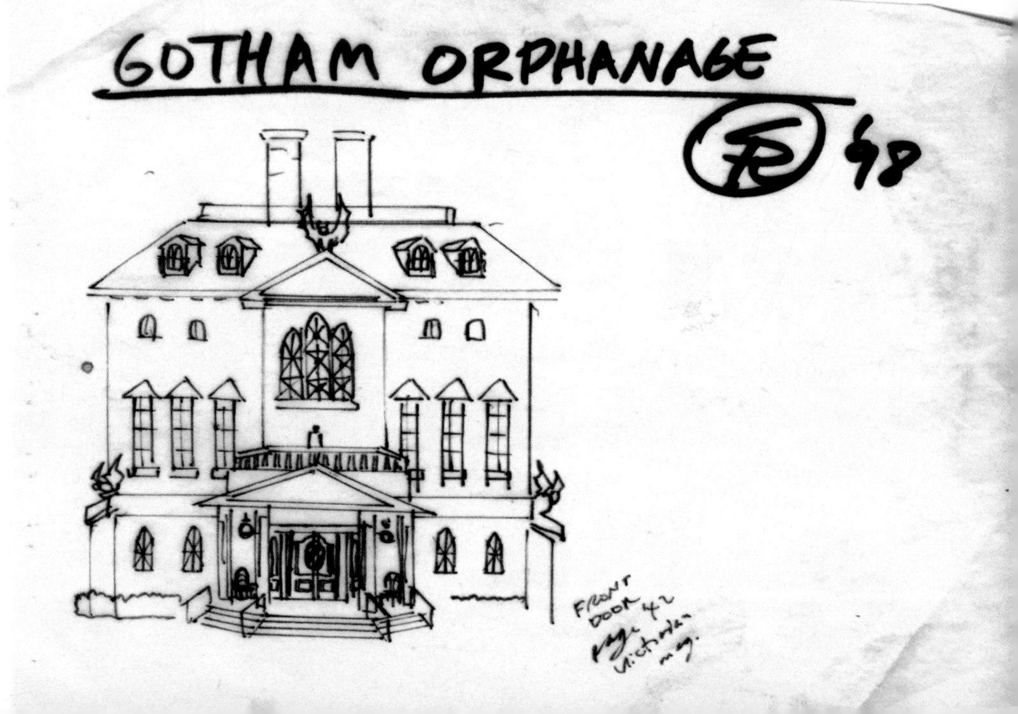
GOTHAM ORPHANAGE
98
FRONT DOOR
42

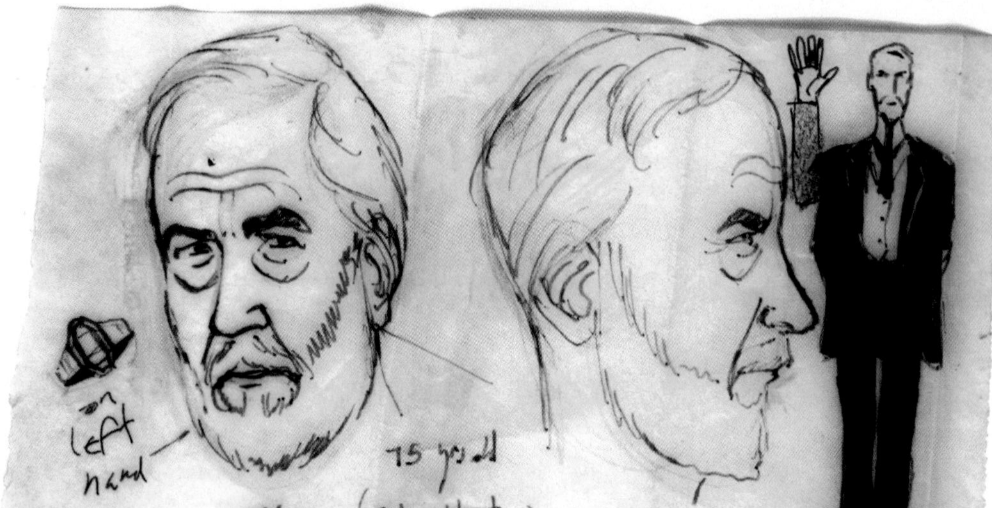
on left hand
75 yrs old
WYLIE (John Huston)

BYRON WYLIE: is, apart from LUTHOR and JOKER, the real villain of the piece. Born in 1907, we see him at various stages of his life; at 39, confident and in his prime; at 45, when things are going badly wrong and at 82, publicly frail and ill but, in reality, almost supernaturally fit and strong after spending 36 years in jail.

He is a tall, wiry, angular figure with a commanding presence. He is well-groomed and dresses in dark clothes. He has penetrating eyes, which are capable of switching from pride to compassion to sudden anger. A distinguishing feature is a large RING, set with a blood-red ruby, which he wears on one of the middle fingers of his right hand.

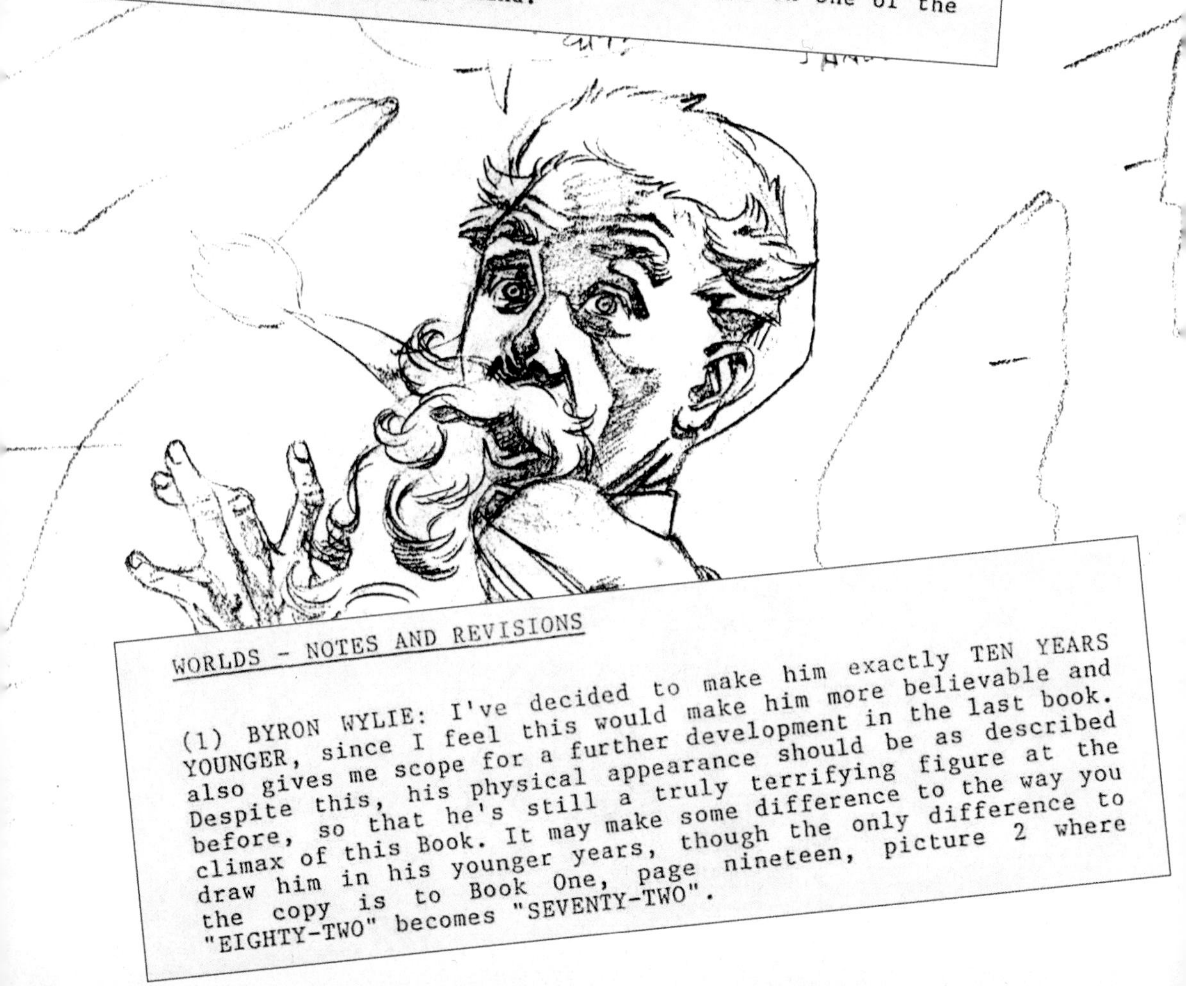

WORLDS - NOTES AND REVISIONS

(1) BYRON WYLIE: I've decided to make him exactly TEN YEARS YOUNGER, since I feel this would make him more believable and also gives me scope for a further development in the last book. Despite this, his physical appearance should be as described before, so that he's still a truly terrifying figure at the climax of this Book. It may make some difference to the way you draw him in his younger years, though the only difference to the copy is to Book One, page nineteen, picture 2 where "EIGHTY-TWO" becomes "SEVENTY-TWO".

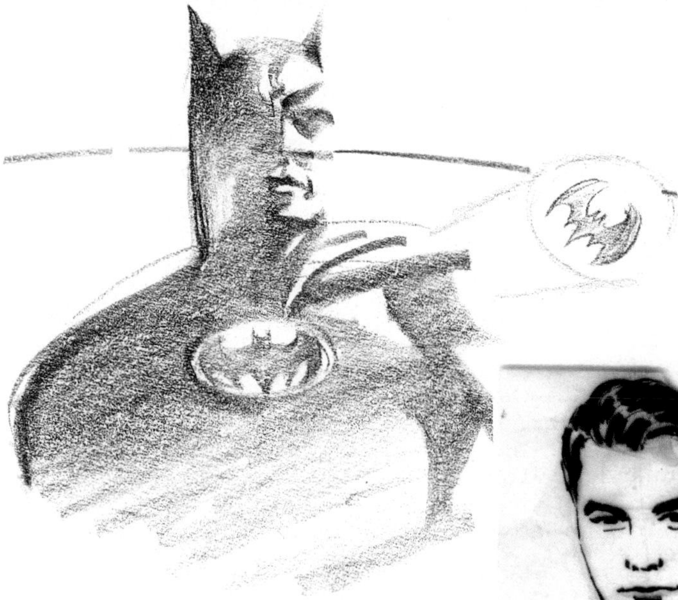

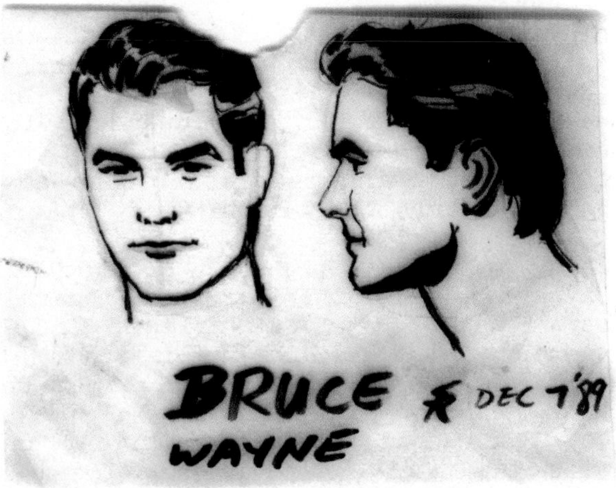
BRUCE WAYNE
DEC 7 '89

If there's anything else you need to know, please call, but otherwise I'll just shut up and let you do your job -- I can't wait to see the results !

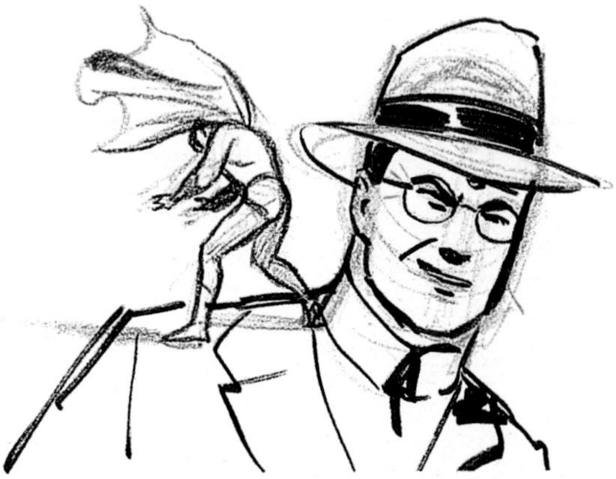

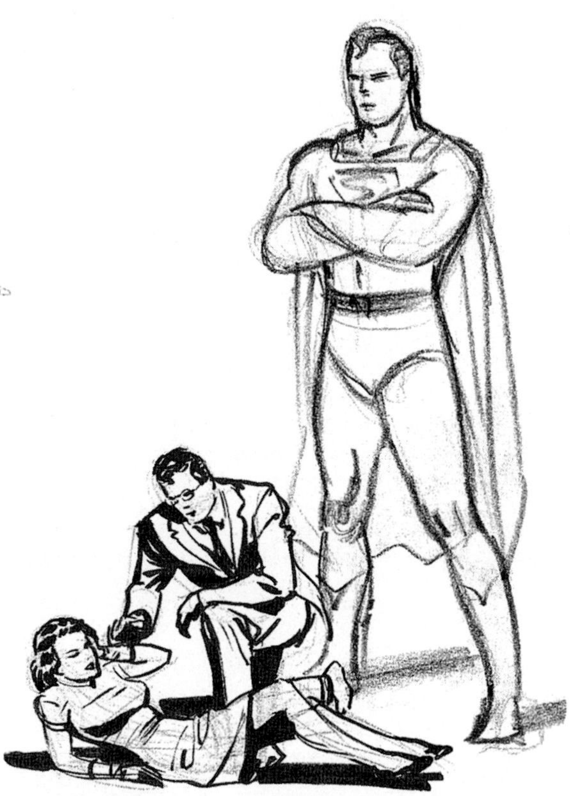

BOOK ONE - 'WORLDS APART'

We open with a full page of GOTHAM CITY at dusk, Babylonian
mausoleums against a guttering blood-red sunset. A single
caption says "Gotham.". Overleaf, we start a three or four page
sequence of BATMAN capturing a criminal in typical style,
playing the visuals for all they're worth - fearful faces,
swirling cape, dark shadows, ornate architecture and hard
physical action. The selection of shots and angles should also
help to make this sequence visually notable, it being
completely silent. It ends with the bad guy eating a suicide
capsule, a grinning death-rictus enveloping his face as BATMAN
grimly snarls the single word "Joker.".

Then to a full page of Metropolis at dawn, clean geometric
skyscrapers soaring into the sparkling air. A single caption
says "Metropolis.". Overleaf, we start a three or four page
sequence of SUPERMAN typically fighting crime, in the form of
some huge super-scientific gizmo. Death rays sizzle, machinery
is torn apart like tissue by rippling Kryptonian muscles and so
on. Again, the sequence is silent and visually striking, ending
with the 'driver' of the device blowing himself up, to avoid
capture. Brow-furrowed and sad, SUPERMAN sighs the single word
"Luthor.".

Next, a sequence which opens with a clock face, showing one
minute past twelve. Two balloons come from off; one says
"Evening, Kent.", the other says "Er, MORNING, Mr. Wayne." We
pull back to see BRUCE WAYNE and CLARK KENT (for it is indeed
them) shaking hands. They are wearing tuxedos and are attending
the opening celebrations for the new GOTHAM-METROPOLIS
ORPHANAGE. Our heroes talk briefly and a little uncomfortably,
whilst we notice other members of the cast mingling. For
instance, PERRY WHITE reminisces with COMMISSIONER GORDON and
we see that LOIS LANE and ALFRED are really hitting it off
together.

A short speech by Reverend WYLIE, the somewhat obsequious
director of the Orphanage, informs us that it has recently been
bequeathed this building, a huge old mansion midway between
GOTHAM and METROPOLIS, by a former inmate of the Orphanage who
made good. This has enabled the Orphanage to move from its
previous dilapidated premises in GOTHAM. He reminds the
assembled worthies, however, that funds are always needed, and
not to relent in their fund raising efforts.

The party winds up and, as the guests depart into the night,
flashguns and microphones are pushed in their faces by
newspersons.

We go into a couple of parallel dream-sequences: the origins of
our heroes re-told and contrasted. In SUPERMAN's dream, KRYPTON

BATMAN-SUPERMAN   FINAL OUTLINE

Right, here we go again. This is a fairly bald exposition,
covering first the new plot, then describing bits of the action
in more detail and tying them to the plot. Please bear in mind
my notes on the subtexts and contrasts from the previous drafts
when reading this one...

In the 1940's there was an orphanage in METROPOLIS's SUICIDE
SLUM, run by a REVEREND BYRON WYLIE, which was a virtual "crime
college" for the city. Eventually the authorities got wise and
sent WYLIE to jail. A new governor, ADAM FULBRIGHT, was
installed and all was well.

Coming out of jail many years later, WYLIE moved into MIDWAY
MANSION, a huge estate he owned, in the countryside between
GOTHAM & METROPOLIS. No-one could prove it was bought with ill-
gotten gains and he lived there until his death, this year, at
the age of 92. A tough old bird.

By way of a death-bed repentance, he has left the mansion to
the orphans of both cities, to be jointly run as an orphanage
by FULBRIGHT and OLIVER MONKS, the director of the GOTHAM
orphanage. In fact MONKS is an alumnus of the SUICIDE SLUM
orphanage and a protege of WYLIE's, whose personal history has
been "laundered" enabling him to carry on in GOTHAM, much as
his mentor did in Metropolis. The MIDWAY ORPHANAGE is to be a
super-duper crime college with hidden rooms and facilities. In
due time, FULBRIGHT will be murdered, leaving MONKS in sole
charge, all this being ordered, before his death, by WYLIE.

To gain respectability, prominent citizens from METROPOLIS and
GOTHAM, such as BRUCE WAYNE, PERRY WHITE and COMMISSIONER
GORDON , have been made trustees of the orphanage. Their role
will be only nominal, since the place is remote and MONKS and
FULBRIGHT are trusted. LUTHOR has bought the old orphanage in
SUICIDE SLUM, intending to develop it and rejuvenate the area .
Despite this, he has not been made a trustee of the new MIDWAY
ORPHANAGE, which irks his pride somewhat.

There is a "gala opening" for the new orphanage at which our
principals are present. PERRY WHITE finds MONKS strangely
familiar and says so to COMMISSIONER GORDON, but this is
inconclusive. The climax of the evening (which proceeds as
noted in previous outlines) is when WYLIE appears on
videotape,to repent his sins and hope that his legacy will
atone. The more astute in the audience are doubtful but the
assembly applauds.

explodes in a nova of light and a small rocket- ship thrusts toward us. Stars flash and twinkle, the ship finally falling toward EARTH and sunlight.

In BATMAN's dream, the flashguns become the lights on a movie marquee (showing 'ZORRO') and the microphones a gun barrel. This explodes in further light, then becomes ambulance lights and so on, finally fading to black. We finish with both men waking up in a cold sweat in their respective beds, orphans in the night.

We cut to solid black. This slowly slides down, revealing itself to be a limousine window, until we are looking at a beaten up building with a weathered sign reading 'GOTHAM ORPHANAGE'. A voice comes from off: "...Luthor? Mr. Luthor? We're here." LUTHOR steps out of his limo and, flanked by sunglass-wearing heavies, walks into the deserted institution. He's here to meet the owner of the site on which the old Orphanage stands, with a view to buying it and developing it, as a first step towards controlling GOTHAM, the way he does METROPOLIS.

Inside, the Orphanage is dark and creepy but, at the end of a disused dormitory, we see the shadowy figure LUTHOR has come to meet. We close on LUTHOR as he realises who it is and spits out the single word "Joker."

The JOKER is in his usual gaudy outfit and a couple of his goons, absurd yet sinister, step from the shadows to equalize the numbers. "Luthor." he replies.

Our villains are as starkly contrasted in their own way as our heroes, from their bald/green haired heads right down to their black business shoes/purple spats. They are equally uncomfortable with each other: a bit like a medieval fool and a king, the one knowing just how far to go with a joke and the other just how far to tolerate the joke.

LUTHOR is surprised and angry to see the JOKER, since he was expecting to do business with Reverend WYLIE. The JOKER waves this aside, saying that he is now the owner of the property, and opens negotiations by asking for a vast sum of money for its purchase. LUTHOR halves the figure. The JOKER laughs at him, then looks sly. He will agree to the lower figure if LUTHOR gives him free run of METROPOLIS for six months. LUTHOR pretends that such a dispensation is not his to give - he's just an honest businessman.

However... he would have thought that three months might be the length of time that the JOKER would be tolerated by whatever crime bosses there might be in METROPOLIS. The JOKER, mightily tickled, agrees to the terms."Let's shake on it, Curly" he says, offering his hand, which LUTHOR takes. Of course, the JOKER has a buzzer in his hand and gives LUTHOR a jolt! "Just joking..."

A shadowy figure watches from an attic room as the worthies depart...

LUTHOR wants to buy the GOTHAM orphanage too, since it appeals to his sense of symmetry and order to make it his beach-head in that city. As described in previous outlines, he is surprised to find JOKER now owns it, but agrees to his terms, namely a smallish amount of money and the "freedom" of Metropolis for a limited time. As an added inducement, JOKER alludes to certain facts he has discovered about the circumstances under which LUTHOR himself was orphaned. Hotly denying this as absurd, LUTHOR is inwardly horrified and makes it a first priority to discover JOKER's source.

The source is in fact MONKS, who knew LUTHOR in SUICIDE SLUM and had seen something vaguely incriminating at the time of MR and MRS LUTHOR's demise. He is unable to prove anything and cannot do anything to LUTHOR , without revealing himself and also having to overcome LUTHOR's impressive reputation. Apart from that, he's terrified of him. The JOKER, however, might be more dangerous. Meanwhile, MONKS has been perverting his own youthful charges (certainly criminally and (?) perhaps sexually). JOKER has discovered this and is blackmailing him, hence the irregular and cheap sale.

Once in GOTHAM, LUTHOR starts to investigate and discovers all the dirt on MONKS. On discovering his real identity, he realises that MONKS must also be JOKER's source of information on him. LUTHOR wants a partnership with MONKS so that he can also use the orphanage as a college for his own nefarious activities, and teach criminal skills more related to the board-room than the bar-room. He intends to incorporate new orphanage facilities into his developments in the two cities, and take over the country mansion as his baronial retreat, the better to rule both cities. He will also have MONKS killed when the time is right.

At the same time, LUTHOR is making things difficult for the JOKER in METROPOLIS and wants to eventually wipe him out, too, since he can potentially 'embarrass' LUTHOR with what he knows.

Similarly, the JOKER is trying to sabotage LUTHOR in GOTHAM, since he guesses what his power-play is and doesn't want to be squeezed out. He is continuing to keep tabs on MONKS, as well, and senses something is afoot.

FULBRIGHT is killed mysteriously - a shadowy figure was fleetingly observed at the scene.

The party is held on CHRISTMAS EVE as before, so that LUTHOR can announce his new involvement with the orphanage - or at least the worthy public aspect thereof. SUPERMAN is present, as a trustee, though not BRUCE. As LUTHOR is about to sign, SUPERMAN melts the pen in his hand. He has been investigating he quips. LUTHOR is not amused but, the deal struck, they go their separate ways.

The BATCAVE, midnight. BRUCE WAYNE silently dons Batgarb, handed to him by ALFRED, as a screen spells out an emergency call. Speeding into GOTHAM from WAYNE MANOR, BATMAN is confronted by a huge runaway demolition rig. A LEXCORP prototype brought in for the new development, it has seriously malfunctioned. BATMAN manages to stop its juggernaut progress, but only just. As breathless and relieved as we ever see him, he murmurs with displeasure "Luthor?"

The DAILY PLANET newsroom, noon. Word is coming in of a crime downtown and CLARK KENT, pausing only to rip open his shirt in the broom cupboard, zooms off, as SUPERMAN, to take care of it. It's some kind of nasty, twisted hold-up which is just about stopped by our hero, though to save innocent passers-by, he has to let the crooks escape. As a peal of insane laughter wafts back on the breeze, he whispers incredulously "Joker?"

A couple of days later, at the Orphanage in the countryside, honorary trustees BATMAN and SUPERMAN are making an appearance, talking to the kids as they are shown round by the Reverend WYLIE. The kids show off their hobbies; stamp-collecting, geology, astronomy, etc., which elicit characteristic responses from our heroes. Eventually, sensing their discomfort with each other and seeming not a little uncomfortable himself, WYLIE thanks them for their time and the kids wave goodbye. But SUPERMAN stops BATMAN as he is about to climb into the BATMOBILE and whispers "Bruce? I think we need to talk."

"Yes, Clark," replies BATMAN. "I think we do."

In the woods overlooking the Orphanage building they talk, wary and uncomfortable, BATMAN keeping to the shade of the trees, SUPERMAN gleaming in the sun. It's a crisp, beautiful fall day. They agree to trade cities, as it were, the better to restrain LUTHOR and the JOKER from whatever scheme they're involved in.

They shake hands, saying merely "Bruce." and "Clark." by way of farewell, and grimly go their separate ways.

while in GOTHAM, too, and has discovered most of the salient
evidence of skullduggery.

As before, LUTHOR is outraged and MONKS is nervous. Then BATMAN
appears, swinging down from the shadowy rafters of the great
hall. He's been checking the place out and has found the "real"
SANTA CLAUS tied up in a closet - he accordingly unmasks JOKER
as before. MONKS breaks down and confesses, LUTHOR denies
everything. The JOKER laughs it off as before, then BATMAN, who
has bigger fish to fry, goes on to start describing what he has
also found, namely a "secret room" in the MIDWAY ORPHANAGE and
evidence that someone is living there. The place is a veritable
warren of secret passages.

Suddenly all the lights go out and the screen behind the podium
(where previously the video tape of WYLIE's will had been
shown) rises to reveal the spotlit figure of WYLIE in the
flesh. His death was a deception. He wanted to see the
new, improved crime college established and running before he
finally turned up his toes, but MONKS (who also thought Wylie
was dead) has ruined everything ! He roundly curses everybody -
the heroes for their goodness, the villains for their badness,
the worthies for their worthiness and particularly MONKS for
his stupidity. He is a frighteningly wrinkled, lunatic
apparition in this scene, which is the first in which we all
discover he is alive. Up until now we've only glimpsed a
shadowy figure haunting the place.

He has dynamite in his hand and has mined the whole building,
since he feared the worst might one day happen and doesn't want
anyone else to have his mansion, particularly pathetic goody-
goody orphans. He's had a long life and is ready to die so he
presses the button - "You can all go to hell with me !"

The whole place is rent with explosions and starts to collapse
and burn. Miraculously, everybody escapes, except WYLIE and
MONKS who are locked in mortal combat (the bony, wrinkled,
angry old man versus the fat, blubbering, terrified younger
one). Our two costumed heroes, not to mention LOIS, PERRY,
COMMISSIONER GORDON etc. are largely responsible for the saving
of life (you don't have to wear a costume to be a hero...). In
the confusion, JOKER goes missing and LUTHOR seems only
concerned about his own skin.

We then continue as before, JOKER turning up in LUTHOR's limo
trunk , SUPERMAN and BATMAN having the 'ZORRO' scene while
overlooking the now-gutted orphanage (the BATMOBILE is hidden
in the woods), and so on.

The kids will be looked after by various charities and
individuals over CHRISTMAS (like PERRY and COMMISSIONER GORDON,
say) and to show good faith, LUTHOR is to rebuild the MIDWAY
ORPHANAGE (this can all be explained as SUPERMAN and BATMAN
talk in the aftermath and on BRUCE's TV at NEW YEAR).

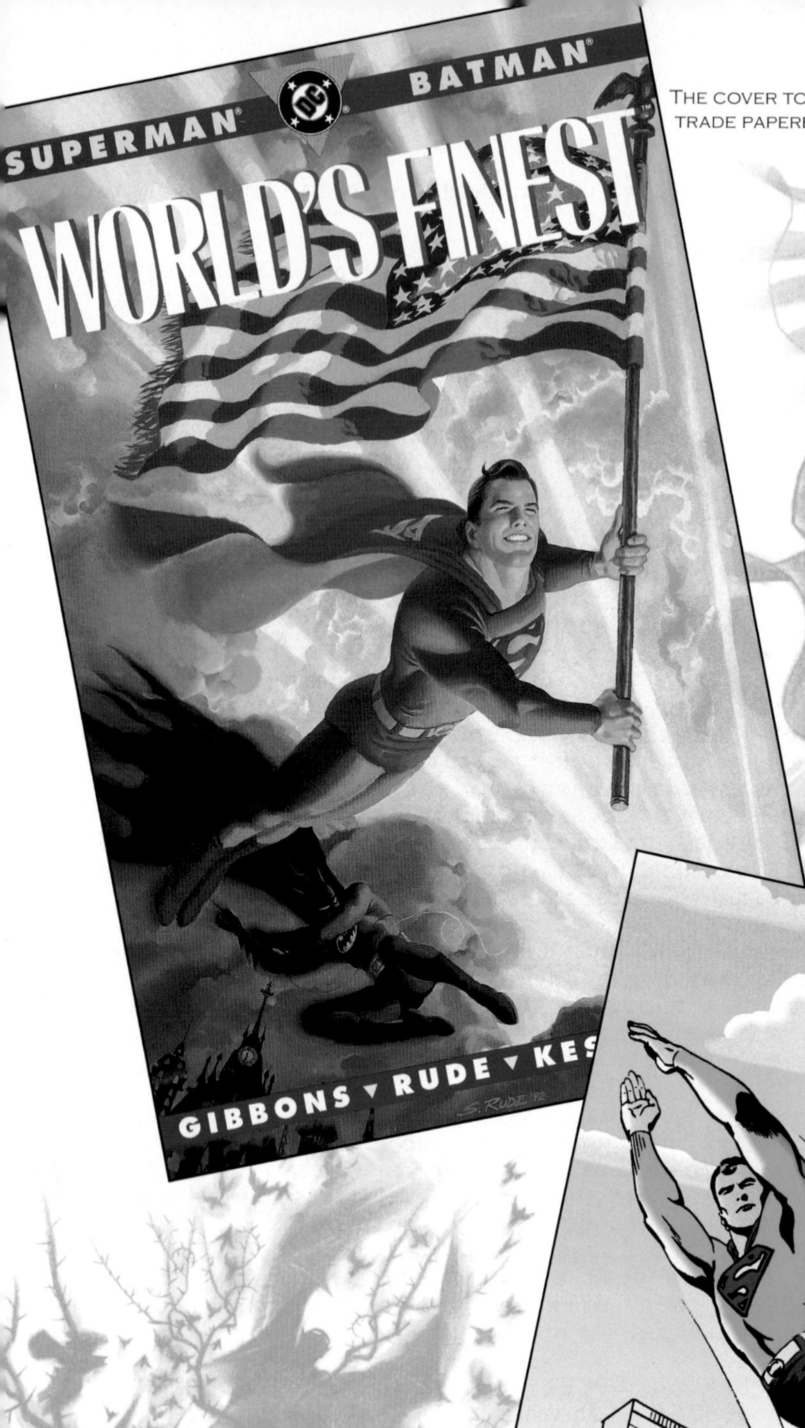
SUPERMAN
BATMAN
DC
WORLD'S FINEST
GIBBONS ▾ RUDE ▾ KES
S. RUDE '92

THE COVER TO THE WORLD'S FINEST TRADE PAPERBACK (1992).

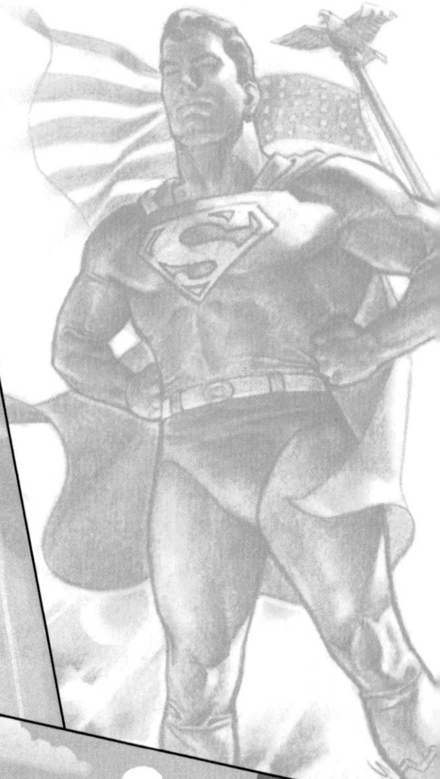

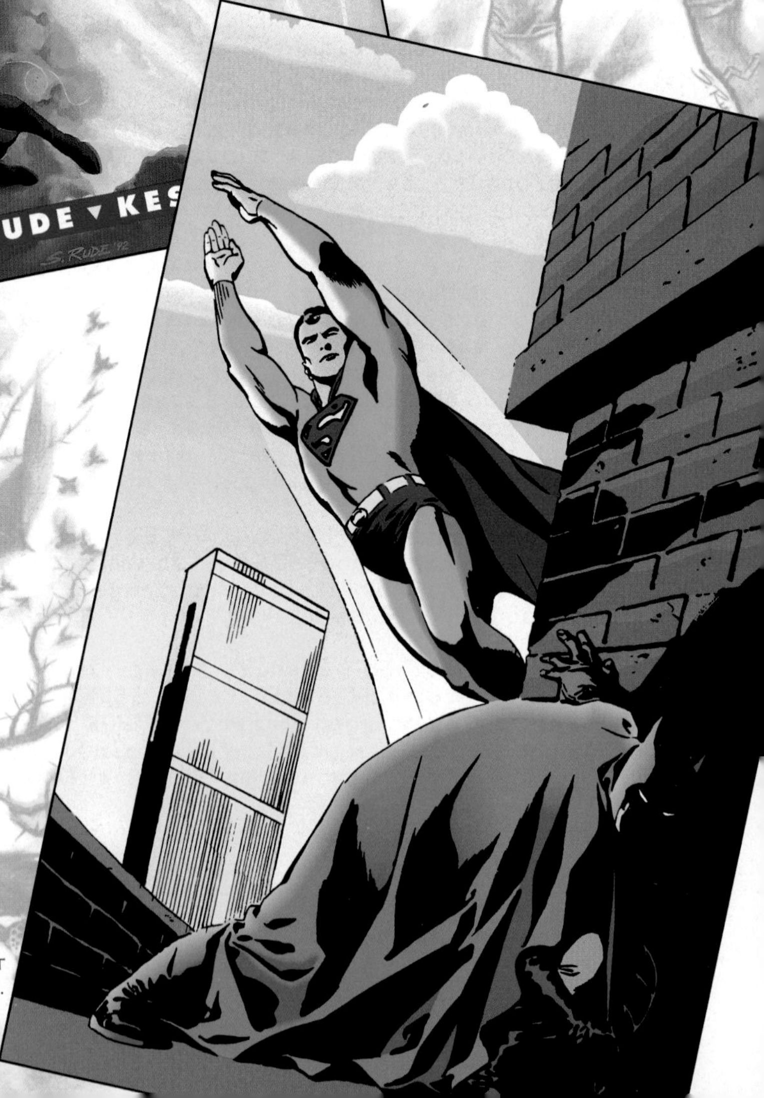

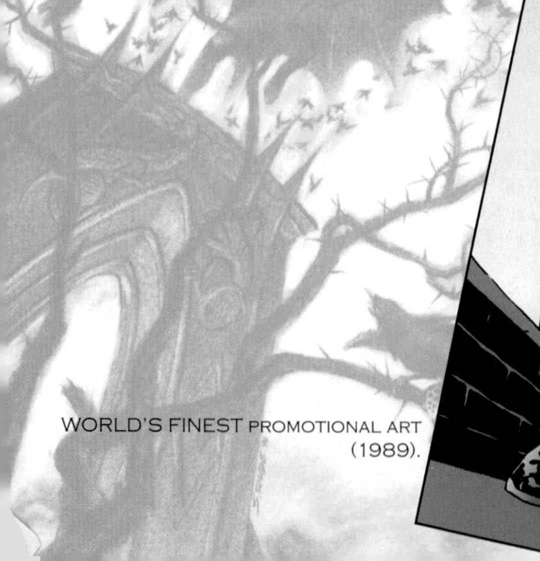

WORLD'S FINEST PROMOTIONAL ART (1989).